TURKEY HUNTER'S DIGEST

By Dwain Bland

DBI BOOKS, INC.

STAFF

EDITOR
Harold A. Murtz

COVER PHOTOGRAPHY
Lovett Williams (Osceola)
Glen Smith (Eastern)
Wyman Meinzer (Rio Grande)
Nebraska Game and Parks Commission (Merriam)
Tom Potter, New Mexico State University (Gould's)

PRODUCTION MANAGER
Pamela J. Johnson

PUBLISHER
Sheldon L. Factor

ISBN 0-87349-000-2   Library of Congress Catalog Card Number **85-73743**

CONTENTS

FOREWORD

DURING a fall hunt for wild turkeys many years ago, I met some men who were impressed with what I knew about the sport and, as they were outdoor writers, they asked me to write an article for their publication. I had read outdoor magazines since I was a boy and, in fact, at one time, my brother Dick and I shot rabbits for the market, spending part of the money to buy hunting magazines.

"Sure," I says, "no sweat, I'll write you an article about turkey hunting." And I did, and I sent it to them a few weeks later.

Boy, was I sick when that thing came on the newsstand. The only thing about the article that was "me" was the photo. Those guys had apparently thought my article stunk. It made me madder'n hell.

I thought, "I'll show you-all. I'll learn to write."

I'm still learning. Never did learn to type with all 10 fingers, and have wore ½-inch off of my two index fingers. But, they just might be the two strongest fingers in the country.

I was humbled that DBI books would ask me to do this book. It is indeed an honor. Of course, it's also one hell of a lot of work. I'm a construction worker, and let me tell you, when I come home at night, my backside is dragging. It's been a tough row to hoe, putting this thing together at nights and on weekends. Not to mention the several hundred photographs which had to be made.

My turkey hunting experience was why DBI asked me to do the book. They presumed that anyone who had done so much of it had surely absorbed a little something along the way. Like the typing, I am also still learning about hunting turkeys. Oh, I've shot at a few, but if my shoes hold out, there are others yet out in the woods that haven't seen me, and I hope they don't. At least, not until after I see them.

During an average year I'll hunt at least three of the five bearded and spurred wild turkeys. Some years I'll hunt all five—the Eastern, Osceola, Rio Grande, Merriam, and the Gould's, a mountain turkey found high in old Mexico's Sierra Madre mountains. I used to think there was a sixth wild turkey, but I have since decided the little Ocellated bird found on Mexico's jungle isthmus couldn't be a real wild turkey. Found in the Mexican States of Campeche and Yucatan, this bird would fit in the body cavity of a big old Eastern gobbler, and what's worse, it hasn't got a beard. Whoever heard of a wild turkey without a beard? Even little "jakes" have a tiny beard. But, what cinched it is that the Ocellated bird can't gobble. Academic! You can't call anything a gobbler if it can't gobble.

These days everyone wants to be a wild turkey guide. Those words seem to have a mystique. I suppose that if a person says he is a wild turkey guide, it makes him some sort of super woodsman, world-class caller, shotgun artist, and public relations executive, all rolled into one. I've been a wild turkey guide for longer'n some of you've been born, and all it's made me is tired. I still do some of it when I get to feeling foolish. One winter I guided for Rio Grandes and Easterns, the next spring I took hunters after Merriams, Osceolas, and Rio Grandes. The following winter my clients took Rio Grandes, Gould's, and Osceolas. I mention these so you can get an idea of how much hunting I do, and how different it can be, switching from one terrain to another so much. Such traveling has taught me about all the kinds of people we have in this great country, what they do for a living, how they farm, cut timber, catch channel catfish out of the Mississippi, and a jillion other things. And, I've learned that what's considered okay insofar as hunting ethics, in one section of the country, may well be thought of as a potshooting slaughter in another. A good guide knows all these things, *before* he hunts in a new and strange area.

Throughout this book I have tried to impress on the reader the need to educate the young people about hunting, that the American hunter wants to keep part of America wooded, with fresh, running streams, the country alive with birds, animals, and even snakes, too. The anti-hunting movement thinks we are the enemy when, in reality, we are trying to stem the losing battle of habitat loss. Unless the country changes its ways drastically, the anti-hunters will have won their fight. There won't be anything but shopping malls, interstate highways, oil wells, strip mines, and clearcut forests. The hunter will be gone. And, so will be all that he stands for—wilderness America.

Throughout the following pages you will also read my mention of shooting at "close range." In fact, you will get darned sick and tired of my saying this. I hope you do. Perhaps, together, we can slow down long-range shooting. There will be fewer turkeys crippled, and less chance of hunters being shot.

You will also probably be able to figure out that I hunt turkeys only with a shotgun—and almost always nowadays with a black powder shotgun. That's my preference because I want to hunt the way our forefathers did so many years ago. However, that doesn't mean that other hunters must follow my suit. I guess what it all boils down to is you do it your way, I'll do it mine.

For the reader who wants further reading enjoyment, or needs state-by-state hunting information or wants to know where to order a game call, there is an Appendix in the back of this book with all of that information.

Recently I was asked, "What qualities do you look for in a turkey hunter?" This is a tough question. Just as different as two people's fingerprints are, no two people are alike. I like to think turkey hunters have some manners, and use them around children and women, and even among themselves. My greatest admiration is for folks who learn from what they see, have a "game eye," and hang in there when the going gets tough. I don't mind if a person has a shot of whiskey, just so they wait until after hunting time to do it. But, they don't have to have it every night, and don't need to drink ½-gallon. I don't mind if a hunter smokes, but I'll come after him with blood in my eye if he sets the woods afire. A turkey hunter will hunt best if he doesn't do these things at all.

Other qualities a person should possess for being a better-than-average turkey hunter are determination, time, patience, and a knack for being in the right place at the right time. Let me explain some of these a bit further.

Turkey hunters gotta have time, is an old cliché well known among older turkey hunters. It hasn't got anything to do with alarm clocks, but is just the opposite. A turkey does not wear a wristwatch and the hunter shouldn't either. Forget the time. Just hunt. You will become better for it.

Patience. Do you know what the dictionary gives as the definition of "patience." *The ability to wait without pain.* A doctor's patients wait with pain, but the turkey hunter must wait without it. Can you wait without pain, for an hour, as a gobbler tears down the woods with his gobbling, while mosquitoes make your face a donor to the local blood bank? The gobbler has so much patience you almost never do see him.

Patience should be lumped together with luck, and sold at the supermarket. All of us would like to go into the store and buy several "lucks." Then, when I need one, I could dig it out of a pocket and use it. Instead, we have to make our luck. I greatly admire those people who successfully play the stock market, because they must have some amount of luck. Or, do they? Too often luck is nothing but hard work. Much of my good luck, or being in the right place at the right time, was nothing but my hunting hard with a good portion of patience thrown in, too.

A turkey hunter should be "sure of hisself." Now, this isn't anything like being stuck up, or as some would say, "sold on hisself." A turkey hunter must have complete confidence in his abilities, because the turkey is working constantly to erode this idea, and unless a person has the confidence, there will be many days when he may as well stay at home. To get this "sure of hisself," the hunter should study the wild turkey, both through books and in getting out into the woods during the off seasons. The hunter should practice with turkey calls, attend seminars, put in time on the shooting range, and compare notes with other hunters. Perhaps then, when the hunter gets into the woods, and his wife remarks to a neighbor, "Oh, he's gone turkey hunting," the hunter will be able to make the best of each small opportunity.

I have "laundered" this book, trying to make it readable to folks who have never hunted wild turkeys. It hasn't got all the "turkey talk" that us turkey hunters use. Maybe I'll see you in the woods. Then we'll talk turkey.

Dwain Bland

The Bearded and Spurred Wild Turkeys

Photo courtesy Leonard Rue Ent.

THE TURKEY, both wild and domestic, is native to the Americas. When Columbus sailed the ocean blue in the 1400s, turkeys were as yet unknown to the civilized world. We aren't even positive that Columbus came in contact with the bird, though he may have seen the smaller jungle turkey, the Ocellated, which inhabits Cuba, Honduras, parts of the Mexican peninsula, and South America.

But by the 16th century, Spanish explorers had discovered the turkey and had also taken it back to Spain. When Cortez, and later Coronado, landed along what is today the east coast of Mexico, they found great numbers of turkeys under domestication by the Aztec Indians. The birds were kept in pens and fed daily by the Indians. History tells us the Indians offered their birds to the conquistadors as food for the terrifying animal the conquerors had brought with them—the horse. Obviously, the natives presumed that such a monster was a meat-eater.

Nobody knows for certain where the name "turkey" came from. As good a guess as any is that these early explorers thought they had found a new route to the countries of the Far East, one of which was Turkey. So, when some of these travelers began carting turkeys back to Spain, the unknown bird was named "turkey," and the moniker stuck. From Spain the domesticated turkey eventually found its way to France and England, and from England it was brought to America by the first Pilgrims. It was the domesticated Mexican turkey found by Cortez and Coronado, then, that is the progenitor of all our present domestic stock.

The turkey, domestic and wild, was an important source of food for many early Indian tribes, though some would not eat the birds due to religious beliefs. The feathers were widely used in decorating clothing and in fletching arrows. However, only the boys of the tribe hunted the wild turkeys. The birds were not so wild then as today, so the hunt was not considered worthy of a brave. Among tribes in which the men did hunt the birds, they often imitated the call of the turkey with their mouths, and used dried tail feathers to lure the birds. (Don't try this today, unless you have little value for life and limb—you stand the chance of being mistaken for a turkey, and being shot!)

During my wanderings in Mexico, and deep in the Sierra Madre mountains, I've seen old Indian pottery decorated with paintings of turkeys. Though this pottery is found where wild turkeys are also found, I am certain that the design celebrated the domestication of the bird. Throughout present day Arizona, New Mexico, Colorado and Utah, drawings of presumably both wild and domestic turkeys can be found on the walls of caves once used by cliff dwelling Indians. From the numerous bones found in and among these cliff houses, it is obvious that the turkey was used extensively as food. It is also interesting to note that Indians who used turquoise for decorations called it "turkey stone," because the color was so close to that found on a turkey's head.

The turkey continued to play an important part in North American history. The woodland Indians of the eastern seaboard states did not domesticate the turkey but hunted it extensively, relying heavily on the turkey for food and its plumage for robes, clothing and garment decoration. Awls and whistles were made from the bones, and arrow heads fashioned from the leg spur.

When the early colonists landed on the northeastern

Indians often painted wild turkeys on their trappings and on cave and rock walls. Turkey feathers were widely used to decorate apparel and equipment, and still are today.

(Left) Both domestic and wild turkeys shared an important part in the lives of Indians before the arrival of the white man on the American continent. This piece is from the Casas Grande Indians in Mexico.

shores of America, they found huge flocks of *wild* turkeys. These were the ancestors of the bird we know today as the Eastern wild turkey. When compared to the domesticated turkey they had brought with them, the colonists noted marked differences in size and coloration between the two, the wild bird being much larger and darker.

In fact, the early settlers moving westward throughout the continental United States found the wild turkey so widespread that over the years hundreds of local geophysical features and landmarks have been named from contact with the birds. Gobblers Knob, Turkey Point, Turkey Feather Pass, Turkey Foot Ranch, and Turkey Creek are just a few examples. There must be hundreds of Turkey Creeks across the width and breath of this country. I know of three in Oklahoma, and probably there are several others.

There are also numerous stories told about the wild turkey and its association with the horse troopers and infantry, as they campaigned throughout the western United States, during the Indian Wars in the latter part of the 19th century. With meat being the main course served at far-flung military outposts, the wild turkey was a favorite target of the trooper's gun. General Philip Sheridan, who headed up the campaigns, together with cronies like General George Crook and General William F. Strong, made numerous sor-

Stories are told of teamsters shooting roosting turkeys, and heading back for camp . . .

(Below) Twenty four wild turkeys can be counted hanging from the meat pole in this early Oklahoma hunting camp, along with a number of prairie chickens and deer. (Courtesy Oklahoma Dept. of Wildlife Conservation.)

There are places all across the United States named after the wild turkey.

An old hunting camp in southeastern Oklahoma, date unknown. The two hunters on the left are holding Model 95 Winchester rifles, the other a Model 1873 Winchester. The two on the left are wearing the "standard" hunting coat of that time. Surely the hunter in the white coat didn't hunt while wearing it! (Photo courtesy Oklahoma Dept. of Wildlife Conservation.)

ties along the rivers of the western prairies, escorted by soldiers and six-mule wagons. In fact, General Sheridan, when soldiering from Camp Supply, in what would later become northwestern Oklahoma, made so many hunts to a favored area along the North Canadian River that the place became known as Sheridan's Roost. From what has been passed down through the notes of troopers, turkeys, numbering in the thousands, roosted along the North Canadian. Stories are told of teamsters driving wagons beneath the towering cottonwoods, shooting the roosting turkeys, and then heading back for camp with only the birds that fell in the wagon.

On one occasion, a detachment of troopers, going into bivouac for the night, suddenly found the campsite overrun with turkeys going to roost. Seeing all this fresh meat running among them, the troopers decided to make the best of a good thing. Throughout the fracas, which thereon took place, one of the horse trooper's animals fell dead, shot through by a bullet meant for a fleeing turkey.

Wild turkey was very often the main course served at the troopers' mess halls, as few western forts were located beyond terrain where wild turkeys could be hunted. A Thanksgiving Day menu at one of these log bunkered outposts included roast wild turkey, wild turkey soup, broiled wild turkey, wild turkey giblets and gravy and, thankfully, a moonshine drink known as "pinetop whiskey." At Fort Cobb, in the early 1800s, a wild turkey could be purchased from an Indian for a pound of flour. By 1900, on the Chicago market, the bird might bring up to $5.

Market hunting had begun to take its toll in the late 1800s, and the bird was doomed for near extinction. During the early 1800s there were thousands of wild turkeys roosting among the blackjack oak forests which blanketed the country. By 1900 all those birds were gone, wiped out by incessant hunting, much of it a simple slaughter. Birds were killed by the wagonloads, and if the load spoiled before getting to market, so what?—there were more where those came from. Today, a few droves of wild turkeys can be found near the small town of Ames, Oklahoma, birds brought back through the restocking efforts of the Oklahoma Department of Wildlife Conservation. There would be even greater numbers of turkeys there, but the great oak forests are gone, having been burned to make room for cultivated crops. On the whole, however, the efforts to reestablish the turkey have been met with success. Though not as abundant as it was when the first colonists arrived, huntable populations exist in 46 of the 50 states.

Learned biologists and naturalists have come to the conclusion that there are two genera of turkeys—the *Meleagris gallopavo* and the *Agrocharis ocellata*. Four of the five subspecies of the *Meleagris* genus are found within the continental boundaries of the United States. These are the Eastern, the Osceola, the Rio Grande, and the Merriam. The fifth subspecie, found throughout the Sierra Madre mountain chain in Mexico, is the Gould's wild turkey (*see Chapter 10*). The Ocellated turkey is the only subspecie of the *Agrocharis* genus. The Ocellated is primarily a jungle fowl, and among the characteristics which separate it from *Meleagris* is the complete lack of a breast ornament, known as a "beard" among turkey hunters. The Ocellated is also smaller than any of the five subspecies of *Meleagris*.

Other differences are that the Ocellated bird has a rounded tail, whereas the wild turkey of *Meleagris* has a definite square looking tail. From what I have been told, the jungle turkey hen has small nubs where the spurs are normally located. The Ocellated turkey also does not have the upright carriage found among *Meleagris* gobblers, nor have I heard of these birds having that "heavy" breast appearance during mating season, or a "breastsponge," the fat reservoir found on the upper chest of adult males.

An Eastern wild turkey
in full strut.

The Eastern is called the "ridge-runner," "mountaineer," and other local nicknames . . .

The Eastern wild turkey is by far the most hunted of the wild birds. It is found over the greatest range, which today takes in the bulk of the country east of the Mississippi River, along with a huge chunk of land west of that river. Among turkey hunters, the Eastern is often called the "ridgerunner," "mountaineer," "piney woods turkey," "Ozark turkey," "swamp turkey," and who knows how many other local nicknames. But, to many of today's traveling turkey addicts, in order to keep the birds separated more or less as to habitat, the Eastern turkey is simply called the Eastern, or "woodlands" turkey.

I'll not go into depth describing the plumage of the various turkey subspecies, as anyone wanting this information should buy one of the fine books on the market today written by wild turkey biologists. I will simply look at the differences as a hunter would, and in particular, as the hunter who is seeing the bird for the first time.

will weigh from 6 to 8. The Eastern wild turkey is dark in plumage, almost black when seen in the woods. The tail and lower rump feathers are tipped in dark chestnut brown. The large wing feathers, the primaries, are distinctly barred with a very dark gray and white. The overall glistening sheen of an adult gobbler will be a burnished coppery-green, though on the back the sheen may take on a purplish and bluish luster. The Eastern turkey, in general, has the finest beard growth of all the wild turkeys, and spur development is second only to the Osceola wild turkey. Foot size is medium, nowhere in comparison to turkeys found in the mountains of the West. Leg length is slightly shorter than that of the Osceola, which exceeds all subspecies in this category. Tail length is longer than all except Osceola, and perhaps members of the Gould's turkey race found in Mexico.

If you were to lay in front of you a gobbler from each of the five subspecies of the bearded and spurred wild turkeys, it would be easy to pick out the Eastern bird. Simply look for the one with the dark brown tipped tail feathers and with the distinctly barred wing flight feathers. A pure strain Eastern male will have these features, setting it apart from all others.

These are the primary flight feathers from the (top to bottom) Osceola, Eastern and Gould turkeys. Note the large size of the Gould's feather compared to the others, and the predominance of black coloration of the Osceola (top).

The Eastern turkey is big, standing perhaps 30 inches in height (adult male) and measuring nearly 4 feet in length from tip of beak to tip of tail. Hens are a few inches smaller in both dimensions. Weight varies considerably from one part of the bird's range to another. Overall, the largest Easterns come from Missouri and Arkansas, though for many years there has been a controversy raging as to whether these birds might have a slight mixture of domestic blood, resulting in weights that tip the scales at between 25 and 30 pounds. Throughout the country, an average Eastern gobbler will weigh nearer to 16 or 17 pounds, while a hen

If you seek the Eastern, you hunt where the trees shed their leaves . . .

The boundary lines of the Eastern wild turkey's original range begins in Pennsylvania, goes south along the Atlantic states to northernmost Florida, continues west through Georgia, Alabama, Mississippi, Louisiana, and from east Texas angles northeast into Arkansas and across into Oklahoma, taking in much of that state; from there it extends north into Kansas. Eastern portions of that state (Kansas), Nebraska, Missouri, a part of New York State, Ohio and across to Pennsylvania—all of the region within was, and is, the historic home of the woodlands wild turkey, the Eastern bird. Early naturalists noted that these birds were to be found only among the deciduous treed forests of this region, and so it is to this day. If you seek the Eastern, you must hunt where the trees shed their leaves each year.

Anyone who has hunted the Eastern will agree that this subspecies inhabits a tremendously diversified zone, insofar as climatic conditions go. During the course of a single fall season, a person can hunt Easterns among ticks, mosquitoes, nasty tempered rattlesnakes, not to mention oppressively hot afternoons, and then a month later be caught in a blinding snowstorm several hundred miles to the northeast—all the while in Eastern turkey habitat.

I was hunting some Ozark turkeys many years ago, during an early fall hunt, whereon by midday the hunting was all but impossible. It had been very hot that summer and dry as a powderkeg. I soon learned that if I was to hunt at all throughout those scorched mountains, I would have to take up calling stands only where I could get a slight breeze, and even then I went without a shirt during the afternoon hours. I couldn't even leave camp without a canteen of water. The limit was one bird thereabouts, which I shot, but only after some extremely miserable sessions. Not 3 weeks later I was lucky to come out of a blizzard alive while trying to find an Eastern among some northern New England hardwoods.

Of course, these conditions can also prevail during spring hunts. How many of us have set out to hunt an Eastern gobbler on a clear April morn, only to be blown off the mountains a few hours later by a fast moving late winter storm. But, for all the fluctuations in the weather, the range of the Eastern has one thing in common—hills and mountains. True, the birds can be found in places such as "inside the levee," along the Mississippi River or in areas where the country might be considered fairly flat. But, these areas are small in comparison to the total habitat. And, like many terms associated with turkey hunting, what might be "flat" country to one hunter, will be "rolling" country to another. Flat country to me is south Florida, the rice country around Stuttgart, Arkansas, the plains of western Kansas, or the

tion exceeds 30 inches a year, and in many instances, 40 or 50 inches. This results in more luxuriant plant growth of tremendous variety, and ever-present streams, brooks, creeks, or swamps—any and all topography associated with abundant water. As I am from the dry prairies of western Oklahoma, Eastern habitat is a continuing source of study for me, and when I'm hunting Easterns, it is difficult for me to hunt uplands if I hear a stream tumbling among rocks. I can spend hours wading belly-deep through creek swamps, just searching for snails, leeches, or in sneaking up close to a sunning cottonmouth. Beaver swamps, river cutoff ponds, sloughs, canebrakes, flooded bottoms, all are indeed interesting to a person from dry country.

Along with the change in annual precipitation and the flora resulting from this moisture will be a change in bird and animal wildlife. In the New England states, ruffed grouse and woodcock will replace the bobwhite quail found further south and west, or the prairie chickens of the Plains. Goshawks, gray squirrels, and red fox will be seen.

Snakes, lizards, and all types of plant and animal life change as a person travels from one ecological zone to another. The hunter who fails to notice these changes will also fail to notice a good portion of the wild turkeys there-

These two hunters wait, listening for the beckoning gobble of an adult male turkey. This is typical Eastern wild turkey terrain of mixed hardwoods and pines. The hunter on the left, with camouflage gloves and facepaint, will not be so easily detected by a turkey as will be the hunter on the right, whose unpainted face and hands are "bright."

Snowbanks are pretty, but they can be problems for a turkey hunter. Due to many freeze/thaw cycles they become crystalized and are quite noisy to walk on. If the hunter wants to get near a gobbler, it's best to either go around it (if possible) or call the bird to him, which is often easier.

Oklahoma Panhandle, and various plantation land of the South and Southeast.

To a western hunter traveling into Eastern wild turkey habitat for the first time, the soil color often looks darker than soils of the West, and appears to be of "tighter" consistency. Probably a hunter from the West will also notice a lack of sand. Hunters from the Plains country will be fascinated with the abundance of rocks, rocky type soils, and the presence of rocks on cultivated lands. Water will be quickly noted by travelers from the dry Southwest, as Eastern turkey country is situated where annual precipita-

abouts. Daniel Boone lived to a ripe old age because he kept his eyes and ears tuned to what was taking place around him. He realized that for each creature in nature, there were other creatures which were its foods and, above it in the chain of evolution, those which hunted it as food. Why hunt a wild turkey in a hunk of woods that has no bird life, nor any signs of small animals? Without these, I would suspect the area is lacking in natural foods, for birds must eat almost continuously. The droppings of small animals can tell us that there are wild berries about. Without berries, there will probably be no turkeys. Or, what about deer droppings? Have you noticed a lack of them? This could indicate an absence of acorn crops the past year or two. No acorns?—again, probably no turkeys.

Climax vegetation, what the average hunter would call "mature trees," throughout the Eastern wild turkey's range, is what divides them into differing zones. Throughout parts of the Deep South, the climax vegetation might be water oak, and overcup oak, mixed with the ever present pines, shortleaf pine, loblolly and long-leaf pine, slash pine, and perhaps pecan, hickory, tupelo, gum, and bald cypress trees. Throughout Arkansas and Missouri's Eastern habitats are found post oaks, blackjack oak, white oaks, with a scattering of pines, hickorys, sycamores and elm. Climax vegetation in a state such as Vermont would be sugar maples, white oak, black cherry, along with the conifers like hemlock, white pine and spruce. In other regions beech would be an important tree for turkeys, as would pecan, ash and tupelo. It must be noted that throughout the range of the Eastern wild turkey, there are few areas without oaks, and, in fact, numerous areas where several species of oak are located. Throughout all of my travels in turkey country, regardless of what subspecies I was hunting, seldom have I noted a lack of acorn bearing oak trees. Truly, acorns are the mast of life for the wild turkey.

In mentioning roost sites, never forget the age of the turkey being discussed . . .

Many times I've been asked if there is a principal tree the Eastern wild turkey prefers over all others as a roosting site. My answer—if they had all types of woods available to them, they would probably choose mature pines. My conclusion here is drawn from hunting turkeys among mixed hardwoods and pines for so many years, along with understanding, perhaps, why a turkey would choose a pine. A mature pine grows straight and tall, with its crown above the roof of the forest constantly reaching for the sun. Since only the fastest growing, healthiest trees survive in getting sunlight, the ones that do make it will jut above the surrounding woods, and this dense crown seems to be a beacon to roosting turkeys. Too, perhaps the boughs of the pine, free of so many gnarled twigs and intervening branches, are favored by turkeys. The long straight trunk appears to discourage predators, and perhaps the turkey, with its wild instincts, feels this.

I've heard a turkey hunter make a flat statement that all the turkeys where he hunted would invariably roost in a "so-and-so" kind of tree and always on the southwest side of a hill. This told me he had hunted turkeys nowhere but on that hill, or that he was hunting in an area where local conditions caused the birds to roost there. I know of stream bottoms, where, aside from the stream itself and a small border along the water course, all the timber has been cut,

leaving only the trees along the stream for roost locations. Yes, the birds roost there. They have no choice. Perhaps the mature trees are the only climax vegetation left on a given hillside, and regardless of what tree species, if these are the largest trees in the area, the birds are very apt to roost in them, if all other conditions are ideal. In mentioning roost sites, a person must never for an instant forget the age of the turkey being discussed, as the roost site varies according to the bird's age. The discussion above has been focused on adult turkeys. Young turkeys roost in smaller trees.

As the old saying goes, "A turkey will eat anything which don't eat him first . . ."

Berries of the *bumelia* are a favorite of the Rio Grande wild turkey. The birds will fly up into these thorny trees, feeding on the berries as they teeter-totter on the small branches. Other birds wait below for berries which fall to the ground.

The foods of the Eastern turkey are as varied as its habitat. Aside from acorns, pecans, wild cherries, beechnuts, and a few others, much foodstuffs are gleaned from understory vegetation. Principal among these are dogwood, sumac, simlax, blackberry, huckleberry and wild grape. Others are grass seeds, cultivated grains, various grass and weed leaves, buds from trees, and just about anything else which will fit in a turkey's beak. As the old turkey hunter's saying goes, "A turkey will eat anything which don't eat him first."

The dyed-in-the-wool woodsman, turned turkey hunter, will notice what foods are plentiful as he hunts, and what type of foods are thereabouts along with where turkey sign is seen. It isn't difficult to tie all these together, then to make a fairly accurate deduction as to what the turkeys in

Grapes such as these are commonly known among turkey hunters as "possum" or "fox" grapes. They are eaten by wild turkeys, though are often not found in quantities which would make them a principal food.

(Below) Acorns are the "staff of life" among all wild turkeys. There are not many areas in this country where the birds are found that oak trees are not present in some form. These are from a blackjack oak. An old saying says that, "A turkey will eat anything which don't eat him first."

by the hunter who has hunted near or among these thickets. I've flushed adult gobblers from them back in Pennsylvania, on days when the woods were crawling with hunters. No doubt many turkeys seek cover in them and remain there even while hunters pass within yards of their hiding places. In less mountainous regions these escape covers are replaced by rank stands of switch willows, huckleberry bushes, canebrakes, cedar brakes, or other dense, impenetrable fortresses of brush, vines, and brambles. Turkeys ordinarily do not go into the worst thickets unless pushed there through hard hunting or other harassments. (Back in the high Sierras of Mexico is found another member of the heath family, the madrona, which grows in sprawling tangled "Hells." The berries of this bush are a favored food of the Gould's wild turkey. Numerous explorers nicknamed the madrona the Strawberry tree because of its beautiful red bark.)

Thanks to restocking programs, executed by numerous wildlife departments, and monied by hunters' dollars, the Eastern wild turkey is hunted in 35 states. With continued out-of-season protection, plus a change of attitude locally, as to poachers and unethical hunting practices, the numbers of these grand gamebirds will continue to increase.

Hunters seeking pure Osceolas should hunt them south of the city of Orlando . . .

Osceola wild turkey in typical habitat. (Photo by Lovett Williams, courtesy Florida Game & Fresh Water Fish Commission.)

that neighborhood are feeding on. When hunting, it's sometimes easier to find foods first, and then look for the turkeys where the food is.

One winter I was gingerly working my way over a ridge, whereupon I suddenly spied a turkey teetering on a branch half way up the side of a buckthorn *bumelia*. Further looksees revealed five turkeys in the tree. Anyone familiar with wild turkeys and buckthorn berries can understand when I say, the birds are crazy about them. The little trees are not prolific, most years, and that particular year, only the trees which were growing along the crest of ridges bore berries. I'd learned that from looking in the trees as I hunted. Once I'd found which trees were bearing, it was only a matter of searching out the ridge-top *bumelias*, and in time I would find the birds. The berries are black, and delicious. Anytime I'm hunting turkeys, and I find these trees with berries on them, I hunt no further. I've killed a good number of birds around *bumelias*.

Throughout parts of the Eastern wild turkey's range can be found what I term "escape cover"—areas where turkeys sometimes seek cover when hunted and pursued severely. These thickets are made up of shrubs, mountain laurel and rhododendron. These members of the heath family often blanket an area, the gnarled limbs forming what has been termed as "Hells," a very apt description, only understood

The Osceola wild turkey is found throughout much of Florida. Turkey hunters seeking pure, full-blood Osceolas, should hunt them south of an imaginary east-west line drawn across Florida through the city of Orlando. I am certain that a great many turkeys killed north of this demarcation will appear to be Osceolas, but, so long as I hunt farther south, I will be sure. The farther north one goes, the chances increase that the birds have interbred with Eastern wild turkeys, resulting in a mixed breed.

In overall coloration, the Osceola looks identical to the Eastern from a distance. In hand, the differences aren't many, but, there is one which is obvious. The white bars on the primary flight feathers, those long black and white feathers of the wings, are not distinct. At a glance, these big wing feathers seem to have very little white on them at all, if the bird is a full-blood Osceola turkey.

These feathers are "broomed" to a spike-like shape and are often found on the secondary feathers of adult Osceola gobblers, located near the body on both wings. This is prominent only on this subspecie, according to the author's observations.

The Osceola wild turkey, found in Florida, has wing markings which set it apart from all others of the subspecies. Notice the tremendous amount of black in the wing primaries toward the left end of this bird's wing. All other turkeys have nearly as much white in these feathers as is there black here.

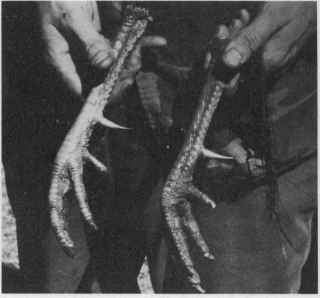

The Osceola wild turkey, found in southern Florida, has the greatest over-all spur development of all five of the turkeys which make up the Royal Grand Slam. Many Osceolas will have spurs up to 1½ inches in length, with a sharp curved appearance. These are true trophies.

On closer examination, I have noticed much brooming of the secondary wing feathers next to the body on adult males during the spring season. Brooming is the wearing away of plumage from the feather shaft, usually caused by the strutting male dragging his primary flight feathers across the ground. I've noted this among other subspecies, but never to the extent as can be found among male Osceolas. Many times these feathers will be broomed to the point that the center shaft becomes a spike. The nearer the body, the greater the brooming.

Beard growth is excellent among Osceolas. From my experiences and observations, the spur growth of the Osceola is unmatched by any of the other subspecies in length and keenness of point. Insofar as spur base circumference,

I believe the Eastern has the edge, but the Osceola outdoes the Eastern's spur in all other measurements. This is on a bird-to-bird ratio. The Osceola does not attain the body weight of the Eastern, and except for longer leg length, is comparable in size to the Rio Grande.

The Osceola hen is easily the most attractive of all subspecies, with a burnished light-brown appearance when in full sunlight. Luckily, the first time I saw a hen I had binoculars hanging around my neck, and I was thankful for the long observation they allowed me. Thereafter, I worked at getting to places where I could study the Osceola hen as well as the gobbler. My initial reaction to seeing an Osceola gobbler in full strut was that he appeared to strut "taller" than the other turkeys and to show more of the lower leg.

I combed that spiney tangle for over an hour, trying to search every inch of it . . .

Osceola country is as flat as a pancake. Once in a great while, a person will come to a long grade which is a few feet higher than the surrounding countryside, and as these are so few in Osceola country, such long gentle swells are highly noticeable. None could be called "hills." Very often, the only high ground a hunter might see will be where soil has been piled up from the dredging of a drainage ditch, or the deepening of a canal.

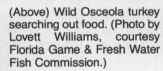

(Above) Wild Osceola turkey searching out food. (Photo by Lovett Williams, courtesy Florida Game & Fresh Water Fish Commission.)

Osceola wild turkeys often roost in giant trees located in bottomlands, along streams, creeks, and rivers. They especially prefer to roost in trees which are standing in water. This is very typical Osceola territory.

Water is everywhere. Drainage canals, roadside ditches, swamps, creeks, ponds, lakes, sloughs, rivers—you name it. If it will hold water, south Florida has it—plus saw palmetto. Saw palmetto is a member of the palm tree family, though this member ordinarily grows to about 20 feet in height. The leaves, which are long thin blades with a spiked end, radiate from a center stalk, and are truly a fan palm. These can and do grow to maybe 15 to 20 feet in width, and form massive thickets which are impenetrable without a machete. I lost a huge Osceola gobbler one morning in one of these thickets. My shots had upended him, but he managed to take wing, and sailed out across a pasture studded with palmetto stands, crash landing into one of these. Though I had the thicket marked well, once I got to

Osceola habitat is flat and sometimes open, with visibility reaching out to a mile. Osceolas wander all over this country, so the hunter must keep a continual watch for the birds. Cypress strands and creek swamps snake across the horizon, and these are where the birds find roost trees. Listen near them at dawn for a gobbling turkey.

it, it was with great difficulty that I could walk in it. I combed that spiney tangle for over an hour, trying to search every inch of it, getting speared in the legs so many times I quit worrying about them, and just kept looking. Nobody hates losing a fine adult gobbler more than I do, so it was with a nasty gut feeling that I walked away from there without the old bird. Though the incident happened years ago, I can still see that big imposing thicket west of Yeehaw Junction.

The saw palmetto, if uncontrolled, will take over a pasture in a few short years, so cattlemen in Florida burn the stuff, which not only helps to slow its takeover, but also keeps check on the rattlesnakes. Once a saw palmetto pasture is burned, wild turkeys can then feed among the burned stalks. Turkeys are extremely difficult to see at a distance in such stuff, so it helps to carry binoculars in Florida. A

Small drove of Osceola turkeys feeding among the southern pines. (Photo by Lovett Williams, courtesy Florida Game & Fresh Water Fish Commission.)

big Osceola gobbler flew over me one hazy morning, going to ground on a "burn," a good ½-mile from where I stood along a cypress swamp. I kept track of him with the field glasses, and a while later was able to call him into easy shooting range.

Florida has another palm which is found where the turkeys are hunted; this one a tree, the cabbage palm. These look no different from a palm tree, the crown made up of large fan-shaped leaves, atop a long narrow trunk which may reach 70 feet in height. Turkeys eat the berries of this tree during the fall and winter months.

Probably the average Osceola turkey hunter would say there are two principal trees to be considered when hunting these turkeys—the live oak, and the bald cypress. Live oaks have evergreen foliage, grow to about 40 feet in height, sometimes 4 feet in diameter, and have a huge, sprawling crown. Acorns on live oaks mature in a single season and are sweet. Throughout areas inhabited by Osceolas, these trees grow in clumps or islands, referred to as hammocks. Often mingled with these hardwoods and towering above them will be the cabbage palms, and underfoot, within these dark shadowy canopies, will be scattered clumps of saw palmetto. Like tattered clothes draped from a scarecrow, Spanish moss will hang from the palms and oak boughs. Turkeys love these hammocks, going from one to another, seeking the acorns.

The landscape will be dotted with long lines of lace-like foliaged trees, standing straight and tall above the prairies, or perhaps in clumps, or standing in the still waters of a swamp. These trees are the bald cypress, a favored roosting tree of older gobblers. Floridians have names for the various stands of cypress. Those forming a long line along a watercourse are known as "cypress strands," while isolated clumps, or a group at one end of a strand, are known as "cypress heads." Cypress swamps, or sloughs, are large bodies of water in which cypress trees are growing, the sloughs often going dry during long periods of little rain. And throughout the swamps will be found the well-known "cypress knee," a root projection that sticks above water anywhere from several inches to 3 feet.

The hunter who finds numbers of big mature cypress within his hunting area would do well to hunt near them at dawn, as these are often used as roosts. I found a fairly

The best hunting for Osceola wild turkeys can be found on private lands, such as the newly opened Fish Eating Creek Hunting Camp, located in Palmdale, Florida. This "pay hunt" offers the finest Osceola hunting habitat in the Sunshine State.

good sized hunk of swamp in Osceola County one afternoon while I was scouting and, on closer examination, eyeballed fresh tracks in the mud along its western boundary. Unable to tell how far across the swamp was, I began wading. A couple hundred yards out, I studied the intimidating trunks, reaching for the open sky, where far above me the gnarled boughs cast a roof across the swamp. The black, tea-clear waters had become belly deep, and because the far side seemed no closer than when I had left the mucky edge, I turned back. Leeches, cottonmouths, moss, airplants—a fascinating world lay in those still waters.

An old bird cut loose far out among the cypress. After he'd gobbled a time or two . . .

The next morning I was there by the edge of that swamp, just as first light was breaking, having walked the better part of 2 miles, crossing two cypress strands in getting there. But, it was worth it. An old bird cut loose far out among the cypress. After he'd gobbled a time or two, I could hear the meek chatter of hens. Though the bunch got together on going to ground, I luckily managed to bag the gobbler. The point is, the big cypress were there, I knew there could be hunting possibilities, which there were, and it worked out for the best.

Various additional oaks make up the climax vegetation in Florida, along with a number of pines, magnolia, bay, sweet gum, and other trees. Acorns are the preferred food of Osceola wild turkeys, which is easily understood, there being several varieties among the habitat. The laurel oak, myrtle oak, and live oak are the principal evergreen trees.

The deciduous oaks are the water oak and the turkey oak. Other foods of the Osceola are wax-myrtle berries, pine mast, cabbage palm seeds, and a great number of grass seeds. I watched an adult gobbler with a few hens feeding in a field of grass one morning, and they must have picked up a jillion seeds from it. Another time I watched while a hen plucked all the petals from a wild iris. The Osceola also fills out its diet with all sorts of insects, beetles and grasshoppers.

The first-time hunter to Osceola country will notice a tremendous amount of wildlife. Birds of all varieties are thick. Ducks, tremendous numbers of wading birds, southern bald eagles, ospreys, swallow-tailed kites, caracara, water turkeys—the list is endless. I would advise a hunter to buy one of the small pocketsize bird identification books for the eastern regions of the United States and carry it along. Small white-tailed deer are abundant. Armadillos are everywhere. The fact is, many times when you think a turkey is approaching, it will be one of these armored critters. Though they appear formidable, they are harmless.

Snakes are plentiful. The swamps, sloughs, and areas where water is prevalent are where the bulk of the cottonmouths are found. I've hunted around these snakes from Oklahoma to Florida, all across the Deep South and have never found them to be an aggressive snake. David Kelley, a buddy of mine from Cocoa, Florida, and I stepped across several cottonmouths in less than 10 minutes one morning while hunting Three Lakes Management Area, near Saint Cloud. Like so many, they simply stared up at us, cotton-

gin's to protect the hunter's lower extremities are popular.

Hunters in Florida should be on the lookout for wild hogs. The ancestors of these animals were domestic, but, once so many of them got loose in the swamps, the animals began breeding there, and now Florida has thousands of feral pigs. The bulk of these will be black or dark red. Some Florida ranchers barbecue these over a pit of oak coals. All else a hunter needs is a hunting knife to cut off the delicious slabs, perhaps some hot bread and butter, baked beans and iced down beer. The appetite will be there once you see the hog basting above those red embers.

Alligators—another reason the turkey hunter should carry binoculars is to study these big-mouthed suits of ar-

(Above) Gallberries are a favorite food of the Osceola wild turkey found in southern Florida. These bushes are prevalant in many areas in Florida and are seemingly a prolific bearer of food for wildlife.

This Osceola threesome sense danger and are high-tailing for the safety of some nearby cover. (Photo by Jake Johnson, courtesy Florida Game & Fresh Water Fish Commission.)

white mouths hinged open like a hissing cat. Cottonmouths are ugly snakes.

Florida has no shortage of rattlesnakes either, these coming in all sizes and species. The feared ones are the giant Florida diamondbacks. At crossroad stores I've eyeballed dried skins which appeared to be near 8 feet in length. From what I've been told, the Florida diamondback will crawl up onto a saw palmetto clump, coil up there and wait for prey to pass by. Florida is excellent bobwhite quail country, so many bird dogs are bitten by these critters. Snake leg-

mor. Gators are wild, wary critters and in approaching an alligator inhabited area, it is best to stalk it much like a drove of turkeys. Alligators spend a great amount of time sunning on the banks of pools or streams. Though the beasts seem to be asleep, they will flee into the dark water at the slightest disturbance. During dry years, 'gators are forced to areas of water and are easily visible, if the hunter takes care in sneaking them. One year when I was hunting the Fish Eating Creek area, conditions thereabouts were very dry, allowing me to observe alligators all I wanted.

The average size of a Rio Grande will be slightly less than an Eastern . . .

The Rio Grande wild turkey is hunted today throughout portions of the Southwest with limited hunting farther north in the plains country just east of the Rockies. Rio Grandes are also found in the east-northeast states of Mexico. Restocking and relocating programs are responsible for much of this hunting, for historically the Rio Grande was found only in west Texas, far western Oklahoma, perhaps along the northeastern edge of New Mexico, and in small numbers along Kansas' southwest border.

Laid out alongside other subspecies, the first thing noticeable about the Rio Grande is the pale buff coloring on the tips of the lower rump and tail feathers. Now I've heard this described as "white" by folks who aren't acquainted with the true strain of Rio Grande, but the color is really a pale buff, or beige. This is very evident on both gobblers and hens, and alone sets them apart from the other strains of wild turkeys. Overall, the hen appears lighter in color than an Eastern turkey hen. Rio Grande gobblers, at a distance, appear black when viewed from head-on. When facing away from the hunter, the gobbler will appear lighter than an Eastern gobbler, particularly throughout the wing and lower back areas.

Beard development is good in the Rio Grande, but I have never seen as many lengthy beards as are found among the Eastern variety, on a bird-to-bird ratio. Nor have I observed beards so thick and bulky as can be found among Easterns.

Rio Grande hens are often found with beards, probably more so than among any of the other subspecies. The average size of a Rio Grande wild turkey will be slightly less than an Eastern wild turkey during the spring months, but slightly heavier during the fall and winter months. Rio Grandes gain weight at a faster pace during the late summer, and throughout the fall, than Eastern birds. Throughout January, February and March, the Eastern surpasses the Rio Grande in weight, particularly among adult gobblers. Spur development is not on a level with the Eastern or Osceola insofar as sharpness is concerned; length is very near equal.

Creeks, rivers, and cow pasture ponds, these are where the Rio Grande is found . . .

The first-timer to Rio Grande country will probably notice a lack of water, as much historic range is what many folks would term as hot and dry country. Many of the tributaries have water in them only a portion of the year. Anyone who has hunted the upper reaches of the Cimarron River has probably heard some cowboy make the remark, "a mile wide and an inch deep," but this is at flood stage. Much of the time a hunter can cross the sandy river bottom and never see water. The Rio Grande turkey, like all turkeys, is found where there is water. Creeks, rivers, cow pasture ponds (what many of us Westerners call "tanks"), these are where the Rio Grande is found, as along them

Rio Grande turkeys are found throughout the shinnoak country of western Oklahoma and Texas. Shinnoak grows in clumps, bears small acorns, and during hot weather provides shade. Due to the interior being a foot or two higher than surrounding prairie, the turkeys in these clumps often see a hunter at long distances. This elevation difference is due to the small clump of trees stopping blowing sands, which build up over a period of time.

(Left) Rio Grande gobbler. (Photo courtesy Gene Smith, NWTF)

(Below) This hunter is searching for sign of wild turkeys near a windmill in the western U.S. This is typically hot and dry country and these wind-powered water pumps are sometimes the only source of water. Unfortunately, many are turned off when cattle are taken from the pasture. The wild game, then, no longer has water and must move on, reducing the game population.

A wintering flock of Rio Grande turkeys feeds across a pasture and, like all wild turkeys, feed most of the day. During winter these birds will subsist on grass seeds, multiflora rose, autumn olive, a jillion weed seeds, hackberries, and acorns, just to name a portion of the foods available. (Photo courtesy David Jackman.)

(Right) The Rio Grande turkey habitat is dotted with junipers, stunted oak clumps, and various grasses. The principal vegetation here is sand sagebrush. This hunter is carrying a nice Rio Grande back to his truck, and it's a sure bet that he wishes he had a sling on his shotgun!

will be the timber for roosting trees. Windmills, which are allowed to pump the full year, will also have resident wild turkeys located nearby. Too often, windmills are shut off, the cattle being rotated to other pastures, resulting in the birds migrating to other sources of water. There are huge acreages of potential Rio Grande habitat which would be home to thousands of these turkeys if water was made available on a regular basis.

Principal climax vegetations found throughout this historic range are cottonwood, elm, cedar, hackberry, pecan, walnut, ash, willow, shinnoak, post oak, blackjack oak, mesquite, sand sagebrush, sycamore, live oak, black locust, hedgeapple and hickory. Much of this region is sandy soiled, supporting bushes and shrubs like prickly pear cactus, catclaws, sumacs, salt cedar and buck brush. Mesquite, sand sagebrush, along with the dense thickets of salt cedar which border some of the tributaries, and the thickets of

stunted oaks, are escape covers for hard-hunted Rio Grandes.

The larger oaks, cottonwoods, elms, and sycamores seem to be the main source for roost sites, though younger birds very often roost in soapberry when small groves of these are present. A woods made up of mature black locust would possibly be used by hens with their young broods.

Like all wild turkeys, the Rio Grande is fond of acorns. The shinnoak supplies great quantities of these almost every year so the birds have them available at all times. Hackberry is a favored food, as are the berries of the *bumelia*. *Bumelia* are very sporadic fruit bearing trees, although the hackberry makes up for this, bearing fruit each and every year. Leastways, the areas where I hunt Rio Grandes have never known a season without hackberries. I am always popping a bunch of these in my mouth, to chew off the sugar-loaded skin, spitting out the large seed. These are the best in the

Young Steven Preston walks toward a large stand of juniper, nestled beneath a towering cottonwood tree. Rio Grande turkey habitat varies tremendously from open prairie-like country to heavily timbered, brushy bottoms.

often, once turkeys are located, it is then possible to stalk to within easy shotgun range. Binoculars are excellent for studying the lay of the land, enabling a stealthy hunter to pick a route to them, unseen.

Binoculars will also let the newcomer observe coyotes, deer, prairie dogs, plus numerous birds like shrikes, sparrow hawks, Harris' sparrows, killdeer, Mississippi kites, kingbirds, scissortails, to name a few. Prairie chickens can be seen in places, along with cottontop quail (blue or scaled quail), pheasants and bobwhite quail, even roadrunners.

Numerous snakes are present throughout Rio Grande turkey range, and though most are nonpoisonous, a variety of rattlesnakes can be found, some reaching 5 to 6 feet in length. Lizards abound, as do horned toads, or horned lizards, whichever you prefer to call them. All sorts of fur-bearers are found—beavers, raccoons, bobcats, possum, skunk (both spotted and striped), badger, coyote and mink.

The Merriam was named after the first chief of the United States Biological Survey, C. Hart Merriam . . .

Wild Merriam tom turkey in full strut. (Credit: Irene Vandermolen, Leonard Rue Ent.)

dead of winter. The glistening black *bumelia* berry is very tasty, though the turkeys will often beat a path to these before the hunter has a chance. As with the hackberry tree, wild turkeys will fly up onto these trees, teeter-tottering up and down on the wobbly outermost limbs as they peck at the berries. The remainder of the flock will run about beneath the trees, feeding on those knocked loose by their compatriots above.

Rio Grandes also feed heavily upon grasshoppers, one commodity the southwestern part of the United States has a great plenty of during an average summer and fall. On numerous occasions I've counted upwards of 200 'hoppers in a single jake turkey craw. The onset of winter kills the grasshoppers, the dead insects scattered across the range the remainder of the winter to be eaten by turkeys, prairie chickens, coyotes, and other wildlife.

Other favored foods of the Rio Grande are mulberries, French mulberry, chickasaw plums, Mexican plums, sunflowers, ragweeds, doveweeds, cedar berries, along with seeds, panicles and leaves from a jillion varieties of grasses and weeds. Rio Grandes, like all the other subspecies, will feed heavily on cultivated crops when these are available, particularly maize, wheat, oats and corn. These crops are also consumed when in the leaf stage. Wild turkeys like fresh small green leaves, particularly after a winter of feeding heavily on acorns, mast and woodland foods.

A hunter new to Rio Grande wild turkey hunting will probably be startled at the nakedness of the flat, rolling terrain. His initial reaction will probably be, ''the turkeys will be able to see me for miles.'' This is true, but the hunter can put this to his advantage, being able to see them at great distances—*if he carries binoculars*! A hunter journeying to the prairies of Texas, Oklahoma and other areas where these birds are hunted should make it a habit to use field glasses. The open habitat lends itself to their use. Very

The Merriam wild turkey, historically inhabiting areas which would become Arizona, New Mexico, Colorado, and parts of Cimarron County in the far west end of the Oklahoma Panhandle, is often known among veteran turkey hunters as the Rocky Mountain wild turkey. The Merriam was named after the first Chief of the United States Biological Survey, C. Hart Merriam. When Cortez and Coronado first traveled north in their search for The Seven

Ponderosa pines are always present in the historic range of Merriam Rocky Mountain wild turkey. These huge pines are invariably used as roost trees throughout these areas, which include large sections of Arizona, New Mexico, and Colorado. Continuous logging operations often cause wild turkeys to leave such areas.

(Right) The *average* wild turkey gobbler will weigh between 17 and 20 pounds—the average for all five subspecies.

Cities of Gold (which was a myth, though they had no way of knowing), they noticed the presence of turkeys among the Indians wherever they traveled. New Spain, as this region was known, was infested with the birds, both domestic and wild. The Indians were expert at bringing home wild birds from the mountains and taming them. Perhaps, the birds found in many Indian villages throughout the mountains of Arizona and New Mexico were what we today call the Merriam wild turkey.

A hunter who has never seen a Merriam gobbler in the wild will, on seeing one anywhere inside of 50 yards, immediately think, *look at all the white on that turkey*. Laid out on the pine needles, this is all the more evident. The dark bars on the wings are smaller, with greater amounts of white on the primaries and secondaries. Just as startling, at least to a first-time Merriam hunter, will be the beautiful snow-white lacy appearance of the tips of the lower back and tail feathers. Such feathering on a full-blood Merriam gobbler will be as white as snow. My first thought on seeing Merriam turkeys was "black and white." The birds are simply that—big black and white turkeys. The hens are very dark, and both birds appear to have more hair on their heads than the other wild turkeys. Feathering reaches up the neck to a greater extent.

Weight is on a par with the average Eastern. Beard development is below that of the other three bird subspecies found in the United States, as is spur growth. The presence of snow and ice throughout the Merriam's habitat could have a bearing on beard length, though this is strictly speculation on my part.

Ponderosas are the predominant roost tree for Merriams at the highest elevations . . .

Ponderosa pine comes to mind at the mention of the Merriam wild turkey. These large timber trees, found in the Rocky Mountain forest region, grow on high mountain slopes, in an area where long cold winters prevail. This region has a short, warm growing season. Other trees which are important to Merriam turkeys are junipers, pinyons, and scrub oaks. At lower elevations cottonwood and cedar could be added.

Ponderosas are the predominant roost tree for these birds when they are at the higher elevations, 6,000 feet or above. Scrub oaks, consisting of scattered stands or immense thickets of Gambel's oak, make up the bulk of the feeding areas, which are interspersed with any number of grasses. Grass seeds and acorns make up a good portion of this bird's diet.

Grass leaves are an important food source, and where man has cultivated Merriam's turkeys will eat heartily of what grains are grown. The alligator juniper is invariably a heavy bearing tree, which results in this standby food being readily available. Sumac stands can often be seen along the bottoms of tiny mountain meadows. I killed a fine old gobbler one afternoon as he fed in one of these thickets. He was easy to stalk in a blinding snowstorm.

Other foods—grasshoppers, beetles, and umpteen other

(Below) Author's friend David Jackman totes a gobbler down from a rocky, cactus-studded ridge in Black Mesa country, in the Oklahoma Panhandle. The Merriam turkeys which call this dry desolate country home have migrated here from far upriver in New Mexico and Colorado, and have been found in this area since the country was settled.

Excellent wild turkey range in Nebraska is found along the Niobrara River, which is Merriam habitat. This is an area of rolling hills, large cattle pastures and cedar trees. This is highly productive territory.

insects—are found on mountainous terrain. Animal foods such as snails and frogs are found at spring seeps and in mountain streams. As with all wild turkeys, Merriams are fond of green leaves when these are in season. Dandelions, muhly grasses, panic, bluegrass, and lovegrasses, are all eaten by wild turkeys. Anyone who has studied the wild turkey has marveled at the manner in which these great birds will attack a stand of mature grasses. I have lain in thick cover, field glasses trained on gobblers as they fed on the grass by grasping the stem with their beaks just beneath the seed head and then, with an upward jerk of the head, stripping away all the seeds. A drove of old gobblers will seemingly do this for hours on end.

The Merriam wild turkey can be hunted in 15 states, as the bird has been successfully restocked and introduced into a number of western states. Rifles are a part of the Old West, so a good many wild turkeys are killed with these firearms.

In the South, the hen will begin laying eggs in late March, but this varies . . .

In order to understand the methods utilized in hunting wild turkeys, we need to know the lifestyle of these birds, from egg to adulthood, along with a study of their habits. Let's begin with the egg. Wild turkey hens lay anywhere from eight to 14 eggs. The nest, which is built on the ground, varies in location from one subspecies to another, with the shallow grass and leaf-lined nest lying at the base of a tree, or beneath a blackberry tangle, or under the overhanging spears of a soap yucca. Wild turkey hens are expert at concealing nests from marauding predators.

I have stumbled across several nests while hunting springtime turkeys. I have no desire to find nests, as disturbance could cause the hen to vacate the eggs, which is a condition I want least of all. But these were discovered usually after flushing a hen at extremely close range, whereon I noticed the eggs, and then quickly left the area. I once observed a most unusual object among a clutch of eggs laid by a Rio Grande hen among vines of wild gourd. One of the gourds, round, smooth and about the same size as a turkey egg, laid in the center of the clutch. This reminded me of my boyhood experiences on a farm here in western Oklahoma, when we often placed "nest eggs" made of wood, ceramic or glass in chicken coops, to encourage the hens to lay. I presumed the gourd had perhaps played the same role, as it was there when the Rio Grande hen had begun laying her clutch.

Many times I have found the remains of nests destroyed by predators. Skunks, raccoons, 'possums, snakes and crows probably cause the greatest egg predation. Predators will break the egg shell randomly and scatter them about, whereas eggs which have hatched will be split apart neatly, leaving a cup-like portion of the shell in the nest.

In the South, the wild turkey hen will begin laying eggs in late March, but this time period varies as one travels north and/or higher in elevation. Weather affects laying and incubation among all subspecies, so there is a great variation among young turkey broods, even in the same area. I have many times observed young turkeys (poults) which were as large as fryer chickens, but within the same area, have seen a brood of tiny poults but a few days old. Anyone who has hunted fall turkeys extensively understands what I am saying because the fall hunter will bag turkeys that vary greatly in size and weight.

Mother Nature's timetables allow the young turkeys to come into the world when conditions for growth and survival are at a peak. Nowhere is this more evident than high in the Sierra Madre mountains of Mexico, home of the Gould's wild turkey. During the spring and summer months, the country is very dry, with little or no new vegetation, and scant water supplies. The summer rains are late, not coming until July and August. Therefore, the hatching season is at that time.

Once the hen has laid her eggs, she remains on the nest day and night incubating them. She leaves the nest for a short time each day to feed and drink. The feeding period varies, and she will often take evasive measures in coming and going to prevent predation of the nest. As boys my brother Dick and I were given the task of finding the nests of the tame turkeys we raised on the farm. The birds were allowed to roam free, so when the old hens began nesting, we had to sneak along after them, to learn where they had secreted the eggs. This often took a great many sneaky trips, as a turkey hen will wander very erratically in going to her eggs. Much of the time we would find the nests deep inside the many expansive thickets of sand plums on our Oklahoma farm. (As a side note, I might mention that Dick and I also found a large cardboard box filled with fruit jars of illegal moonshine late one afternoon as we searched a thicket alongside a little used dirt road. Those was "prohibition days." Needless to say, when we told our father and grandfather of this, they had us quickly show them where the find was, and after toting it to the house, gave us a fare-thee-well understanding to keep our mouths shut and, to stay shy of that bunch of plum bushes in the week ahead. We did.)

The eggs will hatch about 24 to 25 days after the last egg is laid. All of the eggs will hatch within a 20 to 30 hour stretch, and as soon as this is done, the hen will take the brood from the nest area. Should she leave there during the morning hours, the little family may be a ½-mile distant by nightfall.

The poults immediately learn to respond to the hen's voice, and should danger come near, she will run away, trying to lure the danger to her. The poults will run a few feet, and "freeze" in cover, remaining hidden until she calls them back together. No one should attempt to catch poults. These little birds are not much bigger than a bumblebee and are very fragile, insofar as being able to sustain physical punishment. Too, most states have laws against keeping wild game in captivity.

An alert turkey hen watches for predators as her youngsters continue feeding. Should she detect anything suspicious, her "putting" will tell the poults to be alert. (Photo by Greg Butts)

The wing feathers of this young turkey are all sizes, indicating a continuing moulting process as the bird grows from a poult into a more adult-like bird. Rarely are birds this small shot during the fall season.

An alert and spooked turkey hen runs from the photographer. We can tell this is a hen due to the whitish tips of its breast feathers. Many turkeys spread the tail when running, as has this bird, as the tail acts as a steering rudder when dodging back and forth through the terrain.

I can recall flushing a large drove of birds. A youngster which could barely fly tried . . .

At the age of 2 weeks the poults can fly up into small trees, either to escape predation, or, to roost. I have seen them sitting atop bushes which were perhaps 10 feet from the ground after being flushed there by dogs. The person who suddenly finds himself near a scattered band of small turkeys should quickly leave the area. Very young turkeys are extremely susceptible to any number of dangers when separated from the mother hen. Vacate the area. Leave them be.

drove might make contact with yet another drove, and join them for a day or two. By mid-winter, these droves will remain together permanently for the winter months.

The number of birds within a fall or winter drove can vary. I have observed tiny droves of one adult with three or four young hens, "jennies," and young gobblers, "jakes." On the other hand, I have seen wintering droves which numbered over 300 turkeys, of all ages, sizes, and of both sexes. I can recall flushing a large winter drove of nearly 50 birds, which immediately vanished from sight. A youngster which could barely fly tried to go after them, flying a short way, then after running a distance, flying again. From that same scattered drove I called up an adult gobbler. Obviously, the tiny turkey was of a very late hatch.

Ordinarily, throughout the winter months the males and

A wild turkey hen takes her brood out for a feeding period. Notice that these young turkeys have little fear of the surroundings. The foods of most interest to these youngsters are insects (particularly grasshoppers) and weed seeds. (Photo by Greg Butts)

The three young turkeys with this hen are grown to a size that they can fly up into a low tree to roost and, as the birds grow larger and stronger, they will roost in larger trees. Until the birds are about 2 weeks old, they must roost on the ground, where they are susceptible to predators. (Photo by Greg Butts)

Once the youngsters can fly up into trees, the daily routine is one of leaving the roost area, feeding toward water, resting during midday, and after feeding again during the late afternoon hours, flying up to a roost for the night. Such a routine may vary: watering can be at any time of the day; there may be time spent in wallowing a "dusting" location; and there will be times when the birds just lollygag for a few moments, perhaps on a hillside in the sunlight, or on a sandbar near water. Fighting, chasing and quarreling can, and does, take place almost every day. As the birds grow older, there will also be vocal threats, and much chasing and pecking when small family droves meet. Wild turkeys are extremely entertaining to the hunter who wants to study them, for they are seldom quiet. They seem to be feeding or chasing each other much of the day.

With the end of summer, the small bands begin joining together, though this can be on a day-now-and-then basis for some time. I have seen large numbers roosting near each other, but at dawn, the groups assemble separately, and go their own ways. During the daily rambles, such a

females will roost and feed in separate groups. These groups may roost among the same grove of trees, but after gathering at dawn, will go their separate ways. The older adult males, the long bearded gobblers, will very often make up a yet smaller group, which will have nothing to do with the other birds. And, in any territory inhabited by wild turkeys, there are, at times, a single bird, or perhaps a pair of hermit gobblers, which live a solitary life throughout the months, spending the days and nights alone, or in the company of one other old male. These old rascals are what the veteran turkey hunter knows as the most worthy of adversaries. Many of my fondest memories are of fall and winter hunts resulting in dealings with such birds.

With the approach of spring there comes into the wild turkey's world a slow but inevitable change, as the mating urge awakens in the birds' bodies. Gobblers begin to gobble a few times at dawn. The adult males then begin to seek out the large droves of hens and to strut. Fights take place, as the dominant gobblers establish themselves for the right to mate.

Spring turkey hunting is built around the mating urge of the male turkey . . .

A "chesty" male turkey walks along a section of hogwire fence, followed by a smaller, slender hen. The wild gobbler gains weight during the winter months, much of this accumulating on the upper chest, resulting in a fat reservoir known as a "breast sponge." As the gobbler often eats very little during the spring breeding season, this fat deposit enables it to continue breeding. This breast sponge will be gone by late spring, and throughout the summer and fall months the gobbler will be at his lightest weight. (Photo by Greg Butts)

(Right) With a deer for company, a large wintering flock of turkeys feeds in a river bottom in Kansas. Spring breakup will soon begin, as we can see several gobblers strutting in this photo. When this occurs, small groups of two or three gobblers, with several hens in each, will leave the area, seeking other uninhabited areas, where these groups will remain during the spring breeding season. Each group will feed, roost, and breed as a separate unit. After the spring breakup has begun, wild turkeys are often encountered many miles from where the wintering flock had gathered. (Photo by David Jackman)

These short-bearded gobblers are "blue-johns," "buck turkeys," or "shortbeards," but are most commonly known among turkey addicts as "jakes." A month or two shy of being a year old when the spring season opens, these jakes often interfere with a hunter's efforts, as their gobbling often draws a hunter away from the intended quarry—a long-bearded adult gobbler.

great amount of springtime scattering, with birds being seen 15 miles from their usual winter haunts.

Dominant males then establish themselves throughout these scattered territories, and with a small group of hens, remain there during the mating season. During April, May and June, the hens lay, and then incubate the eggs, leaving the gobbler. Abandoned, and with the mating urge waning, the breed males group back together, and for the remainder of the summer these birds will be the most difficult turkeys to find throughout the range. The older gobblers will molt feathers during the summer months, and are exceedingly shy at this time.

The younger males, the birds that all turkey hunters know as "jakes," will react to all this in different ways. Some will form small bands and wander about the country like a bunch of gypsies. Others will simply prowl the terrain alone, seemingly without friend one. Still others will hang around an old gobbler and his harem of hens, though the old bird will not allow the jakes to mate the hens. It is not uncommon to call in an adult gobbler, and find two, or

Throughout March and early April, in much of the country's turkey terrain, an event known among turkey hunters as "spring breakup" takes place. The large droves split apart, resulting in the various members scattering over a much larger area than was inhabited by the wintering drove. Among all subspecies, spring breakup takes turkeys many, many miles from their fall and winter residence. Merriams often migrate 30 or more miles from winter range to where the hens will nest and raise the young. Rio Grandes do a

maybe four or five, jakes along with him. I called in a group of 29 young gobblers one morning many years ago, as best I could count. Probably 15 were strutting. Their combined gobbling was no different than what a turkey farm sounds like.

Spring turkey hunting is built around the mating urge of the male turkey, in hopes that, by imitating the call of a turkey hen, the male will come to the hunter's tolling. Hens will often come to the call too, as will young jake gobblers.

The five wild turkeys which make up the Royal Grand Slam in turkey hunting have a predominant "beard," which is a breast adornment of a hair-like rudimentary feather. This "beard" can grow to a length of 14 inches on the Eastern, Rio Grande, Osceola, Merriam, or Gould's wild turkeys.

Adult gobblers often strut while on the roost branch, as this pre-dawn photo reveals. Though the bird can't walk back and forth unless standing on a huge ponderosa branch, it will drop its wings and fan the tail, exactly as it would do if standing on firm soil. (Photo courtesy David Jackman.)

The daily habits of a gobbler with his bunch of hens are important to all turkey hunting enthusiasts, for around these habits is laid the groundwork for hunting methods. An average April morning finds the old male perched high on a branch, the hens scattered among nearby trees. At the first inkling of coming daylight, he will have the urge to gobble. Though it in no way sounds like a song, it is said to be the male's song, much the same as a cardinal, or a mockingbird. Supposedly, his gobbling also lets the hens know where he is, and once he has flown to ground, they go to him. Sometimes he will leave the tree after only a gobble or two, while on another morning he may remain in the tree until after sunup, having gobbled maybe 100 times.

Very often, after he has flown to ground, he will gobble a time or two, whereon the hens join him, and then he will cease gobbling. There will then be mating activities, after which the hens begin walking toward a favored feeding area. Mating may take place other times of the day, particularly when the mating season is at its peak. The adult may gobble at any time during the day, though the average adult male will gobble predominantly before 10:00 AM.

A spring turkey season is feasible because a hen needs to be mated only once to proliferate the race. Thus, wild turkey seasons are set to open after the mating period, but, hopefully prior to the hens incubating the eggs. This results in less hunter disturbance of hens at this critical time.

The hunting season is also set to open during prime gobbling season. Such gobbling indicates a lessening in male and female relations, causing the male to gobble frequently in order to lure hens to him. It is at this time that the male bird is far the easiest to hunt. Like I've heard it said about men, "He's a sucker for a skirt." So gobblers are "a sucker for a call." The old gobblers throughout much of the turkey range will be removed by the hunters each year, particularly where pursued by veteran hunters. Numerous areas, where my buddies and I have hunted for the past 20 years, have not produced what could be classified as an outstanding

Notice the distinct "hook" or "dogleg" in this beard found on a wild turkey hen. This is very characteristic of beards found on wild turkey hens, regardless of subspecie. Beards seldom exceed 8 inches on hens.

"trophy gobbler" in the past umpteen years. Bluntly, we keep them shot out. There simply are no hermit gobblers, nor birds which attain the long lean curved spurs of the trophy adult. I have been to areas, scattered across the United States, which were supposedly the home of this many or that many hermit gobblers, but, unless the supposed local experts weren't as expert as they hoped to be, the birds were just replacements of those which are killed each season. There are no 5- to 10-year-old gobblers in the woods which I hunt each year.

The wild turkey is found throughout the length and breadth of the United States today. Many of us would like to think this condition will last forever. If it was left up to the American hunter, I could promise you that it would. But, so long as we have the tremendous amounts of land being cleared each year for land development and myriad other uses, in time the turkey will go. The giant timber companies are working at cleaning off the landscape, as bare as a dog's bone on the kitchen floor. If you don't believe me, travel to southeast Oklahoma. Those mountains have been skinned like a cat.

And, the United States government is doing its share too, channeling streams, subsidizing the cost of brush spraying, selling off public lands, and submitting to pressure from self-interest groups. Turkeys are tough. Let's hope they are tough enough.

Chapter 2

Outfitting for Turkey Chasin'

ANYTIME I THINK of hunting and camping equipment, I recall articles I've read by Patrick McManus, staff writer for *Outdoor Life*. The bulk of McManus' writings deal with the how-to's of lashing a complete, overnight, well-equipped campsite onto a bicycle, wading across trout streams, and other pursuits, all told in such a manner as to keep the reader hollering with laughter. Many, many evenings I've been doubled up reading about the shenanigans of McManus' childhood buddies. This bunch of characters have a thing for rounding up a mountain of gear, tying and strapping it all over themselves and heading for the wilds. They were so weighed down with gear that they oftentimes left tracks "2 inches deep in solid bedrock."

McManus has never hinted that any of his cronies are turkey hunters. If not, they certainly have the qualifications. One hot April afternoon, many years back, I thought I'd bumped into one of Patrick's old chums. I was stillhunting toward the Blue Mountain Tower, down in southeastern Oklahoma's Winding Stair mountains, when I met a young bucko coming down the trail. He was in full beard, which was black as coal, had on camouflage pants tucked into 8-inch high lugged-sole mountain climbing boots, and was sweating like crazy. I could see a heavy flannel shirt sticking out around his coat collar, and he had a wool watch cap stuck on his long flowing black head of hair. Worse, he was wearing a down hip-length coat, one which would have been much more at home in a cold goose blind. The pockets were bulging. I supposed he was toting at least a full box of shotshells hidden there for the big magazine gun he was cradling in one arm.

Speaking to him, we passed the time of day for a moment and then I suggested we sit a spell, as I could see the boy needed a rest. Obviously, he had set out before first day was streaking the sky and, thinking it was a little cool, had donned clothes for the time being. Now, hours later, he had no need for his coat, hat, boots and, from the way the sweat was pouring from his face, very little use for his long hair and beard. We sat there for a time, discussing turkey hunting thereabouts. After he'd cooled down, he went his way and I mine. He was young and strong, and chances were the heat wouldn't harm him. But what he was enduring could have very well been fatal to an older person. In such a state, he was no match for whatever chance at a wild turkey should present itself. And, all of this torture could have been avoided with a little forethought in those predawn hours as he left his vehicle.

A case in point. Nowhere on that rolling terrain was there a need for heavy, lugged-sole boots. Lightweight ankletop shoes would have cut hundreds of pounds from his walk. As all the hunting thereabouts is slightly uphill from where vehicles are allowed to park, he should have realized that though it was cool in the predawn darkness, a few hours later his body would begin heating up and therefore he would have no need for a down-filled coat. He would have needed only a billed camo hat to hide part of his long black hair, and a slower pace would have helped guard against his face sweating as it was. I envy him his black beard, as it helps to camouflage his face. Mine will never be black again—*age*.

And, certainly he had no need for but a few shells, as

(Left) A full beard is excellent camouflage for a great many of today's turkey hunters. The author's longtime hunting buddy, Gene Druiett, says he feels naked without his chinwhiskers. He's never owned any face paint.

With high hopes, a group of hunters heads for turkey country. Decked out in camouflage clothing, with a few shells stuck in a pants pocket, these men are not burdened with unneeded gear. Too many of today's hunters are gadget crazy and, having read too much about "survival" paraphernalia, go into the woods laden with equipment they don't need.

the gun's magazine held at least three. Three others, at the most six, would have been plenty. What was hidden in his other sagging pockets, I have no idea. Chances are a good portion of that could have been left behind, too.

The American people, and the American hunter in particular, have become gadget addicted in the last couple of decades. Twenty, 30 years ago, a hunter could walk into the woods carrying a pocketknife, a billfold with his hunting license stuck in it, car keys, and some shells. Probably he felt a little chilly as he headed for the woods, but he soon forgot the cold, what with walking and being involved in the hunt itself. More than likely he wore the same old shoes he worked in the day before.

That's changed. Today's hunter can be far better prepared to hunt, but he can also carry this far beyond the extreme. Let me tell you what a friend of mine had in his pockets on one spring hunt. I might say we were hunting new rough mountainous country, a place we had not hunted previously. I happened to take a photo of what he was carrying, as otherwise I would not have been able to recall each item: a large box call; a slate call; three mouth calls; pocketknife; compass; a small camera; a hunk of strong cord; flashlight; toilet paper folded and secured with a rubber band; a pipe; a pouch of tobacco and a lighter; lightweight leather gloves; handkerchief; billfold; truck keys; two maps; lightweight rain parka; six shotgun shells (besides what was in the gun); a small can of insect repellant; several first aid items; a candy bar; an apple; a sandwich; a small can of tomato juice; and a shotgun.

I hated to be seen near him. The way his pockets bulged, the local law could get the mistaken idea he had just robbed one of those quick stops. I'll agree, he was prepared for about any situation, be it an emergency or going into business. There are those hunters who feel more secure and

thus can hunt with mind at ease if they are always prepared for the worst. Others of us prefer to go light, endure some privations, and enjoy the hunt without weight and bulk.

I wade around in the creek swamps and cypress strands in old Redwing work shoes . . .

Let's take a look at what a turkey hunter should wear. We'll start at the ground and work our way up. What about his feet? Footwear will vary with time of year and terrain. For example, a spring hunt to Florida calls for lightweight boots, perferably ones which are of canvas. The hunter after Osceola turkeys oftentimes finds it necessary to wade water, and the feet could be wet for hours. 'Nam boots,

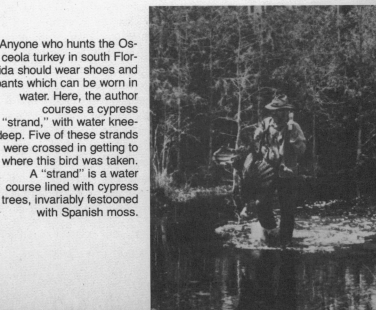

Anyone who hunts the Osceola turkey in south Florida should wear shoes and pants which can be worn in water. Here, the author courses a cypress "strand," with water knee-deep. Five of these strands were crossed in getting to where this bird was taken.
A "strand" is a water course lined with cypress trees, invariably festooned with Spanish moss.

those Army brogans of black leather made famous by United States soldiers during the Vietnam War, are often seen in Florida swamps. I wade around in the creek swamps and cypress strands in plain old Redwing work shoes. They dry out quick, keep their shape in drying on my feet, and are light. I don't wear any socks when I'm planning on doing some wading.

A springtime hunter seeking Eastern wild turkeys can wear most lightweight 8-inch boots, or hightop work shoes. I've noticed hunters in everything from jogging shoes to shotgun top Wellingtons. Lightweight socks fill out the bill.

Hunting turkeys farther west, late in April, calls for something very light in weight, and if possible, a boot or shoe that allows the foot to breathe. It is often hot when you are hunting Rio Grandes in Texas and Oklahoma, and the feet will perspire considerably. Blow sand is sometimes encountered which means a boot with traction will help, but heavy lug soles are a turkey hunter killer in such stuff.

Loose sand can sap the strength from legs quicker than any other ground cover. Weed seeds and sand burrs are also problems in Rio Grande country. So, the best footwear are 8-inch boots, with canvas or light leather tops and a treaded sole. Keep these as light as possible.

The Rocky Mountain springtime hunter, hoping to put his sights on a Merriam wild turkey will probably be wearing 8-inch, or ankletop, lugged-sole mountain boots. Feet need the protection from rocks and the traction that lugs provide. In most instances these boots will also do the trick for the fall turkey hunter with perhaps the addition of heavier socks or a second pair. I know hunters who wear nothing but shoepacs during fall and winter hunts, as the lower waterproof portion keeps the feet dry in water and snow. Too, shoepacs ordinarily have good tread-like soles which give excellent traction on damp terrain. The famous L.L. Bean boot with its rope tread design is a favorite because it keeps feet dry, is light in weight, and the shallow tread

(Below) Today's turkey hunter can buy footwear for any occasion. These extremely lightweight ankletop boots are a sewn combination of synthetic canvas and leather, allowing them to "breathe." This short boot is excellent for use in sand as it has a shallow tread sole, making walking easy.

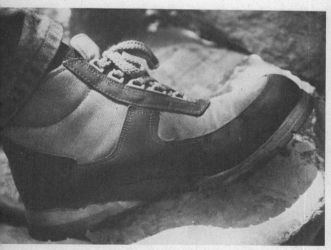

(Above) Shoepacs are extremely popular among turkey hunters because the bottoms are made of rubber to keep out water and the uppers are usually treated leather. Hunters who must spend considerable time in traversing muddy areas, snow, wet grass, and shallow sloughs should invest in this type of footwear. Shoepacs are very comfortable, too.

(Bottom left) Gokey Bullhides offer complete protection from thorns, sand burrs, and snake bites. These have lug soles, are tough as nails, and adjustable at the instep and top.

(Left) Today's marketplace offers an endless number of rubber knee-high boots which are excellent for wearing on terrain where shallow streams must be crossed.

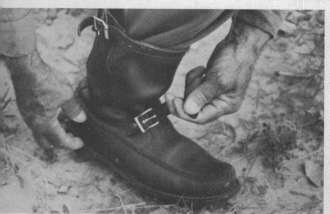

does not allow a buildup of several pounds of clinging mud.

Shoepacs are the favored footwear throughout much of the South during spring hunts. I have a 14-inch pair of Bean boots which have seen me across many streams, swamp ponds, and what have you without my feet getting wet. Even when the water is above the tops, if the boots are laced tight and I hurriedly wade across, I won't take on much water.

Such hightop boots are also some protection against snakes. For those hunters who do fear snakebite, there are 14- and 16-inch hightop boots made of heavy leather which will turn a snakebite. I have a pair of Gokey Bullhides that a rattler tried his teeth on some years back, and he bounced off them like hail off a tin roof. Snake leggings made of lightweight plastic will also work. Many folks scoff at talk about snakebite, but don't be misled. There are few pains which will compare to that which comes not long after a rattlesnake has sunk in his fangs. But whatever you wear on your feet, the main thing you must have are shoes that fit and feel comfortable. I've been in camps where street shoes, work shoes, all sorts of hightopped boots, and cowboy boots were worn. Tennis shoes, too. More than anything else though, the wearer felt good in them.

If you plan on doing considerable walking, you won't need so many clothes . . .

Pants and shirts? Most of today's hunters wear varying weights of camouflage clothing. Heavy or lightweight underwear will make up for what the outer garments lack, and the heavy outer garments can be peeled off as needed. What most hunters fail to take into consideration is what they will be doing while hunting. If you plan on doing considerable walking, you won't need so many clothes. The hunter who plans on sitting and calling for much of the day will need heavier clothing, as he will chill during the early morning and late afternoon hours. During the day, he may need to remove garments so it's smart thinking for the moving hunter to wear a fanny pack, or a small daypack, to carry clothing in. Chances are that sometime during the day he will be on a calling stand for some time and may need to put some of that clothing back on, for once he stops all movement, he will soon cool down. If you plan on doing considerable walking, you should always leave camp feeling a little cool.

I hunt considerably in Old Mexico, back high in the Sierra Madres. Invariably camp will be at a lower altitude than where the Gould's wild turkey is found. Therefore, the first order of the day upon leaving camp is a long hard climb. Before this climb has ended, I will be soaked with sweat. It is cold in the high Sierras, so once I am up where an old Gould's gobbler awaits me, I will get chilled, as my "longhandles" will be wet. But, this does not happen so long as I carry my coat and heavy over-shirt tied to my belt, directly along my backbone and out of the way while

Springtime turkey hunting can be a heat-of-the-day sport. This hunter has partially unzipped his coveralls and removed his cap in trying to remain cool. Camouflage clothing, due to its being of dark colors, and therefore reflecting no light, is hot to wear. Too, this type clothing is usually made of heavy materials, which doesn't help matters.

(Right) Though squatted in partial sunlight, this hunter would go unseen by a wild turkey. Notice how the cap, face mask, gloves, coveralls, and gun blend into one irregular object.

Thin mesh camouflage gloves are easily slipped off and on, hide untanned skin, but are not warm like heavier gloves. These will be ideal for spring mornings in much of the courtry's turkey woods, though they won't provide suitable mosquito protection. These gloves take up very little pocket space.

Several mixed patterns of camouflage clothing have blended this hunter into the surrounding woods. Dark gloves hide fair-skinned hands, and small dabs of face-paint have broken up the large areas on the face. By remaining in the shadows, any glint of light which reflects from eyeglasses will be cut to a minimum. Camouflage tape has been applied to the shotgun to help break up its shape.

(Right) Steven Preston's face blends well into the foliage of this tree even though he is wearing only a simple mosquito net. (Far right) Without the net, Steven's smooth skin will reflect light, presenting large areas which would be easily detected by a keen-sighted turkey. Care must be taken that the net also covers the small, triangular-shaped patch of exposed T-shirt.

climbing. Often I am cold while climbing, but it is better then than later.

As for camouflage patterns, there are many on today's market. Obviously, the hands-down favorites are the jungle or woodlands patterns with the dark browns and greens. Most turkey woods have low shrubs, trees, decaying logs, soils, etc., which span these color ranges but are below the average man's height. Add a pair of gloves, a cap to match, a little face paint or a mask, and by sitting quietly, a person will simply fade into the surroundings.

A new popular camouflage is the tree bark design. This pattern of vertical grays and blacks is designed for the hunter who sits against the trunks of hickorys, oaks and other large trees found in the turkey woods. The dead leaf patterns are best used when hunting over large expanses of oak forest after the leaves have fallen, or where the forest

floor is cloaked with them year 'round. It is particularly well-suited for use on Missouri, Arkansas and Pennsylvania-type ridges during the spring hunt, for those slopes are well covered with dead leaves. I've worn the dead-leaf pattern for years when hunting from shinnoak clumps in Rio Grande country, or in the Gambel oak forests found in much of the Merriam's range, or when hunting the Mexican blue oak thickets back in Old Mexico. It is extremely deadly camouflage when the hunter is shooting from a stretched-out-on-the-belly, or prone, position.

Rain suits, parkas, heavy winter down coats all come in camouflage materials. These will be advertised as windproof or water repellant. Watch what you buy. Make certain it is advertised for the purpose you have in mind. Remember, the tighter the material, the less it will breathe. A garment which will keep the hunter bone dry from the out-

The contrast here between tree bark and snow is as vivid as black and white. This hunter's dark camos seem a stark contrast to the terrain she will be hunting. But, by remaining in the shadows, and by taking up hunting stands in rocks, fallen logs, trees, and brush piles, she will have no difficulty in remaining well hidden from the keen eyes of turkeys.

learned, was with a black powder firearm and whatever clothing they had at the time. Back in those "good old days" the wild turkey was nowhere near as wild as today's bird, so the black powder gun with all its faults was adequate. Range was short, and there were plenty of turkeys. The birds had little fear of man, so it mattered not at all what the hunter wore. But, as the white man advanced across the breadth of the United States settling the lands, the birds were thinned out. What birds did remain after the country was laid "grass side down" (plowed) were the ancestors of the bird we know today as the *wild* turkey.

In my quest to learn what hunting was like back then, I realized I must quit wearing camos, and wear colors that the hunters of those long ago times wore. Dark greens, browns, grays, blacks—these are the colors I wear now. Hats were worn by all men, so I now wear a hat. What have I learned from these "good old days" hunts? Right off, I realized what a boon camouflage clothing is to the modern turkey hunter. Without it, I felt naked when a turkey approached, and still do to this day. Though I have hunted turkeys extensively from New York to Arizona in old timey clothing, I no longer feel free to sit out in the

side elements will often hold in all the perspiration. A hard walk in such clothing can result in the wearer being soaked in his own sweat. When buying rainwear, it is wise to "listen" to it. In other words, due to the type material it is made of, much rainwear will make all sorts of sounds when worn through brushy country. A turkey will hear the coat coming well in advance of the hunter's footsteps. Slip it on in the store, brush your hands across it, brush it against other clothing, making note of the noise it will make in a silent woods once the rain has ceased. You will be able to walk ever so quietly on the soaked leaves, but will your clothes give you away?

Right off, I realized what a boon camouflage clothing is. Without it, I felt naked . . .

Cap? Wear what most hunters stick on their heads—a billed camo cap. It will keep the sun from your eyes, hide your dark hair or your bald head, costs very little should you lose it, and another can be found almost anywhere. Of course in cold weather, a heavier cap may be needed— perhaps one with ear flaps. Any and all can be purchased nationwide, made of varying camouflage materials. There are even camo stocking caps if you prefer that style.

You may notice in the photographs on these pages that I am wearing wide brimmed hats, along with clothing which is not camo. Let me explain. Many years ago I got a hankering to hunt wild turkeys as our forefathers did which, I

Two turkey hunters in vivid contrast. Dwain Bland, left, hunts with a muzzle-loading shotgun and without the benefit of camouflage clothing. Larry Shallenberger, right, carries a modern shotgun, and takes advantage of today's tree-bark pattern of camouflage. (Photo courtesy of Larry Shallenberger)

The camouflage face mask is used by a large army of today's turkey hunters, and though this model doesn't keep out insects, it does allow complete vision freedom. Many hunters don't like the "hazy" vision which occurs when wearing a full mask. Headgear is the popular baseball-type cap.

(Above left) This hunter is wearing what most turkey hunters stick on their heads—a billed camo cap. These baseball-type caps keep the rain and sun off the face, hiding it well, and help to break up the outline of the head. They're also pretty cheap to replace if you loose one during a chase through the woods. (Above right) The author prefers to wear what his forefathers wore in days of old for turkey hunting: clothing in dark shades of green, brown, gray and black, the hat a wide-brimmed style that fits in well with the black powder shotgun. Sorta gives the turkey better odds!

open in front of a tree, watching as a wary gobbler comes to where I am sitting. Now, I must hide behind upturned stumps, in brush piles, blowdowns, shoot from rock outcroppings, any cover which will help hide my clothing which lacks the broken patterns found in camouflage material.

I have been seen by wild turkeys several times, instances where I am positive the bird would not have seen me had I been in camouflage. Two such times cost me very fine old gobblers, as the birds noticed me just as they were coming into easy gunshot range. Ask anyone who has hunted them for years, and you'll learn that those long whiskered old birds can leave your presence about as quickly as anything alive.

I don't recommend that anyone hunt wild turkeys dressed as I do, unless he is willing to forego a chance or two, here and there, at birds he may have bagged otherwise. If he doesn't mind that though, and wants to put some spice into his hunting, he should try it. I can guarantee it will make a far finer turkey hunter of the person who does. The bulk of my old timey clothing, including hats, come from the River Junction Trade Co.

Sweat shirts, T-shirts, underwear, gloves, belts, caps, shoes, boots, everything a hunter wears can be purchased today in camo patterns, so there is no need for anyone to

The turkey woods are full of all sorts of insect pests, so it's wise to spray for them. This hunter is spraying boots and socks for protection against the Rocky Mountain spotted tick. The bite from this critter can be fatal, so it's wise to take precautions against them.

be seen by a wary old gobbler. All you need to add are patience, some black crayon smeared on your face, being in the right place at the right time, an open season and a turkey tag.

As numerous springtime turkey chasers will need insect repellants to ward off mosquitoes, gnats, flies, and other pests, it should be kept in mind that there are face paints on the market with insect repellants mixed in the formula. Otherwise, a person will need to carry one of the small pocket-size cans of spray repellants available. Face nets, a head covering made of mosquito netting, are also popular. New ones fold up into the confines of a camo cap. Lightweight camo gloves will help to protect the hands.

You may need a flashlight. I never leave home without one stuck in the duffel bag . . .

Like so many other hunting sports, turkey hunting usually begins in the dark hours just before dawn. You may need a flashlight. These are plentiful today, in all sizes and colors. Though I seldom carry one in the field, I never leave home without one stuck in the duffel bag. My favorite is an old Army surplus, olive drab two-cell which has a short cord tied to it. After I no longer need it, I tie it to my belt near my back where it is out of my way. I have another flashlight which works well; it uses a tiny lithium battery and drops into a pants pocket.

For the hunter who likes to leave camp well before daybreak, there is an endless variety of small flashlights available to help him find his way through the dark woods. This tiny light has a cord for hanging it from the belt, or it can easily be stuck into a pocket. A flashlight is also very handy to have around camp when the hunt is over for the day. Be sure to pack along a supply of fresh batteries!

known to pile sand on a bandana laid out flat, pull the corners together and tie them, making a small sandbag. It works wonders when I need a firm but pliable base on which to rest a camera when I am making my timed exposures.

I never leave camp without toilet tissue folded into a tiny packet and secured with a rubber band. Nor would I be caught in the woods without a knife. What style of knife is strictly a personal choice. I sometimes carry an old Case knife I've gutted birds with for 25 years, while at other times I'll tote a belt knife. Ordinarily, I pack a belt knife if I know I'll be away from the pickup for several hours, or when I am planning on hunting 2 or more days on end. My belt knives are custom-made jobs, made by an old friend, Larry Marvin from Alva, Oklahoma. Larry knew I wanted a knife with a fairly short but narrow blade, as this

Though this knife sports a big-game skinning-type blade, it will suffice for anything from cleaning a turkey to cutting branches for a blind. Many hunters carry pocketknives, or a small folding-hunter, which slips into a belt sheath and has a snap closure to prevent its loss. The knife is one of the two things the wise hunter will never leave camp without—the other is toilet tissue.

Another handy light for the early morning turkey hunter is the headlamp mounted on an elastic band which fishermen have used for years. This leaves the hands free and the band can also be tied around a belt loop in back when not in use. The batteries are small and can fit in a hip pocket. Head lamps put out a stronger beam than an ordinary flashlight. Invariably I'll carry an extra light as someone will forget theirs, or the batteries will be dead. A hunter traveling back into areas as remote as Mexico's high Sierras should always pack spare batteries. Check them to be certain they work, are fresh and fully charged.

I never hunt without a blue or red bandana. It can be used as a bandage, a washcloth, a gun cleaning rag, or can be left tied to a tree telling friends the direction I've gone. I've toted no telling how many gobblers from the woods with one, using it to tie the legs together. I've also been

would make it easier to field dress a gobbler. But the knife needed to be built solid and strong, as I would also be cutting limbs or doing other whittling tasks. The belt sheaths he made are deep, fairly tight, but do not need snap loops to prevent loss of the knives. You won't catch me hunting strange country, places new to me, without a belt knife. A good knife is one of the best friends you'll have if you get lost.

What I like about a belt knife is that it doesn't take up room in a pocket. Many Westerners tote large folding knives in a belt-worn button-down sheath. I often use a belt knife for spreading butter on bread, maybe to cut a chunk of venison, spear a pickle, or smear applesauce on a tortilla. When it isn't being used for those tasks, or cutting small branches to open up a shooting lane, I can always cut a toothpick with it, and then lean back and whittle.

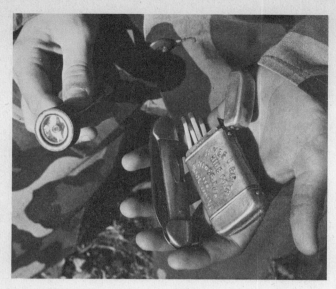

The author never sets foot in unfamiliar turkey country without these three items stuck in coat or pants pockets: a pocketknife; a small tin match safe filled with wooden kitchen matches; and a clip-on brass compass. These could help to see a person through the rigors of being lost.

Many mornings I've arrived too early and, used my matches to build a tiny fire . . .

What about matches? Some folks need them for smoking tobacco. Perhaps if it is chilly while you are standing there waiting for the eastern sky to begin streaking light, you may want to build a fire to warm up. Many mornings I've arrived in some far neck-of-the-woods too early and, while waiting for an old bird to gobble, have used my matches to build a tiny fire. Feels good if you are hunting Rocky Mountain Merriam turkeys up in the high mountains where springtime mornings can be quite cold. Keep the fire small, and the turkeys will pay no mind whatsoever. Make certain you *do not set the woods afire. Make certain that you put the fire out thoroughly.*

I carry my matches in a small tin matchsafe. These are ordinary kitchen matches, wrapped in wax paper, tied in tiny separate bundles, and placed in the matchsafe so each bundle can be removed without bothering others. You may have cold wet hands when you need matches, and they will be more easily handled if wrapped. The small fold of wax paper can also be utilized with wood punk or grass to get a fire blazing. I replace the matches at least twice a year. A person who gets lost should always remember that dry wood can often be found on the underside of small trees which have fallen over and hung up on another tree. Fallen logs can often be kicked apart, revealing dry punky wood inside. If you are hunting piney woods, you can kick a knot free from a downed tree. This knot will have pitch in it

which lights easily. With your knife, you can whittle bark and slivers from dead saplings or branches, as invariably these will be dry inside. Whittling a small pile of these into splinters will give you a little kindling to get the fire going. Throw your cap over your kindling to keep it dry.

Many hunters say they always know where they are. Most have never been in "big country" . . .

When I am hunting large rough areas that I've not hunted before, I carry a compass in addition to a belt knife and a matchsafe. These are the only emergency items I carry, but with them I can easily make do until I find my way out of being lost. True, there are people who claim they never get their directions turned around. I've heard many hunters say that they always know where they are and which way is north. Most of them have never been in what is truly "big country." But, what some don't know is that anyone can become lost on a few hundred acres. A sudden fog, a sandstorm, or perhaps a cold front moving through, with the resultant cloud cover—these and other of Mother Nature's little tricks—can blot the sun, change the wind, and turn the tables on an unsuspecting hunter.

My advice to anyone who suddenly gets the slightest inkling that he is not certain which way is which is to

The smart hunter will carry a compass and a section of map when hunting in unfamiliar country, or in country where sudden fog or a storm could cause him to lose his sense of direction. The person who takes a compass reading before leaving camp, and thus orienting himself with the area into which he plans to hunt, will seldom have any problems with becoming lost.

quietly sit down and study his moves up until the present time. Go over your route as best as you can recall. You may be able to untangle your being lost before it becomes a reality. Study your surroundings. In your mind's eye, picture yourself as you traveled the last few hours. What direction were you headed when you left the vehicle? Did you study the area map before you took off on your hunt?

Very often I will have a section of map in a pocket. I won't need the complete map, as I'll only be able to hunt a tiny portion of it, but I'll study the area as a whole, then cut out the area I plan to hunt. Topographical maps are excellent for this purpose, as they give elevations, creeks, trails, plus a jillion other landmarks which can be used as reference points for the wandering hunter. Ordinary national forest maps will quite often do, but once again, these

These hunters check a map before leaving the road and walking into vast areas of backcountry. Even a game department map with a few of the major roads marked will be a great help should the hunter become lost while chasing a gobbling bird. The hunter who knows there is a road nearby needs only a compass to guide him to it.

are very large, and it is best to cut out the portion needed. The turkey hunter who studies maps becomes acquainted with what is required as turkey habitat for the various subspecies and can then apply this knowledge to his map reading. On his map, he can locate areas which could be very productive. In addition, the person who has done his homework, so to speak, will be able to give all his concentration to hunting turkeys if he is reasonably sure of not becoming lost.

Probably a great number of turkey hunters have become lost, at least for a short time, after chasing a gobbling turkey. On one occasion, I was thoroughly confused for a couple of hours after I'd chased a piney woods turkey around and over some up-and-down hills in the Deep South. I was sure of my directions when I first heard him gobbling, but by the time it was over, the wind had quit, and the sky

had clouded over. I no longer knew north from "sic 'em." What's worse, I didn't get the turkey. After coming to the conclusion that I was walking in circles, I began striking a straight line (by keeping trees lined up as far ahead as I could see) and soon broke out on a road. Since that day 20 years ago, I have been turned around a number of times. In every instance, this was caused by concentrating more on the kill than where I was; I was no longer paying strict attention to my whereabouts, noting landmarks, the distance traveled, and all the things I would have noticed had my mind been free. I have never spent the night in the woods, as a result of being lost, because I have always studied maps of all the areas I've hunted, and by taking a compass reading, and then striking a general line, I have been able to walk out.

Nobody has a greater respect for what the elements are possible of than I. I search out backcountry since I much prefer to walk a few extra miles in getting back to where there are fewer hunters. Therefore, my getting truly lost could have its setbacks. Having hunted many places far from roads and trails in Arizona, New Mexico, and in particular, far back in Mexico's Sierra Madre mountains, I plan on hunting hard, intent on bagging turkeys. So I prepare before I go, and when I get there, I tote along the few items which could mean the difference between walking out, or *staying there for good!* Don't forget to keep your compass a few feet from a metal magnetic source because it will upset its field. *Have faith in your compass!* If you hunt enough in back out-of-the-way places, a time will come when you will read the instrument—only to feel that it is wrong. Compasses don't lie. The needle will point to magnetic north. It will be up to you to decide the direction you should walk.

For all-day hunts, I never carry but six rounds including the two in the shotgun . . .

Aside from a billfold, or whatever it is you wish to carry your hunting license in, plus a turkey call or two, all else you should need are a few shotgun shells. A few, I said, not half a box.

Numerous times I have walked away from my pickup with none other than the two rounds in the double-barreled gun I hunt with. Now, don't get me wrong, these were not all-day sorties, but short hour or 2-hour hunts not far from where I was parked. For all-day hunts I never carry but six rounds, including the two in the shotgun. Turkey bag limits are seldom more than one bird per day. Nobody should need six shots to kill one wild turkey.

Back during the '30s, when my brother Dick and I were learning to hunt with .410 shotguns, we hunted ducks year 'round. We worked hard for the money it took to buy shotgun shells by market hunting rabbits. Growing up on a farm

Successful hunters walk along a country road as the morning sun burns away the fog. Photographs are perhaps the hunter's finest link with past hunts, enabling him to while away long winter evenings while enjoying all the things from hunts otherwise forgotten. Cameras and film are cheap, when compared to moments which, once gone, can never be brought back.

The small, pocketsize Olympus camera is excellent to carry into the hunting field as it takes up little room, and weighs but several ounces. There are many other compact 35mm cameras on the market, comparable in size and quality to this one. Many have auto focussing (and everything else) that allow even the rank amateur photographer to take top quality slides and/or prints.

has no end of work, but when we had the work whittled down to size, we hunted rabbits and made good money at it. So, when we headed for a place we knew as the Drummond Flats, several miles west of Enid, Oklahoma, we were always loaded down with two or three boxes of shells. It seemed like the guns always needed a warming up to the task at hand. But, invariably the last 10 or 15 loads killed the most ducks.

This is the lesson I am getting at: If you carry but a few loads, you will not try those silly long-range shots. You will wait until the turkey is within easy shooting distance and make your shots count. Put only three or four loads in your pocket; it will make a far better hunter of you.

As for extra items you may want to tote with you, you should consider a camera. Viewing slides on a large screen or looking at color photos will bring back all the fond memories of a hunt that otherwise might be soon forgotten. You'll study photographs of old friends you've lost track of and cherish pictures of newly found acquaintances. Others will bring a burst of laughter and a longing to go back to a place you grew fond of in just a few short hours.

You don't need to be weighed down these days carrying a camera. There are a number of compact full-frame 35mm types on today's market the size of a package of cigarettes. I bought an Olympus a couple of years ago which weighs but a few ounces, and I carry it everywhere I go. It's tough. I've belly-crawled on it, sat on it, and who knows what a beating it has taken while in my luggage aboard commercial airlines. Last year, while sitting on Chanante, a horse I ride in Chihuahua, I handed it down to a Mexican, but he dropped it on the rocks alongside a trail. Chipped some paint from the case, but otherwise did it no harm.

I've toted field glasses across much of Chihuahua's high Sierra Madres . . .

Binoculars fall into the same class as cameras. They aren't something you must have, but there is nothing handier. Few people carry them, but those who do will observe wildlife that is not often seen. Wild alligators, particularly the huge "chimeras" of 10 or 11 feet, are too wary for close-up viewing with the naked eye. With field glasses, I've studied the old critters from crooked teeth to armor plating in Florida's backwoods swamp holes. And what a gorgeous big black squirrel you'll see in Florida, more so if you see him through binoculars. Spur length on a live gobbler is difficult to judge unless you use field glasses. But, of greater importance, is using glasses when hunting wild turkeys. Hunting all five of the world's spurred and bearded turkeys, I've toted field glasses all across the States and throughout much of Chihuahua's Sierra Madres. Except when I am hunting areas which I am familiar with, I am seldom without field glasses.

Binoculars should be light in weight, compact in size, and for turkey hunting, have a wide field of view. Do not skimp when buying field glasses. Cheap binoculars often will not focus properly. There are hundreds of cheap binocs purchased each year by hunters who do not know the technique of focusing, and what is worse, few store clerks have been properly instructed in helping them. Take the time to read the brochure included with the binocular *before purchasing*. If the glass cannot be focussed properly in the

Designed with low-light hunting in mind, these Zeiss 7 × 42B binoculars would be excellent for the turkey hunter willing to tote a few extra ounces. They're fairly large but have a wide field of view. The rubber eyepiece cap is attached to the neck strap and protects the eyepiece lenses.

Binoculars need not be bulky nor heavy these days. The pair on the left, being black and shiny, would serve better for turkey hunting if they were coated with camouflage tape or painted with camo paint. Both of these glasses are considered small in size, the ones on the right easily slipped into a shirt pocket. Both the Nikon 9 × 30 (left) and Pentax 7 × 20 are fine for average turkey hunting duty.

store, it won't work any better in the field and my advice is not to buy it. Take the time to find a good glass and spend a bit more money than you'd originally budgeted to get the best you can afford. You won't regret it.

I have owned two pair of binoculars in my lifetime and both have seen an unbelievable amount of use and abuse. Both have excellent light gathering qualities, ideal for dark areas, particularly for early morning and late afternoon viewing, and both have unexcelled definition. The first pair were 7x50s; the ones I am using now are 8x40s. Like all truly good binoculars, they both have individual eye focus. Both of them I bought after looking over many types and styles. In both instances I asked the store managers if I might take the binocular outside where long-distance viewing would not be distorted by store-window glass. Once outside, I looked for a far off shady area, preferably the dark inside of a large open store or garage door so I could focus on the darkened interior. Satisfied the glass would bring out subjects under these conditions, I then picked out a few birds to glass. If the binocular found these quickly, I felt safe that the field of vision would be ideal for picking up distant turkeys. Of course, throughout all these personal tests I observed clarity, and the fine definition of such things as the feathers on the birds I viewed.

Too many folks treat binoculars the same they do a camera. When they need it, it's back in the truck or at home. I'll agree, binoculars are just another something to pack around, but when a priority is placed on what to carry while afield, and what not to carry, then these items should be measured in terms of their ability to make the hunt a success. Time after time, while hunting Gould's turkeys in Mexico, or Rio Grandes on the vast shinnoak prairies of

the Southwest, or Merriam wild turkeys among the Rocky Mountains, or Osceolas among the sprawling palmetto burns on vast Florida ranches, and even Eastern turkeys in various places, you wouldn't catch me leaving the truck without them. Field glasses fall into the same category as the shotgun, shells, calls and a pocketknife.

Today's market offers a tremendous selection of binoculars in size, power, style of construction and some even come with camouflage finishes. The bulk will have a strap for carrying them about the neck. Binoculars should be carried high, in other words the strap needs to be short,

These Zeiss 8 × 20B glasses are small enough to slip into a shirt pocket and are rubber armored not only for protection from bumps and dings, but also for silence should they contact the gun while slung around the neck.

bringing the instrument to a height where it will hang near the middle of the chest. And, as a binocular will often bounce on the chest as the hunter walks or runs, a strap arrangement, known commercially as a Cuban hitch, is needed to eliminate this action, keeping the glasses snug. I invariably slip my binocs inside my shirt or jacket which also dampens this bouncing effect. There have been numerous occasions when I realized my binocular was no longer needed on the stalk because I would be crawling on hands and knees or belly-crawling and the binoculars would just be a nuisance. In such situations I'll take them off, leaving them to be picked up when the hunt is done. Both my pairs have lain along scads of cow paths, near trees, on rock piles, just any place. One hot muggy spring morning, deep in Mississippi, while after a lone old slinker that was gobbling high and dry amid a spring freshet, I left my billfold, turkey calls and binoculars atop a cow pie, as from there my bellying would have to be in water about 6 to 8 inches deep. The creek was in flood, leaving this the only alternative if I was to kill the turkey where he stood on a tiny point of land. My luck ran out when I'd closed the range to about 45 yards. Deep water saved that old bird, but my field glasses showed me that gobbler in the beginning, as they have on heck knows how many other occasions. It's up to me to do what remains.

backpacks snag on many branches. Shoulder pads should be used if the wearer is not accustomed to wearing the pack often. Three things should always be kept in mind when buying camping items to be carried in a pack: light weight, tough and durable, and if possible, items of multiple use. If the hunter thinks much of his rest, he should buy the finest sleeping bag he can afford, preferably one that is down-filled. Dehydrated foods are another backcountry backpacking item the turkey hunter should look into. Numerous food processing companies are into the dehydrated foods business nowadays, offering a wide range of menus to a hunter far from the nearest fast food restaurant.

A hunter packing far back, where he will be "out of touch" for a few days, should stick a new compact first aid kit in his pack, along with a small book on first aid medical treatments. The hunter may want to add special items, such as cough drops, cold tablets, or any special medications needed. Hunters who have pre-existing physical problems—for example, a heart condition—should make this known to anyone they are with, plus give them instructions as to where emergency medications will be located, and how these should be administered. Such medicine containers should also have the instructions clearly marked for easy reading. If the medicine is to be taken aboard airliners, or across borders into other countries, it

If you don't sleep like a log, due to your buddies' snoring like a bunch of hogs . . .

For the hunter who is planning on being away from vehicle or camp from before dawn until dusk, I would suggest a small rucksack, fanny pack, or back-slung daypack for toting along a lunch together with a bottle of water. Fanny packs have become quite popular, as these belt-slung bags are easy to get into, regardless of the layers of clothing the hunter may be wearing. My first one was made of green canvas and sewn to my specifications by the local canvas company. Fanny packs were not even a foggy idea back in those days. Today, these packs can be bought with zippered pockets, padded waistbands in contour design, and the whole thing made of rain resistant camo material.

Day packs fit over the shoulders, ordinarily have a back pocket plus side pockets, and come with, or without, internal framing. The old models had wooden frames. These will tote a canteen, spare jacket, rain gear, and lunch, with room left for other small items.

From day packs, the backpack grows ultimately to the Alpine pack, in which a small spike camp can be carried. It is possible to stillhunt while shouldering a large backpack, though if the hunter plans to do this often, he should buy a model with a narrow frame. This will allow slightly better gun movement. Whatever pack a hunter chooses, he should strive to buy one of tough, durable material, as

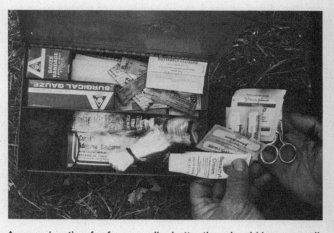

Anyone hunting far from medical attention should keep a well-stocked first aid kit handy, either carrying it with their gear in a travel bag, or in the vehicle. Such store-bought kits should be supplemented with special items, such as scissors, tweezers, eye and ear drops, cough drops, pain killers, and other items of personal preference (or need).

is wise to tape the prescription to the outside of the container.

People who wear eye glasses should pack an extra pair if they are seriously handicapped without them. I have a friend who had one set of prescription lenses mounted in a set of frames to which a camo headnet is glued. Works like a charm. He takes his turkey hunting seriously, so the expense was justified.

If you sleep like a log, you should pack an alarm clock.

Or, the next time you need to buy yourself a wristwatch, get one with an alarm. You'll always have it handy, plus that'll save space for other gear.

If you don't sleep like a log, due to your buddies snoring like a bunch of fat hogs all through the night, you owe it to yourself to go to the drugstore and buy a couple pairs of ear plugs. I never leave home without them.

David Jackman and I were back in the high Sierras one winter, and after crawling into our sleeping bags, I could hear a couple of Mexican cowboys chattering as they lingered over the wood cook stove. Digging out a pair of the ear plugs for myself, I handed my spares to David, as I felt sure he'd never tried them. We'd scarcely crawled from bed the next morning when David told me he'd never have made the night without them. He's carried his own since that hunt, plus spares. If they ever hold a "snore off" in this country, I have a buddy or two who will walk off with all the hardware. There have been nights when Tom Preston and I have staggered to our feet at 3 o'clock in the morning and dragged our beds 50 yards from camp to escape those torturous melodies.

The noise stoppers I use are made of a soft plastic-like material, which allows them to be form-fit to the wearer and then inserted into the ear. The soft material can be pushed and molded in the ear opening, making them all but soundproof. I can still hear the alarm clock if set near the head of my sleeping bag. These soft ear plugs are cheap, disposable, clean and easy to carry.

Liquids of all kinds can be taken afield in varying types of containers. This hunter has water in a large canteen, whereas coffee is kept hot in a stainless steel thermos bottle. Taking a number of "coffee breaks" during the day helps keep a hunter alert and fresh and can make the hunt more enjoyable (and safer, too). Note how the camo'd gun blends with the foliage.

The only water I'll drink is when I can see the source, be it a spring or artesian well . . .

Drinking water! Are you going to drink from the streams or take it with you? Time was when I drank from streams all across the country. Nowadays, I'm leery of doing this, mostly due to all the hoopla about pollution. About the only water I'll drink today is when I can see the source, be it melting snow, a spring, or an artesian well. And, the stream must be small in size. In many areas of the West, streams will go underground for long distances, surfacing well filtered. In Mexico it is not uncommon to find a dry streambed that, immediately after a heavy mountain shower, runs a foot deep, but downstream a few miles where it has not rained, the streambed is dry; the water has gone under.

The log house camp which I hunt out of back in Mexico's Sierra Madre mountains is not a stone's throw from a tiny stream trickling through a pasture where the horses are kept penned at night. For years we have boiled water from that streamlet, and none of us have shown any ill effects from it which simply proves that boiled water is reasonably safe. Boiled water is extremely "flat" to the taste, but is ideal for making tea and coffee.

There are also a great many additives on today's market which make water safe to drink. A tiny bottle of this stuff plus a cup to mix it with water is all that's required. The directions are on the bottle. Another device which will purify water is a long plastic straw-like tube through which water is drawn, straight from the creek into the hunter's mouth. It is as much trouble to carry as a fountain pen and gives the user the option of drinking as much as he pleases. These little devices make drinking time-consuming, but if a person is thirsty, the time is well spent. David Jackman, one of my longtime turkey hunting cronies, carries one much of the time. Some water sources have a laxative effect on humans, and whether one of these filters will prevent this, I do not know. The Poteau River in southeast Oklahoma is one of these. Its water is often called *Poteau punch* for is laxative qualities. This stems from a chemical content, giving the water a faint milkish cast.

When I am hunting within a reasonable distance of camp, I'll tote my water in a fine silver brandy flask Charlie Elliott gave me years ago. These hip pocket flasks do not hold much, but not much water is required except on hot days. I get around this by drinking plenty of water before leaving and after arriving back in camp. Another item which will tote water for two or three hunters is a canvas water bag, the same kind made famous years ago as it hung from the side of a truck, or a tractor. The vehicle's motion helped to evaporate the water seeping through the bag's material, and this in turn cooled the water inside. The bag has a rope sling and can be carried over the back, hanging near the belt.

Quite often I'll stick a couple of oranges or a small can of juice in my pockets, utilizing these as water sources. A small tin of canned tomatoes is another excellent item to stash in a coat pocket for quenching thirst. Of course, a hunter seeking Osceola wild turkeys in Florida has it made; Florida oranges are plentiful and hard to beat.

Because I call with a trumpet caller so much of the time, very often you'll find a roll or two of Life Saver mints in my pockets. These can be quickly popped into the mouth to prevent "dry mouth," which is so common when using trumpet calls. The Quill Call, made by V.O. Johnson over in Arkansas, the Turpin Yelper, sold by the Penn's Woods people up in Pennsylvania, or even a section of river cane cut on the spot, all require a moist mouth if the calling is going to be satisfactory. Very often, in the excitement of listening to an old gobbler sound off, or hearing the whistling of scattered young birds, the hunter will suddenly suffer "dry mouth," resulting in not being able to make a decent note on the call. Mints or coughdrops will ease this quickly. Ask any athlete, and he'll tell you that lemons and limes are excellent for relieving this dryness of the mouth. But, not many turkey hunters are apt to lug around or cut up a lemon or lime when things get hairy.

Discussing equipment, let's look at how he's going to get to where he plans to hunt . . .

the shotgun hunter, on horseback, should fit his gun with a sling, or carry along his personal shotgun scabbard. I advise the latter because the horseback turkey hunter will be among trees, and with a gun slung across the back, tree branches will be catching on it continually. In packing saddlebags, packboxes, or backpacks, remember to pack the items you'll use throughout the day in side pockets, or on top, where these can be easily gotten to.

In discussing what kinds of equipment a turkey hunter might use, let's look at how he is going to get to wherever it is he plans to hunt. This has a bearing on how much equipment he will have at his disposal when he walks out of camp, motel or whatever. The close-to-home hunter will undoubtedly be driving a vehicle. Like so many of today's hunters, he will want to drive the car just as near to where he hunts as possible, which is often too near, but he will do this anyhow. Since he will run the risk of getting stuck in mud, sand, or perhaps snow, he should keep a shovel, crosscut tree saw, a length of chain, a few 4x6 wooden

Whiskey flasks make excellent hip-pocket water containers. These can also be filled with fruit juices, or tomato juice, which is excellent for satisfying thirst. The flask takes up little space and doesn't weigh very much.

Many turkey hunting camps are little more than a truck or two parked near some trees. Trucks can provide a place to sit, sleep and eat, as well as carry many comforts which otherwise would be left at home. The author's pickup provides a complete first-aid kit, fire extinguishers, tools, tow chains, saw, hammer, bailing wire and umpteen other things.

Hunting from horseback offers a wider selection of what can be taken along for a day's hunt. The essential gear is the same, though a spikecamp including a lightweight tent, sleeping bag, coffee pot, and other such stuff can be stuffed in saddlebags or packbox. A rain slicker can be tied on the saddle. Few outfitters furnish scabbards for shotguns, so

blocks, and a couple 8x10 sheets of heavy-duty plastic in the vehicle at all times. The chain is for pulling the thing out, providing someone can be found who will give him a pull. The wooden blocks are used in stabilizing the jack, should the vehicle need to be jacked off the ground in unstable soils. The plastic sheets are used when it is nec-

Air travel is a familiar mode of transportation to the hunter who wants to hunt all five of the bearded and spurred wild turkeys which make up the Royal Grand Slam. Hunters *must* check air travel regulations concerning firearms before entering the air terminal. Failure to do so could easily find the hunter in jail, charged with serious offenses. Special attention must be paid to packing guns before entrusting them to baggage handlers, so get a good, sturdy case for shipping them.

essary to lie in mud or snow in order to perform tasks on a broken down vehicle. I am never without a full set of hand tools, from hammer to nails, wire, pump pliers, lineman pliers, socket wrenches, spare fan belts, jumper cables, a spare tire, and the jack. In the kit bag with all these are extra fuses for the truck, and spare light bulbs.

I'm also never without a water can, nor a grub box with eating utensils and some cans of food. Wooden matches, a can of insect spray and spare mantles for the gasoline lantern can be found in the grub box, too. Paper towels and a couple of complete changes of dry clothing, including socks, are always in my pickup, and there have been a number of times when I, or a buddy, have been darned glad these were along. A large well-supplied first aid kit remains in a compartment in the vehicle, as do two fire extinguishers, one in the cab, the other in the pickup's camper shell.

The hunter traveling by private vehicle can lug along all the things he has room for, or that his buddies will tolerate. This explains why most hunters will drive long distances to hunt. The comforts of having all the paraphernalia at hand make up for the distance traveled.

When I want to make a trip far from home, I'll invariably fly. The time I save will allow me to hunt longer. The money I will save in motel bills, gasoline and food, will easily pay for the airline ticket. The ease of flying, in getting there rested and relaxed, will allow me to hunt harder once I get into the woods.

One of the problems arising from air travel is in getting about once a person has flown to the general area. Ordinarily this is by rent-a-car. Otherwise, the hunter will rely on friends to pick him up at the airport, and cart him around throughout his hunt. I've done much of both. But, if you rely on buddies to haul you hunting, make doggoned well certain that you return the favor. *Back up your intentions by asking them to your area to hunt.*

The average hunter traveling by airliner will need to scale down the hunting items he carries. This is not due to the restrictions airlines place on numbers of pounds allowed per passenger, but in being aware that the hunter will be digging through luggage each time he needs the tiniest article. So the less bags he has along, the less digging. Having been a turkey hunting guide for óver 20 years, I've had folks arrive toting all sorts of equipment. One man arrived

at my doorstep with five bags of varying sizes. I couldn't believe it. He spent as much time looking through them as we did in hunting.

I take two pair of footwear, wearing one, with the other in the baggage. I'll bring a set of clothes for eating out, etc., if such occasions arise. When hunting backcountry, I'll hang my good clothes on a nail, leaving them there until ready to head for home. Often I've worn or carried a coat on board an airliner, lessening the baggage weight. I'll pack one set of hunting clothes, whereas at home I would perhaps have two in the truck. I'll count the days I'm to be gone, then throw in socks and underwear for each, plus one. Very often I'll leave the shaving gear at home, to worry about that when I get back. I do pack a large towel and washcloth. I put in a small flashlight; it could come in handy on the hunt or when searching in my luggage for something. The alarm clock? If I know a buddy will have one, I leave it at home. I carry a camera and hope it doesn't get busted, plus, an extra roll or two of film. Last, but very important, *two or three heavy-duty large plastic trash bags*, folded compactly, and tied with a short wire. I'll get back to these later.

I was sitting in the air terminal at Orlando, Florida, one hot afternoon, just passing time, watching all the strangers go by, as I waited to catch a flight back to my native Oklahoma. Soon I noticed a good-looking young lady coming toward me, followed by a porter with a four-wheel dolly on which was stacked her luggage—a mountain of it. She walked up to a ticket counter nearby and I immediately thought, *Now, if anyone has got too much stuff to get on an airplane, this gal is number one.* After all, there were signs hanging everywhere about how many pounds were allowed each passenger. The porter finally got it all wedged into the checkout opening, she handed him a tip and he stalked off. Whatever she handed him, he'd earned. Those folks at the ticket counter did not bat an eye, they took it all. Truely, she was traveling with everything but the kitchen sink. At least, I presumed it was not among all her baggage. Course, you never know what anyone is toting. After all, in the luggage I'd just checked in were two froze-hard-as-rocks Osceola turkey gobblers—birds I'd taken in the few days I'd been in south Florida. That's what the plastic bags were for.

Chapter 3

Wild Turkey Calls and How to Use 'em

SOMETIME BACK in the dark ages, an early hunter was foraging whatever meat he could bring to earth, probably armed with a throwing stick, a spear, or perhaps a primitive bow. Wild turkeys were "thicker'n hair on a dog's back," as the saying goes. One day the savage likely mimicked their calls with his own voice. He probably didn't know why, it was simply something which happened. Undoubtedly, he was surprised when a bird answered his calls and came toward him. There's no way of knowing if he said anything to himself about this wondrous discovery, but today's hunter would probably remark, "Hey, man, this is alright."

The primitive hunter told the other hunters in the clan about his discovery, and so it was that turkey calling probably began. The human voice was widely used in imitating the notes of the wild turkey, but in time it was also discovered that some of the notes could be made with a bone whistle. In time, bone whistles were used while luring the birds with turkey tail feathers which had been dried in the fanned position. The savages' keen use of surrounding cover, together with the calling and the use of the tail feathers, enticed birds into close range. Some were even caught by hand.

This sly trick came into use in a far more treacherous manner as the settlers began making inroads on the Indian lands. Diaries and other handwritten accounts of the early settlers' lives tell us that pioneers were duped by the calling of turkeys—they would see the tail moving above the bushes and, thinking it was a potential dinner, stalk into the Indian's ambush. Suddenly, the hunter had become the

hunted. But the question also arises in my mind as to how many Indians may have taken a dose of shot that was intended for the strutting gobbler. I can promise you, I would not dare try this trick in today's turkey woods.

The Apaches were known to use the gobble of the mountain turkey as a signal to each other when on warring raids, and when engaged with white soldiers. Though I have heard the owl's hoot used as a signal among Indians in cowboy and Indian movies, I haven't found any mention of this in

This box call was made for the author by an Apache Indian. It's made of mountain mahogany and has an unusual opening.

Bland's small gunstock Apache turkey call is stroked on a chalked shotgun fore-end. It has called wild turkeys far from where it once called Rocky Mountain birds.

historic accounts. The owl was considered an omen of death, so I doubt that Indians imitated its mournful wailing.

I have hunted among Apaches a few times and have talked turkey hunting with them, though I've never known one who could call a wild turkey with his voice. I do have a quaint box call made by an Apache. It's made of mountain mahogany, and has such an unusual opening that it must have evolved somewhere in tribal history. The notes are made by chalking a spot on a gun stock and drawing its sounding edge lightly across this.

The call we know today as a wingbone call is an offshoot of the bone whistle used by the Indians. It seems ironic that the bones from a turkey's wing can be turned against others of its kind. This goes one step further in that the wing bones from a young gobbler are best suited for calling young gobblers, and the bones of a hen turkey's wing will make excellent notes of the hen turkey, and so on.

Sections of river cane can be used in a like manner, but these must be small like the hole through a turkey's wingbone. Several times I have been hunting where I would come across small stands of cane. I would cut a section between the nodes, and after running a weed stem through the center of the cane, I could make turkey sounds no differently than can be made with a "store-bought" Turpin yelper. The hole through these canes, or through a turkey's wingbone, must be near 3/32-inch in diameter if you want to use it for calling turkeys.

After the wing bones have cooled, cut off the ends with a fine hacksaw blade . . .

Making a wingbone call is not difficult, though it does take time and patience. Far the best bones are the two small ones found in the second or middle section of a mature hen turkey's wing. These should be laid aside after the bird has been cooked and eaten, and then boiled in a shallow pan

for a few minutes, with just a few drops of liquid dish-washing soap added to the water. The soap will make the call taste better when it's finished.

After the wingbones have cooled, cut off the knob-like ends with a fine-toothed hacksaw blade. Then, with a long pipe cleaner, the bone marrow can be cleaned from the insides. Now, by experimenting, these bones will usually telescope together enough that the two sections can be glued together, but only after they have dried for a couple of days. Once glued, I always make a cork mouth-stopper and glue it onto the call so my mouth will butt up against it in exactly the same position each time. This is made from a simple bottle cork whittled to the size desired with a sharp pocketknife. Don't glue the cork stopper until you've moved it back and forth along the mouthpiece and found the spot

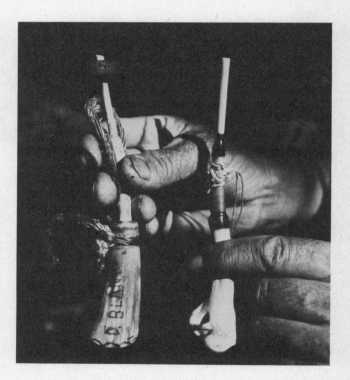

These are both homemade wingbone turkey calls. The one on the left has a cork mouth-stop that makes it easier to position the lips for consistent notes throughout a series of calls. See text for instruction on how to make this call.

that results in the best notes available. The notes are made by sucking or pulling air quickly through the call. Clucks are made with a kissing action. Yelps are made by using the throat muscles, best described as a gulping action. It takes a lot of time and practice to master any of the trumpet or wingbone-type turkey calls, so this is why you won't see many in use. Lots of hunters carry them, but few can actually call turkeys with them.

Among my black powder gear are a couple of ancient clay pipes which were dug from a confluence of the Ohio River, having been made from clays there, and then fired

Ed Merrow, a longtime Vermont turkey hunter, demonstrates how he has called turkeys with the barrel of a fountain pen, using the instrument exactly as he would a Turpin yelper.

(Left) Wingbone calls are as popular nowadays as they have been throughout many decades of wild turkey hunting. These are made by gluing sections of bone from a turkey's wing together with one telescoping into the end of the other. The ones shown here are large bones, probably from a young gobbler's wing, and will make the notes of a young turkey gobbler. As with all trumpet-type calls, the wingbone call requires a great deal of practice if the notes are to be of good quality.

in a brick kiln, apparently back in the early 1800s. I have inserted a section of cane in these, which was the correct method for making a smoking pipe back then. With either pipe, I can make kee runs, clucks, and yelps. Amazingly, they still taste like smoking tobacco. Many of today's modern smoking pipes will make the notes of a wild turkey if the owner knows how to use a Turpin yelper or a wingbone. Ed Merrow, a Vermont turkey hunter, was with me one afternoon, and he called up a small drove with the hollow barrel of a fountain pen. He discovered he'd walked off without his Turpin call, but found the pen stuck in his shirt pocket. Yankee ingenuity did the rest. Of course, Ed knew how to use a trumpet call, so the fountain pen yelper was easy for him. This just points out that any hollow tube, used properly, and with the right tone and resonance, can be transformed into a turkey call. Anyone who wants to learn to use a trumpet-type call should ask a friend to listen to his calling and critique it until it's right. This practice should be done out in the woods under natural conditions.

These calls have a tremendous carrying range and can be heard at great distances, so it's easy to call too loudly. Yelps are not easily made, and this swallowing, drawing in air through the yelper takes time to master. These notes can often sound too quick, and more like a bark than a yelp. Too many yelps in a series often results in a call that doesn't even slightly resemble a turkey.

Excellent kee runs can be made on a trumpet or wingbone, but these must be practiced over and over to be anywhere near authentic. The kee part of the calling is done with the air being sucked through the call with a greater intensity than is done with a yelp, which causes the note to break much higher on the musical scale. This is part of the lost young turkey's vocabulary. These must be quick, with all the pleading in them that is possible.

The hunter practices for weeks, has all the calls "down pat," and with the call slung around his neck, heads for the woods on opening day, hoping for a chance to call to a scattered band of turkeys. At last, the opportunity arises, but he can't make a sound. Why?

Simply, with the intense action of the moment at hand, a person's mouth goes dry from all the excitement. You can't use a trumpet call with a dry mouth. I often carry mints or cough drops just for this purpose. I have cut short sections of sassafras branches and chewed on these, or willow, locust, elm, hickory, and manzanita. Placing a small rock under the tongue will also induce salivation. Wetting the mouthpiece of the call by simply licking it will also help. If there is dew on the grass, rub the tip of the call in this, but make sure it is thoroughly moistened.

The commercial version of the wingbone call is known as a trumpet call. It isn't blown into as a trumpet would be, but used with the kissing, sucking, smacking actions mentioned earlier. Trumpet calls are often referred to as Turpin yelpers, named after Tom Turpin, a turkey hunter who made them well known in his writings about hunting wild turkeys. He also made and sold these calls commercially. Today, Penn's Woods Company sells this same basic yelper, which comes in a hard plastic, metal, and wood version. I've seen untold numbers of this famous yelper all across the United States.

This is an old-time Turpin yelper. The modern turkey hunter has now applied the moniker to all manufactured trumpet yelpers. Very few examples of this call will be found in turkey call collections. Today, this same basic call is made from hard plastic, metal, and wood.

(Left) Arkansas' V.O. Johnson trumpet call is homemade and was turned out on a wood lathe. Trumpet calls make beautiful "turkey music," but only after many, many hours of practice. Clucks can be learned almost instantly, but the yelps and kees take time.

Another version of the trumpet yelper is made and sold by V.O. Johnson, in Arkansas. This man's grandfather made the original version back in the 1800s. This patented call is all wood, turned out individually on a lathe.

A half-hour later, far from our encounter, I discovered "Miss Jezebel" was missing . . .

I had a rather interesting experience one hot afternoon in northern Arkansas with an old wingbone of mine—one I long ago nicknamed "Miss Jezebel," after the wicked woman in the Bible. Lennis Rose and I had been hunting fall turkeys for a couple days, and realizing the birds were well entrenched within the confines of a large spread of private land, we decided we'd best look for them there. The place was not posted against trespassers, but local talk was that folks were far from welcome—turkey hunters in particular.

But, thoughts of success were greater than the fear of being caught by an irate landowner, so we snuck in. The place was well laid out with old roads, though it was obvious these were seldom traveled, and none showed any fresh tire tracks. We wandered up and down the roads, searching and calling for several hours to no avail. We sat down near where we'd found some fresh scratchings, calling from there, when, like a monster turned loose in an amusement park, we suddenly see and hear a big sedan coming down the road toward us. However, big sedans can't run up and down hollows, which is what we immediately began doing.

A half-hour later, walking down a road far from our encounter with the automobile, I discovered my "Miss Jezebel" was among the missing. Telling Lennis about it, we were standing there mulling this over, when Lennis said, "Dwain, that call's got your name on it." Chances were the call would never be found mixed in with all those oak leaves, but I told Lennis I'd best make an effort to go back and look. The folks who owned the place knew me by name, so I didn't want them to know I'd been back in their woods hunting their turkeys. Lennis insisted on going back with me. We didn't see hide nor hubcap of the big city car, but I did find the wayward wingbone, dropped smack dab in the road. Lennis seemed happier than I, probably because folks around those parts knew that he and I hunted turkeys together. They'd soon put together the facts that anywhere a call of mine had been found, was perhaps a place Lennis Rose had hunted, too. Not long afterward, Lennis got permission to go through the front gate of the place.

The finest mouthpiece I have run across in all the years I've used a wingbone is one I made from a hairpipe which, if you don't know anything of Indian regalia, is a bone often used on the breast armour of the Plains Indians. I worked one of these down with a rasp until it was of proper size, resulting in a mouthpiece with excellent tone. You must be careful with the small wingbone mouthpiece as it is easily broken, particularly if you do any belly-crawling. I have broken umpteen mouthpieces, but I can replace them, so I always keep the neck strap tied to the unbreakable main part of the call.

My favorite wingbone is one I have had for years and is embellished with silver. The silver-smithing was done by a Sioux Indian friend who is now gone from this good earth. This silver encasement strengthens the call, beautifies it

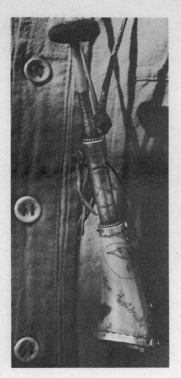

Partially encased in silver-smithing done by a Sioux Indian, the author's well-worn wingbone call, "Miss Heartbreak," has a mouthpiece fashioned from a hairpipe. Hairpipes are the bones which Indians used in making breast armour for deflecting arrows in battle.

immensely, and sets it apart as a one-of-a-kind. The bell end is a section of an old priming powder horn which was made back in the 1800s. I had the wingbone call scrimshawed, and gave it a name—"Miss Heartbreak." My predilection for giving names to favored things such as guns and calls dates back to two happenings in my past. Number one is that Archibald Rutledge has long been my favorite writer, a connection with the storied past of the Deep South. His favorite turkey call was a small box made of willow, one which he christened, "Miss Seduction." Number two has to do with when I was a tail-gunner aboard a Flying Fortress, flying raids over Germany, long, long ago during World War II. We American boys nicknamed our planes with beautiful American girls back home in mind. I can recall bombers with scantily clad beauties painted on the noses, nicknamed such fond monikers as "Miss Delightful" or "Miss Behavin'."

Wingbones, or trumpet calls—either is capable of making the clucking and yelping of a hen turkey as well as any turkey, so the springtime turkey hunter would do well to keep one of these hung about his neck. Use it sparingly, but with full concentration. In time the hunter will master its use.

Trumpet and wingbone calls date back to the times when this country was settled. From left to right: "Miss Jezebel," a wingbone made by the author with a section of cow horn for the bell end of the call; a trumpet call made and sold by V.O. Johnson of Arkansas; a trumpet call made and sold by Penn's Woods Products of Pennsylvania; and a homemade wingbone loaned the author by Allen Jenkins, and made by a Mississippi hunter. These are all excellent calls but, like all trumpet-type calls, require considerable practice to master, and call with forever after.

A large Gibson-like box call has no equal for locating gobblers at long ranges . . .

Box calls date back to the last century, as one box I know of was patented then. The Gibson Turkey call, made and sold by Gibson & Boddie of Dardenelle, Arkansas, has "Patented Jan. 5th, 1897" printed on it in black paint. This large box, with a "shuffling" lid or paddle, appears to be made of poplar or willow, the best woods available for these

Stacy Gibson, a turkey hunter from Wister, Oklahoma, makes "turkey talk" on a homemade box call made by his father. Box calls date back to the late 1800s. The best woods for them are poplar or willow.

Box calls are faily large, particularly those with the shuffling paddle, and there are numerous belt bags available which will carry them. This bag is of camouflage material, hangs from a belt loop, and has leg tie-downs much like some six-gun holsters. This is the safest way to tote them.

(Right) Box calls can easily "talk" when you least want them to, like when laying it down, pulling it from a holster or pocket, or if it's dropped. To prevent this, wrap a long piece of cloth between the box and paddle. When you're ready to use the call, just lift the paddle and flip the cloth aside.

calls. Well-known old-timey turkey hunters Tom Turpin and Henry E. Davis hunted turkeys with them and, in fact, Henry Davis' unequaled book, *The American Wild Turkey*, goes into great depth of this call's description. Roger Latham's fine text, *The Complete Book Of The Wild Turkey*, has a line-drawing plan of the Gibson Box Call, along with instructions for making one. Davis' book can be bought from Old Masters Publishers, while Latham's book is available through the Penn's Woods folks.

I've heard it said that these large box calls were a nuisance to carry, and in his book, Davis mentions this; he also writes that the box was good only for making the turkey's yelp.

For carrying the large Gibson-style box, there are available today any number of cloth and leather bags of the belt-loop variety. I've seen them with a separate small pocket for holding the chalk and sandpaper, as well as others which are nothing but a light skeletal frame to hold the box only. Along this same line, many of today's hunting pants have roomy cargo pockets which will hold a box call, unlike the clothing of times past, which had small pockets.

One problem with carrying a Gibson call which has been a headache to some hunters is its tendency to make noises, or squawk, while the hunter has it in a pocket, and is walking or moving. Obviously, this could spook a bird within hearing range. A simple remedy is to either place a heavy rubberband around the call to keep the paddle in place, or fasten a cloth or leather strap to the box and wrap this around it a few times, allowing the paddle to close on the cloth. All of my boxes are "muffled" in this manner, have been for years, and can be brought into use almost instantly. The strap arrangement serves as a confining strap when I

want to "gobble" the box and, unlike rubber bands, won't rot from heat.

A big box call can do many chores for the turkey hunter, in addition to making excellent yelps. I have heard clucks, purtts, whines, and purrs which would do justice to many wild turkeys made on boxes. But, like all calls, to make these sounds with equally good quality, time after time, when the only thing listening is the real thing, the hunter must *practice, practice, practice*. Few hunters do this. Unfortunately, the average turkey hunting enthusiast doesn't bother to work with "Ole Reliable" until perhaps the night before the season opener. Therefore, none of the notes have a likeness, nor a turkey-like cadence.

As for yelps, few calls can outdo a well-tuned box call. Once the hunter has become thoroughly acquainted with an individual call, and therefore familiar with the required location of the paddle on the sounding edge for various turkey notes, this call can be used to imitate all of the yelps of

A long narrow piece of cloth wrapped around the box and paddle allows the call to be held upside down and shaken to make a good gobble. This takes practice and the method varies with each call. The larger the box, the deeper and louder the gobble.

Read the instructions that come with any box call, because these will tell the hunter what must be done to the call to tune it and keep it in top calling condition. Some box calls must have the sounding edges sanded round, while others need a flat edge. These edges should also be chalked at all times.

(Right) Various instruments are offered on today's market which attempt to mimic the gobble of a wild turkey. Some are shaken vigorously with the hands (left), while others are used much like a "snuff can" call (center). None of these will carry like a gobble made by a real turkey. But, these will often induce another gobbler to gobble.

both young and old turkeys. Properly operated, either with a restraining strap, or as the Lynch-type call is used with rubberbands, a box call will make a reasonably good gobble. Very definitely this gobble will become better as the hunter practices making it. Gobbles are excellent early morning locating calls when hunting springtime gobblers, and will bring a drove to life with a noisy awakening on some fall mornings. A large Gibson-style box call, chalked and sanded, has no equal for locating adult gobblers at long ranges. If the hunter is very familiar in the use of the box, he will know where and how hard he can strike the paddle against the sounding edge to make a note (hen yelp) that will carry beyond a mile. I've located Merriam gobblers all over Arizona's Rocky Mountains, along with a greater number in New Mexico, while using a big poplar-wood box call. Some of the birds have been more than a mile from me.

Tuning a box call is a must because if the thing does not have the true ring of a wild turkey's voice, it won't be effective at all times. Tuning requires sanding the lid and sounding edge with lightweight sandpaper. Sand lengthways on both, and try to keep a rounded edge on the box, as a flat edge can cause squeaks. Once these have been sanded, then both should be chalked, and this must be done again after several series of calls are made, or when slick places begin showing on the paddle's rubbing surfaces.

When listening to notes made by a box, if the person has no "ear" for how a wild turkey sounds, I would recommend having a veteran hunter listen to compare its notes to the calls of live turkeys, or to recordings of live turkeys. I don't recommend listening to recordings of calling champions as these are not true turkey notes, but imitations being

attempted with the call in hand. Anyone who seeks the help of a veteran hunter should also be certain that he has a turkey hunting past which ensures he knows what he is doing. The woods and roadside cafes are loaded with turkey hunters who are experts, but a great majority are more expert with the mouth than gun and call.

Some years back, a man became famous throughout the South, particularly Alabama . . .

Buying a box call is easier said than done. Perhaps I should clarify this statement by saying, to buy a *good* box call is easier said than done. There are seemingly a jillion box calls for sale, in many sizes and made of various woods. The maker of each will say flat out that his call is the best there is, with endorsements by this turkey hunter or that. A great many would be best used for kindling wood.

Sadly, most calls are nowadays packaged so the hunter can't try a few notes in the store before buying one. So, unless the clerk will allow the call to be removed from its wrapping, the hunter will have to buy it untested. Lately I've received a good number of calls, many of them of the box variety. None are now here, simply because none were of good quality. Long ago I learned that I would do best to stick with the old reliables, when buying hunting gear and that goes for buying calls, too.

As late as the 1930s, about the only turkey call that was advertised in hunting and fishing magazines was made by the P.S. Olt Company, the same Olt company who so many of us have associated with duck and goose calls over the years. Though the Olt game calls had their beginnings in 1904, they didn't bring out a turkey call until 1931. I have one of these early cedar models, which is about 5 inches long, and close to an inch square. Like many of these small boxes, this one can be rubbed on a chalked surface, including a gunstock. These are almost the opposites of the

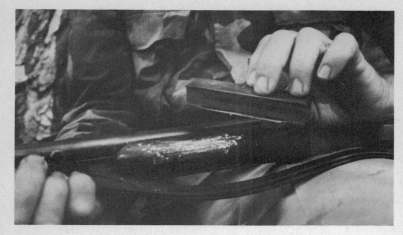

Many small, slender boxes can be stroked on a chalked area on the gun-stock, and that's how they came to be known as "gunstock" boxes. Today's average hunter doesn't look on a shotgun as a tool, and so does not want it marred with sandpaper and chalk. So, these calls come with a small wooden block which is toned for use with the instrument. The call shown here is an Olt box made back during the early 1930s. The Olt company is a prime supplier of many turkey calls to this day.

(Right) Allen Jenkins, owner of M.L. Lynch, makes and sells thousands of this very popular turkey call each year. Though it seems the double-edge box is most often seen, Allen sells a great many single-edge boxes as seen here. Allen's company is located near Liberty, Mississippi.

large Gibson box, as they can be carried in a shirt pocket. This little Olt call is delicate to handle, so it could be easily broken. P.S. Olt makes and distributes fine game calls to this day, enjoying the oldest continuous name in the game call business. Such a reputation is built on but one thing—quality.

Some years back a man became locally famous in small towns throughout the South, particularly in Alabama. He held demonstrations on street corners and peddled his homemade turkey calls. As the years rolled by, and the name grew, they (both he and his wife worked at the game call business) offered a shuffling box call, a peg-and-slate call, a squirrel call, and a book describing the use of turkey calls, and how to hunt the birds. The man's name was M.L. Lynch. The box would become the now-famous Lynch's World Champion Turkey Caller, made in a small backroom operation in Birmingham, Alabama. The squirrel call was known as Lynch's World Champion Chatter Box. Lynch dubbed the peg-and-slate call the Lynch's Big Chief Turkey Call, maintaining he got the idea for this one from the Indians' use of slate rubbed with a narrow pine lighter stick which had been inserted into a corn-cob.

One of the boys who was drawn to this turkey hunter's Pied Piper was a lad by the name of Allen Jenkins. Allen got a job helping put together these turkey calls during his school years and, in time, was able to buy out Mr. Lynch's business. Allen moved the business near the small town of Liberty, Mississippi, built a modern well-equipped and staffed plant, and these days ships thousands of turkey calls

each year. Allen Jenkins works hard at maintaining quality standards, from selecting the woods that go into the calls, to seeing that each is attractively packaged. Just to prove how good this call is, many companies have copied its style. Only a true Lynch call can carry this famous name. I wish I had a nickel for each turkey that has been tolled to a hunter's gun with a call stamped Lynch's World Champion Turkey Caller.

One advantage of the Lynch-style boxes is that they aren't as large as a Gibson box, so they're more apt to be stuck in a pants or coat pocket. These boxes will not "carry" as far as a Gibson shuffling box, but the tone has a slightly higher pitch, as they're made of walnut and mahogany. Many of them have a rubber band arrangement which allows them to be held by the end of the box to make a gobble. Other models have just one sounding edge, allowing the lid to be tapped against the blank side for making clucks.

The smallest shuffling box call I have seen is one made by Lou Stevenson, and known as "Stevenson's Turkey Talker." This extremely narrow one-piece box was made of mahogany and is now a desired collector's item. The one in my collection has with it a small vial of powdered rosin which was used in place of chalk. Also stored inside the box was a small instruction sheet. If there is one thing to be learned from reading this sheet, it is to *practice at every opportunity*.

Virginia has been the home of many very fine turkey call boxes, especially the small flat box which is often stroked across a section of slate, or a chalked piece of wood or even a piece of chalk. I have also found that many of these can be drawn across a chalked gunstock, though many of today's hunters would shy away from sanding and chalking their gun's stock. My guns are old and strictly hunting tools, so a little blue chalk won't hurt them. I use blue carpenter's chalk with most of my calls, but there are calls which work best with the harder white chalk. The Roy Rhodes box seems to work best with white chalk applied to both the edge of the sounding chamber and the edge of the striker.

The edges on these small boxes should not be sanded to a round contour, but should be flat, unless the maker has sanded the edges otherwise. Many of these calls are tuned by the makers, and he will have chalked the edges, too, so the hunter can use the color of chalk showing on the box edges.

John Grayson, of Bristol, Virginia, has been putting his feet down in turkey woods for nigh onto 50 years, and sells his well-known "Lost John" box from that town in the southwest part of the state. This long narrow box is patterned from an old one his granddaddy carried back before the Civil War. The original was "rived" from a hunk of old cedar fence post. Cedar is an excellent wood for calls because it withstands wear, does not sand off excessively fast, and will take considerable abuse. Properly tuned, cedar has the clear resonant sound much like a wild turkey. John Grayson hand-makes his "Lost John" boxes, and also individually tunes them. Fifty years of listening to wild turkeys have resulted in Grayson's having an ear for what a turkey call should sound like.

Up near Appomattox, Virginia, lives a man by the name of Frank Hanenkrat, who hand-makes a small, unusually shaped box call. Frank is another old-time turkey hunter,

so his calls have that built-in tone which a good call must possess. Frank's calls are hand-tuned, and though I don't know if he still does so, he used to mark the exact location on the call's sounding edge where the striker should be rubbed. Frank Hanenkrat's fine book, *The Education Of A Turkey Hunter*, is guaranteed good reading on those long winter evenings when you want spring to bring you a gobbling turkey. Frank's calls also have a sheet on hunting turkeys included with the instructions. The wood for Hanenkrat's calls was grown on the Appomattox battlefield. Like many boxes of this style, this one will drop into any

These small flat calls are sometimes called "Virginia" boxes because of their popularity in that state. Hanenkrat's "Old Master" call (upper left) has the sounding edge marked where the striker should be rubbed. These calls require a fair bit of practice to sound authentic.

(Right) This small group of old calls are but a sample of what could have been found around the country years ago, as most calls were homemade, and never sold on the retail market.

Dick Bland holds a small box call belonging to the author, which is today considered a valuable collector's item. Many turkey hunters are also serious call collectors, avidly searching for calls made famous from use, for unusual calls, and for one-of-a-kind homemade calls.

shirt pocket. Amazingly, all of these little calls will make notes which have excellent carrying ranges, and turkeys can often hear them a mile away. Like all turkey calls, the hunter must be thoroughly acquainted with them to use them properly, which means handling them by the hour, and learning where each call of the turkey can be reproduced on the call's sounding edge. No two calls sound alike, even though they may be carefully built to exactly the same dimensions.

Time was when there was another small, flat box made in Virginia which had a fork-type handle, and this fork could be used for scratching the leaves. Anyone who has called in a turkey with leaf scratching is aware that once fall turkeys have been scattered and called extensively, the birds will become so call-wary they will run off at the sound of a call. Very often the only way a hunter can call in one of these wary birds is by locating in a cove, or under acorn bearing oaks, beechnut trees, wild cherry, or in a leaf-carpeted location, and then attempt to scratch in the leaves as does a feeding turkey. The handle on this call, known as a "Virginia Banjo," was used in making these dragging scratches. These are "scratch—short pause—scratch, scratch, scratch—short pause—scratch, scratch." The pauses simulate the turkey changing from one leg to the other, as ordinarily a turkey will make one scratch with the left leg, followed by two or three with the right, then one or two with the left. Perhaps somewhere the Virginia Banjo is being made for turkey hunters. I use a short stout tree limb to make the scratches.

Down in Florida is a man whose calls have made a huge dent in the Osceola turkey numbers, this being Tom Gaskins. I've talked to many a Florida "cracker" who was toting one of Gaskins' little boxes. His shop is located near the town of Palmdale, but it is easily found if you simply follow his unique signs along the highway.

Some of the small gunstock boxes will make kee runs if the hunter will take the time to find where to make them on the call. The easiest method is to begin with yelps on the center of the box, then to work out toward the end, particularly the end held by the other hand. By exerting pressure on the sides of the box with his holding hand, the yelp can be made higher on the musical scale. I have never found a large shuffling box which will make kee runs, as the amplifying chamber is not conducive to creating high-pitched notes.

Back in 1929 there was a game warden near Staunton, Virginia, named John Todd, who was succeeded as area warden by his son Jack when the senior Todd passed away in 1934. These men introduced a peg and slate call to a boy from Staunton, W.P. "Bill" Tannehill. After many years of hunting with it, and making adjustments, Tannehill at last felt that the call was marketable. He hand-made these calls in his antique shop there in town until his death in 1969. Today the business is owned and run by Lewis B. Wood, Jr. and his mother. Made at times of both mahogany and walnut, this slate call has a fine tone, easily slips into a pocket, and makes all turkey talk except a gobble. Some

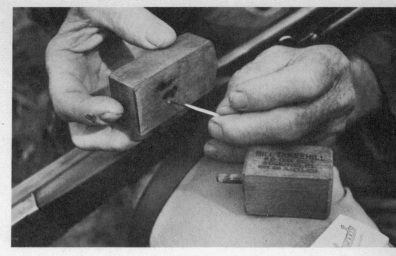

The peg and slate call is perhaps the easiest of all calls on which a hunter can learn to make "kee-kee runs," the often used call made by a lost young turkey. The hunter should follow the directions which come with the call, learn how the sounds are made by watching more experienced hunters, or by attending one of the excellent seminars staged throughout the country each year. The hunter here is holding a match to the slate to burn away any moisture which may have gotten on the surface. Before using, the surface must be lightly sandpapered.

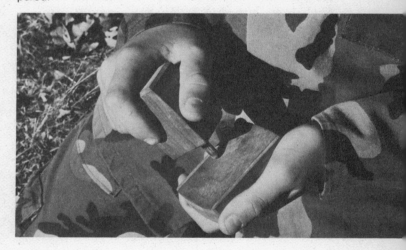

25 years ago I bought one from Bill Tannehill and still use it. I can recall bagging a big adult gobbler with it the first morning I carried it with me, a bird which had an 11¾-inch beard. Luckily, I was carrying a book of matches and a tiny slip of sandpaper that morning. The leaves and brush were wet with dew, and while making calls to the bird, I got the slate surface wet. It was quick and simple to hold a lighted match beneath the overturned slate surface, dry it with the heat, and resand lightly. Hidden in a thick clump of oak sprouts, I couldn't be seen by the approaching bird. Though older hunters may prefer these old-style slates, a good many new slates have space-age plastics in their makeup. To each his own.

Turkey hunting has become so popular over the last decade that today it seems every hunter in the country is

Slate calls must be sanded *lightly* from time to time, otherwise they will not be reliable, emitting screeches and squawks when these are not wanted. Proper and ongoing maintenance will keep a good call in top shape for years.

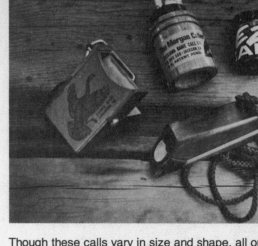

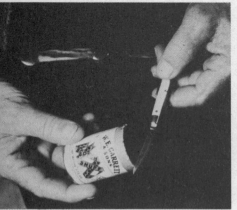

The wild turkey's vocabulary can be mimicked on an endless variety of instruments and can even be made by dragging a pocketknife blade across the cardboard edge of a snuff box. The knife blade must be sharp. But, the notes can only be imitated after considerable experimenting with various containers, and sizes of blades.

Though these calls vary in size and shape, all operate on the principle of air passing over a thin rubber membrane. The sounds made are therefore very much like those made with a mouth call. People who can't use a mouth call because of false teeth can ofttimes learn to operate one of these so-called "snuff can" calls. This term has been used in describing all calls which fit this category.

(**Opposite page**) This hunter is holding the slate and peg portions of this call properly for making notes of the wild turkey. The peg section must be held at about a 45-degree angle to the slate surface. The slate surface must be kept free of any moisture, even body oils from the hands. If moisture gets on the surface, it can be removed by holding the slate upside down and holding a lighted match beneath the surface for a few seconds. The tip of the peg should be charred with a match, then lightly sanded before using. If the call eventually begins to "screech" or to "whine," the surface of the slate needs a light sanding.

making and selling a turkey call of one kind or other. Few, if any, are making a worthwhile living at the business. Sadly, commercialism has taken over this grand gunning sport also.

Turkey calls have been made of anything from turtle shells to sections of rubber hose. I don't doubt that a turkey could be called with a rusty nail and an old milk bucket. Why I have never seen a hunter strolling through the woods with a saxophone is a mystery, for surely, many musical instruments are capable of making turkey sounds.

But, just because a call is offered on the market doesn't mean that it is a good buy. Charlie Elliott, the veteran turkey hunter who wrote *Turkey Hunting With Charlie Elliott*, and I were once hashing over turkey calls, and he told me that one time he went through the better part of a large

store's inventory while searching for a call with the proper tone. In fact, he tried 53 calls before finding one which sounded right. Of course, Charlie has an ear for what a turkey should sound like, after chasing birds around over the country's turkey woods for 50 years.

Charlie is right—few calls have that just right tone. During the past few months, my mail has probably brought me 30 calls, and only a handful have stayed out of the trash basket. Today's hunting magazines are chuck full of ads extolling the virtues of this call or that, and I've got $100 that says one out of every two would not be worth carrying into the turkey woods. Of course, many of these are available only by mail, so the average hunter will have to go through a trying-out period to find one that he likes. This can be expensive, too. My old Florida buddy, David Kelley, who lives in Cocoa, used to own a Jeep Wagoneer, which was mainly used for hauling all the calls David had purchased over the years. I think Dave had two or three of each and every kind made. He just couldn't find one with built-in turkey, as few calls have this quality.

Acquiring an "ear" for wild turkey sounds is best done through years and years of hunting and listening to the birds in their natural habitat. This is where the makers of numerous calls have fallen short, as they haven't heard enough turkeys to know when a call sounds like a turkey, and when it is off key a note or two. An older experienced caller can make up for what a call lacks by knowing when and how much to call, and cover any bad notes with those that follow. The novice turkey hunter is unable to do this though, so a bad call in his hands just sounds bad. The turkey shies away, naturally.

Knowing when to answer is often the difference in going home with something to pluck, or just going home . . .

Turkey hunters everywhere are always demonstrating calls to each other. By having an *experienced* turkey hunter listen to your calling efforts, you'll be able to improve your calling and eventually sound like the real thing. Calling contests are not the best examples of wild turkey sounds. Probably more money is spent each year for turkey calls than for any other aspect of the sport.

Cadence, and knowing when and where to call from, have more bearing on successful calling than do the notes themselves. Too many of today's beginning turkey addicts try to learn turkey hunting and calling through listening to tapes of calling experts, or by attending turkey calling seminars and contests. No one has put this more aptly than my great friend, John Lowther, in his book, *Spring Gobblers*. Let me quote him: "Most beginners are geared to hearing the beautiful musical sounds that emanate from turkey calling contests. They go hunting and listen for this uniform flow of perfect yelps and clucks. I'll say this, if one would put a real turkey in a contest, it wouldn't get 10 points."

John has chased ridge-running old gobblers over enough of West Virginia's mountains to know exactly what I am talking about when I say that a wild turkey can ofttimes be a very poor caller, but not many hunters can imitate this poor calling; for those who can master these imperfections, their calling becomes far deadlier than the calling of the average turkey caller. Knowing when to answer a yelp with a quick cluck or two, or when to make a soft trill in thick cover, is often the difference in going home with something to pluck, or just going home. And, though John Lowther

and I and some other old boys I know could write 10 million words on how to call, or how to hunt turkeys, the bulk of learning boils down to learning the hard way. It harkens to the Smith-Barney ad so often seen on television, which goes, "We make money the old-fashioned way—we earn it." I learned to hunt turkeys the old-fashioned way—I worked at it. I earned each one I put shot into.

But, for the fledging turkey hunter, a full schedule in this fast-paced living we do in America too often leaves little time for lollygagging about in some far-from-town woods, hoping a drove of turkeys will talk it up, just so he can hear them. Wild turkeys have never had a reputation for doing anything on cue, so a hunter can spend lots of time in good turkey country, often days, and not hear a single cluck. The next best thing to do is to listen to them at a turkey farm, or where a few are being raised by a local farmer. Recording equipment is excellent here, for if a hunter can't listen to live birds, on-the-spot, then he can listen to recordings of them.

I have an excellent tape, made and sold by Austin Baggs, of Route 1, Poteau, Oklahoma, 74953, recordings he made of Eastern wild turkeys in the mountains near that town. The tape contains the two basic notes made by wild turkeys during the spring and fall seasons—the hen's mating yelp and the kee run. The hunter who learns these two notes, knows when and where to make them, and can shoot straight will kill all the turkeys anyone would want in both seasons.

Though I don't keep up with what is available, I feel certain there are numerous recordings of wild turkeys which can be bought by mail order. These can be played over and over, the idea being to imprint the sound into the hunter's memory so that when he attempts to make the note with a call, he'll know what it is he is mimicking. For many, remembering the hen mating yelp is easy, but the kee run is hard to recall. So, before the fall season, a hunter should listen to the kees as made by real wild turkeys which have been scattered, and if he can do this every evening during the season while sitting at home, his confidence will increase, and as it does, he'll become a better turkey hunter.

I have been a judge at many calling contests, and have learned that a great many hunters copy what they hear at these exhibitions. Sadly, never have I heard a contestant who could imitate the kee run with any degree of success, including so-called national and world champions. In judging on a one to 10 basis, with 10 being the best, I have yet to give a four on kee runs, though it is one of the two most important notes a hunter must learn. My old Mississippi buddy, Ed Norwood, in using a mouth call, makes far the best kees I've heard a hunter make.

Enough has been written about the notes in calling wild turkeys to fill two or three small libraries with a bunch of my past writings thrown in for good measure. But, the truth is, telling someone about this, and doing it, are two different things. Nobody can tell someone else exactly how to call a turkey, how a call is used, how it should sound, all about the proper cadence, when to make a note and where

Wingbone calls such as "Miss Jezebel," being used here, make excellent clucks and yelps for hunting of fall and winter turkeys. The cowhorn section on this call acts as an amplifier, allowing the call to carry better. Completely muffled notes are excellent for locating turkeys yet on the roost at daybreak. These notes are known as the turkey's "tree call."

There is an endless variety of mouth calls available to today's turkey hunter. The hunter should buy as many of these as are available, in each style, and then in trying each, he can choose the one which seems to fit the mouth most comfortably and which makes the notes he desires. The author uses five or six different mouth calls throughout the year, using those which best fit his hunting methods.

to sit while doing all this. These things best come from hard earned experience. So, while you're reading what I say about these things, keep this in mind.

Nobody can tell someone else how to call a turkey, and where to sit while doing this . . .

Let's discuss time of day as it relates to wild turkeys, and our calling to them. One thing is certain: turkeys are most vocal during the early morning hours. This often begins with a very soft yelp, a pert, or clucking note. These notes can't be heard, even on a quiet morning, for more than 100 or 200 yards, and usually less. The notes are made singly, much of the time with a few seconds between them. They are ofttimes referred to as "head-in-the-barrel" notes because they sound muffled, like the turkey has its head in a barrel. These are the wake-up notes the birds make back and forth to each other just as day begins to break. A hand muffled mouth call, or a wingbone, is best for mimicking these tree calls, and the hunter should practice them as he walks toward a place where they may be used, making adjustments in volume as he goes along. No two mornings are alike insofar as how sounds will carry, particularly if the hunter has been hunting one terrain, and then switches to another.

When I'm hunting fall and winter turkeys, and think I'm near an ideal roosting area, or even when simply walking

unfamiliar woods, I'll make these tree calls as I go, hoping to make contact with an awakening drove, or just a bird or two. This will work for only a short time, for just as soon as the sky brightens, the birds will then stand erect on the roost branches, and change from the faint tree calls to yelps, and clucks. While making the tree calls, the birds are usually hunkered down on the branch, head drawn in on the shoulders. Hunters use the tree call for no other purpose than in trying to locate treed turkeys. It has no use in calling them to the hunter.

The yelps, kees, and clucks, which will follow, are used to bring in the bird. If a hunter hasn't heard these sounds *many* times over, the best thing he can do is to listen to the birds making them, and then try to copy the calls. This is often what I do when calling them from the tree if I think there are but a few, or if the birds' callings indicate they will be, or are, flying down before I can get close to them. Very often an undisturbed drove will make lots of racket while in the trees, with mixed in kee runs, whistles, yelps, clucks, perts; sometimes a young gobbler will try to gobble.

I go out into turkey country before the season, just to find an awakening drove, and listen as they group for the morning. Sometimes I will run in among them scaring them good, and after they've flown or run all about, I'll then hide, and listen as the birds regroup. For the hunter who spends a great amount of time in pursuit of fall turkeys, there is no better preparation. On occasion, I'll practice calling them, trying out a new call, or proving to myself that I've not lost my touch. Much of the time I'll be carrying a camera, so any called-in bird can be photographed.

But, my main pre-season concern is to imprint the calls of the birds on my memory, particularly the kees and yelps of young gobblers and, if I am carrying a call, to learn how these notes are made on that particular call. With practice, most boxes, whether gunstock or shuffling style, will imitate these coarse young gobbler yelps. The hunter who can "swallow" the slower yelps as made on a trumpet call can also make them, but these are more easily made on mouth calls. Because it is so versatile, the mouth call can duplicate the hoarse, drawn out yelp, or make the raspy, barking yelp of a jake gobbler. At the same time, the hunter can exert more pressure on the rubber, which will cause it to break into the higher pitch of the kee itself.

The birds will continue to call once they leave the trees, but after a short time they will be grouped, and the drove will then wander off in search of food or water. Very often the talk will be over for the day, all the more so if the drove is small. Large droves of 20 birds or more will yelp back and forth as they walk along, but as they day progresses this will lessen.

Florida's creek swamps are ideal for the calling hunter. With endless places from which to call while hiding, the notes "carry" well throughout the quiet terrain. Visibility is very limited, which means the turkey can't often get together with other turkeys by sight, so it must walk within a short distance of a calling hunter.

Scattered turkeys separated by the hunter just before sundown often will not respond well . . .

This hunter pauses alongside a pine tree and makes a few calls with a mouth call. He is attempting to get an answer from a young turkey which has been scattered from a drove during an early fall season. If a bird answers, he will then take action in moving to another location or, perhaps, sit down against the base of this large tree and continue calling.

So, for the hunter who depends on calling to put a bird in the oven, the chances to succeed with separated turkeys are best at dawn. I cover lots of ground at first day, simply because I want to hear birds then, and attempt to make a kill, or scatter them, before they all go silent. It is no different than when hunting a gobbling bird during the springtime—I want to get near him while he is gobbling,

as this tells me exactly where the bird is located. The kees and yelps tell me where the drove is, and with a little luck perhaps I can run among them and make a kill. If I'm in a two-bird area, I can then call one of the little yelpers to me. One trick that shouldn't be overlooked while hunting a bunch of well scattered turkeys is that when you hear them calling back and forth to each other, don't forget that these turkeys are apt to go to each other's calling. If it is possible, get between two of them and chances are good a kill can be made. The main problem, of course, is doing this without spooking the birds. Very often the birds will keep to high ground when going to each other. The cover certainly need not be wide open, as some people think, as scattered young turkeys will often walk through thick cover to reach each other. When trying to flush them out, I have had to walk into stuff so thick I couldn't shoot one in it. Older turkeys won't go into such cover as they know the dangers of such actions.

Scattered turkeys can be called at any time of the day, though those separated by the hunter just before sundown often will not respond as well. They will, however, usually come to calling the next morning at dawn. Many late afternoon flushes will result in birds alighting in trees, and though they may fly to other trees before dark, very often they will stay "up" for the evening. If the hunter is a good stalker, and has an eye for locating turkeys perched high among tree crowns, it isn't difficult to walk within good shooting distance of one. Some shots will be at resting birds, while others will be at them once they flush. This

These two hunters are trying to call a gobbler from posted land onto land on which they have permission to hunt. This is but one advantage of using a turkey call, as birds will sometimes scatter to a posted area. The wise hunter will try to call them back "in bounds" rather than hunt where it "t'aint legal."

high crossing shot among trees is a very difficult one, so if you aren't an excellent wingshot, don't try it. Let the bird fly away, mark its course, and then get between it and the remainder of the drove at first light the next morning. Such a well separated turkey can often be easily called into range with a few yelps or clucks.

The neophite fall turkey hunter should remember that turkeys will sometimes fly to calling, alighting in a tree over the caller's head. This is an easy shot, certainly not to be confused with roost shooting. This seems to upset some hunters who then simply throw the gun to cheek, and fire. Treat these chances just as you would an approaching turkey on foot—bring the gun up smoothly, take careful aim at the bird's neck or head, and then squeeze the trigger.

Many times a hunter will hear several turkeys calling, and then realize the birds have grouped nearby. This situation is bad for the hunter, as this bunch will call others to it, so the hunter's only choice is to attempt to scatter them once again. This is best done by running toward them as fast as possible. I don't recommend shooting over them. Such birds have already been separated once, and too much excitement could result in their not gathering for days. Simply run toward them and watch to see if they have flown off in different directions. Then, take up a calling stand between the scattered birds, wait until one is heard to call, and then begin calling. There will be less calling on this second scatter so your calling must match theirs.

Whatever the season, a hunter's calling must have some semblance of sounding like a turkey. And, regardless of

how good the hunter sounds to himself, his calls may not sound so hot to a turkey. Therefore, it is very important for someone who has heard and hunted lots of turkeys to listen to another's calling, and be frank enough to tell him if it sounds good or bad. I have a friend who makes two or three soft clucks after each series of hen mating yelps. Each and every time he makes a call, these clucks are added. I haven't told him about it yet, but it would do him a great favor to reveal this little habit, which does not sound at all like a turkey hen. Obviously, the hunter who has incorrect calling habits is going to call up few turkeys.

One spring, three buddies of mine, and myself, made a sashay down into the Gila country of New Mexico and across the state line into Arizona's White Range, hunting Rocky Mountain Merriam turkeys. All of us did well, except for one hunter who didn't get a shot. The truth was, he hadn't killed a springtime gobbler for the past 2 or 3 years. On the long trip back home, we got to discussing calling, and it dawned on me that his luck was so bad that something else was the cause. Maybe luck hadn't turned on him, perhaps it was his calling. I told him to dig out a call and let me listen to him. At no time while we had been hunting had there been a chance for me to hear him. Nor had I hunted with him for the past few years.

Fetching out a mouth call, he made a few hen yelps. Though these were hen yelps to him, the notes were too deep, too slow, and not at all those of a hen turkey with love in mind. My buddy was making perfect gobbler yelps. He was amazed when I told him what was wrong. Once back home in the East he called three adult gobblers to his gun and told me of his good fortune, happy to be back on the Hallelujah Trail.

Be careful in choosing another hunter to listen to calling. Choose a friend who will be honest, but still listen objectively. It won't do any good if you're told your calling sounds fine even if it doesn't. In fact, you'll just keep on getting worse. This listening to calls by another must be done in hunting terrain, and at varying distances, due to the need to perhaps soften the notes at near ranges, and maybe at longer distances, too. Sounds vary according to humidity, denseness of low ground cover, and slope of terrain. Wind has a tremendous effect, and this is many times associated with time of day, as the wind usually picks up with the sun's climbing in the sky.

If you hear a bird answer your call, *cluck cluck* back to it as quickly as possible . . .

The all-day hunter must realize that turkeys are most vocal at dawn, and with each moment of passing daylight, the calling lessens. The hunter must not lose sight of this fact. Too much calling later in the day is apt to alert turkeys, make them spooky, and after much of this, make them call-shy at all hours.

yet another may not answer but will come to the call silently. Each year there are countless numbers of these silent turkeys which come to a call, but are never seen because the birds will eyeball the hunter while approaching. Complete camo, plus the ability to sit quietly for long periods

Allen Hawkins (left) and David Jackman listen hopefully for an answer to Jackman's "blind" calling with a shuffling box. If they get an answer, they should give an instant comeback with two or three clucks.

Complete camo and the ability to sit quietly for long periods of time are essential to putting a turkey on the dinner table. Here, Monty Montgomery of Enid, Oklahoma, makes yelps on a large shuffling box. Hand movements should be kept to a minimum.

Therefore, a hunter who is "calling blind," in other words, simply calling in hopes of getting an answer, as he travels through turkey woods, should make only an occasional yelp, kee, or cluck, and then call to any responding bird with a like number of notes. Very often, when a hunter hears an answering yelp or cluck, this surprises him, and he just sits or stands there for a moment, trying to decide what to do next. This is exactly what he should do, but he should do his thinking *after* he gives an instant comeback to the turkey. If at all possible, clucking back to a bird two or three times should be done the second the hunter hears the bird. Turkeys that are separated over a period of time do this as it is their way of saying, "Boy, am I glad to hear you. I've sure been lonely." Frequently his instant clucking will result in the bird flying or running to the hunter. Remember, if you are hunting birds which have been scattered for some time, or you suspect the birds in the area have been hard hunted, call very sparingly as you ease through the woods. If you hear a bird answer your call, *cluck, cluck* back to it as quickly as possible, one right after the other, just loud enough for the bird to hear them, and with all the reassurance in them that you can muster. Don't make clucks which are sharp, loud, and spaced apart.

After opening day, particularly in country infested with lots of hunters, we can expect to find numerous turkeys already separated, feeding and roosting alone. These birds will readily regroup. However, one bird may answer a hunter's calling, but another will completely disregard it, and

of time, will put many of these birds in the oven. Hand movements while manipulating a box, slate, or trumpet call, must be kept to a minimum, and a sharp lookout must be maintained for any turkey walking into view. I've killed several turkeys after waking from a nap in deep woods, perhaps birds I would not have bagged had I been awake and making movements, no matter how slight. Lying there sprawled out, sound asleep, the bird has seen no movement from me. All of these birds have awakened me with alarm clucks, but as the birds have been within yards, I have had time to come up shooting. Thus far, I've not lost any such golden opportunities. Probably there have been others which eyed my dozing form, or heard my snoring, and made their escape silently.

Older turkeys which have been scattered often respond to calling but approach silently . . .

What kind of note to make while calling fall turkeys depends on what notes the birds are using in talking to each other. The older the birds, the more this is true, whether within a season, or not. Older turkeys do less calling, except during mating season, and turkeys which are several years old will probably go for days without making any sounds. I have been near groups of older gobblers during

Choosing a calling location can vary with the age of the birds hunted. These hunters are both sitting in the shadows in fairly open terrain which is good for older, hard-hunted birds. If a turkey does approach, they must "make like a rock" and not move to remain unseen by a bird.

Slouched against a tree trunk, Ed Norwood makes "turkey talk" with a big shuffling box. He must be extremely careful not to make any moves detectable by a gobbler while using the call. Because it requires two hands to operate the box call, the hunter must lay his gun down while using it.

fall and winter hunts, and have never heard these birds make a note, day after day. I presume they must talk to each other with extremely soft purrs and clucks which cannot be heard except at very close range.

Older turkeys which have been scattered often respond to calling, but are not seen by the hunter; they'll approach silently, and are more wary than a young turkey, so will come in head high, and on the lookout. Any caller who is poorly located will surely be seen due to insufficient screening foliage, or while making a calling movement. A solid blind works best when dealing with these older turkeys, but this is often impossible to build, or would not be feasible. Choosing a calling location which will be approached by older, hard-hunted turkeys is quite different from choosing one that a young bird would approach. The surrounding cover must be less dense, offering better visibility. Yet, if the hunter locates out on an open flat, the bird will often "hang up," failing to go nearer the call, probably because it can't see the bird which is apparently calling from there. Day after day, regardless of season, far the best place to call is from cover which is dotted with low bushes or hanging tree branches which are situated on rolling uneven ground. Such terrain gives the spooked turkey, or even a springtime love-struck gobbler, sufficient visibility to allay its fears about hidden predators. It forces the birds to approach within easy gunshot range, but before it can actually see the spot where the call is coming from. What I prefer as the "best" place from which to call is one where, once

Clad in a buckskin coat and gripping a muzzle-loading shotgun, the author watches a wild turkey that has come to his calling. By crouching on his knees, he can now raise up to shoot, or ease the gun forward over the log and shoot while hunkered over. This crouching position is one of the author's favorites. It gives complete freedom of the body from the hips to the shoulders, allowing for any swinging action which may be required.

I am seated, I can see over nearby humps in the terrain, but yet my calling location, whether with a box call on my lap, or with a wingbone, is not visible to the turkey until it has approached quite near. This type of cover can be found anywhere that wild turkeys are encountered though it may vary from having to hunker on a sagebrush hill to hiding in a downed treetop on a mountain ridge. *Never* do I attempt to call turkeys while located on large open hunks of flat terrain. Even if ground clutter is present, I will make every possible effort to remain low to the ground, particularly while actually calling. The turkey *must come looking for the caller; and it is preferable that the bird not see the calling location until well within gun range.*

This is comparable to hunting geese, when a hunter sees jillions of them flying about a wildlife refuge. They're nice to see, but you can't shoot any until they fly into range. A turkey, standing alert 100 yards out on an open flat is nice to look at, but the bird would look a darned sight better at 20 yards, just above your shotgun's bead. Like the geese, the turkey can be called into range, but without a whole drove of decoys, your chances of doing so are best if you can keep it from seeing where the supposed turkey is calling.

Last season Don Wildman and I drove up to a hunter who was looking at a big gobbler sprawled out on the ground in front of him, and about the first thing the man says was, "Well, after all these years, at last I called up a turkey."

The hunter's eyes were shining with excitement, and I wasn't surprised when Don asked, "So you got one by calling, huh, how close did he get?" Don knew this man hunted with a combination rifle-shotgun, but like me, I don't think he'd given any thought to the chance that maybe the hunter had unloaded on the gobbler with the rifle. I know I hadn't, after he'd made the statement about calling to him. "Oh, he was about 125 yards from me when I shot." I all but broke out laughing. Don, however, never flinched.

Later, driving along a country road a mile from there, both of us heehawed. A "called up" turkey to us is a few yards nearer than 125 yards, in fact, about 100 yards nearer.

I've run into this fallacy all across the country, having heard numerous hunters tell stories about calling in wild turkeys, only to learn the birds had never walked within shotgun range. Many hunters consider a bird called in if it answers them and takes a few steps toward the call. I'm not a good caller, and I envy folks who can call birds with ease. A buddy of mine recently told me he'd called in 40 gobblers just this past spring. 'Course, I didn't believe him, because he was in hard-hunted country where there hasn't been 40 gobblers killed in the past two or three seasons. If he had told me that he called up these birds before the season opened, I would have lent an ear to his story, and this is probably what he did. Some hunters count all turkeys which come into range as "called" turkeys, even though they may be hiding near a food plot, near water, or in a blind overlooking "bait."

The turkey hunter in south Florida has perhaps the finest concealment cover possible for use in hunting wild turkeys. A hunter calling from this oak hummock need only cut and place two or three fronds from a cabbage palmetto in the soil around the tree trunk and, presto!, a blind is built. The author poked the gun barrel from this one so you would know his location.

It helps to be crazy to hunt turkeys because turkeys will do many crazy things . . .

Whatever call a person chooses to use, most will make a number of notes which will bring turkeys to the hunter, providing, of course, the hunter is located where a turkey will come to, the notes and the rhythm of the call sound like another turkey, and there is a reason why the bird will go to the call. A hunter can make very nice sounding yelps during the spring season, but if any listening gobbler is with hens, the chances are 100 to one the bird will stay with the hen already present. A lost young turkey can stand on a ridge, calling its head off, and if the hunter's calling is coming from where none of the scattered drove has flown, it probably won't go to the call. What it boils down to is knowing a great deal about a turkey's lifestyle, from when it is a small poult until it is a grown adult gobbler or hen. Turkeys are birds of habit, flying down, feeding, watering, loafing, feeding, loafing, flying up, day after day. These habits change slowly as the weather cycles, as food availability causes them to move to other areas, and as their bodies develop. Their calling to each other is a result of these parts of the lifestyle and in their response to threats from predators.

The person new to calling turkeys can do no better than to spend all the time possible in close contact with the birds, listening to them as they go through each day, and do this day after day, making every effort to learn what makes them tick, or in this case, yelp. This will reveal to the would-be hunter the whys and why-nots of calling, and if he becomes a student of animal behavior, the reasons why a wild turkey will do this or that become apparent. One afternoon another hunter and myself were doing a little ''blind'' calling, not knowing if a turkey was within a country mile. All of a sudden, a hen strolled out in front of us, not paying us any mind, and as we ''made like stumps,'' she began pecking at the weeds and grasses. I suppose she decided that since she'd come here, she might as well make the best of it and do some eating. Anyhow, she'd been there a few minutes, when suddenly, she stood erect, then bowed her neck. I whispered to my friend, ''Don't move, there's turkeys coming.''

A few seconds later, a little bunch of jakes walked into view, but they didn't hesitate, and went to pecking along with the hen. My buddy eased up his gun, and made a kill.

After it was over, he said to me, ''How did you know those turkeys were coming? There wasn't any way you could see them, and I never heard them call?''

''No, they didn't call, and I couldn't see them,'' I answered. ''But many times I've seen turkeys being approached by other turkeys, and they began acting belligerent. I've noticed that they'll bow their necks like that hen did. It's got something to do with the different flocks' social structure, I suppose.''

''Well,'' he said, ''I saw the hen bow her neck, but I thought you'd gone crazy when you told me to get ready, that turkeys were coming.''

It helps to be crazy to hunt turkeys because turkeys will do many things which seem crazy to human beings, and how they respond to calling is part of it. My advice to anyone just beginning to hunt wild turkeys is to buy a call and a taped recording of *live turkeys*, and then *practice, practice, practice*. Talk to other hunters about their calling, if you want; read what others have to say about it, but just remember, nobody—me, your best friend, or 100 of the best callers in this country—can truly tell you how to call a wild turkey into shooting range. It must be learned while hunting the real thing, a wild turkey.

Nor will you get good at it overnight. It's taken us all these years to learn a little about speaking English, and nobody has come near to mastering it yet.

On second thought, you should buy a whole bunch of turkey calls. Who ever heard of a turkey hunter with only one call?

Learning about the lifestyles of the various wild turkeys is far easier done by reading about them than can be learned otherwise, due to the great amount of time which must be spent near them at all hours of the day. The books available today cover all aspects of hunting the wild turkey, from learning what one looks like to the cooking of the birds.

Gobblin' Time Is Huntin' Time

Dick Bland, the author's twin brother, hefts a spring-killed gobbler. Springtime hunting is far more popular than fall hunting, simply because the turkey's gobble tells hunters where they are located. If wild turkeys had never gobbled or strutted, there would never have been springtime hunts.

GOBBLING TIME, or as others will say, gobbling season, is by far the most popular of the two hunting seasons for wild turkeys. Why? because the turkey gobbles. This reason alone causes people to jump out of bed at ridiculously early hours, leave home without breakfast, file for divorce, spend outlandish sums of money—all for the privilege of lolly-gagging around on some wooded hill, listening for a bird to make a crazy sound.

If all the turkeys in this country would quit gobbling next spring, the country could return to some sort of normalcy. Bosses would see employees they ordinarily do not see in April, and little children just might get daddy to take them to school.

The gobble is why so many hunters take to the woods in March, April and May. The hunter hears the quarry, so knows it is there to hunt. Without the gobble, the average hunter is lost insofar as knowing how to cope with the shooting of a turkey.

How many times have we all had someone ask us, "Did you hear a bird gobble this morning?" I think I've heard that question a thousand times, just while walking little used Arkansas backroads. As pickups drove past, the hunters would stop to chat a moment or two and invariably they would ask that question.

Truthfully, the question, "Have you heard any?" is rather silly. It's akin to asking the man who catches great numbers of fish what he's using for bait, and where he's been catching 'em. I'd be a fool to tell some stranger where I heard two birds gobbling this morning, when he has just told me he hasn't heard a single one. This thing about

gobbling has gotten out of hand though, as we now have hunters who have seemingly forgotten that the idea of hunting turkey gobblers is in bringing the hunter's gun to within range of one of these birds. Not just in counting gobbles.

Ed Norwood and I had a friend in Mississippi who kept us posted on what "his turkeys" were doing each morning. We'd very often bump into him at a crossroads store where we'd stop to buy a bottle of soda pop after the morning session of hunting. The first thing we'd ask him on arriving at the store was, "How many times did they gobble this morning?"

"A hundred and fifty-three," or perhaps "eighty-six," would be our buddy's answer. He would count each gobble each day. We came to the conclusion years earlier that this man could not care less if he ever got the birds into shooting distance, just so long as they gobbled. Ed and I would ofttimes get him quite upset by telling him we were going after "his turkeys" the following morning. Of course, we never did, though the birds were on public land. We miss him now, as he's gone on to the Happy Hunting Grounds. I hope turkeys gobble there every day, just for him.

Many, many hunters would quit hunting turkeys if the birds ceased all gobbling, mainly because they would no longer be able to locate them so easily. This is why spring turkey hunting far outstrips fall hunting in popularity. The American hunter's association with spring turkey hunting has grown into a fondness which has resulted in many facets of the sport being given slang terms. A bird's gobbling is oftentimes referred to as "sounding off," "firing back" or "cutting loose." You may hear a hunter remark that he

Jay Brown, of Natchez, Mississippi, photographed here while hunting one spring morning with the author, uses an old turkey hunting trick in an effort to elicit a gobble from any gobblers within hearing distance. This is to hoot like an owl. Jay's "owling," as this is known among turkey hunters, is the best the author has heard.

Owl hooters are sold today for hunters who can't imitate the sound of this bird with their mouth. These calls are simple to operate, mimic the owl's tone perfectly, and cost little.

(Right) A sight to gladden the heart of any wild turkey hunter. But, for what season? The protruding "heavy belly" look of this adult long-bearded gobbler tells us that this bird is in prime condition for the spring mating season. An adult gobbler during the fall and winter months has a sleek appearance.

heard a bird "bellering his head off," or the bird's gobbles "sounded like the Bells of St. Mary's." I have heard old-timers state "the old turkey was rarin' and gobblin'," or, "he gobbled and it jarred the ground," all terms of endearment to men who love the sport.

Wild turkey gobblers are known to go into "gobblin' sprees"—they "yodel," and they "holler." All of this when it is "turkey struttin' time." Birds who don't gobble are known to have "shutmouth." The hunter who attempts to cause a turkey to gobble is invariably attempting to "raise a gobbler." You may overhear a hunter remark, "I was owling, but couldn't raise one." What this means is that the hunter was imitating the call of an owl in hopes that a wild gobbler would sound off at these sounds. Or, a hunter who does much calling may be attempting to "crank up a turkey," to cause a bird to gobble over and over.

The result is a season that opens after the birds have mated, but before the hens have laid eggs . . .

Folks who do not hunt may wonder why there is a spring hunt for wild turkeys, whereas for other hunted fowl the hunting season is closed during the mating season. Probably, if this hunt had no roots back into the last century, there would be no spring season. The pioneer hunter began

the tradition, and the hunting methods associated with the sport, using a call and a shotgun, rifle or musket, also soon became tradition. The calling itself is steeped in tradition, as anyone who has read the directions accompanying one of the calls made back during those "good old days" knows. The time-honored method instructed the hunter to make two or three soft yelps, wait 5 minutes, make three yelps, and then call no more. The calling of a wild gobbler to the hunter's gun was considered the ultimate of hunting pursuits. Local men who were successful at this sport year after year became legends.

But the spring season is based on more than just tradition. The modern day hunter knows that it is possible for us to have a spring wild gobbler season because of the lifestyle of the wild turkey. A few simple facts will help explain. Wild turkeys mate during the spring, and unlike ducks, doves, and other game birds, do not pair during the mating period. A single adult gobbler will gather from one to several hens and mate each many times over a period spanning

Chuck Hartigan, president of DBI Books, Inc., admires the spurs which are called "buttons," just beginning to show on the leg of a young jake gobbler. By the end of the second year of life, the spur will have reached ½-inch in length, and grow accordingly as the bird ages. The world record for a spur now stands at 2 inches, attained by a several-year-old gobbler bagged in south Florida.

several weeks. Turkey hunters refer to a group of hens as a gobbler's "harem." I have counted as many as 13 hens with one adult gobbler.

For those readers who do not know, the turkey hunter refers to all male turkeys past 1 full year of age as *adult gobblers*. Such birds are also known as "longbeards," "old gobblers," "boss turkeys," "patriarchs" or "hermits." The gobbler from the previous spring's hatch of turkeys, not yet a full year of age, is known as "shortbeard," "blue-john," or as the bulk of turkey hunters will call him, a "jake." A jake is a young gobbler with a beard which protrudes from the breast feathers for perhaps 3 inches, seldom more, very often much less.

Once that adult gobbler mates with a hen, the hen no longer needs further mating; this one time will see her through the egg laying season for one year. (Jake turkeys are not yet able to mate, biologically, and though these young gobblers are often observed with hens, they cannot proliferate the race until their second spring of life.) Thus, once an adult gobbler has mated with the local hen populace, he can be considered "surplus," insofar as turkey numbers are considered. His demise will not have any bearing on continued turkey populations. But, to lessen hunter disturbance of nesting hens, the season must be set so as not to interfere with hens incubating a full nest of eggs. The result is a season that opens after the birds have mated the one time necessary but before the hens have laid the clutch of eggs and while the adult male is still gobbling. (Once the hen has laid all her eggs and has begun incubating them, she no longer seeks out the male's company. Soon the gobbler's mating instincts wane, causing him to cease gobbling.)

Numerous states have spring hunts which begin at a time of day when all the hens are with the gobbler. This causes much gnashing of teeth for the turkey hunter who hopes to lure the male with a hen call because the wild hens have

already done so. Various states have hunts which end each day at noon, or thereabouts, to prevent disturbing the turkeys the remainder of the day. According to hunting pressures, there are states which have long seasons, while others have seasons which last but a week or two. Obviously, the hunting of wild turkey gobblers during the springtime has little effect on future populations. A great many states have had such hunts for decades, with turkey populations today as good as the terrain will permit.

Springtime is gobbling time, and gobbling time is the time to hunt . . .

Gobbling time is something else; it is springtime. New green shoots are spearing upward across the great palmetto pastures that have been burned in Florida. Indian turnips stand like tiny sentinels at lonely guard posts in a Vermont woods. Woodhens, or what the non-turkey hunter knows as a pileated woodpecker, ring the piney woods with their jack-hammering in search of wood borers. Or, perhaps a thin blanket of an overnight snow lays dazzling white in the Rocky Mountain sun, etched with the drag marks of an old turkey's strutting. With all this, the gobbling of a wild turkey is just more icing on the cake.

Why does a turkey gobble? Biologists tell us this is the male bird's lovesong, though it doesn't much seem in the same category with a mockingbird, or a cardinal. But obviously it is, because the birds seldom gobble at other times of the year. All of us who have hunted fall and winter turkeys extensively have heard gobbling then, too, but it is sporadic, to say the least.

Wild turkey gobblers will sometimes gobble at the cawing of crows, which brings forth another trick in the hunter's bag—the use of a crow call. The hunter using this call should make two or three quick loud "caws," then stop and listen. If a gobbler is apt to answer, it will be to these first sudden callings. If a gobbler does gobble at these, the chances are good the bird will not do so again at least for 20 or 30 minutes.

The Legend Of The Dogwood

There is a legend that at the time of the crucifixion the dogwood was the size of the oak. So firm and strong was the tree that it was chosen as the timber for the cross. To be used thus for such a cruel purpose greatly distressed the tree, and Jesus, nailed to it, sensed this, and in His gentle pity for all sorrow and suffering, said to it:

"*Because of your regret and pity for my suffering, never again shall the dogwood tree grow large enough to be used as a cross. Henceforth it shall be slender and bent and twisted and its blossoms shall be in the form of a cross . . . two long and two short petals. And in the center of the outer edge of each petal there will be nail prints, brown with rust and stained with red, and in the center of the flower will be a crown of thorns and all who see it will remember. . . ."*

Throughout all of wild turkey country there's a saying that goes, "When the dogwood blooms, it's turkey gobbling time." It is the season to hunt wild gobblers.

Many different sounds can stimulate a turkey into gobbling. Apparently, these are simply what could be referred to as reaction gobbles. The most common sounds which elicit gobbling are the hooting of owls and the cawing of crows. I've heard gobblers sound off at the wailing cries of sickle-billed curlews, band-tailed pigeons, jays and the drawn-out yodeling of coyotes. Honking a car horn will sometimes cause a gobbler to sound off, as will slamming a door, clapping the hands, or shooting a gun. Many times I have heard a farmer talking about a turkey gobbling when he was out calling up the cows. I threw a battered dishpan into the side of a rusting car body one day in Mississippi and was answered by a nearby gobbler. However, the turkey will usually gobble only one time at these sudden sounds, and further attempts to entice more responses will be ignored. Continued gobbling is often brought about by only two sounds—the voices of hen turkeys, or the gobbling of other males.

But, there will be mornings when you will hear no gobbles even though you are certain the birds are present. Shutmouth turkeys defy all explanations as to why they do not gobble. Weather, time of day, etc., any or all conditions can be exactly like so many other days when the birds will cut loose time after time. After a few days of this silence, it is common to hear hunters remark, "they ain't gobbling," or "they was gobbling 2 weeks ago, but they quit since then." I heard this from many hunters during the recent 1985 season. That spring I hunted in south Florida, hearing only one bird gobble a few times on one morning, this over a period of a week. Everyone in Florida was wailing about "they ain't gobbling." Later in Oklahoma, Arizona and New Mexico, it was the opposite. Turkeys were gobbling morning, noon and night. When the birds are being "shutmouthed," the hunter can either pack up and go home, or endure the long hard days of stillhunting, ambushing, or just hope to call a bird to the gun.

Next to hunting fall and winter adult gobblers, the hunting of "shutmouth" birds in the spring season is probably the toughest there is. During my travels to various turkey woods, I have noticed that I must endure far greater numbers of "shutmouth" turkeys in Mississippi than in any other state. Who knows why? Perhaps Mississippi has had springtime turkey hunting for so many years that the birds have become less vocal, the trait genetically passed down through the generations. Perhaps not. Springtime is gobbling time and gobbling time is the time to hunt. How do we locate a turkey gobbler, if he is not gobbling yet, or make a bird sound off?

Let's presume we have done our homework, and through scouting, or further endeavor, are positive that we are in known turkey country. We did not arrive before season, so must begin hunting as soon as we can find a bird to hunt. We need to make a turkey gobble.

The hunter who is on strange grounds, in an area he has never been in previously, will do best to remain near a road until he can make contact with a gobbler. It's too easy to walk a jillion miles in unknown country, the end result being that you don't hear anything resembling a turkey. Anyone who has hunted turkeys but a few times has already observed that within a given area there will be places where a turkey gobbler never travels. This is a constant fact, regardless of which subspecie is being hunted, no matter what the terrain.

As I do not like waiting for a bird to gobble, I instead sound off with a mouth call . . .

To the beginning turkey hunter, I suggest a person's best chances of finding a turkey, or getting one to gobble, are to drive country roads, woods trails, or even little used blacktops, and listen for a gobbling bird. This is best done just as daylight is washing white onto the eastern sky and can last well past sunrise. Throughout hilly or mountainous terrain, it is wise to stop the vehicle every ½- to ¾-mile, shut off the engine, quietly get out of the vehicle, and then listen. As I do not like to waste time in waiting for a bird to gobble, I instead try to get a gobbler to sound off by gobbling with a mouth call. Gobbling is also imitated with tube-calls, elongated rubber tube devices, and with any number of box calls of the shuffling-lid variety. I use a mouth call as this type will far exceed the others in volume. I use a gobble because I have found that many turkey gobblers will not respond to the hoot of an owl which is so popular around the country. Too, many gobblers will respond only one time to this "owling," but will gobble more

often to repeated calling. I have also had responding turkeys approach my gobbling which they have not done when I was imitating an owl.

Another trick I have often heard is to stop the vehicle, quietly get out, and then slam the door. Gobblers may react to this with a gobble, but like many sounds of this type, will not gobble at it often, nor can they be relied on to gobble at it initially.

Of course, if the hunter is on foot, any attempts to elicit a gobble should be made every several hundred yards along the way, and it is wise during the few hours just past daybreak to cover ground fast, so as to increase your exposure to a bird's gobblings during this prime gobbling time. Don't give up too early though, for many gobbling turkeys have been heard at high noon. I can recall hearing gobbling turkeys several times when I have been at the truck eating lunch. Turkeys can and do gobble all day.

It should be kept in mind that there are areas where the hunter need not drive the backwoods roads, as local turkey populations will be so good that all a hunter needs to do is walk through the woods and listen. Missouri is the best example of this to be found, but it is still easily possible to have large areas without turkeys. Time was when I always did all my listening while afoot, but after having hunted so much unfamiliar country the past couple decades, I nowadays drive backroads, pinning my hopes on hearing a bird sound off from the pickup. Areas which I have hunted extensively are hunted on foot, as I know where the birds will be found though some areas are exceptions.

The exceptions are the historic ranges of the Merriam and Rio Grande wild turkeys. These two subspecies can, and very often do, travel long distances in migrating from

Wild gobblers are often heard from well-traveled highways. Locating a gobbler along such roads often entails nothing more than driving along, with stops every ½-mile or so, and when one is heard, to park the vehicle and hunt. Sometimes the gobbler can be called much nearer the highway, which means you won't have to carry the heavy bird very far once it has been shot.

A number of instruments are available which will make a sound much like the gobbling of a turkey. This bellows-type call must be shaken to render a gobbling sound. Many hunters hope that by imitating a gobbling turkey that any bird in hearing range will likewise answer with a gobble.

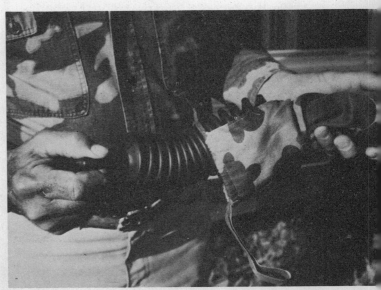

Rocky Mountain country is "big country"—rough, well timbered and at high elevations. It's best avoided by anyone with heart or respiratory ailments. A gobbling turkey can be on a nearby peak, but the hike over to him may result in an hour's hard walk, with difficult, gasping-for-breath panting and puffing thrown in for good measure. The Merriam turkey knows this as home, and hikes up and down these mountains like they are mole hills. Don't hunt this country unless you're in good physical condition.

their wintering flock range to their spring residence. In addition, though a flock will winter in the same area for years on end, the birds, making up this flock, may not take up spring residence in the same location year after year. This is particularly true of Merriams.

Three years ago, three of my buddies and I hunted Merriam turkeys in Arizona, in an area where Merriams have roamed since time began. I had hunted thereabouts a year earlier, so knew the area. The birds were there. Last year I returned but not a turkey could I find. The conditions seemed identical, and like the two previous years, plenty of aging winter signs were present. Regardless, the birds were not in the area. Knowing the wandering habits of these true mountain turkeys, I began a search and found the birds at a higher altitude some 4 miles distant. Next year, who knows? I may again find the turkeys back at the original spring range.

Rio Grande turkeys often do not return to places which are within the flock's spring breakup-nesting area. These variances can be attributed to food supplies, the quality of nesting habitats, land use changes, water, and winter flock populations. My observations indicate that small wintering flocks will nest nearer to the wintering area, especially Osceolas, Easterns, and in part, some Rio Grandes. Where large wintering flocks are evident, flocks numbering 50 or more, the birds are more likely to be scattered over a larger area at nesting time.

In looking for turkey sign, keep a sharp watch around water like this small pond high in the Rockies. Many times the spring turkey season will occur during a dry spell in the far West. Droppings and feathers will indicate if birds are in the vicinity. Examine these carefully because dry conditions can keep them looking fresh over longer periods of time than is often the case in Eastern turkey range.

I can run the risk of dealing with them as a group, or charge in among them . . .

Regardless of how you locate a gobbling turkey, the next thing is, "What now?" Before you do anything, make sure the sound is a gobble. But if you are positive you've heard a bird, be certain you have a fairly good bearing on the direction the gobble came from. Invariably I try to get a bird to gobble two or three times, then I'll decide my next moves. Very often the gobbling of a bird will cause another to gobble; this one could be closer. Or, even though it is not closer, perhaps it is situated where I can approach it more easily, or perhaps I know something of the terrain thereabouts.

Throughout all of this, every effort is made to listen for the yelps of hens in the area. Are the yelps those of a hen, or could it be a hunter calling? Can you hear an owl hooting? Maybe it isn't an owl.

What about topography? Can you get to the gobbler's location? Can you tell how far the bird is from you? Can you tell if the gobbler is up on a tree branch, or has flown down to the ground? Did the turkey gobble without your stimulating it, or could you tell? Has it gobbled since?

A hunter must consider all these variables, but in less time than it takes to read this. So long as you are some distance from the bird, each second counts. You need to get within a couple hundred yards, preferably before the bird quits gobbling and while it is still in the tree. Gobblers are apt to sound off to a greater degree while on a branch. Once they go to ground, the hens (if present, and you must always assume they are, until you know otherwise) will join them. Very often after the hens have made company with the gobbler, he will then go silent. If you are in a position to observe the group at this time, the gobbler will prance about in full strut, often continuously, and tag along behind the hens as they begin walking away toward feeding areas.

Judging the distance to a gobbling bird can be extremely

difficult if the hunter is on unfamiliar grounds. Sounds bounce back and forth over differing types of terrain according to barometric pressures, plus the added effects which wind, rain, fog, heat and cold may exert can change them. Add to this a bubbling mountain stream, a truck droning along a distant blacktop, cows mooing, and it is a wonder we even hear a gobbler cut loose. If the hunter over estimates the distance, then gets too close, there is also the chance that the bird will then be spooked on seeing him.

My brother Dick and I heard a bird gobbling just after daybreak one May morning, which we both estimated to be within ½-mile. Walking and walking, we thought we'd never get to the bird, which turned out to be well over a mile from where we'd begun. I can recall hearing birds gobbling on a fall morning, at least 20 years ago, which turned out to be nearly 3 miles distant. I don't think I would have heard a single gobbler at that distance, but there were a bunch of them.

Getting a good "fix" on the location of a gobbling bird becomes critical if the gobbler is located on a spur ridge, point, or in any location where the hunter must circle it to some degree, then work closer from another angle. Very often it will become necessary to lose contact with the bird for a short period of time, then as you draw nearer, hope to be close enough to regain contact through calling or even sight.

John Waters, a longtime hunting buddy, and I have often teamed up on Arizona Merriams. Merriams can often be heard 1 to 2 miles, but on getting nearer, the turkeys would quit gobbling if we quit calling and it would become difficult for both of us to attempt to hunt the bird. There are numerous times when a hunter can crank up a gobbler, and keep the bird gobbling by doing a great amount of loud calling, making the hen yelps over and over. But, as in the case of the Arizona Merriams, once the hunter realizes the bird is not coming to the call, then it is best to go to the turkey. So, while one of us stays behind and calls, keeping the bird cranked up, the other makes a circuitous stalk, easing in near the bird to either take over the calling or make a stalking kill. John and I have hunted so much together that we think alike and have an idea of what the other is doing, so seldom do these tactics fail us. We know that the early morning habits of Merriams differ from many Eastern gobblers. Merriams tend to go downhill, whereas the average Eastern gobbler remains on a ridge or some high elevation until later in the morning. These are little facts that put turkey gobblers in the back of pickup trucks. But, when the Merriam hunter locates a gobbling bird which refuses to come down-mountain, then the bird is treated the same as an Eastern; the hunter must get above or on a like level with the bird and try to call it to the gun.

Before I begin my approach, I make a quick study of the situation, and though I may be in unfamiliar country, I try to analyze the terrain. Gobblers are far more easily called when the hunter is on the same ridge, within the same hunk of woods, on the same side of the creek, or along the same side of an open pasture. Throughout Old Mexico's high Sierras, a hunter is wasting his time calling at a gobbler which is on another mesa; the hunter must be on the same flat with the bird.

When I first hear a gobbling turkey and then hear hens clucking and yelping nearby, I can also make a decision as

The author makes a yelp on a wingbone call as the note will easily carry throughout the country to the near ridge. Very often a gobbler can be located in this manner if he gobbles at the sound. Should a bird answer here, the author would not walk directly toward the bird, but would continue one way or other along the road, and make a large circling move toward the bird. There is very little chance the gobbler would approach him at this location, because the surrounding clearcut is blanketed with tall weeds, grass, wild blackberry, and oak sprouts.

(Left) The author works a large shufflin' box for a gobbling bird and is standing up to get a good fix on its location. Once it has been "spotted," he'll circle to it, call some more, and get it (or himself) into shooting range.

to what I want to do about them. When I am hunting on strange grounds, I realize that once they get together with the gobbler, the whole bunch could easily get away from me, since I don't know the terrain. I can run the risk of dealing with them as a group, or charge in among them, hoping I'll get a good scatter, and then attempt to crank up the gobbler with hen yelps, and call him in to me. When I'm on terrain which rules out any stalking of the group, I will sometimes charge into a gathering harem. Mexican turkey country falls into this category, as does much Merriam range. Neither has weed clumps, ground clutter, bushes, and tiny humps which allow a hunter to stalk.

On one hunt, I'd approached a bunch of turkeys deep in Chihuahua's Sierra Madre Occidental Range early one morning, but as it appeared they would group and leave me like a bride at the altar, I charged in among them. Watching the boss turkey fly across a deep chasm, I marked him down on the neighboring mountain, then made the long struggle to get on the mesa with him. The trouble was, I overshot him, and after making my calling stand, heard him gobble one time some 400 yards from me. I knew that one gobble was disastrous for me, as that was the only call he needed to let the hens know where he could be found. Running as best I could in the thin mountain air, I plunged into the manzanita thicket where I thought he was, catching a glimpse of the old bird and a couple of hens. We all busted out the far side, but this time I watched him glide across another deep barranca, sailing north toward El Paso. I was too tired to follow though no hens sailed off on that tangent. You win some, you lose some.

Once I decide to go toward a gobbling bird, I run if possible, wanting to get to within 100 yards of the gobbler before he can move off. If you just lollygag along, too often the bird will shut up before you get near and then you won't know where the bird is. Walk fast if you aren't up to running or trotting.

You may want to stop a time or two, hoping that the bird will gobble, thus maintaining a good fix on its location. I don't like to make hen yelps while approaching the bird, so I either rely on the bird to continue gobbling, or stimulate the gobbler with crow calls, owl hoots, or gobbling. Earlier I mentioned throwing an old dishpan against a car body, which was simply an attempt to make a bird I knew was in the area gobble. When nothing else works, I will often make a hen yelp, though I prefer to wait until I have drawn close and make the killing stand before I use this call.

Seldom will I approach a gobbler on a straight line, particularly the last 100 yards. By then, even in unfamiliar territory, I will be utilizing screening cover, and since it is a must not to let the bird see me, I will take whatever route the cover provides. If by this time I know the bird is on a ridge, I would want to get on it with him and, if I have an inkling that the bird's located along a flank, will want to come in on the ridge slightly above the gobbler. This could mean circling completely around a mountain, but the time will be well spent, more so if I am dealing with an Eastern gobbler. If I am hunting open prairie gobblers such as Osceolas and Rio Grandes, I would want to remain in a strand of cover as long as possible and not risk crossing open pastures. Sneaking near a gobbler on a long slope sparsely dotted with mature timber could easily mean a jog of a mile in order to get within a 200- or 300-yard calling range.

The droppings of adult male turkeys, the birds that hunters know as "long-beards," "hermits," and "boss gobblers," are long in shape, often about as big around as a pencil. Some are curved like the one in the top of this picture.

By comparing the toe marks of these tracks, a hunter can tell that two birds walked across this sand. The large tracks are those of a gobbler, the small ones a hen.

(Right) Guide Neal Reidhead points out a fresh dropping on a well traveled road. Due to its piled shape, this dropping is that of a hen turkey. This one has not been run over by a vehicle, so we know it is fairly fresh. Like the old saw, "Where there's smoke, there's fire," so it goes with wild turkeys during the springtime—"Where there's hens, there's gobblers."

I settled into a clump of salt cedar seconds after he gobbled, then yelped again . . .

Longtime turkey hunter Earl Woodbury makes hen yelps with a handmade corn-cob-and-slate call, a call easily made by anyone. The slate call is best operated when the user concentrates on the notes, watching his hand movements over the slate to utilize the portion which sounds best. This area is learned and remembered during before-season practice sessions. Many hunters will mark this "best place" with chalk.

(Opposite page) Throughout many states it is legal during the spring season to shoot any bearded turkey. Therefore, bearded hens are included in a hunter's bag. Notice the difference in size of the bearded hen (left) when compared to the size of the adult gobbler. Both of these wild turkeys are of the Eastern subspecie. Check your state's regulations.

If a hunter had no better look at these two turkeys, it is still easy to tell the sex of each. The black feathers on the belly of the bird on the left tell us that this can only be a gobbler. The bird on the right, a hen, has breast feathers with light tips.

Once the hunter has closed the distance to less than 100 or 200 yards, visual contact should be made if humanly possible. Today's endless array of small pocket-sized binoculars are excellent for searching out turkeys in thick terrain. Too many times though, the hunter will attempt to look for the birds with just the naked eye and in moving closer to get a better looksee, the hunter is seen by the turkeys. Consequently, the birds run off, spooked, leaving him to ponder their whereabouts, after he has spent valuable hours calling to nothing but trees, bushes, and rocks. Visual contact will reveal the number of turkeys, sexes, and ages. Further action hinges on all these factors. And since many young yearling jake gobblers have lusty gobbles, the hunter who is after nothing but older long-bearded turkeys will want to abandon a chase if he sees the bird is a short-bearded jake.

Numerous times I have heard a hunter remark that he could invariably tell the gobble of a jake from that of an adult gobbler. This marks the hunter as having little experience with the various subspecies of wild turkeys. Some yearling gobblers can gobble as well as any adult. Many old turkey hunters have heard adult gobblers that did not gobble well and assumed it to be a jake turkey. They were later pleased to run their fingers over its long beard. Savvy turkey addicts check out all gobbling birds before deciding whether one is a bird they will, or will not, shoot.

Should it be possible to make visual contact, the hunter

then can decide whether to stalk the group, attempt a scatter, call, or just maintain contact and hope a plan arises as the morning wears on. Keeping in visual contact with a group of turkeys is risky over a period of time. The birds will move a great deal, and as the hunter attempts to keep them in sight, he is often seen. Of course, if this distance is stretched out to a few hundred yards, chances are the hunter can maintain contact, but this is often difficult in heavily timbered or rugged country. Too, should a sudden opportunity arise to make a stalk, the hunter who keeps near the birds, within 100 yards or so, will be in a position to do this quickly. As the birds move through thick cover, these opportunities may be fleeting, but the person who is willing to run the risk may be successful. This often calls for quick decisions, with action to match, such as fast running, belly-crawling as fast as possible, perhaps wading waist deep across a creek.

Two years ago, while working my way through thick cover, I was answered by a gobbler as I made mouth yelps while I walked. He was somewhere around 60 to 80 yards from me, as best I could judge from that single gobble. I settled into a clump of salt cedar seconds after he gobbled, then yelped again. Though the bird fired back at me a few times, I could tell he was going away. I'd never hunted thereabouts previously, but after quickly sizing up the situation, I realized the bird would get away from me if I didn't take instant aggressive action. Sneaking back and

very often this may be much earlier, between 8 and 10 o'clock. When the hunter sees that the gobbler is alone, the time is excellent for making some hen talk.

The hunter who cannot make visual contact will still have all these problems and decisions, but in not being able to see the turkeys, he won't know what conditions exist. All too often, the hunter hears the bird gobble, and right then, without giving it another thought, decides the gobbler is all alone. The hunter makes a call; the bird gobbles. This goes on for a time. After a while, the hunter makes a call, but there is no gobble. He assumes the bird has left, and that he has made a bobble somewhere along the line. The truth is, and this happens a jillion times each spring, the gobbler was with hens, and though the bird would gobble back to the hunter's callings, the bird was not going to leave his hens for a hen it could not see. The hunter had made no mistakes. He just did not have all the facts laid out where he could see them.

Quite often, when a hunter calls to a group consisting of gobblers and hens, one of the hens will cluck, yelp, or make herself vocally known, letting the hunter know there are hens present. Having learned this, the hunter can attempt to call the hen, hoping she will come to him and bring the group with her, or shut off all calling.

Who knows how many times each spring hunters will sit and call to a gobbler with hens, this going on for hours, the end result being the turkeys going their way, and the hunter heading back toward the pickup. I am guilty of doing this as are you and all turkey hunters. I suppose it's because there have been times when the whole bunch, or a single gobbler, came to our pleading. Only last spring David Jackman and I walked near a gobbling male, but then we could hear hens noisily carrying on all around him. We stuck around for an hour, calling to them, fully aware there was very little hope of the gobbler coming our way. Finally,

away from my calling place, I then made a fast walking circle onto higher ground from where the gobbles had come. Stealing in and out of thick cover, I hadn't covered 100 yards when I spied a hen feeding across a small gap between two dense junipers. Luck was with me. She didn't see me as I backed into the confines of another juniper and cocked the muzzleloader as I brought it up to my shoulder. Just as I had the gun to shoulder, a second hen, then a third, strolled past the gap. The next bird was a big, heavy-bellied longbeard. Distance perhaps 14 or 15 yards. Though the old turkey never knew what hit him, the white cloud which blasted from those junipers scared the living daylights out of those hens. I have taken a great number of turkeys during such on-the-spot, quick-acting, nothing-ventured-nothing-gained episodes. When I look back on them, some were ridiculous, but they were also successful.

The hunter who has maintained eye contact with a group may notice there are two or more gobblers. An attempt can be made to call one from the group. One gobbler will be the dominant bird; he will remain with the hens. The other may also be dominant, but there is always an outside chance he can be tolled away from the group. There is nothing lost in trying.

If the season is set at a late enough date, the hens will be sneaking off from the gobbler after a few hours. In this situation the hunter can try calling the bird to the gun. All of the hens may not leave the male until near noon, but

The tips of these primary flight feathers have been "broomed" severely. This wearing off of these feathers has been caused by the old male bird dragging them on the ground while strutting. Coarse sand, rocks, and coarse soils cause the wear. These feathers are on the wing of a Merriam turkey.

The mouth-call has become the most popular turkey call in America. Its use leaves the hunter's hands free to hold the gun. Cheap in price, the mouth call will make all of the notes made by wild turkeys.

softly, but if you get no responding gobble, make the notes slightly louder so you are assured the bird hears. If the gobbler is lusting for the company of a hen, he will gobble to your calling.

What the hunter most hopes for, and dreams of, is to have a turkey gobble back time after time to even the slightest calling. One gobble instantly followed by another is known in turkey hunting circles as a "double gobble," three is a "triple gobble," etc. Now and then the hunter

David Kelley, left, and the author hold aloft adult gobblers bagged on a rainy morning during a spring hunt. Warm rains have little effect on the daily lives of wild turkeys. These long-bearded birds commenced gobbling at daybreak, in a slow drizzle, no differently than would they have done if the morning was bright and clear.

we got no response. They had drifted off. A short time later, and several hundred yards along the mesa's edge, we located another group of hens and a gobbling turkey. Same old thing. Eventually we lost contact with them, too. We had both taken Gould's gobblers a day or two earlier, so we were not aggressive.

But, as each coin has two sides, suppose the hunter has heard no hens. If contact has been maintained with the gobbler since the bird was on a roost branch, and during this time no hens have been heard, the chances are good that no hens are present. Hens are usually noisy before leaving the trees. However, exceptions are common in all turkey hunting, and the hunter can't be certain that the gobbler has no hens until visual contact has verified this.

If a hunter has made contact with a gobbling turkey an hour or so past sunrise, there is no way of knowing if hens are with the gobbler. By this time of morning many hens have quit making any sounds. The same hens which were noisy at first day could still be with the male but are now ambling along, pecking and feeding and may not make another note of any kind throughout the day. All turkeys are most vocal at dawn, and this is why it pays to hurry toward them then.

There will be numerous times when a gobbling turkey is alone on the roost. After he flies to ground, this bird offers the best chance for the hunter to bag what he came after. On hearing a gobbling bird, and having cut the distance to less than a couple hundred yards, if it seems that he is still in a tree, I advise clucking to him. Make these sounds

comes across a gobbler which can be easily "cranked up," and by doing lots of calling, the hunter can stir the bird into gobbling time after time. Incessant yelping with a raspy shufflin' box is hard to beat if the hunter wants to crank up an old gobbler. Chuck Hartigan and I cranked up a gobbler last spring which must have gobbled 200 times in the short time it took to get the bird up in front of Chuck's autoloader. I only paused for a few seconds now and then to rest, then I'd lean into the calling again. The bird made the hollow rattle with his carryin' on, though we never could see him until he popped into sight at about 11 or 12 yards. The next morning I fired up three jakes, kept them cranked up as they walked across a ¼-mile of open field, and they were still gobbling when I whispered to Chuck and Ed LaForce to "take em." A heavy fog prevented our seeing those birds until they were within long gunshot, but their cranked up gobbling kept us posted as to their route. We could not go to them as they were deep in posted lands. But, in getting them cranked up with continuous yelping on a noisy shuffling box, it was easy to toll them out of there.

The average early morning spring episode doesn't result in the bird doing considerable gobbling, as once the gobbler flies down and joins the hens, he will then stay with them, gobbling now and then to stimulating sounds, or even to a hunter's imitations of hen turkeys. Once in a great while a gobbler will leave his hens and come to the hunter, but ordinarily this does not happen. Later in the morning, the hens slip away, and then the hunter will have a chance to call the bird to the gun.

Numerous gobblers will not have hens near them at daybreak, and these are the birds we all hope to hear gobbling. Very often a gobbler found in such circumstances will gobble each time the hunter calls, perhaps double gobbling, giving the hunter time to sneak to within a couple hundred yards while the bird is in the tree. In heavy timber it is often very simple to walk to within 75 yards of a gobbling turkey. Just be careful not to be seen.

of a gobbling bird. The instant I see these, I then align the gun, firing when the bird's head comes into view. I have no silly qualms about shooting a turkey in full strut. A turkey's head is vulnerable whether the bird has it stuck up on a long neck or on a short neck. I would shoot at a turkey's head if the old bird was standing on it. So long as the bird is in strut, I know he isn't spooky, so the mark is secure. A bird with his head held high, and alert, can jerk that head down, in preparation to flush, quicker than any

David Jackman, complete with camo mask, calls with a Lynch box as he and Antonio Corrales wait, hoping to hear the gobbles of an approaching bird. Note how the hunter has sprinkled pine needles on his outstretched legs, added insurance against being seen by an incoming bird.

(Below) Each year more ladies take up the sport of hunting wild turkeys. Some of the gobblers are almost as big as the girls who hunt them. Sally Jackman let her hustband carry this big 22-pounder back to camp.

I would shoot at a turkey's head if the old bird was standing on it . . .

Having closed to within these short distances, the hunter can then attempt to call the bird into gunshot range. Few veteran hunters will continue to do much calling so long as the gobbler remains in the tree, but will shut off calling in hopes the bird will come to the few calls already made from the calling stand. I prefer to hear lots of gobbling, so I often do considerable calling from where I intend on shooting the bird. This may delay the gobbler's coming to me, either keeping him in the tree, or causing him to dawdle along the way, stopping to strut. But an added advantage to this technique is that the bird keeps me posted to his route with all his gobbling. By the time he is in near range I have the gun well aligned. Again, let me remind the reader that I strive to call from places where the terrain prevents the bird from seeing exactly where my hen calls are coming from until he is within easy shooting range. Quite often the roll of the ground will do this, but it is otherwise accomplished with weeds, rocks, logs, brush, bushes. In many instances I will turn my head, or hide the call box, endeavoring to give the hen yelps a muffled sound, as if the hen is behind cover. Many, many times the first inkling of an approaching gobbler has been in seeing the upper tips of the bird's fanned out tail feathers, so I watch for these in the direction

hunter can stop his trigger pull. True, a gobbler shot in full strut will have a few shot pellets in the upper body, but once I decide to shoot, I intend to end the bird's life as quickly and completely as the gun will permit.

Taking a calling stand which gives the hunter excellent visibility does the same for an approaching gobbler. What this means is that the hunter must not make any movements, perhaps over a long period of time. The hunter using a box call must be extremely cautious, as must anyone using a call which requires hand movements. If you locate and call from an area that an approaching gobbler can scrutinize, you will not be able to make calls once the bird draws near for fear of being seen. This causes old turkey gobblers to tarry, pause, and look for long periods of time, and in particular, to circle the hunter. Anyone who has made extensive notes concerning approaching gobblers, or any wild turkeys responding to calling, knows that these birds are far more apt to come directly to a call that is not visible until they are near and to a call that does not stop. A wild turkey which is talkative does not suddenly quit calling unless it becomes suspicious or danger appears. Your calling has this sameness.

If you have located to call, and after doing so, realize a gobbler is coming to you on a course which will reveal you to the bird at 40 yards, look around for a place which won't allow the bird a long-distance look. If the bird is not yet in view, hustle to it, even if it means crawling on your hands and knees. I've moved umpteen times in the last moments before a gobbler comes into view, seeking a location which would require the bird to walk to within easy shooting distance before it could eyeball me. There have been times when this commotion resulted in making lots of noise in dry leaves, but since turkeys also make these sounds, I don't fret about making noise. Nor do I attempt to hide any noise I make. I simply move at a moderate pace, as a turkey would do. A wild turkey becomes suspicious of anything making sounds, except when the sound is similar to one it has heard often, such as other turkeys walking. If you don't try to hide your movements the chances are much less that you will spook the bird. Have you listened to a drove of turkeys walking and feeding on dry fall leaves? They sound no different than a group of children walking home from school.

Very often the gobbler will answer a hunter's call, fly down, gobble to the call a few times, walk into shooting range, and the hunt is over. There is nothing difficult about this, except the carrying of a heavy body back to camp.

Spring turkey hunting can be mixed right in with a fishing trip, as Steve Preston is doing here. Fish are often biting during the spring months, and what can be more fun than going after a gobbler just after dawn, and then picking up the fishing rod for a try at trout or bass.

The turkey answered, seemed interested, but did not show. What happened? . . .

All of us who have hunted, many, many springtimes have had lots of hunts which did not have such happy endings, and others which did have happy endings, but only after an hours-long hunt, well laced with sessions of calling, sneaking from one location to another, and resorting to all the tricks in the book.

Invariably, these episodes got underway like the successful ones. You located a gobbling turkey and moved nearer, even got the bird to gobble back a few times, but then the whole hunt seemed to come apart. Long periods of waiting were followed by the appearance of nothing but mosquitoes and gnats. The turkey had answered, seemed interested, but just the same, the bird did not show. After so much of this, the gobbles cease, and stark reality whispers in the back of your mind "the bird is gone." What happened?

The bird could have approached the hunter and caught sight of a tiny movement, or a shining face, or the glint of sunlight bouncing from a gun barrel. Maybe he didn't like the location the calls were coming from, became suspicious and vamoosed. The hunter can guard against these in the future. But, for now we are dealing with a gobbler that has seemingly wandered away from the call, after gobbling to it earlier. What now? I would leave the area for 2 or 3 hours, then come back to it and attempt to raise the gobbler again. Stimulating the turkey into gobbling can be done by making sudden loud noises or using hen yelps. I've used both, but usually imitate the hen, often with sudden, loud yelps, noisy and fast, six to 10 in number.

Twice this past season I went back to places I'd heard a gobbler, bagging both birds just before 10:00AM. I was very near the first gobbler just after dawn, when a rifleman cut down on the bird, missing him (and me), and scaring the

With his blind quicked out around the base of a large tree, the hunter now sets up a plastic hen decoy on an abandoned road on private land. The use of decoys can be hazardous if hunters are unaware of their presence. All of us must remember that there are hunters who will shoot at anything resembling a turkey, hen or otherwise.

This portable blind rolls compactly, has its own carrying strap, and is made and sold by M.L. Lynch Co. It can be set up in just a moment or two, making it an ideal hiding place for hunters who can't sit perfectly still.

Decoy in place, the hunter can now make hen calls from the blind. Any approaching gobbler will have its attention riveted to the decoy. Often photographers cut holes in these type blinds, and take photos through the openings.

gobbler into full flight. I watched the bird's path, noted the rifleman going after it, but made a note to go see about the gobbler later in the morning, provided I hadn't made a kill. On returning to that area, I made a fast series of yelps, was answered immediately, shooting the gobbler in full strut not 15 minutes later. I repeated the performance in about the same amount of time 3 weeks later, in New Mexico's San Francisco Range. I'd gone back later in the morning to where I'd heard a bird gobble at sunup. I'd assumed this bird had been with hens at first daylight, as it never gobbled after going to ground.

So, unless I want to remain and search for a gobbler which has quit gobbling, I leave the area. If I decide to stay, I seldom follow the bird but make a long circling walk in hopes of intercepting him in another area. Very often I will change calls when I try to raise the bird from this new location. I usually carry a shuffling box, a wingbone, and a few mouthcalls with me. I also change the rhythm of the notes—anything which will make this ''hen'' sound different from my last calling.

There have been times when I've circled, hoping to get in front of a gobbler traveling with hens, and then have taken up a location where I can see and hear, waiting to see what develops. Scads of times I have been leaning against a tree when a hen would yelp nearby, or the male would gobble. After I've heard the hen, I stop my calling. Hens are tough competition, and in this case I'd be better off stalking the bunch, or getting near enough to scatter them.

If I scatter them, I can watch where the gobbler goes, follow him, and then my chances to call him are excellent. I don't wait long to begin this calling, usually making my first calls within 10 minutes after separating the birds. My first yelps will be soft, only two or three in number with just enough time lag between notes to give them a ''where-are-you?'' sound. If there is no answering gobble, I remain alert to the gobbler that may come to me without gobbling; the birds will do this sometimes. I won't locate out on a large flat and will invariably seek out the highest ground in the area, though I will not do this if it means there is any possibility that one of the hens could then be located between me and the male bird.

Should I hear the bird gobble before I begin calling, I will answer him very quickly. But if the bird does not gobble back to me, I then get edgy as to what the bird will do. The bird's gobble is his way of letting the hens know where he is located after the scare, and since they are in the habit of grouping at his location, the male expects them to come to his call. This is why I prefer to call soon after locating, in hopes that he will come to my calling before he has time to gobble.

Once the gobbler takes up a calling stand, there is always the chance he will wait for the hens to come to him, refusing to go to them. This happens umpteen thousand times each spring, particularly if the bird is 4 or 5 years of age. These older gobblers will stake out a small gobbling and strutting territory, often on a narrow ridge, out in the flat of a pasture clearing, or in open woods, and go there each morning after leaving the roost tree. The birds call and strut there, the hens going to them. I located such an old bird in Mississippi one morning simply through noticing all the strut marks a bird had made over a period of time since the last rain. I never did see the gobbler. I told Tom Preston about my find that evening and encouraged him to go there the next

every morning, and one local complained that the bird's fired up gobbling woke him up most mornings. He claimed this same old turkey had been showing up on this ridge over the past few years, and he had also caught glimpses of the bird at other times of the year. The turkey was always alone. A true hermit gobbler. I was lucky to bag the old devil the first time we met, and probably would not have done so had he not strayed far enough from the strutting ground to allow me to belly-crawl to within shooting distance. When he came stalking back, me and ole Sue Betsy were there to greet him with a load of No. 5 chilled shot.

Long drawn-out sessions involving a gobbling turkey and the hunter who is trying to coax the old bird into shooting range are often heard told or we read about them in hunting magazines. All turkey hunters place the ability to call a gobbler above all other endeavors in life, from making a marriage work, to being top dog in the local social register. To be able to tell a long tale about one's prowess at calling old gobblers to the gun is far more important than how much money is in the bank. So long as we have turkey

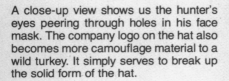

A close-up view shows us the hunter's eyes peering through holes in his face mask. The company logo on the hat also becomes more camouflage material to a wild turkey. It simply serves to break up the solid form of the hat.

day, as I was certain a boss gobbler was staking out that flat each morning. As sure as first day turns into full daylight, the gobbler showed up the next morning, and Tom killed the biggest Mississippi gobbler I have seen to this day. It was not easy because Tom could not wait out on that open field but had to hide in cover at the field's edge, well beyond shotgun range. Nor would the bird march over to Tom's calling, at least not near enough. Biding his time, though, Tom watched the old turkey. After noticing that the bird's movements led it near a clump of wild blackberries from time to time, Tom was able to slip into those bushes and shoot the gobbler.

I made contact with a gobbler on a mountain ridge which would not come to me but instead marched back and forth along the spine of the ridge, gobbling like crazy. I immediately sensed that the bird probably had a habit of going there daily, strutting and gobbling, and that the hens thereabouts went to him on his "strutting grounds." Later, I learned that this was true. The old bird could be heard there

hunting, we will have to endure this stuff. But, if this is given some thought, these episodes would probably have never taken place if the hunter had been doing things right from the first. Those of us responsible for some of these stories have but to reflect back on the tales surrounding those gobblers which took so long to call, and if we do a little soul searching, then be truthful with ourselves, the whole mess would have been avoided had we not made a big boo-boo.

I've been lucky, as I have had very few turkeys which hung back, lingering in the shadows beyond gunshot. With some I've had to make 200 calls to convince them to come to me. Or, to make a few calls, and wait endless hours, knowing the gobbler was there, hidden from view, reluctant to walk my way. But, when I study the actions leading up to these drawn-out sessions, in all but a few instances, I made a boner which brought the longer hunt about.

The bulk of the time my mistake has been in locating badly when I first called the birds toward me. Before the

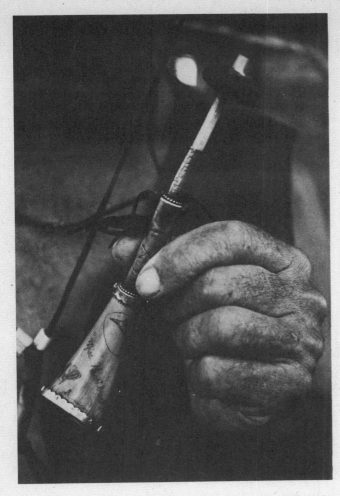

The wingbone call is excellent for making the yelps and clucks of the hen turkey during the spring mating season. Such handmade calls are made from the wing bones of small turkeys bagged by a hunter. This is the author's much used and revered "Miss Heartbreak."

know any or all the reasons.

There isn't much sense in continuing to call to a turkey that has been gobbling back for a ½-hour. It's best to quit the calling and move out of eyesight of the area. Just by chance, should the gobbler go to the area searching for the hen that was calling, there is no chance it will be spooked by the hunter and run off for good.

Two years ago in April, I bellied out on a dirt bank on which an oil-well tank battery was located. My pickup was parked 20 yards behind me. Eyeing an adult gobbler some 200 yards downslope, I called at him with a wingbone call. He gobbled, then began walking to the right, seemingly not too pumped up about my charms. I laid there, calling several times, and though he gobbled a few times, he walked from my view off into brush, apparently leaving the area.

Crawling back, I then took off on a dead run, planning on getting around in front of the bird. Sundown was less than an hour away, so I knew he was heading for woods where he would find a big tree to spend the night. It was hot and humid, so when I got over to where I thought he would be, I was soaked with sweat. I made a quick series of calls, excited like. The bird gobbled back. Where from? He was standing up on the dirt bank not 20 yards from the pickup. We had just traded places. Worried about sundown, I hadn't waited. This story goes to show you that it's senseless to make a call and jump up and leave there, without waiting to see if the calling is productive. Anytime a gobbler gobbles back, there is always a chance the bird will come to where the call was made.

Whenever I have heard a bird gobble incessantly, but not come to me, I then back away, make a circle, and try to make visual contact, and if at all possible, make a stalk. Having another hunter along is a tremendous asset, because one hunter can keep the bird gobbling, which makes pinpointing and stalking the bird easy. I have found that gobblers are far less wary when answering distant calling, enabling a stealthy hunter to slip into gunshot if a minimal amount of cover is present.

My main concern in keeping a turkey gobbling over any length of time is that other hunters will hear the bird. The longer the gobbling goes on, the greater the chances of someone else taking advantage of this. So, if the bird hangs up, and does not come toward the call, then it is best to quit calling.

I became suspicious that I was going to be like the bride left waiting at the altar . . .

Far the worst gobbler to deal with is what many of us know as "walking gobblers," or "traveling gobblers." If you hear a hunter remark, "Boy, I couldn't do anything with that old bird this morning, he was traveling on me," chances are the bird was gobbling at every call the person

birds came into range, they became wary for two reasons. One, I was making calls from open terrain in locations where the responding gobblers realized they should be able to see the hen that was calling. Number two, I had located in a position that found me under eye-to-eye scrutiny by the turkeys so I couldn't continue calling. The birds became suspicious, and though in all but a few cases, I did in time kill the birds, it was only after difficult relocating and calling maneuvers. Invariably, my longest most time-consuming kills while calling were from having taken a calling stand where there was not enough cover to screen me well. Had I taken care to select slightly heavier cover, chances are the bird would have walked within range in searching for the calling turkey, me.

You will hear of an endless variety of reasons why a gobbler will answer the hunter's call, but refuse to go to him. The hunter calls too much. He does not call enough. The hunter should have clucked instead of yelped. He made a move which the bird spied. Seldom will a person ever

Can you tell at a glance the sex of these two turkeys? It's easy. No other wild turkey but a hen has a "hook" or "dogleg" in its beard. The bird on the right is a hen, the other a gobbler. Also, sex can often be told by the overall size and, invariably, by the size of the head, and its color. Notice the white pate on the crown of the bird on the left, a distinct characteristic of a male bird.

made, but kept walking. Walking and gobbling, walking and gobbling—one of these gobblers can cover lots of distance, draw numerous hunters to an area and create no end of turkey calling efforts.

I have seen a good many of these strolling gobble-machines, some had hens with them, some didn't. There is no way of knowing whether the next one I hear will have hens for company or not. And, there is no way of knowing this unless the hunter makes visual contact. Of course, if hens are present, it is easily understood why the gobbler will not leave them to come to a call.

But, when it is determined the bird is alone, the whole

thing becomes slightly maddening. I have observed this type of gobbler walking past hens without slowing down, as though they weren't even there. Though he will gobble at hen yelps, he seemingly has no urge to mate. Once in a while, he'll come to gobbles made by another male, but a so-called ''traveling gobbler'' will seldom pay any heed to a male's gobbling either. I have had some luck when circling them, waiting in the bird's hoped-for path. The bird's gobbling often makes this easier, and though the hunter always has an urge to call to a gobbling turkey, it is best to cease all calling and try to do the bird in through stalking, ambushing, or stillhunting.

Last but not least, by far, is the bird that remains in the general locale, gobbles now and then at the hunter's calling, not always, and though seemingly interested in the hen, refuses to come to where the hunter waits. And, there is a world's plenty of this kind of turkey gobbler.

Such a turkey can be encountered at any time of the day throughout any and all springtime turkey range. I have found them among all five strains of bearded and spurred turkeys, so don't think you have a corner on the market just because your woods are full of these old reprobates. Thank God for them because these are the turkeys that bring us back into the woods each spring.

The last one of these old cusses I dealt with was in New Mexico, in the Gila Forest. While driving a little used forest road, I raised the gobbler when I made a stop. I shut off the engine, got out, yelped a loud few licks on the wingbone call, and this turkey gobbles. Leaving the truck there, I chased off in the woods toward him, stopping a couple times as I got nearer, calling, and getting answering gobbles, until I figured he was about 150 yards distant. The scattered juniper and oak was not too thick so I realized I better not press my luck and perhaps get too close. I might

(Right) Spur development varies throughout the subspecies of wild turkeys, with the Osceola turkey having the best, while the Merriam has the least. This spur is on the leg of an adult Merriam turkey gobbler bagged in Arizona. The blunt rounded tip is typical of the average Merriam spur found on 2-year-old gobblers.

Like the Merriam wild turkey found in the western United States, the Gould's turkey found in the Sierra Madre mountains of old Mexico does not have as good a spur growth as the Osceola. The bird being examined has good spurs for a Gould's. The author has killed Gould's gobblers which had no spurs, nor any sign of them.

be seen by the bird and then there wouldn't be any hunt at all.

I'd made but two or three series of calls when I became suspicious that I was going to be like the bride who was left waiting at the altar. More gobble calls and 15 minutes later, I knew the bird was not budging from a knoll in front of me. Slipping away from my calling stand, I made a circle which appeared to give me the best route up the backside of his hill, but I never did see the old critter. Nor could I crank him up afterward. I will never know if I was seen, or if the turkey walked off. Maybe he didn't walk off alone; there could have been hens with him. Or another gobbler, or both. Who knows?

I can remember back when I first began hunting turkeys, I would spend hours fooling with one of these turkeys. Calling, waiting, watching, calling, all the while the bird would keep up my hopes with a gobble from time to time. None would react the same. A bird one day would stand gobbling in place, while another the next day might walk back and forth from one end of a ridge to the other, gobbling back and forth. Others would just start walking away gobbling, with me following, almost running. Some I'd see, some I wouldn't. A few I killed. A whole bunch I didn't.

I learned enough about this kind of gobbler to be able to recognize them. Today, if a gobbler does not come to my calling, or does not head my way inside of 20 to 30 minutes, then I go to him. Many of these turkeys have fallen to my gun because I have been able to slip within easy killing distance. Aside from this, I have devised other on-the-spot tricks to bring about their demise. Anyone could do the same. It is simply a matter of studying the situation, deciding on a course of action, and then following it through.

If the turkey is traveling on a course that the hunter feels

Surrounded by hens, two gobblers strut near a heavy woods. Gobblers often fight during the spring mating season, these brawls sometimes bringing blood. Contrary to what a famed ornithologist said, none of these combats end in death. Successful combatants maintain their place in the flock's special order, and make an effort to surround themselves with a large harem of hens. (Photo courtesy David Jackman.)

he can intercept, this can be done. There will be gobblers that walk fast, not leaving a hunter enough time to circle around them. They are often heard gobbling as they leave the hunter's hearing range. Just let them go. Such a bird may return hours later, sometimes on nearly the same path. You may hear the bird gobbling much later in the day.

I've circled turkeys, and then called them to me, though this can be risky with a bird who has ignored your calling thus far. It is possible to circle the bird, station yourself in its path and make a call. However, the gobbler may veer off, going by you 100 yards away, or he may turn back on his course. If I try to circle a bird, and think I am within gunshot of its path, I rarely call. I would prefer to take my chances without the call, simply because the bird did not come when I had called earlier. True, he may have gobbled back at me 100 times, but he was reluctant to come to the calling.

All of us who hunt spring gobblers on mountainous terrain, hills, knobs, ridges, whatever you want to call them, have run across gobblers who have marched back and forth along a wooded ridge or perhaps across a glade dotted with trees, the ground littered with dry leaves. The watchful hunter may discover a hole in the bird's defenses, allowing a sneak into gun range. Again, this is risky because there is always the chance the bird will detect the hunter. But this is the chance a person must take unless he wants to sit all spring and count gobbles.

Now, I have moved off from a gobbling turkey who would not come into gunshot, only to have the bird walk to my old calling stand when I made calls from my new location. If you have a bird pull this stunt, you can do what I did one day in Arkansas. I moved to a new stand, made a call, the old turkey gobbled back, and then I ran back toward my previous calling stand and was still out of breath when I spied the gobbler coming. This trick won't work on flat terrain unless there is a lot of intervening cover. I was in the ridges and coves on a mountainside. I have killed gobblers simply by continuing to call—loud, noisy, and plenty of it—while at the same time walking straight toward them. I've done this even when there was not a solid wall of cover, hoping that if the bird detected any movement, he might think it was the hen he could hear walking his way. I killed the last two gobblers I tried this trick with— both were gobbling considerably, both were all alone and had been for over an hour, and neither would budge an inch in coming to my enticements. I shot each at less than 25 yards. Risky? I guess you could say that. I suppose the one I tried it on before those two is probably still running.

I have taken this kind of turkey when moving to a location on higher ground. After waiting until the bird had seemingly quit gobbling, I made a couple of clucks. That Mississippi gobbler never did answer with a gobble. I am certain it was him because the bird I shot came from where I'd heard the earlier gobbles, and was strutting up to me less than 10 minutes after calling.

By the same token, I have called reluctant gobblers with what I term as too much calling. The thickest beard in my collection came from a gobbler who would not come to my calls, though I could not make a note that he did not gobble back to at least once. That old monarch finally began coming my way when I began calling without letup. During the calling, I would detect a gobble or two, but much of the time I couldn't hear the bird for my own calling. I must have called 400 or 500 times while the bird made his way, inch by inch, to a point where I could shoot. I have taken others with this incessant calling, at least two of them during the fall season.

Shutmouth gobblers come to a call like so much smoke. One minute they aren't there, the next minute . . .

How many times have all of us heard, "I have some good news, and I have some bad news." This applies to turkey hunting, in particular to the hunting of springtime gobblers. The good news is when they gobble. The bad news is when they don't.

How many mornings have you been in the woods just as first day was washing the eastern heavens? The damp pungent smell of oak leaves covers you, the still morning air lays like an invisible blanket across the ridge where you wait, and below, in a hollow, a light fog plays peek-a-boo with the gnarled twisted boughs of aging oaks.

The clear lovesome whistling of a redbird rings from a towering pine. A gorgeous morning. Surely they'll gobble this morning. Your eyes search far off places. You scarcely dare breathe, for fear you'll not hear a distant gobble. Before you will give up so easy, you hurry to another ridge, another point, or that old favorite, where you always hear

Keeping ice in the pop cooler is no problem when hunting where snow is present, as it often is in much Merriam range during spring hunts. Light snow showers are common while hunting, though raging blizzards have forced the author down from higher elevations on occasion.

'em gobble. ZERO! They aren't gobbling today. They are "shutmouth." There is no way of predicting what mornings the gobblers will be silent. If there was, it would save an army of hunters the trouble of getting out of bed. When the birds don't gobble, very few hunters will hunt them.

Why? Simple. The turkey's gobble is a beacon to the average springtime turkey hunter, and when the beacon is not working, the hunter does not know where the gobbler is located.

Along with this, there are other things running through the hunter's mind, such as "maybe somebody else has shot the bird," or "the birds have moved someplace else." These undermine the morale, getting progressively worse the more the hunter thinks about them, so he gives up before even giving it a try.

I learned a lot about hunting shutmouth turkeys when making trips far from home. When the birds did not gobble, I decided I could either wait until the next day, in hopes they would gobble, or hunt them anyway. Very seldom have I ever had the opportunity to hunt wild turkeys within 75 miles of home, so regardless of where I have been hunting, I have hunted every morning whether the birds gobbled or not. Coffee shops and sideroad stores have never been handy in the country I hunt, so I couldn't very well join other turkey hunters over morning coffee, cussing the day's bad luck. Nor would I want to, as those things can be done when a person cannot hunt.

On mornings when the gobblers are not sounding off, the next best thing to do is to go into areas where it is thought the birds are, or have been when the conditions were nearly identical, and listen for any hens which might be talking. And, though this hen talk ordinarily stimulates the male to gobbling, I have heard hens on many mornings when the gobblers did not gobble. If hens are heard, the hunter should move in as near to them as possible without being seen, and then call to them with the same notes and vocabulary they are using. If the hens can be called to the hunter, any gobbler with them will tag along. Perhaps the hunter can get to a position where the hens are in sight, and be able to tell if a gobbler is there.

Many gobblers will gobble but a time or two, usually while on the roost branch, and then fly down, not gobbling as the hens collect around him. The hunter who gets into such an area a moment or two afterwards will not hear anything and will think the birds are all shutmouth. And in reality by the time he has arrived, this is truly the case.

One April morning I was fast-walking some old logging trails far back from the main road, when I thought I heard a distant sound which was maybe a gobble. I knew that unless the bird kept gobbling from time to time I would never know if it was a bird's gobble or not. Having hunted the area, I was fortunate in knowing that there was a favored hill toward where I thought the sound had come. By the time I got there, I had heard no other gobble, nor did I get a gobble in answer to my hen yelps.

I did have a hen cluck back to me over a period of 10 minutes, but she quit. I thought she was coming to me at

Coffee in hand, these hunters stand listening along a country road, hoping to hear a gobbler cutting loose. In most states it is against the law to hunt from a public road, which means a person cannot actually hunt on the road, and/or its right-of-way. Shooting is forbidden. But, the road can be used as a path, and the hunter can walk it, so long as he does not hunt, shoot, or carry a loaded gun on it. Most states also prohibit shooting across a public highway. Read the game laws of any state you intend to hunt.

one time. A few minutes later I was happily surprised to see a gobbler approaching, though I never had any indication there was a gobbler thereabouts. My mind's eye can picture the big Merriam longbeard which appeared just as suddenly one afternoon in the Rockies, in full strut, but never a gobble had he made that day. Or, if so, I'd not heard him. Hunting shutmouth gobblers is that way, and though a hunter can hunt them day after day, in prime turkey country, the end result may not be even a glimpse of wild turkey. Turkeys which do not gobble are hard on morale.

Beginning at dawn, I move from place to place, trying to hunt the places I think that particular subspecies will inhabit, taking the time of day into consideration. Hen turkeys go to feed not long after flydown, so I want to hunt much of the morning in areas where the hens will be searching for food. If I can find them, the gobblers will probably be with them. During the midday hours, the hens should be nesting, leaving the gobblers to while away these hours loafing, standing in the shade, preening, and dusting. Later in the afternoon the hens will again feed, and toward sundown, all of them will head for roosting sites. By constantly keeping in mind what a turkey is most apt to be doing at different times of the day, I can pace myself to hunt these areas. Along with this I must never lose sight of which strain of wild turkey I am hunting, and having studied the bird before the hunt, will have an idea of what terrain the bird seeks at various hours.

Calling techniques can vary according to the hunter's whims. I will call on each calling stand considerably as the day begins, but cut back as the morning wanes. During the afternoon hours I call very little simply because this is a quiet period for all wild turkeys. By late afternoon I will all but cease calling, making only inquisitive clucks, these few in number and well spaced. I will also move from one calling location to another. Turkeys cover lots of ground during the late afternoon.

Shutmouth gobblers which come to a call will do so like so much black smoke. One minute they aren't there, the next minute there they stand. When I am hunting shutmouth gobblers I choose calling locations which give a greater field of visibility than when I am calling to a gobbling bird. This is because I hope to see the bird a ways from me, so I can take precautions to sit unmoving, and be ready with the gun. Anyone who does considerable calling, spring or fall, will have birds show up unannounced. And, if the hunter has been engaged in this standoff over a period of several days, remaining alert is all but impossible. A turkey, suddenly standing at close range, quickly makes up for all the silence, but far more quickly if the hunter can take advantage of the opportunity.

There have been times when I have been hunting shutmouth gobblers, not having heard a gobble for days, only to suddenly have a bird gobble back and continue gobbling as it comes to the call. This cranked up bird is what we all hope for on such days. I was walking up a pine-flanked hill one hot afternoon, hadn't heard a gobble for 2 days, but stopped to make a call. A big bunch of slash pines had been piled on top the little knoll, and it happened that I stopped just as I walked up to them.

I called, and a gobbler cut loose on the other side of the brushpile. I fell forward, and stretched out belly down, gun up on my elbows. I slid off the safe just as a red-headed turkey gobbler came around the stack of dead limbs. Obviously the old bird was coming up the hill from the opposite direction, but probably I would never have known the bird was there if I hadn't stopped to call. If I had walked on a few steps, the gobbler would have seen me, and skedaddled, and me never being the wiser. There is luck in all turkey hunting.

Just because he made the first call, gives him no right to the turkey . . .

Too often, in this day and age, you will hear what seems to be another hunter, who is calling to the bird you had considered your turkey. First, you should ask yourself if you are dead certain that the calls are not those of other turkeys. I've known of veteran turkey hunters backing away from a situation when it seemed another hunter was pulling a bird away from the gun, only to make visual contact and learn that the "other hunter" was a well-feathered wild turkey hen. A turkey call can be made to sound exactly like a wild turkey, and a wild turkey can also sound exactly like a turkey call. Time after time I have heard hens who where perfect imitators of box calls. To me, there is no call which sounds so like a wild turkey as does a shuffling box if the user is well versed in its use and in copying the various notes of wild turkeys. But, let us assume you are positive the calling is being done by another hunter—what now?

This conflict should not happen on private lands, but often does due to a lack of communication between all parties hunting within the confines. Much of the time, a group of hunters will decide who hunts where so each person will more or less stick to an area, and not hunt another's turkeys. This not only saves hard feelings but gives all an equal opportunity. Even then, there will be times when a bird will gobble from an area which both hunters feel is within their territory, and both will hear the other calling. I have been involved in these episodes—a buddy calling to a gobbler, and me not hearing him, nor him hearing me. I've known heated arguments to arise when a gobbler has left one hunter's area because it was called over into the other guy's area and killed by him. The best thing to do when hunting private lands is to try to learn where all hunters are going to hunt and to abide by whatever ground rules are established for the hunt. If it's "everybody for himself," then anything can happen and usually does. I hunt on a large spread where this is the case, and over the past couple decades there have probably been a thousand turkeys which owed their lives to one of us messing up somebody else's opportunity. But, I've never known of one single heated word in all that time. We are longtime buddies, so we will look for another turkey. A bird is not that hard to come by.

But, "everybody for himself" can be dangerous. The only reason none of us has been shot by another is that we are veteran turkey hunters. We only shoot when we know the mark is a turkey. No rifles are allowed, so there is no chance of a projectile traveling a long distance and striking someone.

Oddly, the few deaths with which I am most familiar, those having taken place near my home woods, have been on private lands, at close range, and two out of the three involved shotguns. All involved the use of turkey calls, and all incidents involved inexperienced hunters who were "new" to turkey hunting. None of the hunters could positively identify the mark at which they were shooting as that of a turkey, but all admitted shooting at slight movements from where turkey sounds had come. None of this would have happened had these people decided prior to the hunt where, when, and how everyone intended to hunt. Three hunters are dead because of a lack of communication and lack of experience.

Most of us hunt public lands, not because we want to, but because so few land owners will allow hunting. A wild turkey on public land belongs to us all. There are large areas in these United States where a gobbler can cut loose with gobble after gobble and will never be heard by a hunter. This happens all across the country, on any given

Tom Preston waits out a springtime shower under the overhang of an old abandoned house. The hour immediately after a morning rain is often an excellent time to hunt turkey gobblers because many of them will resume gobbling at this time.

morning of the week in various localities. But, too often just the opposite is true. A bird gobbles, and anywhere from one to 15 hunters come alert, tense to the sound, each striving to get a fix on the gobbler's location. Realizing there are others listening, many of these folks will hit the woods running, almost before the sound of the gobble has faded. Whose turkey is it?

Any one of them could make a call without the others hearing it, so just because a person thinks he has made the first call, gives him no right to think he has sole rights to the turkey. A wild turkey on public land belongs to us all.

Ethics often play an important part in settling such disputes because there are hunters who will back away, once they hear another hunter "working" the bird, leaving the gobbler to the other hunter. On the other hand, there are hunters who consider the matter ethically resolved by simply looking at it as a competition, and "may the best man win."

I hear grumbles every year about the unsportsmanlike conduct of hunters sneaking between another hunter and his gobbler, or hunters calling to birds which are already answering another's calls, or even of those who will walk directly toward a gobbling bird, spooking it away, rather than let another hunter get a shot.

So long as we all hunt wild turkeys, some of which will be on public lands, these things will continue. Perhaps we should look on turkey hunting as we do other little things in life. "All is fair in love and war, and turkey huntin'."

Hunting Fall and Winter Gobblers

FALL IS the traditional time of year for hunting. The very mention of autumn, September, and the fall season causes millions of Americans—men and women and kids—to think of going hunting. Doves, quail, grouse, prairie chickens, elk, snipe, the list of game birds and animals which become marks for the hunter's gun goes on and on. Summer was for fishing. Fall and winter are for hunting.

For thousands of hunters, fall is turkey season. It's a time to head for the woods and bag a wild turkey for Thanksgiving dinner. Among those of us who year after year have been shooting a wild bird for Thanksgiving, the hunting has become as much a part of this day as is the bird itself. We plan on having a wild gobbler for the table on the traditional day of thanks. To fail in this endeavor would be the deepest of insults and personal humiliation. It would be a severe case of "losing face."

Since killing my first fall turkey many, many years ago, I have brought home birds for the family table every year since. Most years, I have brought home several by late November, as I hunt additional states to my home state of Oklahoma. I don't want anyone to think I am bragging when I say this, as there are many American hunters who do likewise each fall. I say this to emphasize my love for turkey hunting during the fall and winter months. I'm fortunate to be a person who has no favorite time of year to hunt wild turkeys. I favor any time the season is open. Springtime hunting is one kind of turkey sport, the other is fall and winter hunting. The two are as different as night and day.

Throughout the months of late February, March, April and May, the springtime turkey hunter prowls the woods, hoping to hear a bird gobbling. Gobbling is the key to the sport's popularity. Without it, there wouldn't be a handful of turkey hunters in turkey country. The same hunter is nowhere to be seen in November. The old gobblers he prefers to hunt are there, but they are now silent. The old birds are no longer whooping it up, yelling out, "Here I am, come and get me."

In addition to these adult males, younger turkeys are also killed during the fall hunts. Assuredly, the young birds are the easiest to bag of all wild turkeys, though the droves can be extremely difficult to locate, moreso for the hunter traveling into strange new country. The droves of young turkeys, hatched from the egg the previous spring, and therefore some 6 months of age, will be with the mother hen. At times, there will be added barren hens tagging along with these family broods. As the fall season progresses, such small bunches will join together, forming larger droves of 15, 20, 30 or 40 turkeys. Ordinarily, the older adult males will be palling around together in groups of two to 10, perhaps even more. Or, these older gobblers will be seen wandering about as singles all by themselves. By late fall, November and December, the hunter could bump into a drove made up of any combination of sexes, ages or numbers of turkeys in small bunches. But by mid-winter these small groups will ordinarily be made up of birds of a like sex. Age can vary.

Let me give as an example the birds I found on a short fall jaunt 3 years ago. I encountered three young turkeys (all hens), a band of six gobblers (mixed ages, both short

(Above) A wild turkey hen and two nearly grown youngsters feed in a clearing, but are still close to cover. (Photo courtesy of Greg Butts)

(Below) Shooting old turkey gobblers during the fall and winter seasons is far more difficult than the hunting of these same birds during the spring. The mating call of a hen no longer interests the older gobbler, nor does he have any curiosity. If you want to hunt the toughest wild game in the country, try hunting long-bearded turkeys during the end-of-the-year months.

Few fall-killed wild turkeys are as small as this one. Though this bird will be excellent when fried, it will only weigh between 4 and 6 pounds.

bearded and long bearded birds), two young gobblers, a single adult gobbler, a group made up of one young gobbler and three hens, a single adult, and two gobblers 1½ years in age. These were all Eastern wild turkeys and were found in country that had been hunted moderately.

The following season, again in October, I encountered a large drove of perhaps 40 to 50 birds, and another of four young turkeys (two hens and two gobblers). In the same area the next year I found a small drove of 10 young birds and a drove of six or seven and one adult gobbler. This past fall I came upon a drove of seven young turkeys, a single adult hen and a single jake gobbler. (Feeding and water conditions were varied over this period of 4 years, which is why the number of birds varied so greatly.)

From these hunts I bagged seven young turkeys, one adult hen, and three adult gobblers. In breaking down these hunts further, I can say that I bagged these birds by the following techniques.

Ambush	1 adult gobbler
	3 young turkeys
Stillhunt	1 adult gobbler
	2 young turkeys
Call	1 adult gobbler
	1 adult hen
	2 young turkeys

I mention these examples to point out the mixed bag possibilities during fall and winter hunts for wild turkeys, and the numerous hunting methods that can be utilized by the hunter in taking fall and winter turkeys. Numerous times I passed up shots at young turkeys in hopes of getting a chance at an older male.

I always choose an area with far fewer birds if hunters are all but non-existent . . .

In planning a fall or winter hunt, the first matter of concern is to take a hard look at the options—where to hunt and when. This is made easier for those hunters who belong to the National Wild Turkey Federation (NWTF). Each year the organization magazine *Turkey Call* runs a report by Bob Gooch giving a state-by-state rundown of license costs, season dates, prospects, etc. Additionally, the report points out major state hunting regulation changes which may affect the turkey hunter.

The hunter should choose several states which sound appealing, and then write each, asking for a complete set of regulations governing fall turkey hunting. If the hunter is not a resident of the state, ask for regulations applying to non-resident hunters. On receiving the material from the chosen states, the hunter can then narrow down the choice after studying bag limits, weapons allowed, daily hunting hours, etc. I prefer to hunt areas with multiple bag limits of two or three turkeys. Nor do I choose a place to hunt where I must cease hunting at 4 o'clock in the afternoon. I want to hunt all day.

What birds are legal? Is it an "any turkey" season, or can "gobblers only" be killed? What about the weather? Are there public or private lands where I can hunt? It would be silly to travel several hundred miles without considering these queries, plus umpteen others which will surface. And yet I've known folks who have gone on a hunt without asking these questions and then could not understand the adversities which arose. Each year I have hunters call me searching for a place to hunt which is not overrun with people. My home state of Oklahoma does not have many public areas with good turkey hunting, so when the season opens, those areas sporting fair turkey populations are crowded with hopeful gunners. Both Oklahoma and Texas have a great many wild turkeys, but the majority are on private lands. Obtaining permission to hunt on private property is difficult at best, and impossible much of the time. Locating a good place to hunt has always been the number one priority for me when I am planning a fall hunt away

sought for a state's various counties. Studying the breakdown of reported kills, a hunter can decide upon areas which warrant further investigation. This is when I study a map showing a state's county boundaries. I will note which counties have the largest kills, the size of these counties when compared to others, if there are public hunt areas, national forests, or other areas open to hunters. Seldom will I plan on hunting the county with the greatest number of kills. Why won't I hunt a place which appears to be the obvious best choice? The answer is simple. Publicity. Once an area is listed as the top county in numbers of birds taken, hunters will gravitate to it like bees to a clover field.

Added pressure may even result in a larger kill the following year. True, the area may be the best insofar as turkey numbers are concerned, but probably fringe counties will have good turkey hunting, and far less hunters. As I prefer turkey populations which exceed hunter numbers, I will always choose an area with far fewer birds, if the hunters are all but non-existent.

Kill reports are also subject to scrutiny. The hunters in one area may consider it such an honor to kill a wild turkey that they are proud to take it to a check station. Checking the bird is proof of their hunting ability. Five hundred miles from there the hunters have been exposed to turkey hunting for a longer period of time, and while just as proud of birds taken, see no use in taking a bird by a check station. Many will have the attitude, "I checked the birds for years, and

Pennsylvania hunter Frank Piper examines the primaries of a young turkey. Fall turkey hunting is by far most popular as in the Keystone state, where opening day brings thousands of hunters into the woods. Parking lots along woods roads are filled with vehicles, and shots ring out all day as the camouflaged "army" searches for Eastern wild turkeys.

from my usual stomping grounds in western Oklahoma.

Game departments often give glowing reports of populations which can be found on department managed areas. This may be true, only *if the hunter can be on the area at the season's opening and provided he also knows where the game is located.* By late that afternoon, extremely hard opening morning pressure could result in a large kill, and assuredly this can mean the droves will be widely scattered, resulting in anything but a quality hunt.

One indicator which can oftentimes be obtained through state game divisions is turkey kill statistics. These can be

nothing came of it, so why fool with it any longer."

I study kill reports, take into consideration the number of years that turkeys have been hunted thereabouts, and ordinarily add 100 percent to the kill figures. This will give me a rough idea of how many birds may have been taken in that county. I will then study the areas open to hunting in surrounding counties, and if possible, look for areas which are 2 or more miles from roads. If these are numerous, I then catalog the area as a possibility. From there I go to bag limits. I seldom will travel far to hunt an area with a one turkey limit. I have hunted hard all my life, so

Wintertime turkey hunting can be a cold business, as these hunkered-up hunters will attest. Morale is extremely difficult to maintain when the temperature is in the lower 40s, or below, especially if the hunter is attempting to call a bird, and must sit completely motionless for extended periods of time. Each second drags by and, when the hunter's feet and hands begin to numb, his mind keeps saying, "Let's get out of here, there probably isn't a turkey inside of a mile of here."

Sudden snow squalls are possible in many areas of the U.S. and Mexico during both spring and winter turkey hunts. These can be hazardous to the hunter who doesn't know terrain features, and who is not carrying a compass. Monty Montgomery, well-known writer for the *Boston Globe*, was caught in this snow shower on a ridge in Vermont's Green Mountains with the author, while hunting that state's late October fall season.

when I pick up the gun, and head into the woods, I intend on walking out with game in hand. Turkeys are no different. I intend on taking a bird the first day.

If the area is "one turkey," what then? Is the area open to "either sex," or "any turkey?" Or is it "gobblers only?" If the area is heavily wooded, I prefer "any turkey" bag limits. Why? Wild turkeys are difficult to identify in terms of sex, particularly young turkeys, and especially in the dim light often found in wooded forests. Combine this with the poor light found at dawn, and an early fall when the leaves are yet on the trees, and you have conditions that are extremely bad for identifying a young hen from a young gobbler. The average hunter has enough trouble in telling them apart when the birds are dead, lying at his feet.

There are numerous hunters who are heard to say, "I don't kill any hens. I don't think anyone should kill a hen turkey." Such statements only tell me that the hunters know nothing of population turnovers due to natural mortality. Game department turkey biologists have made intense studies of turkey flocks within their jurisdiction. When these folks say it's okay to kill hens, then it is okay. The hens are apt to be a part of the year's natural loss, so the hunter should benefit. Doe seasons often arise for the same purposes. An area becomes overrun with deer. The answer is to cull out some does. Wild turkeys do not overrun an area

in the same sense, but when the flocks have reached a saturation point, natural causes will skim off the surplus, be it hens or gobblers.

My home state of Oklahoma allows hunters in specified counties to shoot "any turkey." Hunters pursuing turkeys in another group of counties are limited to shooting gobblers, while another group of counties has no fall hunt, as the populations do not justify the potential kill. So far as I know, Oklahoma is the only state which uses the term "tom turkey" in referring to gobblers. A tom is any bearded turkey.

Fall turkey hunting is extremely popular in my state, which also has a hunt for Eastern wild turkeys in far southeastern Oklahoma. Oklahoma's traditional turkey hunt for Rio Grande wild turkeys is a late October and early November affair. Though for many years we have had a large fall hen and tom turkey kill, Oklahoma has as large a wild turkey population today as I can recall. Two areas on which I have hunted fall turkeys extensively for the past 20 to 25 years, today have turkey populations that border on the greatest numbers I have ever observed.

I have always advised new turkey hunters to keep the weather in mind when choosing an away-from-home location for a fall turkey hunt. Parts of the American southwest would be too hot for some New Englanders, as I have witnessed days when the temperatures would climb well into the high 80s. A camo-garbed hunter, toiling up a steep slope on such an afternoon, will question the whys of hunting fall turkeys under such conditions. On the other hand, I've hunted winter birds when I was laden down with all the clothes I could get on and wished I had more. A sudden snowstorm caught Monty Montgomery (the great writer for the *Boston Globe*) and me one October morning high on the slopes of Vermont's Green mountains. We were lucky to escape. We did have the foresight to dress for bad conditions, having heard the weather forecast the previous evening. But by the time we came off the steep slopes, we had abandoned all hope of locating turkeys. We just hoped we could find the parking area. Such conditions can crop up unexpectedly throughout much of North America's turkey ranges. But when hunting the larger mountains, such as the Rockies or the Sierra Madres, a hunt can turn into potential danger for a hunter.

So, when choosing an area for a fall or winter hunt, never let the weather extremes escape your scrutiny and make equipment adjustments for these adversities. Unless you are hunting areas with which you are reasonably familiar, you should never leave the camp or your vehicle without a map of the nearby surroundings, a matchsafe, compass, sharp knife, and perhaps a small container of water. All of these items take on added importance if you have not been keeping tuned to local weather conditions and if you are hunting big mountain country. White coveralls, or a snow parka, can also add to your hunting skills should you suddenly find the landscape blanketed in snow.

Many such locations will become check stations once the season begins, and this alone will tell a non-resident hunter that he is in the region where turkeys can be found. Again, don't rely on check station numbers of birds killed as true indicators. Too often a check station can be surrounded by woods inhabited with numbers of birds, but there won't be a handful of birds checked in to it.

The hunter who arrives in a distant area before the season opens can often locate turkeys simply by driving forest roads, keeping watch for droppings in the trail, tracks where soil conditions permit, and the birds themselves. Eyeballing turkey sign while driving a road takes practice. The beginning hunter will have to drive at a snail's pace, but in time, he will begin to recognize areas which should be watched closely, and those which he can cover quickly. Obviously, a road covered by small pebbles and gravel, will not reveal tracks as does one of sand, mud, or even better, covered with a light snow. But, even a rocky road will not obscure a large dropping in a wheel track. Or a primary feather which has recently fallen from a bird's wing.

Making short hikes along abandoned roads can be very productive. Turkeys walk all roads within their territory, so a quick fast walk for a mile or so along one of these can reveal local turkey possibilities. Fall turkeys are often vocal, so there is also the added chance that the scouting hunter will hear birds. Probably the greatest factor related to walking roads is that these are built for vehicular traffic and are therefore kept on high ground. Turkeys like high ground. If there is food on it, they will use it if it is within their range. Therefore, the hunter should keep an eye open

If the traveling hunter has chosen a good area to hunt, this will become obvious . . .

Having settled on an area you intend to hunt, your hunting success often hinges on what you do once you arrive. Chances are you have decided to hunt a public hunt area, or a national forest, or its equivalent. Once there, you may be able to make a local contact, enabling you to hunt on private lands, but for now you will have to make do with a very large area of heavy woods which you hope is loaded with wild turkeys.

I don't advise anyone to just park the truck, jump out, and head into the woods. This could come later, if all else fails. But, first try some other tactics. Talking to local people is number one. Idle chatter with a gas station attendant has brought me results more than once. The same goes for folks who take your money at quick-stops, as such people are in daily contact with local hunters who stop for a cup of coffee, a doughnut, or fuel. The smaller the store, and the further its location from a large population center, the greater the chances that the proprietor will know what gives with the local hunters.

Adult gobblers go through a moulting process during the summer months which causes them to be so shy that it is seldom a long bearded turkey will be seen during July and August. This gobbler's tail feathers had not yet grown to full length when the bird was bagged during an early fall hunt.

The craw, or crop, contents reveal what the bird has been eating. The clues about where to search for feeding turkeys are told in studying these insects. Grasshoppers are found where grass and weeds are present. Grass and weeds are found in Eastern turkey range along old roads, trails, and in clear-cuts and pastures.

Dogwood berries are a favorite food of wild turkeys. The hunter who is hunting areas where more than one bird may be taken, should examine the bird's craw contents, if one has been killed. He will then have an inkling of what food areas to search.

for acorns, dogwood fruits, wild grapes, grasshoppers, anything that is a preferred wild turkey food throughout the area. There are a couple of disadvantages to arriving in a strange area prior to season, one being that there will probably not be any locals traveling forest roads, and secondly, there will be no shots to tell the visiting hunter if others are into turkeys.

If the traveling hunter has chosen a good area to hunt, this will become obvious the instant the season opens. Road traffic will increase tremendously. Shooting will do likewise, though the hunter should be aware of other game species that have become huntable on the same day. Squirrel hunting is probably the nation's most indulged in gunning sport, so a hunter must be careful that he is not misled by shots taken at bushytails. Numerous states have coinciding fall squirrel/turkey hunts.

And, while increased traffic and shooting are ordinarily reliable indicators of wild turkey activities, both cannot always be relied upon. I have hunted numerous times throughout reasonably good turkey country, yet observed little to no road traffic, nor heard a single shot. This would seem difficult to believe to the average Pennsylvania hunter, who on opening day is accustomed to thousands of turkey buffs in the woods. Just this past winter season, in far southeastern Florida, I heard but a single shot on opening day. Why? Fall and winter hunting has not caught on in some areas as it has in others. From what I can learn through conversations with hunters is that they simply do not know how to locate the birds. This same area in Florida is hunted extremely hard during the spring, when the birds are gobbling. But on mornings when the birds fail to sound off during the spring hunt, the hunters thereabouts all quit soon after first daylight. And thus it goes for fall and winter hunting. The birds are not gobbling on December morns, so the hunter is handcuffed. It is best to forget the whole thing until spring. Turkey hunters, such as me, are amazed

at this reluctance to attempt to locate the fall and winter drove, for in doing so the turkey hunter acquires a well-rounded education.

But, in the average turkey hunting area, once opening day arrives, there will be enough hunters traveling the roads, firing shots, and checking birds, to give the visiting gunner some insight as to where birds are to be found. Numerous times I have envied a hunter the bird he was toting on some strange slope. In my mind's eye I can still see the fine young jake a bearded hunter was carrying down a mountainside, one nasty winter day in Vermont. I'd not seen a track that morn, as it had rained like crazy and washed them away. The day earlier had been worse. The bird he had in hand could have weighed 40 pounds or 5,

Turkey hunting must be bad, or else these men would rather eat fried squirrel. In states where the season is open for these small animals, the bulk of shots heard will be at squirrels. Anyone hearing shots in such areas must not always assume other hunters have scattered turkeys—they could be shooting bushytails!

and I would have cared less. It was a fine beautiful bird much moreso than the one I did not have.

Throughout many areas, such as Pennsylvania, parts of Arkansas, the Virginias, western Oklahoma, and others, opening hour usually brings forth volleys of gunfire as local hunters get into droves of young birds. This is heard at some distance, and the traveling hunter can then head toward the sounds, and as he meets hunters, can locate the exact place where the birds were shot into. Hunters who are not knowledgeable of fall turkey hunting practices will ofttimes leave those areas, thinking them to be the very last place to hunt a turkey. Which, of course, at least for the first few days, is not so. Quite the contrary, the hunter should get as near the exact place from where the drove flushed as he can, as here is where the birds will reassemble.

When I hear gunfire which I presume are hunters firing into a drove, I follow a rule-of-thumb from my own experiences. If I suspect that the area is not inhabited by a

Many fall turkey hunters turn to squirrel hunting if things go sour with the turkeys. Ed LaForce only needs to wash this carcass, then it will be ready for the frying pan.

great number of fall turkey hunters, I will give some thought to working toward the gunshots, as probably there will be few other hunters to interfere with while calling. On the other hand, if I am hunting an area where there are great numbers of expert fall hunters about, I'll forget about it, and continue to look for other birds. Many of the eastern and northeastern states fall into this category, as those areas have the country's greatest number of veteran fall and winter turkey hunters.

Just because you saw one, don't get the idea that that area is good for fall turkeys . . .

I have noticed that many springtime turkey addicts presume that turkeys can be hunted throughout the same terrain during the fall and winter seasons. Though fall and winter birds can often be found on their spring stomping grounds, there are so many exceptions to this that we should stop here and take an in-depth look at this part of a turkey's life.

The statement can be made that all five subspecies of the bearded and spurred wild turkeys *can be found during both fall and spring seasons on some areas of their home range.* With this statement another can be added. Throughout the ranges of all subspecies will be areas where the birds *will be found during the spring seasons,* but *will never inhabit as a drove or wintering flock* during the winter season.

The magnitude of these tendencies, call them migrating habits if you wish, varies with local terrains, and the subspecie of turkey being dealt with. This traveling about, migrating, or just wandering, as I often refer to it, is due to several factors. Rocky Mountain wild turkeys, often known as Merriams, must travel back and forth over separate ranges because of bad weather conditions. Heavy snows and severe winters cover the food supplies and cause the birds to seek lower elevations where food can be found. This up-and-down traveling can result in birds being located here today but 40 miles distant next week. Two springs ago I hunted Merriams along a ridge in the Gila National Forest, found plenty of them and planned a hunt for last spring to that same area. On going back last April, snow blocked the

Foxtail millet is food eaten by nearly all wildlife, including wild turkeys. When consuming such so-called weed, or seed heads, the bird will grasp the stalk just beneath the seed pod, and then with a quick upward stroke, glean the seeds from the plant. Turkeys will do this over a period of time when feeding on small grass heads.

high roads, so I knew the birds would be lower. I found them at the foot of the mountains, some 5 miles from the former location. Had conditions been as bad there I would have found them at still a lower elevation. Certainly nothing difficult, just a factor to keep in mind when hunting Merriam turkeys.

We also know that once the large wintering flocks begin to break apart and scatter during February and March jake gobblers, on being left to themselves, have a tendency to "see the country." How many times have all of us observed a young gobbler, on a bright day, many miles from where we are accustomed to seeing turkeys. I've seen heck knows how many of them miles from where I have ever seen turkeys, and perhaps have never seen another there again. So, when it comes to young jakes, just because you saw one of them in a given area, don't get the idea that that area is good for hunting fall turkeys. Only through further observation, or from years of experience, will a hunter learn one from the other. The same holds true for small bands of hens and gobblers during the spring months. So many times I have located a gobbler with hens in areas where I have not found them earlier, perhaps over a period of many years. About the only thing we can assume from any springtime observation is that there is a reasonable chance the turkeys will be found within a few miles of the area during the fall months. Again, this depends largely on the subspecie, the severity of the late summer and fall weather, along with local feeding and watering conditions.

The hunter who goes on an *early* fall hunt can usually expect to find the birds scattered throughout those same areas during his spring hunt. This is because the hens that nested there will probably still be utilizing the range where they reared their broods. By November, these small family droves join into larger flocks, and the areas will become vacant as the flocks band together into the big wintering droves of 50 to 100 birds. There are exceptions to this, as tiny bands of older gobblers will oftentimes shy from joining the large flocks and will continue to wander the territory throughout the winter among their own kind.

When I go into strange and new country during a fall or winter hunt, I will talk to anyone who I think will divulge information as to local turkey abundancies though I do not expect them to tell me exactly where the birds can be found. If I am then satisfied there are birds in the region, I go looking on my own. This takes the form of driving roads, looking for signs, and looking for the birds themselves. I will walk abandoned roads and trails, and when doing so, I will walk fast, so as to cover as much ground as possible. The walking will be silent which enables me to hear any vocal turkeys. In this manner, I will locate a drove, or whatever number of birds. In most instances I will begin this searching on or after the beginning of the season, which means I will be hunting. Last fall, I drove into a completely new area of a national forest, parked well before a hint of first day, grabbed the old black powder burner, and headed off down what appeared to be an abandoned logging trail.

Come first day, I was probably ½-mile from the truck. It was a gorgeous October morning—warm and no wind, just a great day to be in the woods. Pausing on a knoll among giant pines, I fished out a wingbones call, licked on the mouthpiece to make the bones call easier, then cupped my hands around the bell end, and made a tree call. Seconds later I made another, then another. It was so quiet you could hear a woodpecker yawn. I didn't hear a sound. A couple of minutes passed. Easing the call back to my lips, I made about three hen yelps. You can imagine how I felt when, off from the northeast, a turkey yelped, then a second cut in, a young jake from near the first. Before I knew it, turkeys were answering each other like a bunch of magpies. Feeling like a child in a field of Cabbage Patch dolls, I muttered, "Hot Dogs," to myself, and began hotfooting down the trail which seemed to angle toward the birds.

A hundred yards down the trail, I could still hear the birds awakening, but I could tell I would have to leave the woods road. Down a slope, jump a tiny stream trickling across rocks, up slope, I at last topped out on a tiny spur

Conrad Vollertsen (left) and Stacey Gibson stand on a high ridge, quietly listening for sounds of a wintering drove. Droves of wild turkeys, when feeding during the morning hours, often talk back and forth as they feed, and these sounds are often detected by hunters when there is no wind or other outside noises.

Notice how the dark-hued clothing blends in with the oak-cedar surroundings. If a young turkey approaches, the hunter need only lean back into the cover, sit still, and the bird will come into range. Young, well scattered turkeys are not as wary as older birds, so the hunter who utilizes terrain, and treats them as though they are older turkeys, will have little or no problem in luring them into short range.

ridge which angled upward toward where I could hear the birds talking back and forth. A young jake made one of those blue-john gobbles, which is half-croak, half-gobble, and half-nothing. I couldn't help but grin. This was nothing but shining times. Oak leaves are noisy, like walking on broken beer bottles, but thankfully, it had rained thereabouts the day before, which made my sneaking up onto the ridge with the birds somewhat easier. Now, it seemed they were maybe inside 200 yards and slightly higher along the ridge's crest. Not knowing the country, I would simply have to play it by ear from where I was and hope for the best. Settling down alongside the gnarled trunk of a big oak tree, I leaned over against it on my right side, leaving my left side free, so I could easily maneuver the gun. My legs were drawn up under me so I could come to my knees, or my feet, if need be.

False calling on the bones a couple of times, I then smacked it soft-like, making a cluck, followed by another, then three or four others. Apparently the gathering drove paid me no mind at all, as I could hear them carrying on up the ridge from me. From what I'd heard, the calls must have been from perhaps a small bunch of eight or 10 birds, as I could hear hens, plus at least two young gobblers. The bunch was now on the ground. Soon, they would tire of this foolishness and begin walking toward whatever feeding area lured them at this time. Pushing the bones caller back inside my shirt, I then whistled at them, no differently than a very young poult would do in the early fall. For those of you who've never heard this sound, it is very much like the peeping of baby chickens, but perhaps drawn out into slightly longer notes.

Straight back to me, a hen clucked. Hard, loud, clucks. I whistled again. Back she came a second time. There was no doubt in my mind that I had gotten her attention, but good. "Well, now," I said to myself, "we'll see about this." I laid on heavy with the whistling.

In jig time I could tell that the hen was angling my way. No longer could I hear any other turkeys. Just this one. The harder I called, the closer she came, clucking each step

of the way. I must have whistled 500 times which, if you have never been engaged in this kind of calling, must be nonstop and must imitate the sounds of a young turkey which seemingly is caught, and cannot go to the answering hen. Invariably, the answering bird will be a mother turkey, and in many instances, the remainder of her drove will tag along. I have called up many droves with this cheeping whistle, sometimes to within a few feet of where I was hiding. The sound, as I make it, is done by blowing the breath through the teeth. It is not loud which gives the illusion that it will not carry far, but as none of us have the hearing ability of wild creatures, probably the whistles can be heard a lot further than we think.

When I first began using these sounds, I had never heard of anyone else calling like this, never read of it, nor been told of such a practice. I can recall the first time I did this was on a sudden impulse one fall afternoon when answering a drove that seemed to be doing much whistling. "Kee runs" had been popular up until that time, but these are made with various calls. The whistle is done solely with the hunter's mouth. Nowadays it is not unusual to read of a hunter calling young turkeys by whistling.

When the hen stepped into view, fading in and out of sight among the oak and pines, she was near 80 yards range. Clucking loudly and sharply she would walk a few steps, stop, cluck, look, all the time seemingly very suspicious. I laid on with the whistling though by now my jaws were tiring of the practice. I was nearly whistled out. I'd slipped back the hammers on the old scattergun earlier. It was laid barrels forward along the top of my left leg, my left hand gripping the straight stock at the wrist, my right hand cradling the splintered fore-end beneath the side-by-side twist barrels. In each barrel's innards was packed a measure of DuPont black powder, downbore from a healthy bunch of lead No. 5 chilled shot. Remington percussion caps held tight onto each nipple. Me and this old circa 1840 10-gauge had killed turkeys from one end of the good ole U.S.A. to the other, and if the bird up there in the woods eased down into 30 yards, it was in deep trouble.

The woods was too open for my comfort. The hen would call, but she hesitated in coming to me, as she probably realized she should be able to see the young turkey. I'd situated at a slight rise from her original direction, but she had circled somewhat, so the rise was no longer between us. Gingerly the bird closed the gap. It seemed like an eternity passed before I felt that she was within range, whereupon I slipped the gun to my shoulder as she passed behind a tree trunk. I let the right hammer down when the bird cleared the oak.

Anyone who's shot a lot of black powder knows that when shooting on a still morning, in deep woods, the hunter can't see anything for a few seconds. White smoke blots out the aiming point. I scrambled to my feet, charged through the white cloud, ran up through the woods and grabbed the turkey which was thrashing around among the leaves. Sure enough, an adult hen. She'd come to see why a poult was in trouble. This one had not had any followers, as many I have called to me have had. Heck knows where the bunch was by now. But, it didn't matter. The bag thereabouts was two Eastern turkeys, and I had killed my other bird the first day miles from there. My hunt was done.

Success will be had only by the hunter who can think and make instant decisions . . .

The methods utilized in hunting autumn turkeys are so numerous as to all but defy description. And, along with these are infinite numbers of on-the-spot tricks which a hunter improvises to fit the situation he may suddenly be faced with. I doubt if there is a gunning sport which, by constantly changing tactics, can be so often brought to a successful culmination, time after time, than is the hunting of wild turkeys. But success will be had only by the hunter who has the ability to think, to keep an open mind, and to make instant decisions. The decision to act may result in instant, fast movements, or a long, slow deliberate course of delayed action. Fall turkey hunting, for any and all ages and sexes of wild turkeys, is best done by the hunter who possesses all the afore-mentioned capabilities. He must be able to think freely, to make lightning-like decisions, and then to act on those, whether in the blink of an eye, or later, and to be able to determine one from the other just as quick. Among those of us who travel incessantly in quest of wild turkeys, it must never be forgotten which bird we are hunting, therefore applying habitat adaptations to our hunting techniques.

The *springtime* hunter has little planning to do, insofar

as a "game plan" is concerned. Ordinarily this is spelled out when a turkey gobbles at dawn. Then and there, the greatest part of the hunt is over. The hunter knows where the quarry is. Perhaps three or four birds have gobbled meanwhile, so the hunter knows there are others about. If he cannot coax the first into gunshot range, there may be a chance at another. Gobbling is why springtime turkey hunting is so extremely popular. A hunter does not need to spend endless hours searching the woods for game.

Fall and winter hunting on the other hand is not pursued by such armies of hunters, solely because the birds do not call out and locate themselves for the hopeful gunner. Once a person walks into the woods on an autumn morning, he must locate the birds through any number of means, the least of which is being able to hear the birds as they call.

Luckily, there are droves of turkeys that do call back and forth to some extent during the fall months. Sometimes this calling cannot be heard at any distance, and a good deal of luck is often needed for a hunter to hear the chatter. I can recall a winter morning when six of us had scattered in a large woods, knowing a drove of birds was roosting there. I had heard a yelping at first day, but realizing two of the boys were somewhere in that vicinity and would undoubtedly get into the gathering drove, I held back. Suddenly a bird went flashing past me, flying all out, off to my left some 40 yards. Running hard, I topped out on the ridge beneath the path he'd taken, and stopped. I hadn't taken a deep breath when I could see another turkey heading toward

(Right) Steep rugged canyons course through much Rio Grande turkey country. These are heavily wooded, providing excellent protection for the birds during bad weather, and as escape cover when pursued.

Being fairly proficient at wing-shooting is an asset when turkey hunting because the big birds are quite fast and adept at cruising through heavy woods. Many times they're seen for only an instant. Photo by Irene Vandermolen, Leonard Rue Ent.

me, dead-on, perhaps 50 yards out, flying like his tail was afire. Thumbing back the hammers, I swung on him as he thundered past, for in that instant I could tell it was a big jake. I smoked him with a load of No. 5s. As I ran to where he'd crashed, I heard another shot. A moment later I bumped into Tim Olsen, who was toting a jake just like mine. Soon after that we talked to the two boys who'd flushed the birds, but who couldn't get an open shot because the trees were so thick. The point I am getting across here is that when a hunter hears turkeys during the fall season, particularly those which he suspects are yet up in the trees, he should be ready to shoot. I had a few seconds to get prepared, as I was aware that other hunters were about. On seeing the first bird pass my position, I had the savvy to run to the area I saw him land. Past experiences have taught me that the path one bird of a flushing flock travels can well be the path of any others that follow.

When I am hunting strange woods, don't know where birds are located, and the morning is calm, allowing a person to hear well, I will walk at a brisk pace, stopping every 200 or 300 yards to call and listen a moment before continuing my journey. The mixed drove of hens and young birds are most vocal at daybreak, so my chances of walking to within hearing distance of a group is highly increased with the amount of territory I can cover. As the morning wanes, I can slow the pace, as the birds will slacken calling considerably once they arrive at feeding places.

When I am lucky enough to hear an awakening drove, I can then weigh the options. What to do? Of course, the first thing to do is to walk nearer, preferably placing myself at an elevation above them if possible, and if I know the terrain sufficiently. Having drawn as near as I can without

spooking them, I then attempt to learn if the birds are yet in the trees. Birds sitting among the upmost branches can be called to in hopes one flies to the hunter. Once a few of them alight on the woods floor, chances are that all will join them there. True, some may glide to earth off to the side, but on average, the drove will assemble where the largest number has flown down.

Two hunters working together can bag birds with ease from an awakening drove at first day. It is often a case of one hunter circling them and then walking toward the birds as the other hunter also begins walking toward them. The last time I tried this was when Rick Greene, a New York turkey hunter, and I were hunting some Ozark birds. I'd slipped around the bunch which was located on a heavily treed ridge of mixed pine and hardwood. I instructed Rick to give me time to walk around them, then begin walking due south along the side of the hill. I spooked a bird which flew up into a tree near Rick, and at his shot, he scared a few past me. We met a moment later, both toting turkeys, marveling at our good fortune. Rick Skiles, a West Virginian who was with us, called in one of the separated birds a short time later. These turkeys were talking back and forth quite loudly when we first heard them, as it was well past daybreak, and legal shooting time. The season was only a few days old, and a late summer found all the leaves on the trees and shrubbery. Obviously the little drove had not been hunted. All of these things combined to make for an easy hunt. Had we decided to make the attempt, we probably could have settled among the cover along that ridge and called birds directly to us from the tree branches. However, there are serious drawbacks to calling birds which are roosting together within a relatively small periphery. In most instances the hunter will not be able to sneak near enough to the birds without being detected. Undisturbed turkeys, when flying down, often give just a flip of the wings, and glide to earth very near the roost tree. Birds on the outer edges of the roosting flock will fly a longer glide path, but will head toward the center of the bunch. Complete flydown can take but a moment or two for a small drove. So, unless a hunter can slip close to the birds, almost in among them, his chances of calling in a bird from an unsuspecting, unmolested close-roosting drove are not good. Chances for calling kills are far greater if the hunter simply walks in among the birds, or runs, as I do, scatters them from the trees, and then after a short wait, uses the call.

Lennis Rose, my old Missouri sidekick, and I had a few birds separated up in north Arkansas one October morning,

Eastern wild turkey habitat is very often mountainous, deeply cut with gullies, and well laced with spur ridges, hogbacks, coves, and flats. Tiny streams provide a year round supply of water, and oak trees provide the turkey's principal food, the acorn. Many hunters who will tromp these rugged hills all day in search of a bird would not consider working this hard if their regular job should demand it.

smack atop a narrow spine blanketed in hardwoods. We'd watched one bird sail off from the others, apparently settling a couple hundred yards from us, out on a point jutting from the main ridge. We sat down against a couple of oaks after walking in the bird's direction a short distance, and a few moments later I kee'd the bird to us. Tom Preston had spooked the birds in the beginning after hearing them in the trees in a high cove. Walking up to them from directly below, he'd dropped a mature hen as the flock flew from the trees. Harley Rose, Lennis' brother, had gotten into the same drove the afternoon before and killed a bird as he flushed them from where they were feeding on acorns. Harley had stillhunted into easy shotgun range, as he silently walked an old tote road.

Any type of call will turn the trick when calling to roost scattered turkeys. The birds will make all kinds of calls,

and those which have not been hunted will become extremely noisy, as bird after bird joins in regrouping. Young gobbler yelps, half-gobbles, hen yelps, kees, whistles, clucks, you name it—a bunch which has been separated makes all the notes in a turkey's vocabulary when gathering. Except the alarm call. Make the mistake of letting them see you, and you'll hear it too.

I don't concentrate in one tiny area, but work a range of a few square miles . . .

But, let's pretend you haven't heard any birds at first day, and it is now mid-morning. Still no sound of turkeys. What next? The hunter must keep in mind the routine which a turkey will follow on an ordinary fall day. The birds gather at the roost location, and from there amble toward water, or a feeding area. The bunch will peck at anything edible along the journey, and it should be remembered that wild turkeys, like all wildlife, spend most their lives engaged in the pursuit of food. The drove will linger during the midday hours, preening, dusting, standing, sleeping, and in general just being lazy before again taking up the hunt for food during the mid to late afternoon hours. The fall turkey hunter must keep this routine in mind and build his game plan around it.

Thus, the mid-morning plan should involve a hunt for turkey foods, and in searching for those, the hunter should make contact with the birds. At this time of morn I will be covering lots of country, noting what foods are abundant and if the turkeys have been feeding on these. By reading such signs, I will know where to be extra alert and where I can probably find birds. I don't concentrate in one tiny area, but work a larger range of a few square miles and note the types of terrain which could be productive.

The first time I made a winter hunt back into Mexico's high Sierras, it became obvious by noon of the first day that finding turkey foods was not going to be a problem. Everywhere I looked there were so many things for a turkey to eat that the birds could simply wander about pecking blindly and eat their fill in nothing flat. I'd hunted the region during spring hunts, so knew the birds were somewhere within the general area. I would simply need to locate what feed the birds were choosing from nature's banquet. Two days later, I began cutting lots of tracks across a mountaintop mesa. Less than a mile away as a crow flies, I found what I'd been searching for—an old cornfield, tucked back near the base of a towering peak. From then on in, the hunt was simple. I was there the next morning and at dawn could hear the awakening drove, high up in a saddle, yelping and clucking back and forth, from a stand of chihuahua pines where they'd spent the night. Two hours later I struck gold—two birds bagged from the bunch.

During those 2 hours, I had located the birds' principal

path to the old corn patch. Gun laid across my lap, I was ready when they came by. The fierce December cold of the high mountains is not so cold after all when the sight of wild turkeys warms your blood.

During fall hunts to unfamiliar areas, my principal method in searching for birds is to walk fast, stop to listen from time to time, watch for signs of turkeys, keep an eye peeled for major food sources, and all the while, keep alert should I bump into birds. This sounds like an unreasonable number of things to be engaged in but with time, it becomes a habit. It is no more than being extremely alert, utilizing the senses of sight and hearing, while taking a hike through the woods. A great many hunters never truthfully see all there is about them. How many snakes have you seen while hunting? What about lizards, or a snail? Deer? Hummingbirds? Mexico's mountains are laden with these birds, though you may not always see the little jewels. You'll hear the buzz of their wings. Do you look up into the trees? Few hunters do. Is there a good mast crop this year, or did you notice? Have you noted where the bulk of the roost trees are located in your home turkey woods? In numerous areas, these will be located along a north slope. Do you know why?

Wild turkeys utilize cultivated fields, as does all wildlife, feeding on the crop which man intends for human consumption. Such fields, like this one of standing milo, are excellent locations for the fall turkey hunter to search for recent sign. If there is indication the area is being heavily used, the hunter can wait in ambush, hoping to bag a bird when the drove feeds past.

So much of your hunt boils down to being super observant. You will need to study the woods from sod to treetop. Your hunt will take on a much deeper enjoyment. Rocks in a tumbling stream, rough brown bark, the red leaves of autumn, a tumblebug pushing its burden along a cow path, a goshawk coursing through northern hardwoods—all of these things will become part of your hunt. You should see all that takes place around you, because if you don't, you are not being as observant as you could be.

You can do all of this, still remaining alert should you walk into shooting distance of unsuspecting birds. Such alertness will enhance the chances of spying a drove of turkeys. Too often a hunter ambles off into the woods, keeps his mind on what he's doing for a few hours, then becomes rather lackadaisical. From then on, he's just wandering. Won't see a turkey unless it flies into his face. Worse, he will not be able to take advantage of any nearby unexpected chances to bag a turkey.

Perhaps the major difficulty faced by inexperienced turkey hunters is in keeping up hope or maintaining a positive attitude that the hunt will be successful. With each passing hour that game is not found, morale becomes all the more difficult to keep in check. Those same gobblers which were gobbling during the spring, are now silent. It is easy to give up. Thousands of fall turkey enthusiasts do give up after only 1 or 2 days of hunting.

A gradual loss of hope is invariably tied to the unseen, the unknown, and the uneducated. The veteran hunter who has faced these obstacles day after day, realizes that success is there, but it is up to him to ferret it out. This is true hunting. This is hunting in its purest, rawest form.

When I am walking through the woods, popping up and down over sandhills, easing through the dark confines of an oak motte, wading a swamp, or easing through the clawing brush of a manzanita thicket on a mountain's flank, all the while searching for turkeys, I try never to lose sight of my one objective—I am hunting turkeys. Watch close, but watch at a distance, too. Listen at all times. Keep both eyes searching for recent turkey signs. Don't forget the trees, turkeys are a tree oriented bird.

Though I constantly work at being alert, I recall walking along a trail in deep woods one morning and having the bejabbers scared from me by a big gobbler flushing from a small dead oak. No, I couldn't excuse myself for this blunder. The oak was not 40 feet tall, no leaves, and why the bird remained there as I walked toward him, I will never know. He flushed at a range of 20 yards, at most. I was not ready, so he simply flew away. My behind needed kicking badly. It needed the same treatment another morning, probably around 8 or 9 o'clock, when I scared a bird from a pine tree hanging over a little used blacktop road. Who knows why the bird was there at that time of day, with the sun streaming down. It flew straight down the road. An easy shot, but I was standing there with my mouth hanging open. I was wandering about like a zombie. I had no business being loose among the birds and the beasts.

When a drove of turkeys is sighted by a walking hunter,

there are a number of things he should strive to learn. Of course, if the birds are within easy gunshot, the hunter will attempt to make a kill, whether the birds are running or flying. Even then, if he is with other hunters, who may want to hunt the scattered turkeys, he should make an effort to ascertain where the separated birds flew, and then mark those areas in his mind's eye, so he can relay the information to his friends.

Belly-crawling is often the only method to bring the hunter those last few yards . . .

But let's assume the hunter has spied a drove of birds well beyond killing range. First, have the birds seen him? If so, he must take action instantly if he hopes to scatter them. This can sometimes be done by running toward them as fast as possible. If they do not fly, but commence running, he will need to shoot a time or two into the air. With few exceptions, this will put wild turkeys into the air. Watch where they go. Did they all fly away in the same general direction? Did they scatter to the wind? What age were the birds? How many did you see?

Make an effort to answer all these questions while the birds fade from sight. But, let's presume you have been trodding an old logging trail, have just passed through stands of huckleberry along the road, then suddenly eye turkeys pecking beneath a few wild cherry trees scattered across a flat. They haven't seen you. They are well beyond gunshot. Freeze—but gently ease to earth, lowering your body closer to the ground. No matter what part of the country a hunter is working, turkeys at 100 yards distance will have trouble eyeballing the hunter who has settled to a squatting position, simply due to the intervening brush, grass clumps, rocks, and the jillion other things which clutter the outdoors. The average turkey addicts' camo clothing will do the rest, helping to fade the hunter's form into the background and nearby foliage. From this lower vantage

point and by moving with extreme caution when the birds are seemingly not acting wary, you can study the birds so as to determine what the best course of action should be.

I cannot over-emphasize the caution which must be maintained while studying a suddenly found band of turkeys. Particularly important is the hunter's need to ''make like a rock,'' if the birds should quickly become alert, whether just one has its head erect, or the whole bunch. I've been involved in many a long drawn-out staring down contest, where turkeys and I have stared back and forth at each other, all of us making like so many rocks, for up to 10 to 15 minutes.

A turkey's fantastic eyesight can truly zero in on a hunter crouching in the woods. If the bird is suspicious, the hard

The hunter who discovers a drove of young turkeys during the fall season should note a number of things about them as they scatter. What sex were the birds? How many were there in the bunch? Did they scatter to all four quadrants of the compass? Did a single or two fly off to one side alone? The answers to these questions could mean the differnce between success or failure.

Hat and powder horn thrown on the ground, the author watches a drove of fall turkeys through a screen of brush which is grown up around a fence post. These turkeys are eating weed seed, though it appears that two of them have noticed something amiss. If the birds become spooky, the author will have no trouble selecting one bird. But, if they remain grouped, he will have to be careful to pick a bird off to the side of the bunch to kill only one turkey at the shot.

look will last longer, and during this intense stare, the least little move by the hunter will mean *goodbye turkey*. But, if the hunter can bear the pain of perhaps aching bones due to being caught in a bad position, the bird will invariably at last be satisfied there is no danger and go back to its previous activities. Should the bird begin walking slowly, the head up, and perhaps move behind cover, do not move unless you are dead sure it cannot see through the screen, or that it will not walk past the intervening object, pop out again, and go through the whole stare down procedure again. I hunt much of the time with small binoculars hanging high on my chest. Once I am pinned down by the stare of a turkey, I do not dare blink my eyes, but wait until the bird goes back to feeding, or walks behind a solid object. In most instances, just as quick as this happens, I will put the binoculars to my eyes, focusing in on the bird when it walks back into sight and begins to stare anew. With the added vision power, I can then study its actions. Let me tell you, I have coursed suspicious wild turkeys for 100 or 200 yards with field glasses, and the same bird which normally could not be seen by the naked eye but is now in sight, is still alert, still stopping to stare, and obviously wound up like a jack-in-the-box ready to go off the second I made a move.

So, if you see a bunch of birds, and they have not seen you, make every attempt to drop from their view, where you can decide what to do next. An unspooked drove of turkeys is far easier to hunt than one which is hightailing it for the next county. Doubly so if the hunter is well out of range.

The fall turkey hunter who suddenly comes upon a small party of wild turkeys must act instantly if the birds are within easy gunshot, and to get a shot at them before they take evasive action. If the birds are slightly beyond gun range, the hunter should run at them, firing the gun into the air, in hopes this will cause them to scatter widely. If that happens, a call can be used to bring them into range.

Turkeys that see a hunter at long distances, before or at the same time the hunter sees them, are very difficult to hunt thereafter. The birds will ordinarily head for the next county without any further notice. Super wary now that they are aware of the hunter, the drove will also not scatter. The whole bunch can stay on the alert which means just double as many eyes to keep a vigil.

Birds the hunter sees before they have noticed him, at longer distances, are sometimes the easiest of all turkeys to hunt. This is when binoculars are extremely valuable as a visual aid. The terrain can be studied inch by inch, as seldom will there be areas where a stalk cannot be planned. Or, the birds can be kept under scrutiny with hopes that they can be hunted when moving to a different location, or travels studied in hopes of planning an intercepting route.

Two qualities which will see a hunter through such episodes are supreme patience and sufficient education about the everyday habits of wild turkeys to be able to decide what they will do next. Of course, of utmost importance is to cut the distance between hunter and turkeys *without them becoming suspicious*. The nearer the hunter is to the birds, the quicker he can strike should the opportunity arise. Quite often, the hunter who makes moves from time to time, in closing the distance, will suddenly realize that one more move will bring him into killing distance.

Crawling on the hands and knees, or better yet bellycrawling, is very often the only method which will bring a hunter those last few critical yards. This works well during the fall months when leaves are still clinging to bushes, and the bushes stand aloft from the summer growth of weeds. We all cuss weeds that peep up from our lawns, but if it hadn't been for weeds, a passel of wild turkeys would have escaped my gun.

Over in northern Arkansas years ago I was walking a county road which, being a highly traveled route, seemed an unlikely place to find a turkey. The area I had in mind was down the road a piece, where I knew a very dim trail led up a steep incline, then gently flowed around a long ridge. It was hot and dusty, and being the second week in October, it meant that the turkeys thereabouts had been hunted hard. Squirrel hunters have always been thick in those parts, but I never knew one of them to pass up a shot at a turkey. My old Hapgood muzzleloader was stuck back over my shoulder, soldier fashion. I was wearing some old clothes, and a faded old brown felt hat. Topping a long rolling hill, I glanced back up a side trail, as I passed the place where it broke out onto the main road. It led to a little acre sized hunk of cultivated ground which I'd been to the day before. Never looked too much like a place for turkeys. You could have knocked my eyeballs off with a marshmallow, when I looked back there. *Turkeys! Real live honest-to-goodness wild turkeys*.

I hit the ground, rolling the gun off onto the ground in front of me. Gingerly, I eased up, using my elbows, and took a looksee through a few limbs lying among the groundcover. Seventy-five yards from me, straight up the trail, and out along the edge of the tiny field, I could make out

These turkeys have become suspicious. Their alertness will "telegraph" to the others, resulting in much standing tall, necks outstretched, and with a lot of "perting." The hunter should charge toward this drove in hopes of scattering them in all directions. Such a scatter could result in an excellent calling opportunity.

(Right) Late winter hunts can often take place in a woods barren of foliage. Such terrain offers little to the still-hunter and stalker. Far the best method here is to scatter a drove and then call one back to the gun.

the backs of three or four feeding turkeys. One of them paused, stood erect, looked things over, and then went back to pecking. One bird faded from sight off to my right, screened from me by brush, weeds, and other stuff cluttering the woods floor. My best chance would be to wait until all of them, did this, and then belly-crawl down the trail where noise would be slight. I hadn't laid there 3 or 4 minutes when the last one eased from view. I quickly began bellying, at the same time, keeping my eyes on the field. The second a bird came into view, I would have to freeze. This happened several times, but in being careful about my moves and stopping when a bird was where it might see me, I worked my way to the field's edge in a few minutes. At last, belly down behind a small mound, ridged up with fallen leaves that had caught in a branch lying on the ground, I raised up just to where I could study the clearing. Four, five, six—I could make out the backs of six birds pecking at the recently upturned soil. The nearest was about 25 yards. Poking the gun out through the brush, I eased back on the right hammer. *Click*—the nearest bird's head shot up. *Booomm!* Running out to where the young turkey was flopping, I watched as the others fanned out. Excellent. My two buddies could try calling them. I've crawled on all fours from one end of this country to the other with part of Mexico thrown in for practice. It is the simplest method there is for stalking wild turkeys.

Invariably, the hunter who has seen turkeys at a distance can work himself to within scattering distance if not within gunshot. By making a sudden run toward them, he can affect a good scatter. The birds will fan out, though all will fly off toward one general direction. Now is the time to mark them down to the best measure possible and immediately go in that direction. I run as much of this distance as one good leg, and one bad one, will allow. Why? Wild turkeys, being gregarious birds and having grown up together, are used to having each other's company. On being separated, even for just a few moments, they will quickly strive to find the company they have been accustomed to. So, if the birds are young, have not been hunted much, nor been separated before insofar as the hunter knows, they will begin regrouping the second they come back to earth. If the woods is open without a heavy screening canopy of leaves, and the woods floor is void of brush, the birds will probably see each other alight and get together by sight. This is also true on prairie hunts and in open meadows, or on a great many mountain hunts in the Rockies, as much of this country has a park-like topography.

One December afternoon three of us scattered a small drove of Eastern turkeys alongside a well-used blacktop. The birds flew uphill into heavy pines but were not separated across a very wide front. We instantly headed up the center of what we presumed was the birds' route, Conrad Vollertsen off to my right, and Stacey Gibson to my left. Hurrying as best we could, though steadily walking uphill, we were "guns up" alert, hoping a bird would be spied in the treetops. No such luck. Near the top of the ridge, we got a last look at the bunch, running in a group above us as they broke over the rim and then from our view. That ended our chase. We simply hadn't gotten a good scatter in the beginning, nor could we effect one on them later. Following them would be a farce, as the birds would be as skittish as a snake during cotton chopping time.

The birds eyed me and made a running takeoff, flying back into heavy, hardwoods . . .

When I bump into a drove of birds, I strive to learn the age and sex of the individuals. All further techniques must be built around this knowledge. Without it, the hunter has his hands tied. The hunter calling to a scattered drove of young jakes would not want to try to call one to him making hen yelps.

Last October I tried sneaking to within easy range of a band of seven turkeys I'd spied, feeding along the edge of a pasture. It was drizzling rain, so I'd left my binoculars back in the truck where they would stay dry. The birds eyed me from afar and made a running takeoff, flying back into heavy, mature mixed hardwoods and pines. I presumed the little bunch was a single hen with a small brood. Trotting back to where they seemed to have flown, I began stillhunting, paying no mind to the ground, just watching overhead. What with the light rain, and it being past 4 o'clock in the afternoon, chances were the birds would alight in the trees. I knew one thing: if the birds were not young ones, I would not walk to within gunshot of one. At least, I probably wouldn't be able to get in a killing shot. As it turned out, I eyed a bird a short time later and killed it right there on the limb. Walking over to where it tumbled, I saw that it was a young turkey. I could send my two companions to this spot the next morning and be able to tell them how to hunt.

Wintertime turkey hunting is often a cold, nasty sport which brings forth the heaviest clothing a hunter owns. These parka-clad hunters sit waiting in a drizzle, hoping a bird will come to their calling. Only diehard hunters will stick with this sport. Sitting for long periods of time, with a menacing cold settling into feet, back and fingers, can soon undermine a hunter's morale.

Had the birds flushed wildly, and had I not been able to make positive identification, I might have decided the birds were older which would have meant different techniques in calling. Young unhunted turkeys, particularly on a rainy late afternoon, should be approachable by a stealthy still-hunter. I knew this and was able to take advantage of the fact.

As the season advances and if the birds have been hunted moderately for 2 to 3 weeks, hunting will become progressively more difficult as each day goes by. Once they've been hunted for this long, by only a handful of hunters scattered throughout their territory, my experience indicates that the birds will have attained a superior wildness, which means they will simply be tough as hell to hunt for the remainder of the season. Even if it lasts for 2 months. Such birds will flush at the sight of man though the range may be ½-mile. They will roost with greater distances between them, and will feed less with much time devoted to standing absolutely motionless, head and eyes slowly moving searching the surroundings. Probably they will be call-shy. If you think they aren't, get into a position where you can see one, then make a call. You'll know the answer if it makes for the next county like a scalded cat.

Late December hunts can be tough, due to bad weather and a lack of foliage to name just two adversities. When you add snow and cold to not being able to find a place to hide, things get tough. Hunting a bunch of scattered, spooky wild turkeys makes it all but impossible. Many of the well-known ''name'' hunters will no longer make the scene though the birds are still in the woods. Those same good old boys who earlier had said that fall and winter hunting was easy are now hiding in the house, huddled around a fireplace, dreaming of spring. I have never bumped into one of them in turkey woods when winter's winds are howling.

Throughout many areas of the country, the bulk of fall or winter turkey kills will be made when the hunter has an opportunity to waylay a turkey while hunting other game. Ordinarily, the hunter will be after deer. My home state of Oklahoma has often had coinciding deer and fall turkey seasons. Quail season is often on, too. I can recall numerous occasions when a party would hunt geese until noon, then spend the afternoon in searching for turkeys. I can look up at a picture on the den wall of my son-in-law, Tom Preston, my brother Dick, his son, Dick Jr., and me. With us are four adult gobblers plus a big eight-point whitetail. We didn't hunt quail that day though we could have, as we were headed back toward home by 2 o'clock on that fine November afternoon. Just never occurred to us that bird season was open, I suppose. Among my mementoes are numerous photos showing hunters with turkeys, plus ducks, geese, deer, prairie chickens, quail, squirrels, fish, and even mushrooms.

Many of these turkeys are killed with a rifle, since the hunter is usually in pursuit of big game at the time. These hunts have been taking place for years, often for decades, so any argument about a rifle having no place in the hunting

Turkey hunts often coincide with seasons offering other species of wild game. This eastern turkey was taken on the same outing as the ruffed grouse, or "patridge," as a Vermonter would say. The author often plans hunts where two or three kinds of game can be hunted in conjunction with that of wild turkeys.

Fall and winter hunts coincide with other numerous hunting seasons, but the serious fall hunter ignores these, trying to bag what he came after. The fall turkey hunter in northeastern states can also hunt grouse and woodcock.

and shooting of wild turkeys has no place with these hunters. Such a statement will be met with a cold stare, and a look which means, "anybody who would say that ain't too smart." There are a passel of grizzled veteran hunters in the western states who have been killing deer and turkeys with the same rifle for years. They know the gun. They know how to shoot it. All of them are aware what the load will do to a turkey gobbler's breast.

Each fall when the season begins to draw near, my mind invariably drifts around to the hopes that in the weeks ahead an old gobbler will loom above the barrels of my trusty side-by-side. Maybe there'll be two big, old, tassle-bearded turkeys, or dreams of dreams, what if a person could get shots at three. Enough of the daydreams, let's just talk about the chance of one decent shot at one long whiskered turkey gobbler. What are the chances that the hunter will get a shot at an old bird, perhaps at 25 yards?

Such hunting can be compared to gambling, and playing cards, along with the term, "the luck of the draw." There is a little bit of luck involved, and regardless of how much work a hunter puts into an effort, if Murphy's Law is working against him, he may not be successful. The hunt for old gobblers during the fall and winter months is this way. These birds are all of the things which the word *unpredictable* is meant to be. No matter how hard the hunter hunts, he could go the entire season without firing at one of the older turkeys. Perhaps they've ranged over onto a neighboring area, and this could be miles from where the bird was during the spring months. And though it is savvy thinking to presume these old turkeys spend the average day high on a timbered ridge, scratching among oak leaves, they may have found easier diggings nearer of the creek.

But, as luck needs all the help it can get, I would prefer

to work with it. You've heard the term, "people can help their luck," or, "luck is what you make it." I think these were coined about turkey hunters. Some folks have it, some don't. But, all of us can seemingly make it better. The turkey hunter can do this by being alert, always ready to take advantage of the least opportunity, practicing to improve both his hunting and shooting abilities, and by using the one sense which makes man the primary predator—the ability to think and reason.

Why don't you get an old felt hat and a muzzle-loading shotgun and go with me. Now you're talkin' turkey . . .

There are no "best" methods for hunting older gobblers from October to January. All of the techniques utilized in fall hunting for any turkey will work on an older male bird, be it bushwacking, stalking, calling, plain walking, or lying in ambush. The one difference is that it often requires a greater number of attempts to bring about a successful hunt. By this, I mean that whereas a hunter might walk 3 miles before flushing a drove of young turkeys, he could very well walk 10, or even 20, before crossing paths with a big gobbler. There just aren't as many of these birds, so it will take more time to find and kill one.

If you'll recall the instance I mentioned toward the beginning of this chapter, and the small table of kills I made in relation to four fall-of-the-year hunts for Eastern turkeys,

The author examines a pair of fall-killed young turkeys. This is typical Ozark fall terrain, the bushes and trees with leaves yet untouched by frost. (Photo courtesy Larry Shallenberger)

you will see that I killed adults by three methods—still-hunting, ambushcade, and calling. The only method by which I did not kill an adult during those hunts was by stalk which was only because the opportunity did not present itself. These were run-of-the-mill hunting trips with no advance plans insofar as kills are concerned. I just take a come-what-may attitude, and let it work itself out from there. I simply love hunting, and though these tactics I mention might seem like hard work to the average person, I doubt if anyone is so relaxed throughout as I am.

So, if the hunter will take his time, but hang tough, stick with it, and make up his mind that he wants to hunt until he bags an adult bird, in time this can be possible. But, this is possible only if he is a good shot, hunts with dedication to the hunt itself, can make quick decisions, and has a complete knowledge of the turkey he is pursuing. For instance, consider that numerous adult gobblers can often be found alone. No other turkeys around. The fact is, there may not be a single one within a mile. This little fact, seemingly harmless, has cost many older gobblers their lives. The bird has but two eyes, so when it is engaged in feeding, watering, or whatever, it is then susceptible to a predator.

Wayne Bailey, in his excellent book, *Fifty Years Hunting*

Wild Turkeys, recalls a hunt on which he, Frank Piper, and me, all killed adult gobblers on a single October afternoon. Wayne was walking an old tote road, popped over a tiny hill in the road, and was face-to-face with an Eastern adult. Wayne is savvy about how a hunter must always be ready, so he dropped the turkey as it thundered up from the trail.

Frank had been hunting a large area of heavy woods, but toward noon made a beeline for the road, so as to meet up with Bailey and me. On nearing the road, he was aware that it had little traffic, so instead of blundering out onto it, he first took a look both ways as he walked from the brush along its edge. You can imagine his surprise on noticing a gobbler in the center of the grade, coming toward him. The old turkey was too busy chasing grasshoppers to notice him, and so Frank dropped from sight. Easing his gun around, he waited for the turkey to walk into easy range which it did. Along about the same time, I was a couple miles from there and had just scattered a small band of gobblers. In due time I called one of them to me—a single adult. All three of us had killed adult gobblers near noon of the same day, and all of these birds had been loners, when shot. Had any of them been with other birds, the chances would have increased by that number that we would not have been successful. Older gobblers are ex-

These hunters take a breather after a hard morning's outing for wintertime turkeys. These birds were killed with the use of turkey calls after being scattered in and among sizeable thickets of shinoak. These thickets, like this one where the birds are hanging, are comprised of small oak trees, and are dense and often difficult to walk through. Wild turkeys like the small acorns, and spend hours in these clumps or "mottes," known by locals as shinnery clumps. This shinnery oak is found in far west Oklahoma and Texas.

(Left) The use of "flushing" dogs while hunting fall turkeys is quite popular in some areas of the country. Here, Bob Besch, of New York state, watches his German shorthair working some turkey woods near Albany. These dogs are trained to run into a drove of birds, flushing them into nearby trees. The dog's barking will bring the hunter to the area. Then, with the dog lying quietly nearby, the hunter hopes to call one of the scattered birds into shooting range. This is an old hunting method which works well, provided the hunter has a well trained dog.

ceedingly wary. They seem to have eyes in the back of their heads. Together, they are all but impossible to accidentally walk upon within shotgun range. There are just too many eyes.

Now, if the hunter can detect a tiny drove of these old birds from a distance, sneaking or stalking them is often possible. I've made kills from a good many droves numbering four to 10 or 12, older gobblers. Throughout the bulk of these incidents, the birds were busy feeding which made the sneak easier, as there are times when all will be headsdown, gathering foodstuffs. During these crawling stalks, there is no way a person can be too careful. If the woods are silent, noise is magnified, and this must be minimized to below a whisper. Of course, the main worry is being seen. This includes taking care that none of the brush suddenly moves, should the hunter bump it. He cannot move a twig. The birds will catch quick movement like it's a magnet, so a crawling hunter must pass through cover as silently and easily as a copperhead snake. Moving when the quarry is not alert, being stone-still when it is alert, and having the patience of a 'gator watching a young deer come to water, is all necessary for a successful sneak.

Calling long-bearded gobblers during the fall and winter months is truthfully a lesson in very little calling, lots of listening, and the patience to watch a leaf turn brown. There are two situations which make calling a viable hunting method—calling separated birds, and calling adult gobblers that are roaming and feeding. Calling feeding adults is done only by a person very well acquainted with the patterns of resident gobblers. Even then the plans can go awry, as older gobblers are extremely unpredictable. Though one or several may feed for days in a cove on a mountain's flank, as sure as a hunter takes up a stand there, they could very well be feeding the next day a mile from there.

If the hunter can scatter a small gang of old gobblers, the chances become far greater to call one of them to the gun. Of course, the hunter must realize he is dealing with long-bearded turkeys, so identification is a must, along with knowing which way the scattered birds flew, how far it appears they have gone, and at what time of the day the scatter takes place. A scatter late in the afternoon could be no better than none at all, as the birds may not call so near sundown.

If the birds fly away on a like quadrant, the hunter should take after them on the dead run because they will regroup by sight quickly once they have landed. The hunter must get to where the birds appeared to be going as fast as possible, and then scour over 100 to 200 acres of the woods, always keeping in mind that regrouping adults seek high ground. This doesn't mean that the birds will go to the top of the nearest hill. If it appears they flew toward bottom land, the birds will regroup on lands up from that bottom unless it is a very large area.

Now, when speaking of regrouping in relation to adult long-bearded gobblers, this can mean simply the getting together of just two birds, or perhaps more; I have never known of older birds lolling around until all the members were together before moving off. Once old gobblers are spooked, they do not hang around the neighborhood. One or two may join up, perhaps others if they are along the trail taken to leave the area. Very often when a hunter comes up near older gobblers, and suddenly flushes them, the birds will fly away on a like quadrant, fanned out in a like direction. After the hunter has hurried to the area and worked it thoroughly, further scattering them, then it is best to go beyond the area up to a ¼-mile, take a calling stand uphill from where the birds seemed to go, and do any calling from there. Sit facing back toward the scatter area.

I would not advise making the first note for at least 15 minutes after sitting down; if the birds are in a hard hunted area, it would be best to wait ½-hour. The calling should only be an occasional cluck, with a yelp or two after the first hour. A couple hours of calling should add up to three or four clucks, and two or three yelps. Now, should your clucking be answered by a cluck, or yelp, it is very advisable to instantly call back with two or three clucks. But, *do not get carried away with the calling.* Old gobblers are shut-mouth throughout all of the year except during the spring gobbling season, so excessive calling will only arouse wariness in an answering gobbler. Once the bird has answered your calls, the gobbler knows where you are, and if he has decided to come to you, he will. If he has decided not to come to you, all of your calling, or your not calling, won't change his mind. Make yourself comfortable when you begin calling because the session may last until dark, and you may never hear a cluck, or see a feather. Forget the time. Make like a stump. Keep your gun in hand. I learned long ago that the hunting of springtime gobblers is a pushover when compared to killing old turkeys in October, November, and December. Winter campaigns against old boss turkeys are what makes hunters look forward to spring.

I guarantee you this, if you have nothing but troubles in April, you just *think* you've seen "hard times" in the turkey woods. Go back out in the woods next fall, those old birds are still there. No, there won't be any gobbling to tell you where. Now you'll know what is like to hunt a wild turkey. Why don't you throw away the camos, get an old felt hat, and a muzzle-loading shotgun and go with me. Now, you're talking. Talking turkey.

Chapter 6

Shooting Turkeys—
It's Not What
You Use, It's How
You Use It

THE CULMINATION of all the practicing on calls, reading, studying maps, scouting, and hours of hunting, is the shot itself. I can easily remember when this was absurdly simple. Back then, we shot whatever gun we were lucky enough to be using because sometimes we had to borrow one from a friend or neighbor.

My earliest "serious" shooting was at ducks, a task which my brother Dick and I tackled with unrelenting vigor. Shotshells weren't easy to come by, so when a duck flew away unscathed, the feud just grew to a fever pitch. Both of us were small, and in the early years sported .410s, mine a borrowed side-by-side with hammers and Dick's a magazine stuffer. Teal hummed around those Drummond Flats by the hundreds, and best of all, we had no competition. So when we had the hulls, we'd wage war from first light 'til last light. We soon outstripped the little guns and moved up to double-barreled 12 gauges. Duckville no longer could ignore us. With our stool of old wooden blocks, we mounted a new assault.

Duck shooting, with all its great variety of shots, probably prepares a person for a lifetime of shooting in finer style than any other sport. Pass shooting, decoying, birds running with the wind, birds heading the wind, jump shooting, you name it, all-round duck hunting offers all the shots in the books. But, beyond this, each subspecie of duck or goose flies in a different manner and reacts differently to any given situation. Some are easier to knock down than others. Add a high-balling prairie wind to all this, and you'll get to be a good shot or go home empty-handed.

Doves and quail had our undivided attention when the

ducks were elsewhere. Cottontail rabbits we hunted with .22 rifles, as the market wouldn't buy them spiced throughout with shotgun pellets. One thing about those days, each of us always had competition—each other. Twin brothers who hunt together year after year soon learn to shoot fast, and sure.

But, we never did get to choose our guns; we used what was handed us. Never questioned whether another might be better suited for the job at hand. The same old long-barreled double that was a hazard to the duck population worked equally well when busting up coveys of quail. What it boiled down to was simply, it isn't so much what kind of gun is used, as how it's used.

Turkey hunting has been much the same for me. I began killing turkeys with an old side-by-side "Monkey Wards" 12 bore, the same one I'd scotched ducks with on the Drummond Flats. It stove in old gobblers like they'd been run over with an 18-wheeler. It began coming apart, so I moved on to another double, then an over-under, then to muzzle-loaders. Throughout my guiding days, I've had to loan my gun on occasion, either because my shooter wasn't equipped properly or in a couple instances, his gun failed to arrive on the same airline flight. So, I've fallen back to carrying anything from pumps to magazine guns, 20-bores too. I am possibly the only guy in the country who has killed a strutting gobbler with a sawed-off riot gun. An Apache lawman loaned it to me after I'd given mine to a friend.

Herein lie the facts about being a good killing shot with a shotgun, or any other kind of weapon. The person holding

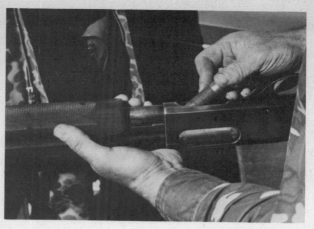

Most automatic shotguns are loaded by inserting the shells into the magazine through the bottom of the gun. Most hold five shells, though some of the newer models are limited to three. Older hunters ofttimes call these guns simply "magazine" loaders for obvious reasons.

The author's old Remington side-by-side is coming apart, but the old Indian method of patching gunstocks with rawhide is holding it together for the time being.

(Right) Today's sporting goods stores offer a variety of excellent guns for hunting wild turkeys. Roger Grove looks over one of the newer models. The short barrels allow the gun to be handled easier in brush.

the weapon must never lose sight of the fact that there are range limitations. The temptations, which will arise endlessly, those that are beyond the weapon's capabilities, must be ignored. Right here is where all but a handful of hunters fail. This is because they either don't know what the weapon will do or don't care. Too often it's a case of "maybe I'll get him." Of course, the other alternative is a crippled turkey. Lost to everyone.

If a person wants to hunt wild turkeys, then he'd do well to buy a 12-gauge . . .

Today, unlike those years back when, the hunter has limitless options in selecting whatever it is he chooses to hunt with. Shotguns, rifles, bows, crossbows, pistols—you can certainly find something to suit your fancy.

The first thing I'd advise any hunter to do is to read the regulations for whatever game he intends to hunt. What's legal, insofar as hunting weapons, varies from state to state. Numerous states have restrictions governing shot size for shotguns. Others do not allow rifles, and among those which do permit rifles, there will be regulations pertaining to legal bores, and what ammunition is legal.

Shotguns are legal throughout all the whereabouts of wild turkeys and are considered the average choice of the American turkey hunter. There doesn't seem to be any preference as to shotgun type among hunters, though from my own observations, it appears that greater numbers of hunters carry automatics and pumps than double-barrels and over-unders. Most will be bored Full choke.

The 12-bore is the hands down choice insofar as size is concerned. What all this means is that if a person wants to hunt wild turkeys, then he'd do well to buy a 12-gauge, in any style except single shot, bored Full choke, and with chambers which will take either 2¾- or 3-inch shells. Barrel length should be kept under 28 inches, as this will facilitate swinging when hunting from cramped conditions. Experienced hunters won't back themselves into such predicaments, but newcomers to the sport sometimes do. The instant a person takes a shooting stand, they should make a swing with the gun to check for clearance before getting settled. Though minor, this is an added advantage of double-barrels, as they will average out a few inches shorter than magazine guns, whether pump or automatic. Of course, this is due to the double's not having the long action found on the other two. Anytime I'm handed a magazine gun, my first reaction is to its length. Seems like a broom,

Winchester's Model 1300 Featherweight pump gun now comes with interchangeable Winchoke choke tubes and a 22-inch barrel. It's easy to tailor loads to shoot best in the gun with the choke-tube system.

Mossberg is offering the popular Model 500 pump in 12- or 20-gauge with Accu-Choke, their version of choke tubes. It is a good value for turkey hunters.

The Ithaca Mag 10 autoloader is heavy, but in the short barrel version this 10-gauge Magnum would be a real turkey killer in the woods.

The Browning BPS "Buck Special" has rifle-type sights that can be a great aid to the turkey hunter. The gun also comes with the Invector choke-tube system and is available in either 12- or 20-gauge.

Remington is enticing turkey hunters with their Model 870 pump (above) and 1100 auto "Special Purpose" guns (below). Both are bored for 12-gauge, have 3-inch Magnum chambers and come with non-glare finish on both metal and wood. Vent rib and camouflage sling are standard.

and balanced about as badly. Of course, I was raised with doubles and use them to this day. Men who have grown of age with a pump feel likewise on throwing a double to cheek I am sure.

Almost all of the major shotgun manufacturers have come out with guns suitable for the turkey hunter. Winchester has the Model 1300 pump with a 22-inch barrel which uses the Winchoke system. The barrels have a non-glare matte finish, and the stock and fore-end are also finished with non-glaring surfaces. Browning offers their BPS

pump, the 24-inch barrel complete with Invector chokes, and it's available in both 12 and 20 bore, both taking either 2¾- or 3-inch Magnum loads. Mossberg also has their Model 500, sporting a 28-inch barrel with the Accu-Choke choke system.

Remington decided turkey hunting was here to stay, so they went after the market in true Remington fashion. They have the 870 and the 1100 Special Purpose guns, both with 22-inch and 26-inch barrels (respectively) bored 12-gauge, and with Magnum chambers to receive the 3-inch loads.

These babies have Full-choke barrels, vent ribs, and sport a camouflaged sling. Barrels and receivers have a non-glare finish. The stock and fore-end are oil finished so these areas won't be apt to throw back a glint to an old gobbler's eye, spooking him into the next county.

Ithaca is offering a Magnum 10-gauge autoloader, bored Full choke, which comes in 26-inch barrel length. This young cannon would be heavy to anyone who is accustomed to toting doubles, but it should be very lethal in the turkey woods.

A hunter searching for an answer to "what-gun-to-buy-for-turkeys?" will notice the numerous guns sporting short barrel lengths. Though this will be a decided advantage in bringing the gun to bear on an advancing gobbler when surrounding brush and tree branches are a problem, anyone buying such a gun should definitely make plans to do extensive patterning before firing it at a turkey. Short shotgun barrels seem to result in many hunters shooting high, moreso as the range is extended. In fact, a gunner not accustomed to the short sighting plane is apt to be off target when the gun is fired. Certainly such short-barreled guns are not made for long-range shooting at moving objects. Of course, any turkey hunter worthy of a gobbler will pattern a gun whether new or old prior to heading to the woods. Moreso each time he buys a box of shells not previously tried in his gun.

I'm not going to tell anyone what kind of gun to use.

The only thing I ask is that, to quote Robert Ruark, "use enough gun." Twenty-gauges, .410s, 28-bores, these are not for the average turkey hunter. Some folks slight of build, or disabled, may have to use such guns, but I would definitely say they are further handicapped by using them. My grandson killed his first few gobblers with a .410, but just as soon as he could handle it, his dad, Tom Preston, and I put a 12-gauge in his hands.

Today's hunter can choose from a tremendous selection of shotguns, and among the options will be camouflage finishes and detachable slings. And, there are magazine guns with sights front and rear, much like those found on rifles. Front and rear sights would certainly be an advantage for many hunters, particularly those who don't have the opportunity to spend many hours on the shooting range before season. Double sights will keep the barrel aligned, preventing the gun from shooting to one side or the other. Misalignment is easily done by a person less experienced in gun handling, moreso under the stress of actual hunting. Add to this a gobbler angling toward the gun, and the pounding of the heart.

Camouflaged gun finishes are not a surprise anymore, and obviously eliminate a problem which many hunters worry about—gun glare, barrel shine, whatever you want to call it. Though I have never consciously been concerned with this problem, I have developed a set of habits which take gun glare into consideration. Keeping in shadows,

The folks at sporting goods stores are always ready to help a customer with any questions about equipment which is available. Roger Groves, owner of Groves Outdoor Sports in Enid, Oklahoma, talks with Scott Maloney about the latest things in turkey hunting gear.

(Right) The difference in camouflage (and lack of it) is starkly evident when looking at these two guns standing side by side. A great many turkey hunters have used the stick-on tape, which is removable if the hunter no longer needs it on a gun. Too, it's easily replaceable.

(Above) Greg Butts, a lifelong hunter and one-time Texas game specialist, hunts with a side-by-side double-barreled shotgun. Such a gun gives him the instant choice of two choke bores, and two different loads, if he so desires. For easier carrying while afield, particularly when toting a big gobbler from the woods, Greg's double sports a sling. Its quick-detachable swivels allow him to remove it just before shooting.

keeping the gun at my side, laying it across my lap, are some of the habits that come to mind. Though I realize it's not always so, I would like to think that the only thing a turkey will see of my gun are the two holes at the end of the barrels. And, when he sees them, then it's too late.

Anyone who's ever let the hammer down on one of those big, gobblers will be glad to have a sling . . .

Slings? On shotguns? For a turkey hunter, who at the end of the hunt should be toting a turkey, there isn't anything better. And, a sling leaves your hands free to use binoculars, scale a dirt bank, or use a pair of walking sticks to wade a fast stream. Some slings are little more than a leather strap which ties or loops around the barrel or stock. Others have quick-detachable mounts, allowing the sling to be taken off and stored in a pocket.

I wouldn't advise a person to keep a strap on a gun while shooting if he hasn't tried this beforehand. It can become easily tangled, especially if the hunter is sitting in or near brush and attempts to bring the gun to bear on an approaching bird; the sling catches. When shooting from a standing position, the weight of the sling beneath the barrel could cause a miss, especially if the hunter has been moving and the sling is still swinging slightly at the shot. I long ago made it a habit to catch and hold the sling in my right hand (being left-handed) where my hand grips the fore-end of the gun. Thus with the slack taken up the sling cannot

swing. Anyone who's ever let the hammer down on one of those big old Ozark ridge running gobblers will be mighty glad to have a sling on the gun while carrying the turkey, being as it is probably three hills and four "hollers" back to the truck. Try it, you'll like it.

Supposing you got a fine modern shotgun, shoots 3-inch shells, you got her "camo'd," and a good stout leather sling. What's the best turkey killer you can stuff into "Old Sue Betsy?" I don't think a hunter could do better than to load up with a 3-inch load of copper-coated, buffered No. 6s, followed up with a like load in No. 4 shot. All of my friends are using these loads today on tough, feathered game birds such as ducks, geese, and wild turkeys. The bulk of the new turkey guns are chambered to take 3-inch hulls, therefore allowing these to be loaded with the extremely lethal loads manufactured today. Just one step down would be the 2¾-inch "baby magnum" that so many of us have been loading for these many, many years. These high-velocity shells have been a boon to shotgunners, though I am certain a great number of older shotguns may have been ruined as continued use can result in the gun's loosening about the receiver and/or chambers. I've relegated two old model doubles to the bonepile as a result of shooting the baby mags, but I considered the end results in game killed to be worth the sacrifice. Anyone shooting these high-powered loads should never lose sight of the risk involved both to shotgun and shotgunner, though apparently this has been all but eliminated nowadays. The modern shotgun is built to withstand the punishment of the modern load. True, when fired, some of these handheld cannons have a healthy kick, but it requires a man-sized gun to do a man-sized job.

Time was when the hunter went into a store to pick up

A favorite shotshell load of many hunters is a Winchester "baby magnum," with No. 5 shot. These lethal loads are made for use in all guns with 2¾-inch chambers. Other favored loads are in equivalent shells, but of No. 4 or 6 shot sizes.

(Left) Slouch camo hat, army web sling, army surplus camos, and a snap-on gun cover keep this hunter ready for the ponderosa pines of New Mexico's turkey slopes. Hunter Darrell Giacomelli's gloves have the fingers cut off which allows him a sure "feel" and easy operation of the gun.

Almost all shotshell makers have loads which are excellent for the killing of wild turkeys. Longtime hunters agree that the best shot sizes are 4s, 5s, and 6s. Though the ammunition people extoll the virtues of loads that will kill at long range, the hunter who knows what he is doing never needs to shoot at turkeys at long range. Instead, he waits until the bird is inside of 30 yards before shooting.

(Right) Lennis Rose, a "flinter" turkey hunter from Washburn, Missouri, examines the flints on his custom built side-by-side shotgun. Flintlocks are seldom seen in the turkey woods, as the lag time between trigger pull and the shot getting to the mark can cause a miss when dealing with game so wary and fast as wild turkeys.

a box of shells, and didn't know what to buy for turkeys. He was told that according to the chart put out by "so-and-so" ammunition company, the best thing for turkeys were the smaller size buckshots, No. 2s and BBs. 'Course, the folks that made shotgun shells didn't know anything about turkey hunting back in those days either. They just assumed that anything as big as a turkey would need a lot of killing, so they thought this called for big pellets. Thankfully, this has come to an end. Nowadays, the people who make shotgun loads will recommend 6s and 4s and, perhaps as a last resort, No. 2s should an unlucky hunter have a cripple escaping at long range.

I went through the same learning process. I'd put in a lifetime in the pneumonia holes which have ofttimes been erroneously referred to as duck and goose blinds, and realizing what kind of load it took to regularly bring down a winter-coated honker, I began turkeyin' with size 2 shot. My mistake was not giving thought to the fact that a wing-broke gobbler can't be run to earth as can a goose with a busted wing, or even one which is wing-tipped. I soon switched to No. 4 shot, then as I became a turkey caller, to 6s and 7s.

Too many of today's supposed expert hunters are recommending long-range shooting. However, the very essence of turkey hunting is in making a killing shot at near

range. The greater the hunter's abilities, the more easily this is accomplished. There is no reason for a hunter to take shots at 50 yards unless he has no faith in his prowess to reduce this range.

I have been hunting turkeys with old-time vintage muzzle-loading shotguns for several years. Scatterguns, I call them, as these old guns have little choke boring. I don't recommend anyone hunt with original black powder guns unless they have been thoroughly checked over by a gunsmith. Many old originals may not be safe today, even with standard slow-burning black powder. If you want to shoot black powder, buy one of the modern replicas. I took on the use of such guns just to prove to myself what it was like for the hunters back in the good old days.

Range has become the most important consideration for me with such a gun in hand. I have experimented with various combinations of powder and shot and wads to no end, constantly trying to work out a combination which would let me have some leeway beyond 30 yards. But to this day I must limit my shots inside of this distance, resulting in shots at the bulk of my birds inside of 20 yards. Previously, I had been pulling the trigger at the 30-yard mark, when hefting one of my modern shotguns. With the muzzleloaders, turkey hunting certainly took on a greater degree of excitement. Of course, at such point blank ranges there are no cripples. But knowing the gun's limitations beyond the 30-yard mark, I realize that should a bird attempt to escape, I must make the effort to prevent it inside of that distance. With modern shotguns, the serious, considerate hunter must try for the killing shot at 10 yards inside of what he considers to be his gun's killing range, so that he will always have the chance to put a backup load to work while it is at its most effective range. Too often a hunter will try for a gobbler at long distance, and then when the bird is suddenly transformed into an escaping cripple, the backup shot is taken at too long a range with little or no result. Escaped cripples are seldom found.

If the hunter is not expert in its use, he won't hit what he's aiming at . . .

Patterning is the only answer to knowing what load is best for anyone serious about turkey hunting. No two loads shoot exactly alike, nor do two similar guns. Patterning will bring to light what loads are best, along with what positions the hunter should use in getting time-after-time killing shots. Old style side-by-side shotguns have what many of us term as English stocks, which means that the gun is smooth and continuous at the wrist, without today's ever present pistol grip. Such guns were made strictly for wing shooting, the style lending itself best to shooting at moving objects. Today's modern shotgun with its pistol-grip stock and often raised barrel rib with both forward and rear sights, seems to be made to shoot more like a rifle.

Of course, in the beginning, while searching out the best load, the hunter should shoot from a benchrest to maintain a steady sight on the pattern paper. Only after ascertaining which load is best should the hunter then begin shooting from various positions to learn about his shotgun's point of aim and pattern center, while simulating actual hunting shots.

The person who has made up his mind to shoot within predetermined ranges, and who has the guts and personal fortitude to do so, will invariably choose small shot, 6s or 7s, for his first load to be launched at a turkey. His shot will be close, inside of 25 yards, probably at a standing bird. Even if the bird is flying or running, the dense pattern of such tiny pellets will bring an instant kill. Any wise all-round turkey hunter, one who hunts both spring and winter seasons across all the country's numerous terrains, learned long ago that it is pattern density which kills wild turkeys. Such a hunter will encounter all sorts of shots throughout a year's time, and will learn that the gun is but an extension of the arm. However, only through continuous use and handling will a gun become an entirely dependable and familiar tool. The young or inexperienced gun handler should make every effort to shoot as often as resources will allow in order to become a master shot. Don't ever lose

sight of the fact that though the "fast gun" was a part of the Old West, the honcho who wrote an end to many gun-slinging careers was maybe not as fast, but he hit what he shot at. It doesn't matter a whit how fine a gun a person is carrying, nor what lethal loads it is stoked with; if the hunter is not expert in its use, he won't hit what he's aiming at.

Try several brands of loads on the patterning papers, and once you have chosen a couple which seem best suited to your gun, then try them at varying distances. If these loads continue to hold up to expectations, it's time to take shots at the bull's-eye from various shooting stances but without any rest. Shoot from the offhand, standing, or sitting po-

If this pattern is any indication, this boy's small .410-gauge shotgun is anything but a lethal turkey gun. None of the shot string has entered the circled aiming point on the paper plate.

sitions, or while stretched out on your belly in the prone position. Very often the results of such position shooting will tell a person if the point of aim jibes with the center of the pattern on the patterning papers. Sometimes an off-center pattern is the shooter's fault, due to an improper hold on the gun or by simply misaligning the sight(s) (if any). Rifle-type sights or front and rear beads on the shotgun can go a long way in eliminating this problem. Cheaply made guns can also be to blame, as well as a bent barrel, but just because a gun isn't expensive doesn't mean that it won't shoot straight. Some fine, very costly shotguns may not print their patterns where they're pointed, too. It all boils down to the fact that whatever gun your budget allows, be it cheap or expensive, shoot it, pattern it, try it out before taking it into turkey woods. If the gun won't perform, you've wasted time, effort and money if you can't hit a bull in the behind with it.

I got into camp, back in Chihuahua, Mexico, late one night, so I didn't have a chance to pattern a borrowed gun

I was using before going up on the mesa the next morning. The over-under was made in Brazil and didn't fit me even though I had removed the buttplate down to bare raw wood. Sure enough, I called in an old Mexican gobbler that first morn and missed him coming and going. Didn't touch him. Like I've heard jokers remark about over-and-unders, "you shot over it the first time, and under it the second."

Taking the gun out to where I could shoot at a dirt wall, I only had to run a couple hulls through it to learn that, indeed, it was shooting over the mark. Way over it. My next opportunity to shoot was at a drove and this time I laid a bird out with each tube. I just compensated in the

The serious turkey hunter will spend a considerable amount of time in learning how and where his gun shoots, and what loads it shoots best. These gunners are examining the results of patterns fired on "flying" targets drawn on pieces of cardboard.

(Left) Young people should be taught the basics of handling firearms when small. That way they will develop safe gun handling habits as they mature. Hunting is a great sport and we must promote it every chance we get. These youngsters will grow up with a great appreciation of our game and the out-of-doors.

Ed LaForce studies a cut out cardboard turkey head which has been nailed onto a long narrow board, placed in heavy brush, and shot much as a person would shoot at a turkey. Shots can be made from sitting, standing, prone, and crouching positions, the results telling the hunter if his shooting will be correct when actually shooting at turkeys.

sighting, and instead of aiming at the bird's head, I held on the upper chest. I've been killing birds with it ever since.

Before a person quits shooting at paper, there is one last test—shooting paper turkeys. If you can't draw a reasonable facsimile of a turkey on a large hunk of cardboard or paper, turkey targets can often be purchased at sporting goods outlets. Shots taken at varying ranges will soon tell a hunter if the gun and loads are up to the task of killing the birds. Again, shots should be made from various shooting positions. It may be that there will be a position which the hunter should refrain from using in the field, or one from which he must take extra precautions. Having witnessed so many hunters miss easy shots at standing turkeys from a sitting position, there are obviously quite a few people who can't shoot while not standing upright. Again, it is familiarity with the gun which pays off when a feathered bird takes the place of the paper one.

Just for kicks, or if a bunch of you are out for an afternoon shoot and want to wager a few bucks on whose gun

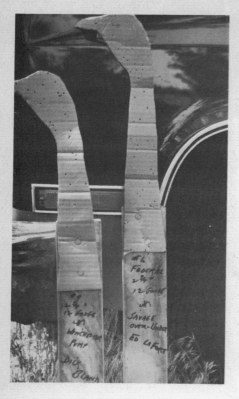

These comparisons indicate that both of these hunters are using shotshells which are deadly on wild turkeys. Dick Bland was using the left head as an aiming point, Ed La-Force was aiming at the middle of the neck. Both were shooting Full-choke barrels at 30 yards. One hunter preferred No. 4 shot, while the other used No. 6s.

Dick Bland examines a cardboard simulation of a turkey's head which he has just shot. The hunter who tries various brands and shot sizes of shells in his gun will soon learn that none of them react alike. The best patterning load is the one the hunter wants to use.

is the best for gobblers, cut out the outline of a gobbler's head and neck, tack these to tall stakes, and take a shot. Walk off a 30- or 40-yard range and then count the shot that hit the mark. If these affairs are impromptu, just for good times, not only will such an afternoon provide a lot of laughs, but it's a sure bet that somebody will head for home determined to find a better load. "Old Sue Betsy" just didn't put 'em in there like she was supposed to do. There is nothing like proof.

Should the hunter have interchangeable or adjustable chokes, patterning will reveal which choke is desirable afield. Suppose the hunter must make most shots at close range due to terrain features. It could be entirely possible that a Full-choked barrel would be too restrictive, resulting in a too-tight pattern at near ranges. In such restrictive situations, another choke tube (or setting) might be of advantage.

Most double-barreled shotguns have two different choices of choke, the bulk of them being bored Modified and Full. The right-hand tube is usually bored Modified, while the left-hand is Full choke. A few of the newer guns on today's market are available with interchangeable choke tubes, like the autos, pumps and over-unders. I think we'll be seeing more guns offered this way in the near future. A gunner using a shotgun with two triggers has instant choke selection between the two. Those who carry such guns into the turkey woods have made it a habit to fire the Full-choke barrel, the back trigger, first. On close shots, I've had hunters tell me they then went back using the Modified barrel, or front trigger, first which is the natural way to shoot a double with two triggers.

As with all guns, doubles, be they over-unders or side-by-sides, definitely should be patterned. Anyone not acquainted with the sighting picture presented by a side-by-side will need to spend time on the trap or Skeet range to be able to acquire the proper sight picture. Likewise, a person who has handled a double will be surprised when handling a pump or autoloader, as gun weight is not distributed in the same manner. Nor will a hunter who is unaccustomed to a pump gun be able to reload quickly.

So why take the chance? Hidden well, I stayed put, scarcely daring to breathe . . .

It has been my good fortune to shoot wild turkeys with all sorts of guns. At one time or other I have hunted with magazine loaders, pump-actions, over-unders, side-by-sides, a single shot, and a sawed-off Winchester pump riot shotgun. Gauges have been 20s and 12s, while shot size has varied from No. 4 buckshot (loaned with the gun) to tiny No. 8s. All killed wild turkeys, but with several I realized the handicaps present and took action accordingly. For instance, one fall afternoon I felt it best to loan a visiting hunter my old 12 bore, which resulted in my having to shoulder the little 20-gauge over-under I used for quail and doves. Worse yet, the only loads I was packing along were low-brass 8s, definitely low-velocity quail loads, not shotshells intended for killing turkey gobblers.

I had a chance to shoot that day and did, but only after getting the adult gobbler into short range, perhaps 12 or 13 yards. The tiny pellets riddled his head like a pin cushion. Likewise, when I was forced to borrow an Apache lawman's riot gun, I waited until the old Merriam gobbler was inside 15 yards. I realized that if I needed a second shot, it would have to be inside of 25 yards, but even then, I presumed the riot gun might not hold any pattern. And, as I was not used to pumping a shotgun to reload, I would need extra yards should this be a necessity. But, the bird hit the ground like a sack of mush, so no second shot was forthcoming.

Too many hunters take long-range shots which are chancy, to say the least, resulting in too many crippled birds. Today's ammunition manufacturers have put too much emphasis on long-range shotshells, glorifying loads which they say kill consistently at ranges beyond 50 yards. The average American turkey hunter, like the bulk of this country's shotgun addicts, shoot nowhere near enough loads each season to become expert with a gun, so will never be able to hit or kill consistently at 50 yards. Even on standing shots. But what must be kept in mind is that should the 50-yard shot result in a crippled bird, what opportunity does the gunner have for a second back-up load? This back-up shot will then be between 60 and 70 yards, far beyond a reliable range, so the cripple will escape.

Why shoot at a wild turkey at 50 yards? Ask yourself this question. *Why?* There are several reasons why some hunters shoot at turkeys at long range. Many have not observed turkeys but a few times, so they don't know what one looks like at 20, 40, 60 or even 80 yards. Others simply don't care. These are the folks who will shoot at a turkey just as far as they can see. Some hunters fear the bird will escape, so they take long-range shots, hoping they can make a lucky kill. (And, the bird does escape, though wounded.)

A great many hunters, including many so-called expert and veteran turkey hunters, have little faith in their own abilities. Having had birds slip away on other occasions, they begin taking longer and longer shots, hoping to justify these with a kill from time to time—a "nothing ventured, nothing gained" philosophy. I have often thought that if there is anything in turkey hunting which will test a hunter's mettle, it is to watch a turkey that has closed to within 50 yards of the hunter's gun walk away. Passing up a shot is tough. Watching a cripple run and stumble as it escapes into heavy woods is much tougher.

This past spring I was calling a gobbler which came into view strutting and gobbling, and when he passed behind a clump of skunkbrush, I brought the gun to bear, cocking both hammers. Looking down the rib between the two barrels, I studied the bird. Forty yards, 35, near 30. Suddenly,

(Above) The author's black powder shotgun bowls over a turkey at close range. These birds are tough, so they should be enticed to within 25 yards before shooting, regardless of what type of shotgun is being used.

Crawling on hands and knees is often the only way to sneak within easy shooting distance of turkeys. This can sometimes be pulled off if the hunter will remember to stick a mouth call into place before attempting the stalk. Then, if the bird should detect a slight movement of the hunter, it can often be kept there by calling until the hunter gets into range.

Hunting wild turkeys with a muzzle-loading shotgun in sagebrush and sandhills is a true challenge to a hunter's abilities. Conrad Vollertsen, of Sand Springs, Oklahoma, downed this bird when it flushed suddenly. All shots with muzzle-loading shotguns must be at close range, as these guns do not have the excellent chokes of modern shotguns.

Tiny snow flakes fall as Diane Mellilo poses for the camera with a grand Merriam gobbler. Today, more than ever before, women are taking up turkey hunting as a gunning sport. Diane is a dedicated hunter having taken Eastern, Rio Grande, and Merriam wild turkeys with her Browning over-under.

he stopped, then turned and walked from my view to the left. No, he hadn't spooked, but apparently had chosen another path. I could have shot, but my old muzzleloader doesn't pattern well at 35 yards, so why take the chance. Hidden well, I stayed put, scarcely daring to breathe. Three or four minutes passed. Zero. Straining, I listened for the strut. *Gobble-obble-obble*. The old rascal cut loose some 11 or 12 yards to my right rear. He'd circled me. It was no trouble to ease the gun back, bring it around, take a fine bead, and kill the bird. Backed into the dark confines of a dense conifer, the bird was aware of my actions, but could not decipher them soon enough. My holding back on a chancy shot had resulted in an easy sure kill.

I attribute the long-range chance shots many hunters take to some bad experiences they've had when the birds were in close, or while the bird was walking to close range. After such experiences, there are many hunters who decide to take the chance, even if the shot is at 40 or 50 yards. Having been a hunting guide for many years, I know what goes wrong in some instances. Too often it is a simple lack of knowing how to handle the gun. On many occasions I have called birds to within 20 yards of where another hunter and myself were hidden, but upon telling him to shoot, watched as he fumbled the gun into position. Nor could some hunters take quick sure aim, but wrote figure eights in the sky as the barrel wobbled. Others couldn't shoot while sitting down, but had to stand. (Whereon the turkey was not sitting either but making tracks for faraway places.) Under such circumstances, I have seen turkeys run and fly away unscathed after one, two, even three shots in their general direction. This not only is disconcerting to a person who has laid money on the line for just such an opportunity, but

also will not endear the hunter to a guide who has worked his fanny off to make the shot possible. There have been times when I have had to fight off an urge to strangle a client who missed. Conversely, there have been times the hunter with me has shown extraordinary coolness, then backed this up with a fine killing shot. A hunt back into Arizona's White Mountains illustrates my point to the utmost degree.

Three of us, my wife Stella, Diane Mellilo and I had climbed a cold mountainside just as day was breaking, taking care to walk around the crunchy drifts of snow scattered among the huge ponderosas. Stella and Diane had heard a bird gobble up toward the mountain's long ridge-like crest, though I'd not heard the sound because of a tumbling mountain brook. Soon, working our way upward, I heard the bird sound off, too. Placing us on a straight line between the bird and the meadow that was along the slope's base, I situated Diane in a commanding position. She would be doing the shooting. Diane had hunted with me earlier. I'd learned then she was a dedicated hunter, committed to making each shot count. Merriam turkeys often have a habit of going downhill from the roost tree, so I was not concerned about getting above them. Hens had begun clucking so I knew there was company for the gobbler. My tree calls soon switched over to lusty yelping with simulated wing flapping added (done by beating a cap on a sleeve or pants leg). Turkeys do much flapping and re-arranging of feathers, once they've gone to ground. The quiet mountain air amplified the sounds. Two gobblers were sounding off, answering my calls, gobbling time after time.

Shortly, their gobbling seemed nearer and nearer. Stella was hunkered behind me against the massive pine on which

I leaned with Diane around the trunk to my right. I could sense her awareness when she whispered, "See them, two of them, two gobblers." White-pated heads glowing in the dark, I had picked them up just as she spoke, both birds making their way toward us. Range, 50 yards, but closing fast. Nowhere was a hen in sight. Both Diane and I had tags, so I whispered to her, "When I say to shoot, you take the bird on your right, I'll stick to the one on the left after your shot. Don't make a move until I say so, then bring the gun up smoothly, but don't jerk." At 30 yards the birds parted, one easing to the left, headed directly at me, while the other cut around to the right. What an excellent situation. I could not have planned it better.

But, upon asking Diane if she had a clear shot, she whispered that the bird was behind brush, and an intervening pine. I waited a few seconds, all the while watching the gobbler coming at me on the left. Range, 15 yards. Huge, black, and in half-strut, he seemed as large as a barn.

"Diane, can you shoot yet?"

"No," came the soft answer. "He's still behind the tree."

My bird had stopped at 11 or 12 yards—now standing erect, obviously listening to our whispered conversation.

Suddenly from the corner of my eye I sensed Diane's gun coming to her shoulder in a long clean move. "Now, I can see him." Her gun barked, and in the same instant I brought my side-by-side into play. My bird ducked to run at my first shot, and as I touched the trigger, I realized I had shot over the old bird. My second was no better. Another miss as the bird scrambled among the brush, dodging back and forth. A clean miss!

That was unimportant for now. What was important was that Diane's bird was thrashing on the pine straw. "Old One-Shot" had done it again. Diane had handled the situation like a veteran turkey hunter. She made not the tiniest move throughout, biding the time when she could make the one killing shot. Then, when that time came, she went into action in smooth, clean moves which would not spook the bird into taking any sudden, swift escaping actions. Too, the bird was very close, was wide open for the shot, and had it been needed, she would have had the opportunity for a second backup shot. But with close range shots, very seldom is a backup load needed. Diane is a longtime deer hunter, most recently bagging a fine eight-point buck with a flintlock rifle. Being aware of how a gun must fit a person, she hunts turkeys with a 26-inch-barreled over-under. With its short action, this gun is small in overall length, which is what a person of Diane's size needs, as she is small and slight of build. From a sitting or standing position, she can handle the gun with confidence. A 12-bore, shooting the standard 2¾-inch load, the Browning is a match for any turkey. Diane has the experience to know how to use it and when.

Few black powder hunters wear old-time clothing while hunting turkeys because the birds are more apt to see them than if the hunter is wearing camouflage clothing. When you consider that the bird should also be closer than for smokeless shotguns, this makes the task doubly tough.

I've hunted many years with muzzleloaders, and it has made me a deadlier hunter . . .

What about hunting turkeys with a muzzle-loading shotgun? Great! This is down-to-earth, old-time turkey hunting at its very best, particularly if the hunter dresses in dull, drab clothing much like what our great-great grandfathers might have donned.

I've hunted wild turkeys for many years with muzzleloaders, and I can truthfully say that it has made a deadlier hunter of me. This is because I have worked hard at drawing the birds into close range before shooting which, together with no longer wearing camos, has caused me to take advantage of the tiniest bits of cover, to learn when to make moves, and all of the other habits which make a woodsman.

As for the gun itself, I would recommend anyone interested in purchasing such a gun should study the guns offered by various black powder manufacturers in the latest *Gun Digest* (DBI Books, Inc.), edited by my old buddy, Ken Warner. These are well-made guns, manufactured from modern metals and with choking. With proper loading, and some experimenting with various loads, all will

When shooting a muzzle-loading shotgun, there's always a dense cloud of smoke after the shot. It's often advisable to jump and run through the smoke to make certain the bird has not been crippled and is escaping.
(Below) Lennis Rose pours a measure of black powder from a powder horn, which he will then pour down one barrel of the shotgun. Care must be taken to insure placing the powder in the proper barrel and not double-charging one of them.

When patterning or target shooting, the hunter should try all possible positions which may be used in the field. Sometimes this will change the sight picture and alert the hunter that he shouldn't use that particular stance in a hunting situation.

kill wild turkeys. Of course, shooting patterns with a muzzleloader is not as easy as opening the breech and sticking in a couple of shells. Patterning takes time, and it is best to try several combinations of wads, overshot and overpowder cardboards, along with various weights of shot and powder. In doing this, the shooter will become more familiar with the gun, and once he begins the actual hunt, this familiarity will lend the confidence a good turkey hunter must have. I would highly recommend anyone who is interested in hunting with black powder to read Sam Fadala's excellent book, *The Complete Black Powder Handbook* (DBI Books, Inc.).

Safety is always a factor when shooting black powder and a person can't be too careful in its use. But after shooting it for a time, safe habits will build, ensuring that the guns are loaded properly and will shoot when the trigger is pulled. Black powder burns just a tad slower than modern powder, so there is a fractional time lag at trigger pull, which can be disconcerting to anyone shooting at moving

targets. Until a hunter becomes used to the slower velocity of a black powder shot column, he is apt to shoot behind a moving object.

Also, since shooting a black powder firearm sends forth a cloud of white smoke, shooting at a turkey with such a gun is much like shooting a single shot—you make the first shot count, because you may not be able to see the bird well enough for a second shot.

Black powder turkey hunting is one gunning sport where experience counts. A person can't be too careful in readying a gun for hunting, especially removing moisture, and particularly gun oil, before loading. This thorough wiping must not only apply to the inside of the barrels, but also to the area within the nipple's firing ports, and the area where the nipples screw into the barrels. Any moisture which might be left could "taint" the powder charge, causing the gun to misfire. The percussion caps must be kept dry. I've learned it is best to put new ones on the nipples each morning, even in dry weather.

Anytime a person has a misfire, the gun should be treated the same as though it could fire any second, since there is always a chance of a hangfire, or the gun igniting late. So keep the gun pointed where it can do no harm for the moment, taking precautions to never point the barrel toward anyone at any time, including yourself. After any black powder gun has been fired, it is best to blow down the barrel, or through the nipple, as this will "burn off" any spark which might remain. If a hunter is shooting a double-barrel, play it safe. Remove the percussion cap from the unfired barrel before doing this, and/or reloading the fired barrel.

The actual shooting of a called-in gobbler with a black powder shotgun has no equal, at least to me. As the bird draws near, I will ask myself if I've done a good job of loading, am I well hidden, and am I in a position where the bird must come close, inside of 20 yards? I want the bird close because the smoke after firing the first barrel obscures my view of the turkey for a second or two, and if it is just crippled, I won't be able to get in the second shot quickly. No matter what a person hunts turkeys with, there will be a time when one will be crippled, so it is best to take this into consideration *before* it happens.

Getting the bird into near range is easy when wearing camouflage, but without it, calling a wary old gobbler to inside of 20 yards is akin to knowing what it feels like to be "naked as a jaybird." I've had birds see me before getting to where I could make a safe killing shot, and they

ran off for the next county. It will probably happen again, but I make every effort to choose shooting locations which will give me greater use of natural cover in keeping a turkey from seeing me. Of course, the hammers should be cocked before the bird comes into range.

I'd taken a stand in a silly place— a stump hole surrounded with huckleberry bushes . . .

Locating ranks number one when considering the problems facing a hunter who has called a turkey approaching his stand. Thousands of turkeys have been saved from a hunter's gun because the hunter has chosen a bad place from where to attempt the final shot. A bad location can mean an area of too much intervening terrain or one with too little cover and the hunter is detected. It can also be a place where circling birds prevent the hunter from bringing the gun to bear, or a spot where a wild turkey just will not go into.

Too much intervening terrain (brush, trees, rocks, hills, etc.) result in the hunter not being able to make a killing shot because either he is not able to see the bird, or if it is seen, is unable to shoot for fear the cover will stop the shot charge. I can easily recall Allen Jenkins and I sneaking to

(Left) Young in years, but old in the ways of wild turkeys, Jeff Butts lovingly admires his vintage muzzle-loading shotgun. Jeff has bagged a number of turkeys with this 14-gauge, thanks to his extensive knowledge of the gun through patterning, plus hours of getting used to it. Though slightly mottled from age, this old shotgun shows excellent care, the hammers shiny, and the engraving crisp.

The muzzle-loading rifle can be decorated to suit a hunter's wishes. This modern Kentucky, a gift to the author, has an inlaid turkey gobbler on the cheekpiece-side of the stock. The gun is a work of art.

The author shoots many turkeys from the laydown, or prone, position as seen here. It is rare that Bland shoots a bird while leaning back against a tree, as the position doesn't allow enough upper body freedom for pivoting from the waist. Turkeys will approach a hunter with much less wariness if the hunter is in the prone position because the hunter is all but impossible to see. Often the bird will walk within 10 to 15 yards.

(Left) Though this hunter is sitting in front of a large tree trunk, as long as he sits quietly wild game won't notice him. With knees drawn up before him, he can take aim across them for a long period of time without tiring, if necessary. There are no nearby bushes which might hinder his shooting. And, with his vision obstructed to a degree in all directions, a wild gobbler will need to come within shooting range before being able to locate the place where this hunter's calling has come from.

within very close shooting range of a group of birds, only to find we couldn't get a clear shot. We never did, though we watched those birds for at least 20 minutes. On leaving, the bunch walked due away from us. Of course, this was not due to locating poorly, but it had the same results. Probably at the range of 20 yards we could have made a kill. But, what if we crippled a bird?

I can recall but one gobbler I did not shoot because I had located where too much brush prevented me from either seeing and/or shooting. The bird's gobbles told me he was within 15 to 20 yards. This was high on a heavily treed ridge in Mississippi with the terrain cloaked in vines, briars, bushes, various trees, and some down-cover. I'd taken a stand in a silly place—a stump hole surrounded with huckleberry bushes. I never made the mistake again.

Down through the years I have heard, and read, that a hunter should never locate in thickets, canebrakes, etc., all of these being exceedingly thick coverts made up of small-sized poles of varying heights with very often a low overhead canopy. I want to modify this statement: Do not locate in one of these areas *if you insist that the called-to turkey must come into the cover*. I have known times when a bird would enter bad, thick undergrowth, but ordinarily it will not do so. If the hunter will locate within easy gunshot of the edge of such cover, a killing shot can be made on turkeys walking its edge. Many's the time I have taken a calling stand inside a stand of manzanita, French mulberry, huckleberry, and such, and once in the heart of a stand of lemonade sumac. I have called turkeys on several occasions alongside all but impenetrable thickets of switch willows. Such thick terrain offers complete screening for the

hunter, who can easily make a shot from the confines. Don't confuse this type of cover with thickets of shinnery oak, Gambel's oak, or Mexican blue oak. Wild turkeys enter these readily, as the understory is rather open, allowing the birds to feed on the acorns and other mast. These oaks seldom have trunks of any size, due to so many of them growing in close proximity. As such, the trunks of these thicket-oaks do little to hide the hunter leaning against them. I have ofttimes hunted from the prone position when calling from these areas after leaf fall.

Anyone hunting from thick cover must be patient and

wait until a clear shot presents itself. One of my old turkey hunting buddies, Ed LaForce, has on two different occasions shot down small trees while hunting behind saplings. One was an oak, the second, ash. Both were severed and fell to the ground. This was good luck for the turkeys which escaped. In both instances the saplings were only a few feet from the gun's muzzle.

Walking around a bend on a backwoods trail one afternoon in northern Arkansas, I spied a gobbler hotfooting for the next county. Throwing the old muzzleloader to shoulder, I set loose a charge at exactly the same time the bird sped into a thicket of sassafras. I didn't get the bird. Noting that one of the saplings was leaning, I entered the small copse of trees, and you guessed it, the shot string had blown away one side of the trunk.

Cottontail rabbits were underfoot in all the weed patches when I was a young boy, so my brother Dick and I hunted them every chance we got. We could make a little money by selling them to grocery stores. We soon learned that grass and leaves had no effect on the .22 Shorts we were using on the bunnies. Later, shotgunning quail as they blasted upward through the tops of blackjack oaks, we realized that it was wise to follow through on birds that slipped behind leafy covers. Shoot, and then watch for the bird to tumble back to earth. Leaves have little effect on a shot string.

So, when I can discern the skulking shadow of a wild turkey behind a light screen of leaves or tall grass, and the range is 20 to 25 yards, I don't hesitate firing. I never use shot larger than No. 5s. The bulk of the time I am loading No. 6s, and when I am hunting near much huckleberry, tend toward stoking the gun with smaller 7½-size shot. My shots will be within the 25-yard mark, very often near 20 yards.

I have often thought that a great many turkeys are missed for the simple reason that a turkey is so big. The hunter is misled into just pointing the gun in the bird's general direction, then pulling the trigger. A philosophy of, "who could miss anything that big" prevails. It pays to take a dead-aim at a wild turkey just as it does to pick out, then aim at, a single duck in a flock. Knowing exactly where the gun shoots in relation to the point of aim is of great importance when head-shooting turkeys that approach the gun because the hunter must shoot the bird in the head and upper neck. Often this is all that will be visible if the bird is screened behind brush. But, if the hunter has patterned the gun, knows its point of impact, and has full confidence in the load, there is no need to see any more of the bird than the head and neck.

As long as the bird has one eye on the hunter's location, the hunter is nailed there . . .

Due to the circumstances which surround calling wild turkeys, there will be many times when the hunter has but a few seconds to choose a final calling location before the killing shot is fired. When calling to answering birds both in the fall and in the spring, I will stop in one area, make a call, and then move on, just to make contact, but will have no intention of remaining there. I do this because all turkeys move about considerably while feeding and scratching, or will simply just amble from place to place. Too many hunters call over and over from one location which is not what a wild turkey will sometimes do. So, I'll make a call to a bird that is answering, move toward the bird a few yards, and make another call. My next move may be off to one side, or even drift back aways from the bird. When calling to a springtime gobbler, I will move toward one that has answered my calls, very often making up to 10 moves before settling on a shooting location. *But*, when I do choose my shooting location, it will be one from where

(**Opposite page**) This well-camouflaged turkey hunter won't be recognized as a human danger as long as he remains motionless. The four patterns of camo which are visible will cause him to fade into the terrain's features, and though he is wearing plain pants, these are too near the ground to cause any suspicion. With all the mast present on the forest floor, it would be a simple matter to scatter some leaves on the outstretched legs. This hunter will need to be careful when bringing the gun to bear that the binoculars do not interfere.

Knowing where your gun shoots in relation to where it is pointed is one of the most important parts of shooting a turkey. The birds should be shot in the head and upper neck, a pretty small area.

These birds have been spooked by the hunter in fairly open territory. He's dropped one of the birds.

Both these hunters have bagged a bird from a flushing drove. These young Rio Grandes will be excellent eating on Thanksgiving day!

Tim Olson points to where this bird had flown from, his shot dropping it as the bird winged by. Wild turkeys are fast flyers, which brings out the fact that though he is a young buck, Tim is a good wing shot. Brush country hunters expect to kill turkeys on the wing.

I have a commanding view out to 30 yards if possible. As I never wear camouflage unless I'm guiding, I ordinarily pick a place behind cover, as the hunters did back in the good old days. (I do this because a great many turkeys, particularly adult gobblers, will detect me if I hunt in front of cover.)

Also, in choosing a shooting stand, I immediately note any close trees, branches, brush, bushes, anything which could prevent my swinging the gun, or bringing it to bear. If the location is suitable in all those respects but offers little cover to hide me, I then will flop down on my belly and make the shot from there. Very little cover is required to screen a hunter from a low angle, just a tiny bush, a few weeds, or a clump of grass. This position also makes it easy to keep scooting around should the bird take a route which brings it in from the side.

Seldom will I take a sitting stance against a tree, rock, or log, but if I do, I invariably sit on one foot. From this position I can rise up on one knee, or even get to my feet quickly. I will do this if at the last second, when the bird is within easy killing range, I don't otherwise like the shooting view. From the prone position, I will sometimes rise to both knees, shooting from that height. Again, (you'll get sick and tired of me coming back to this time after time) it is important for the hunter to be completely familiar with the gun and be able to estimate the range. Throughout the bulk of wild turkey range, there will be scattered trees,

rocks, downed timber, weed clumps, and a jillion other physical features which will come between the hunter and an approaching turkey. Watch for them, and either take precautions or utilize them to make moves which may be necessary. Veteran hunters use ground clutter to screen their moves when they must change positions quickly, and when bringing the gun into shooting position. I have stood up, walked around objects, run to a better shooting position, and made any number of additional moves at the last second because a turkey was going to be hidden behind some sort of obstacle.

There is one location I shy away from, and this is an area where upward of 100 yards of flat open terrain lies between me and the direction I presume the turkey will be approaching. As a bird comes toward the call, it has the instincts to realize that it should be able to see the bird that is calling (in this case, a hunter). When it doesn't see another bird, the turkey begins circling, or "hangs up." A hung up turkey will stop, but will continue calling and looking from well beyond gunshot. Or it may stop, look, and then decide it doesn't like what it sees. In any case, the chances of a hunter shooting this bird begin deteriorating rather quickly. Of course, there are turkeys which will approach across wide stretches of open ground, but I would rather not take any chances and make plans to do something else when at all possible. Once a bird has walked into view of a calling hunter, even at 200 yards, the hunter can't move until the bird has walked from sight. Even then, unless a hunter is using binoculars and is sure the turkey can't see him, it's risky to move, as the bird may still be where it can see the hunter. As long as the bird has one eye pinned on the hunter's location, the hunter is nailed there no differently than if the area was under machine-gun fire. Move, and you are dead. The turkey is *gone*. The worst of these areas are found inside the Mississippi levee, around the parklands found so often throughout the Merriam's range, throughout the browsed areas in the northeast part of the country, and among the prairies in Rio Grande habitat. Though the hunter hopes for more suitable conditions, there are times when he will have to make do with what is there.

This sounds very unorthodox, but *this is my method of killing wild turkeys . . .*

My favorite area for calling turkeys is in mature woods with a moderate scattering of understory—logs, leaves, and dead branches lying about. Mountainous terrain, with rolling hills, tiny knolls, hollows, uplifts, ridges, etc., is also preferred. This allows the birds to come within easy shotgun range before I can see them, *and before they can see me*. In all but scattered instances, I maintain a talking back-and-forth relationship with responding turkeys which keeps me posted on their route toward me. Surrounded by wooded or mountainous terrain, I can keep myself and the gun pointed on the bird the second it comes into view. I can recall dozens of episodes when I was making moves of various types up until the second before trigger pull. This sounds unorthodox, *but, this is my method of killing wild turkeys*. People who have hunted with me know this, and

probably a number of them were quite skeptical as to our chances of getting a shot.

My last kill is an example of what actions I make after having a turkey respond to calling. The place was Arizona, it was mid-morning, and I had returned to the area where I had heard a gobbler sound off at first day. I could only presume the old bird had hens with him earlier. Hopefully, now that the time was 4 hours later, the hens had drifted away. Working my way downhill into low country, I called loudly on a shuffling box. From what seemed ½-mile distant, I got an answering gobble. Just to be certain, I called again. Once more the bird gobbled. Located on a spur ridge overlooking flatter country, I decided to go directly toward the bird a couple hundred yards, then see what the situation looked like from there.

Closer, I looked around. Typical Merriam habitat. Not much understory, but a good sprinkling of large ponderosa pines dotted among isolated clumps of Gambel's oaks. Larger single oaks stood here and there, many of them old dead trees. What I term as open cover. Visibility when standing ranged from 50 to 200 yards. Chalking the box, I hit it a few quick strokes, like an excited hen. The gobbler fired back. If he had moved, I couldn't yet tell. I headed off to the left, walking another 200 yards. A long slope angled off into a shallow wash a couple hundred yards to my front. To my hard left rose the face of the mountain I had descended. To my far right the mountain flowed into flat country, though this was perhaps 400 yards distant. Nowhere were the slopes more than a gentle climb. Visibility to my front had lessened to just beyond 100 yards, due to oak thickets, the angle of the wash, plus a stand of mixed pines and big oaks. A huge rotting pine lay sprawled at the base of a live ponderosa 20 yards ahead of me.

Hitting the box with the paddle, I called again, hoping the gobbler was making tracks in my direction. And, he was. I called again, then again. He gobbled to me all three

(Left) Mature woods like this, mountainous terrain, and rolling hills are what Bland prefers for turkey calln'. Youngsters like this lad should be given instructions for calling and shooting while on simulated hunts.

Two hunters rush toward a downed bird, one with the gun at ready should the bird suddenly recover and try to escape. Wild turkeys are tough birds, so they shouldn't be shot unless within easy killing range.

One of the author's old muzzle-loading shotguns leans against a pine tree in Florida. The Osceola turkey fell to a charge of No. 6s from the gun. Range was a little over 20 yards.

clump of oak sprouts, I looked down at the box, and chalked out a bunch of yelps. Probably weren't needed, but I just wanted to see what the old dickens would do. Gobbling back to me, he blossomed to full strut. Not daring to take my eyes from him, I stared back. Standing erect, the old turkey gave my area the once-over, decided the hen was not yet in sight, and once more walked slightly to my left as he came around the rim of the draw. Seconds later he dropped lower, whereon all I could see was the white pate of his head. Laying the box down, I picked up the side-by-side, gently drawing the hammers back to full cock from the safety notches. Easing the gun to my shoulder, I raised to both knees just as the old gobbler stalked up onto my side of the wash. His head snaked erect. Range? Twenty-one yards. I know, I walked it off after the gobbler quit flopping.

A typical kill for me. Four moves beside the one where I made first contact. No long periods of sitting, in fact at no time did I sit down. The only times of inactivity were while I was crouched behind the pine, while watching for the bird to emerge from cover, and afterward in keeping track of him as he picked a route toward my locations. By kneeling I was able to raise and lower my field of vision simply by easing up or down. The shot itself was simple because I could keep the top of the turkey's head in view through a light screen of pine needles, thereby knowing exactly where and when the bird would come into gunshot. From this "standing on my knees" position, I could swing from the hips, which is a must for any sudden moving shots, especially should the bird be crippled after the initial shot. This stance is the one from which the majority of my kills are made.

Since my call was hidden at the base of the pine and the slight moves in picking up and using the calls were well covered, I could continue calling right up to the shot. The hen yelps from it were muffled by the tree, and had the added effect of coming from a hen hidden from the gobbler's view behind the pine. Locating near any roll in terrain gives a hunter the added advantage of being able to make moves even though the intended quarry is already within shotgun range.

A turkey answered so close that all I did was look around, see it, then shoot it . . .

When locating to call a young turkey during the fall or winter seasons, remember that these birds are not as wary as the older birds, therefore will be more apt to come right up to the edge of thick cover in looking for another turkey. Imitating the whistles of very young turkeys with your mouth is a deadly trick, particularly when these whistles come from thick cover. Scattered birds will walk the edges, calling in answer, wanting the other to come forth.

times. I got a good fix, indicating the bird had moved slightly to the left since my last calling and he sounded much nearer. The bird was working uphill, and drifting slightly to the south. Kneeling down behind the rotting timber, I studied my surroundings. If the bird kept coming, he would break out of the wash some 50 yards from the gun. With the wide open terrain, he could get edgy. Carrying my old Hapgood muzzleloader, I would need the bird at 20 yards for the initial shot.

Then I noticed a standing pine with a small seedling alongside its trunk just along the top of the wash. Running to it, I knelt down, knowing this would probably be the shooting stand. I say probably because I never know until the last minute if a place I've chosen to call from will be my last before I pull the trigger. There have been too many hunts when I have moved umpteen times after having chosen any number of stands from which I thought would be the last until trigger pull. The turkey hunter who does not remain flexible, and who doesn't think throughout the hunt, will not kill many turkeys. It is a sport of instant decisions. *Correct instant decisions.*

Laying the gun on the pine needles, I stroked the shuffling box gently, though I made a long string of some 12 or 15 yelps. Then, without waiting, I made a second string, then a third. Sometime during the yelps, I could hear the gobbler bellering back. Distance? Sounded like he was on the far slope of the wash among the thick stand of oaks and pine trees. Hunkered down on both knees, I studied the slope as best I could, looking alongside the pine tree behind which I was crouched. There he comes. Puffed up in half-strut, he looked like a big, black feathery ball marching along on tiny stilt-like legs.

Seeing that he was going to fade from view behind a

The hunter who finds a water barrier between him and the answering turkey will do best to locate back from the edge of the water at least 50 yards, as birds will be hesitant in flying across to calling coming from the edge of the stream. Should you draw a young turkey to the edge of the water and it remains there, pacing back and forth, calling excitedly, you can get in the act with some fast excited clucks. These have worked for me where all else failed. Of course, if the river or stream is narrow, and the hunter doesn't mind getting a little damp, the bird can then be tolled out on the opposite bank of the water, shot there, and then fetched. If a person hunts wild turkeys for many years, all of these possibilities will arise.

Trying to tell anyone how to locate is in the same category with telling them exactly when to call. Speaking of these things always reminds me of the first turkey I called to the gun. It was wintertime, a dreary day, scudding clouds, but worse, I hadn't seen nor heard a turkey. What I knew about calling wild turkeys could have easily been printed on a cigarette paper—on the edge of a cigarette paper. But, in talking to a farmer long toward middle afternoon, he did mention that some men he knew had shot at a drove of turkeys along the creek. No, he didn't know if they had killed any. Yes, that was before dinner time. Dinner time in that country was, and is, at 12 noon. He pointed out the creek from where we talked in his barnyard. Hurrying that way, I made a few practice calls with the mouth caller I'd dug from one pocket. I'd scattered a few droves of turkeys before season, listening to them call to each other. I had tried to remember exactly what these sounded

like, so when the time came, I would be ready.

Nor was I sure about the mouth call, now stuck against the roof of my mouth. I'd read about how to make such an instrument in a hunting and fishing magazine, probably *Fur-Fish-Game* (while doing some trapping, I read it religiously). Anyhow, the description wasn't too good, but I pounded some lead fish sinkers flat on the anvil in the barn, cut them in long ovals with tin shears, then folded them over at the center, resulting in a horseshoe-shaped fold of very thin lead. Pliable, it was no task to insert a thin narrow strip of prophylactic rubber between the folds of lead, clinch them shut with my teeth, and then trim off the surplus rubber with a pocketknife.

I all but choked to death on those bare hunks of lead before I got a noise from the terrible, gagging thing. And, what noises. Torturous squeals, squawks, and screeches, but at last, turkey noises. Never having seen, nor heard, such an instrument, I never knew in the beginning if what I had made was as it was supposed to be, or not. (It was to be 3 years later that I first saw another one made by an older hunter from Mississippi.)

I'd practiced at home, but this was to be the first time "for real." Barreling my way into the tangles, I kicked out a small circle near the creek, in head-high horseweeds. (Also, years later I learned that a person is not supposed to call turkeys in such terrible tangles. But, the turkeys didn't know it either.) Hunkering down there, I made my best rendition of what I thought was a young turkey calling to its momma. A turkey answered so close that all I did was look around, see it eyeballing me through a forest of weed stalks, then shoot it. Simple! I had seen times as a boy when my brother and I had far more trouble catching one chicken in the pen.

Hunters, like all people, learn from past experiences, or, in reading, or listening to some tale, or, by trying. Never forget: When you shoot, make certain that you have identified your mark, and that it is not another hunter. Don't shoot at an object simply because it is making sounds like a turkey. It could be a hunter trying to call a turkey. *Shoot your turkeys at close range. You won't shoot hunters.*

When an answering turkey is on the other side of the water, it's best to locate at least 50 yards back from the edge and continue calling. This is a beautiful, big bird.

The aiming point when bowhunting is the backbone and where the wings join the body . . .

What about hunting wild turkey with bow and arrows? It is becoming very popular across the country, even if it is exceedingly difficult. Very few hunters have taken more than just two or three birds with bows, the great majority having taken none.

Vic Boyer, the veteran bowman from Albuquerque, New Mexico, tells me the number one thing for any aspiring bowhunter to do is to practice at least 10 minutes *every* day. Practice shooting from crouched and sitting positions

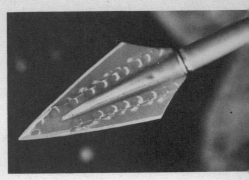

A broadhead used to kill a turkey gobbler has keen sharp edges which allow deep penetration. Wild turkeys are tough to anchor with an arrow, so they must be hit in a vital area, either through the backbone or in the heart-lung area.

Dave Harbour, of *Sports Afield* fame, totes a fine adult Osceola gobbler from a Florida swamp. This old bird was taken with a compound bow. Perhaps Florida's best bowman, Dave writes about bowhunting for wild turkeys in his excellent book, *Hunting The American Wild Turkey*.

The bowhunter must practice shooting at various ranges and at targets placed in actual hunting conditions. The sight picture changes completely when the target is standing among brush, and the hunter no longer has known objects to relate to when estimating range.

and practice shooting wearing the clothes that will be used when hunting. Vic also advocates shooting at dark turkey targets made from styrofoam, and when shooting at these, to place them on rough terrain where dirt banks can be used as backstops to halt the arrow's flight. Broadheads should be used in practice sessions as the season draws near, so the hunter will adjust to the flight variances between practice arrows and hunting arrows. Boyer says the serious bowman will have a friend listen from nearby, when the hunter makes actual hunting practice sessions from cover, to ensure that the bowman is not making any sounds which might spook turkeys. Bow-quiver rattle, or clothing scraping on twigs, leaves, etc., will send the turkey off on a dead run.

Many hunters I have talked to about bowhunting agree with Vic when he says the bowhunter will do best when hunting from a well-concealed blind. A solid blind will allow the bow to be drawn with very little of this action visible to the turkey, and it is during the draw that most turkeys spook from the bowhunter. Obviously, the range must be very close, 10 to 20 yards, and this nearness also increases the chances of a bird spooking, as the turkey's outstanding eyesight will invariably detect any movement.

Dave Harbour points this out in his first turkey hunting book, *Hunting The American Wild Turkey*.

Another point Dave stresses is to practice until a bowman has near pinpoint accuracy, and if he is accurate at close ranges, then to limit his shots afield to ranges that are within his abilities. Harbour also stresses full camouflage for bowhunters, including camo'd bow and arrows. When drawing the bow, do so when the bird has its head turned away, or has passed behind some terrain object.

Many of today's bowhunters use the compound bow which, with its breakover qualities, allows a hunter to hold the draw of an arrow for a longer period of time than was usually the case when shooting longbows or recurved bows. This has a decided advantage where wild turkeys are the quarry, as the hunter can sometimes draw when the bird passes behind cover, and maintain the draw until the bird walks into an area for a clear shot.

The aiming point on turkeys when hunting them with bows is the backbone, and the area where the wings join the body, often termed the "the wing butts." When shooting at turkeys, it is best to shoot high, and then if the bird is missed, the arrow will probably go over its back. Low shots, into the lower breast or gut area, will not kill a turkey

Weldon holds aloft various broadheads which are lethal on wild turkeys. The two outer arrows also support the small "adder" sections, which can be fastened to most of today's hunting arrows. These help to keep the arrow from passing through the turkey, as many bowmen believe that the arrow remaining in the bird slows down any escape attempt.

(Above) Danny Weldon, long-standing member of the Professional Bowhunters Society, is another bowman who believes in full camouflage, from boots to face mask. Danny emphasizes the need for the turkey bowhunter to practice drawing from the place where he intends on shooting, to make certain no limbs, twigs, or other objects, will interfere. Any such associated noises can then be eliminated.

(Left) The bowman should place the decoy very near the area where he hopes to keep a gobbler's attention. This enables the hunter to draw the arrow while the gobbler has its attention riveted to the decoy. The decoy should be placed out in the open. It should be from 15 to 20 yards from the bow, at the most.

immediately, though the bird will probably die after a few days, lost to all. But worse, it is a slow lingering death for a grand bird. Practice keeping the arrows high on the bird targets as you ready for season, and perhaps you won't lose one to crippling. None of the bowhunters I know have advocated shooting at the bird's head or neck. These areas are too small, and the person who shoots at them will become discouraged after so many misses.

Decoys are used by today's bowman to keep the gobbler riveted near the blind, and often these birds approach in full strut. It's no different than when using a shotgun, as the bowhunter can aim dead center at the fanned tail, if the bird is facing away, and the arrow will hit him in the upper back. I have killed many, many gobblers in full strut when the bird was facing away. The hunter can rise from a sitting or squatting position, and whether using bow or gun, take a serious and true aim and let fly. Shoot for plumb center.

Danny Weldon, veteran Oklahoma bowman and past Oklahoma Bowhunter of the Year, stresses the importance of the arrow "staying in the turkey," and not passing completely through, as this helps to anchor the bird until the hunter gets to it, insuring against escape. Like all old bowhunters, Danny Weldon also is a stickler for close-range

shooting, everyday practice sessions, total camouflage, and endeavoring to draw when the hunter is not visible to the turkey. I might mention here that anyone who has watched an arrowed turkey fly from view (and this advice applies to anyone who has shot and hit a turkey, then looks on as it takes flight) should "listen" the bird out of hearing. This simply means to stand quietly, and as the bird flies away, mark its course, but listen very intently, as quite often the bird will die in flight, and in plunging to earth, break tree limbs, or simply hit with a loud thud. Once on the ground, many birds will flop considerably, often several minutes, and the hunter may hear this noise if he follows the bird's course after it has flown from view. Wild turkeys often fly fairly straight paths for several hundred yards.

Vic Boyer remarks that if a bowhunter does everything right, he will score only about 10 percent of the time, due to misses, noises, and other things which face all hunters. Vic has taken turkeys with all three types of bows, the compound, recurved, and the longbow. He is now back to hunting with the longbow. He knows his bowhunting. He was inducted into the National Bowhunters Hall of Fame at the same time as was Howard Hill. To folks like me, who knew Hill as a legend, that's "stepping in tall cotton."

The modern compound bow has elaborate sighting systems, with various pins to denote sightings at different ranges.

The author's quiver holds broadheads which he made 45 years ago. The broadhead on the right was sold by Roy I. Case of Racine, Wisconsin, back in the early 1940s.

White, red, or blue feathers on arrows should be covered (or other colors used) so other hunters will not mistake them for the colors found on a turkey's head. The bowhunter's calls, together with the use of a decoy, are a setup which can attract other hunters. They might shoot at any movement near the setup, particularly if the color that shows is the same as that on a gobbler's head.

Today's bowhunter reminds me of the cigarette ad, "You've come a long way, baby." Bowhunting is about as far removed from the days of Sitting Bull as is cruising down the turnpike in a Cadillac. The modern compound bow is not a primitive weapon. If you are not up-to-date on the sport, you owe yourself the privilege of browsing through one of the bowhunting magazines found on most newsstands. In addition to having the "breakover" tendency, which allows the hunter more time to sight the bow, the modern bow has numerous sights, even a peep sight, bow quivers (which hold several hunting arrows alongside the bow itself), devices to keep an arrow nocked on the string, string silencers, trigger releases, and a device known as a stabilizer, which subdues recoil and prevents the bow from rocking back after firing.

The newest thing in turkey arrowheads is known as a Turkey Thumper, and must be seen to understand its construction and principles of use. Danny Weldon carries his arrows headed with Copperhead Broadheads, to which the Adder has been coupled, which makes an excellent turkey hunting head. Danny purposely files a saw edge on the broadhead's cutting edges, as this breaks bones instead of just slicing or sliding by them. The greater bone structure damage that a bowman can do, the better the chances that any turkey hit will not escape. Danny stresses the use of arrows which *do not have any fletchings which are blue, white, and red*, as these are the colors found on turkey's heads and could be mistaken to be a turkey's head by some other less cautious hunter. Best arrow color is camouflage.

Weldon earned his membership into the Professional Bowhunters Association by proving himself as a bowhunter. He hunts turkeys from a "hide," uses a call to lure them into near range, and practices for hundreds of hours each year. His bow is tuned so that it does not make a sound when drawn, and if he is wearing a back quiver, it lays on the ground near him, so there will be no arrow rattle.

Hunting Wild Turkeys With a Rifle
by Larry J. Hearn

What about hunting wild turkeys with a rifle? A rifle??##!!! Yes, I know, you have not hunted turkeys with a rifle, aren't going to, and that's not all—you don't want anyone else to use one.

Well, I have bumped into turkey hunting riflemen all across the country, and have observed one or two things about them which most shotgunners do not know and probably don't want to hear. Number One: Due to the manner in which the gun must be used, with its defined choosing of a lethal area on the body of a wild turkey, rifles are far safer for turkey hunting than are shotguns. Number Two: Due to the defined aiming point, the average rifleman will shoot at wild turkeys many fewer times than will the average shotgunner. And, regardless of what's being fired, the fewer good shots, the fewer the number of lost cripples. This applies to shotguns as well as rifles.

But, all the same, rifles have been disdained by a hunting public that presumes the rifleman is taking unfair advantage when shooting at wild turkeys at long ranges.

I dug into this rifle controversy, talking to rifle hunters when the chance presented itself, one of them being the well-known Lovett Williams, from Florida, the man who wrote The Book Of The Wild Turkey. *Lovett hunted turkeys for years with a rifle, then drifted into hunting them with a Savage 2400 combination .222 and 12-gauge. Lovett is very high on this gun, and carries it now when hunting his newly opened camp in south Florida. Anyone who knows Lovett Williams knows that he definitely does not carry a rifle so as to blast at turkeys from long distances. Like most riflemen, he hunts with a rifle because of the "degree of difficulty," or, as many put it, because of the challenge. It's like trout fishing—anyone can catch them on a worm, but it takes skill to catch one on a fly, and only the best catch trout consistently on a dry fly.*

Let's let a rifleman have his say, this man being Larry J. Hearn, a native Tennessean. Larry Hearn could possibly be the best turkey hunting rifleman in Tennessee. He does know his rifles, and he knows turkeys. Here's what he has to say about rifles vs. turkeys.

The rifle has erroneously been classified as a long-range tool for killing turkeys beyond shotgun range, therefore providing the hunter with an unfair advantage. There is no disputing that the rifle has the potential to kill a turkey farther than a shotgun; but, the skill and steady nerves required to utilize this advantage in turkey hunting are more than compensated for by the nature of the quarry. To be consistently successful in hunting any game with a rifle, the quarry must present an unobscured, motionless target.

The wild gobbler is seldom still, frequently obscured, and his vital zone presents a very small target under any circumstance. My hunting has largely been limited to the southeastern states where there are vast forests of hardwood, both in creek and river bottoms as well as hills and mountains. In this terrain, one seldom has an opportunity to shoot a wild turkey beyond 40 or 50 yards with any kind of gun. Scattered throughout the wild turkey's southern habitat are open pastures and fields that turkeys regularly frequent. The misinformed would assume that it is an easy feat to slip up to the edge of a pasture full of turkeys with a rifle and easily kill the turkey of his choice, or lie in ambush in the edges and snipe the gobbler the moment he appears. This is simply not so for several reasons. First of all, the visual acuity of the wild turkey is so great as to enable him to detect the slightest movement at long range. I know of no greater challenge than to try to slip within gun range of a wild turkey. Secondly, when turkeys are in open fields, they are rarely immobile, being continuously on the move with infrequent opportunities for a still shot. Since the vital zone for a rifle is limited to the chest cavity or backbone, the target is only 4 or 5 inches in diameter.

Since the rifle is a precision instrument, the foremost requirement is accuracy. All rifles are affected by the trajectory of the projectile they disperse, that is, the bullet does not travel in a straight line. Therefore a bullet cannot

This rifleman relaxes after bagging an adult Rio Grande gobbler. Rifles are popular for turkey hunting in the open country of Oklahoma and Texas and in other areas of the country where fall hunting seasons coincide with other game types.

be perfectly placed except for the exact range for which the rifle is sighted in, and since no prearranged agreement has been made with the intended quarry, one cannot anticipate the precise range at which the turkey will present an opportunity for a shot. We must not overlook the requirements for steady nerves and keen eyes to make a rifle shoot effectively.

If you are hunting in the woods, the serpentine movements of a wild turkey pose a different problem—an unobscured shot to the vital zone. An experienced shotgun hunter can usually overcome the movements of his quarry, requiring only the exposure of the head and/or neck to direct a dense pattern of No. 6s, the size of a wash tub, at 30 yards or less.

The nature of the turkey puts the rifle hunter at a severe disadvantage. The rifleman who tries for a head or neck shot has launched himself into an exercise in futility. If there is anything more difficult to hit with a rifle than the heart and lungs of a gobbler, it is his head or neck. Therefore, the proper tactic for the rifleman is to wait for an open, still shot, preferably within 50 yards: Align the sights to deliver the bullet to the vital zone with precision and place it there.

The rifleman must also make sure that his bullet does not encounter any other object in its flight to the target. A twig the size of a kitchen match can, and frequently will, deflect the missile from its intended path. When using a rifle instead of a shotgun for turkey hunting, the hunter voluntarily assumes a handicap and his chances for a successful kill are, thereby, automatically and substantially reduced. If the reader questions the validity of this statement, let him first try it and be convinced.

I remember the disillusionment experienced when I acquired my first combination gun, a Ferlach 12-gauge shotgun over a .22 Savage High Power rifle barrel equipped with a folding leaf sight, manually operated according to which barrel was to be fired. The .22 Savage High Power cartridge shoots a .228-inch diameter bullet and comes from the factory (Dominion) with 70-grain soft points. The factory load leaves the muzzle at 2800 feet per second. I reloaded this cartridge to give a muzzle velocity of 2100 fps. I found the iron sights on this combination gun the best I've ever used and my confidence was soaring. I was eager to use this ''laser beam'' on some gobblers, having no doubt that the gun provided me with the ultimate tool for killing turkeys. One day soon after I acquired this miracle weapon, I had my first opportunity. I had been lying in a prone position for some time watching three young gobblers 300 yards out in a peanut field. The peanuts had been harvested and the gobblers were scratching and searching for wasted goobers. I waited patiently as they disappeared behind a swale in the field as they fed toward me. A purple grackle dropped from the overcast morning sky to pluck

Despite what many people think, hunting turkeys with a rifle is no easy task. The gobbler seldom holds still long enough for a carefully aimed shot, the vital ''kill zone'' is quite small, and the birds are usually obscured by brush or undergrowth. The shotgun is still the best tool for the job, according to the author.

one measly peanut from a knoll 100 yards in front of me, but he was put to flight short of his objective by a young gobbler who rushed at him with ruffled neck feathers, denying the poor grackle a single goober. Shortly, the other two young gobblers appeared and all three continued to feed in my direction. At 60 yards, the front gobbler stood to his full height facing me and the other two made a 90-degree turn which would put them farther away from me if they maintained that course. I could barely see the 2-inch beard jutting out from the erect gobbler's breast, and I drew a bead on a point just above his beard. To my surprise, the fine front blade sight practically blotted the whole turkey from view. It was at this moment that I realized that what I had thought would be a tremendous advantage in a turkey gun was actually limited to a questionable 10 or 15 extra yards.

Realizing the erect gobbler probably presented the best opportunity I would have, I drew a fine bead from the prone rest and with my confidence waning, I fired the rifle. At the crack of the gun, two gobblers rocketed skyward and planed off into the swamp, but the object of my shot ran a

The Savage Model 340 has been a favored rifle for turkey hunters because it's chambered for some good turkey calibers—22 Hornet, 222 Remington, and 223 Remington.

Remington's "Sportsman" 78 bolt-action is a no-frills rifle that has a 4-shot magazine, walnut-finished hardwood stock, and 22-inch barrel. It's chambered for .243, .308, .270 and .30-06 and with proper handloads could be deadly on gobblers.

The Browning A-Bolt rifle has a 22-inch barrel, short-throw bolt, detachable box magazine, and is available with or without iron sights. It comes in a number of chamberings suitable for turkey shooting, and with glossy or oil-finished wood.

Winchester (U.S. Repeating Arms Co.) offers this Model 70 Mini-Carbine with 12½-inch stock pull in .243 Winchester that is ideally proportioned for young shooters and small-statured women. It comes standard with iron sights.

few steps and fell mortally wounded. Later, upon examination, I discovered the 70-grain soft point had entered the gobbler's back just below his neck and traveled about 1-inch deep the entire length of his back, making its exit at the base of the tail. Obviously, just as I squeezed the shot off, the gobbler reached over to snap up a goober. I never saw that movement and only concrete evidence would have convinced me that it occurred.

Those who make great claims about their ability to kill wild turkeys at long range with a turkey rifle under hunting conditions have succumbed to the figments of their imaginations. This is especially true when the rifle is equipped with iron sights.

Another key factor frequently overlooked is the optical illusion created by the visual presence of a turkey. What the rifleman sees is a target apparently 3 or 4 feet long with a depth of 15 to 20 inches. Probably less than 2 percent of the visual target represents the vital zone.

A mature gobbler in full strut appears as large as a 55-gallon drum at 40 yards, but the vital area for a rifle is only about 3 or 4 inches in diameter. I would guess that about 50 percent of that gobbler's optical illusion is pure feathers and air.

I have hunted with a wide variety of rifles for the last 28 years, during which time about 50 wild turkeys have fallen to my rifle. The range of calibers included a wide variety from the .22 Long Rifle to, and including, the .30-06.

My preference in a turkey rifle is a centerfire .22-caliber of light weight, accurate to one minute-of-angle at 100 yards and short enough to manipulate in tight places. I presently own my first choice of any turkey rifle I've ever seen. It is a custom rifle in .224-caliber using the .221 Remington Fireball case. It has an L46 Sako action with 17¼-inch Hart barrel and a petite Circassian walnut stock. This rifle is equipped with a Leupold Vari-X III telescopic sight with a variable power from 2½x to 8x. The scope has the duplex reticle and is mounted in Sako rings. I use a 1-inch sling on all my turkey guns, shotguns included. From the bench, this rifle will group five 55-grain bullets within ½-inch at 100 yards—consistently. It has a silent safety and weighs 6 pounds, 9 ounces.

I also own several other rifles and a combination shotgun/

This hunter has permission to hunt on posted land. He has placed his gun on the ground, crossed the fence, and now will pick it up for loading. This is a safe method, but the hunter must be careful that dirt does not get in the action, and that it is unloaded. It's wise to make it a practice to never be in front of the barrel.

rifle that all qualify for turkey hunting. The trigger on a turkey rifle, like any other precision gun, is extremely important. My preference is a crisp trigger with no apparent travel and with a pull of 2½ to 3 pounds. Although some of my turkey rifles and my combination gun are equipped with a set trigger, I never use them. They frequently fire prematurely under the pressure and excitement when the rifleman places his trigger finger for the shot, and it's easy to forget how easily they activate. The trigger should tolerate a firm hold but not require excessive pressure.

If ever there was an overrated advantage in turkey guns, it would be the drilling, or three-barreled gun. In my opinion, a better choice is a good combination gun with the shotgun on top and a .22 centerfire rifle barrel underneath. I acquired a Ferlach 12-gauge over .222 Remington in 1965. The front trigger fires the rifle barrel, the back trigger fires the shotgun. The safety is mounted on the tang like traditional side-by-side and superposed shotguns. The barrels are 24 inches long and the shotgun delivers 80 percent plus of No. 6s to a 30-inch circle at 40 yards. The rifle will deliver minute-of-angle accuracy at 100 yards. It is equipped with a 1½x to 4½x variable-power Bushnell Scopechief IV telescopic sight with Command Post reticle. The Command Post provides instant selection of either a crosshair or post. Both the shotgun and rifle shoot to the same point of aim using the scope. A manually operated rear leaf sight is optional for the rifle. I've probably killed 50 turkeys with this gun—at least 20 of which with the rifle barrel.

Although I've had good success with combination guns, I prefer to hunt with either a singular rifle or shotgun. It is difficult to think in terms of both shotgun and rifle simultaneously as a gobbler approaches. In addition, your thinking is further complicated by considering scope versus iron sights and even further by the selection of scope power and reticle. There are simply too many options, any one of which may be a mistake.

Almost all, if not all, rifles will shoot a particular load better than others. This can be discovered by experimentation. However, accuracy is not the only factor to consider. An accurate projectile of sufficient energy and velocity to instantly kill the largest old gobbler when delivered to the chest cavity is a necessity. At the same time, the bullet should not be excessively destructive. In my experience, factory loads have proven too destructive for turkeys. For example, the factory .22 Hornet cartridge delivers about 2690 fps at the muzzle with a 45-grain soft point bullet, and is excessively destructive to the soft flesh of a wild turkey. To overcome this problem, I reload all my turkey ammunition to minimize damage.

My preference in .22-caliber centerfire ammunition is a 50-grain soft point with a muzzle velocity of between 2200 and 2400 fps, depending on what velocity within this range gives the best accuracy. As the weight of the bullet increases for larger caliber bullets, decrease the muzzle velocity accordingly.

One problem encountered in cartridges for turkeys is the powder capacity of the case. The .22-250 shoots a .224-diameter bullet just like the .22 Hornet or .222 Remington. However, when making reduced .22-250 handloads for turkeys, you wind up with excessive space in the case so that the relatively small amount of powder shifts in the case according to the position of the rifle. This inconsistency affects accuracy and some experts advise against the condition from a safety point of view. Therefore, my choice of a cartridge for turkeys is one which is compatible to reloading in reduced loads where this excessive space is not created.

Until the advent of the .221 Remington Fireball, the .22 Hornet and K-Hornet set the standards for a turkey cartridge. The .222 Remington is also an excellent cartridge when loaded down to proper velocities. I have found, on the average, that the .221 Remington Fireball and .222 Remington give better accuracy than the Hornets. A 1-inch group is about the best I could ever achieve with any Hornet I shot. I would not recommend any rifle for turkey hunting that could not achieve this kind of accuracy at 100 yards.

Although the .22 Magnum will kill any gobbler that lives, out to 75 yards *if* the little 40-grain bullet is perfectly placed, the combination of its inherent inaccuracy with human error creates a combination conducive to failure. A 40-grain bullet leaving the muzzle at 2000 fps is not quite enough for the tenacious wild gobbler.

The best and most accurate rifle in the world can do no better than the man behind it. If the gun is not properly aligned on the target, the missile it launches will be ineffective. Although good marksmanship comes about primarily as a result of practice and talent, the single most important human element is vision. You can't consistently hit that which you cannot see.

Where precision bullet placement is required, the telescopic sight provides visual detail far superior to iron sights. Also, the margin of human error is reduced by use of the glass as opposed to iron. When using iron sights, four factors come into play: (1) the target, (2) the front sight, (3) the rear sight and (4) the eye. By contrast, the telescopic sight reduces these factors to three—the target, the reticle and the eye. With iron sights, the farther away the target, the smaller it appears and the larger the relative size of the front sight becomes in comparison to the target. Regardless of how accurate the rifle, as the distance of the target increases, more guesswork is imposed upon the shooter by the use of iron sights. I consider the effective range of iron sights in competent hands for shooting wild turkeys not beyond 50 yards. Anything beyond this gets to be a guessing game and this has no place in turkey hunting. The telescopic sight compensates for distance by its magnification of the target. Hence, a target at 100 yards would be as clear through a 4-power scope as would appear to the naked eye at 25 yards.

My choice of sights for a turkey rifle is a high-quality scope with a variable power of 2½x to 8x. Depending on the distance of the turkey and surrounding conditions, one has the option of adjusting the magnification power. My first preference in reticles is the medium crosshair in conjunction with the post. This reticle gives the hunter the instant option to use either crosshair or post-crosshair reticle. Under poor light conditions the post is much more visible than the crosshair. My second choice is the multiplex reticle which utilizes heavy crosshairs which taper or step down to medium crosshairs at the center. Thus the variable power scope, coupled with a choice of two reticles, is a compatible rifle sight to most conditions one will encounter when hunting turkeys.

In selecting a scope for your turkey rifle, you should try to select one that is compatible in size and weight. A 3x–9x variable would be the upper limits, even for western hunters. Even then, the larger scope wouldn't look good nor balance well on a petite 5½-pound Hornet rifle. A fixed-power scope is not a bad choice, and if that is your preference, I would advise a 4x.

The proper rifle combined with a proper cartridge and equipped with a good scope is like a scalpel in the hands of a trained surgeon. It is very sharp but you must know how, when and where to use it. ●

Regardless of what you use to bag your turkey, if you are flying to the area you've chosen to hunt, you need to be aware of airline restrictions on transporting firearms.

Flying isn't new to me. Nor are restrictions as to what can be carried aboard. *Do not attempt to carry a gun through an air terminal or aboard an airliner. You will soon be in jail if you do.* Call the airline you plan to use, and ask them what requirements they ask of hunters wishing to travel with a firearm. Once you arrive at the terminal, take your gun directly to the ticket counter. *Do not attempt to take it through a security checkpoint.* Tell the people at the ticket counter what it is, and they will instruct you in how the matter will be handled until you arrive at your destination. I have never had the least trouble when traveling with a firearm, which proves to me that the airline people are not out to hassle a hunter. They are trying to prevent some nut from blowing up an airliner filled with innocent travelers, or from making a side trip to Cuba, while some demented soul points a gun at the pilot's head.

If a hunter expects to travel much by air, he would be wise to invest in a good case for his gun. These are extremely tough, foam-lined boxes. However, a person should open the case, after retrieving it at the luggage checkout area, to make certain there is no damage to case or contents prior to leaving the terminal. If damage is present, it is best to immediately go to the claims office to file for damages. Baggage handlers for airlines are far harder on luggage than the gorilla you may have seen in TV commercials.

Pocketknives, belt knives, folding knives, all of these I put in my check-in luggage. I buy ammunition at the destination. Going through the security checkpoint at an airline terminal can be an experience. I've been asked to explain the workings of metal encased camouflage crayons, along with having to explain why a pair of my binoculars have a leather covering. One security officer asked to hear a wingbone which brought a quick response and approval. I'm positive the officer had no suspicions about the call, but possibly just wanted to know what it sounded like. I've noticed folks who seemed irritated at going through the hassle of checkpoints, but long ago I learned that far the best way to handle this was in being courteous to them. They are like you and me, they simply have a job to do. I hope they do it to perfection. After all, when I'm headed for turkey woods a thousand miles from home, I don't want to take any sidetrips around the world. Particularly, with anyone foolish enough to be walking the aisles with a hand grenade. I don't like being late for turkey hunting.

Stillhunting, Stalking and Ambushing

The stillhunter must approach clearings slowly, eyes constantly scanning the clearing as it comes into sight. Turkeys are often "heads-down," all of them feeding, and the alert hunter who sees them can ease down into cover when none are watching.

I'M NO different than the average wild turkey hunting buff—I prefer to hunt the birds with a call. It is far easier to bag one with this method, in both the time and the effort put forth. There are great numbers of new hunters who consider it impossible to bag a wild turkey by any other means. Too, there are veteran turkey hunters who have never killed a bird by any means but calling, which indicates a lack of knowledge about the wild turkey and hunting it, along with no true sense of woodsmanship.

The techniques of stillhunting—ambushing, bushwacking, dry-gulching, stalking, whatever term you apply to them—are applied best to fall and winter hunting when the birds are bunched. These droves most often consist of adult hens with their 6-month-old poults hatched the previous spring. Not yet wary to all the dangers found throughout their habitat, these young birds are less difficult to hunt. Of course, springtime gobblers are also vulnerable to the methods we'll discuss in this chapter. After all, there are countless days during spring hunts where a gobbler will gobble the whole morning, and yet will not come to the hunter's call. Can he be hunted? As sure as the sun sets in the West, provided the hunter has two legs, can walk, and doesn't mind using them.

In discussing these techniques, the reader must keep in mind that due to an endless variety of terrains, terms will be used in generalities. The reader will need to apply the terms to his local habitats as they relate to each other. A ridge in Missouri, often steep, of good elevation, cloaked in oak trees, and covered from top to bottom with dead dry leaves, will not resemble a ridge found in the Merriam's

country at 8,000 feet, with its scattered ponderosa pines, clumps of Gambels oaks, with a rocky ground covering. But, in relation to turkey hunting, both are ridges. Turkeys feed on the acorns found on them, and roost in the trees found on their flanks. An old bean field in the deep South can be a treeless area of several acres, grown 6 feet high with weeds with all indications that it hasn't seen a plow in years. Such a field farther west could be as flat as a pancake without enough cover to hide a turtle. Creeks can be anything from runs to brooks, streams, drafts, or spring branches, but to me, they are all "cricks." Arroyos are ordinarily dry but can be awash many feet deep after a sudden mountain cloud burst. Canyons, gullies, washes, all of these drain water from higher ground but, as used by most western Americans, are dry much of the time. Keep these things in mind, and if you associate them with local conditions, you'll more easily understand the hunting methods we will discuss.

Throughout this book, any time I mention "at near or close range," it should be understood that I'm discussing the shooting of a shotgun which to me is within 30 yards. I'm known as a hardhead on close range shooting, but it is wise to look at it in the following manner. If the hunter shoots at a wild turkey beyond 30 yards, but only cripples the bird, his next follow-up shot will be in the neighborhood of 40 yards, too far to prevent the bird's escape. Many, many turkeys are fired on by today's hunters at distances up to, and beyond, 50 yards. Sadly, gun and shell manufacturers are responsible for much of this, as they continually beseige the hunter with ads making all sorts of claims about long range killing guns and loads. I have come upon a number of crippled birds which I've finished off, saving a bird that another hunter had crippled. And, I have found dead birds, recently crippled, which had escaped the hunter, but then had died. Don't cripple. Become a dyed-in-the-wool true turkey hunter, shoot them inside of 30 yards. Twenty-five yards is best.

Walking, sitting and bending will take its toll on the stillhunter who is not tough . . .

What makes the best stillhunter or stalker? Truly, the finest stillhunters are those who adore the great outdoors. People who simply like "being out," who like listening to a tiny spring brook as it trickles from rock to rock, or gaze at the black leaves lying dead in a stagnant pool. The person who trods along, not finding anything which causes him pause as he passes through the woods will not make a good stillhunter.

Together with this, the stillhunter-stalker will need physical stamina. Walking, leaning against trees, sitting, bend-

ing, will take its toll on the stillhunter who is not physically tough. Much stillhunting requires but little walking, for if the hunter has studied local turkey flocks, he will be able to place himself where these birds are known to spend the bulk of their time, increasing his chances of making contacts quickly. But, in stillhunting a strange area, there are times when it's best to cover a lot of ground by foot, seeking out sign of turkey habitations, and the birds themselves.

Mental toughness? What about it? As with all phases of turkey hunting, stillhunting and stalking calls for a hunter to "hang tough" until it runs out of his ears. You will sometimes be told to "hang in there," or "stick-with-it."

These all mean the same thing—to make up your mind to stick to it and accomplish the task at hand, with little regard for the obstacles. Mental toughness comes with being educated, insofar as turkey hunting is concerned, for the person who doesn't thoroughly study the wild turkey's habits and habitats will soon be demoralized once he goes into turkey country to hunt. The farther from identifiable habitat

Two lady hunters pause to admire the beauty of the morning sun's coloring of some piney woods in New Mexico. Much of the far West's Merriam turkey terrain has little understory, being open beneath the towering ponderosa pines. With visibility reaching out to distances of hundreds of yards, the shotgun hunter has little chance of stillhunting for wild turkeys.

(Left) A hunter who is new to this type of terrain will probably see very few turkeys, and ponder how so many tracks were made in the sand. But, this is excellent stillhunting country, the hunter needing to slip silently over each sandhill, gun ready, attempting to remain in the shadows as he does so. This kind of hunt is only for those who don't mind putting in a few miles each day on foot, often when the weather is too hot, or too cold, and very often with a gale blowing.

that a hunt is conducted, the tougher will be the mental strain. This is best pointed out by recalling all those days in April when the hunter hasn't heard a bird gobble.

For me, there have been lots of such hunts, for throughout much of my early turkey hunting travels years ago, there was no one to tell me where the best areas were, so I had to ferret them out solely on my own. I would hunt an area and hear no gobbles, yet I would find sign indicating that there were birds in the area. Were the birds still there, or had they migrated to another segment of their range? Should I move my hunting location, or hang tough? No gobbles, no turkeys? Or were the birds just being silent? If so, why?

The stillhunter can walk into easy gunshot of wild turkeys. It's certainly not done every day, but if a hunter doesn't mind walking, loves just being in the woods, has the will to become a good wing shot, and can remain alert, the chances are good he can "walk up" a turkey. The walking stillhunter must make it a habit to watch ahead as terrain flows into view, constantly looking for birds. The more the hunter does this, the better "eye" he'll develop for seeing the birds.

Once located by stillhunting, stalking wild turkeys is then best done if the bird is by itself, because one or more turkeys in a group often have their heads up, and this does not allow a hunter to move as often as is the case with single birds. But, it must be remembered that single turkeys will tolerate less detection of movement than will a drove. Apparently, turkeys feel safer in numbers.

A classic example of this happened to me and my son-in-law one April in Mississippi. Tom Preston and I had hunted for 3 days without hearing a single bird sound off, yet Ed Norwood, our longtime buddy who lives in that state, insisted the birds had been gobbling prior to our arrival. Nowhere was there an abundance of sign, but that's not unusual in deep South turkey habitat. An abundance of scattered foods, together with nesting habitat, plentiful water supplies, and the highland grounds cloaked in pine needles, made conditions ideal for widely scattered sign.

But, as Tom and I had traveled all the way to Mississippi to hunt, we were determined to get our birds. We stillhunted the bulk of the days. Both of us would attempt to entice a male into gobbling for 2 or 3 hours after dawn, then we would ease among the ridges bordering the Homochitto River, hoping to make visual contact, or to hear a gobbler. Such hunting is extremely difficult, as the terrain lends itself to the bird spotting an approaching hunter. And as the day wears on, the heat often becomes oppressive, bringing on thirst. A sense of hopelessness will grip a person not toughened, nor dedicated, to the sport.

Tom and I met back at Ed Norwood's place the evening of the third day. We both had finally met with success. Tom had bagged a fine old thick-bearded gobbler late that afternoon which was a match to the one I took. Both of us had been stillhunting, had made visual contacts with gobblers before the bird eyed us, taken cover, and then made the kill as the birds walked into easy gunshot. Tom was hunting a ridge back from the river, whereas I was walking within 100 yards of the river when I spied my gobbler pecking at the forest floor far down the woods from me. Falling to the ground, I bellied into a tangle of honeysuckle vines from where I could study the bird. At one point I

considered calling, as it appeared the bird was going to pass me beyond shooting distance, but, the bird swung back onto a course directly to me. The shot was anticlimatic to the pounding of my heart and the dry-mouthed tenseness of lying there hoping the bird would come my way. I made a second kill through stillhunting and all the way back to Oklahoma, Tom and I basked in the glory that we had met our quarry on its own ground and had won. Calling would have been our chosen tactic, but for that hunt, calling was out. Later, Ed told us the birds began gobbling a few days after our departure. We would have liked to have been there. Like many traveling turkey hunters, we had to make do with the time we had to hunt. We couldn't wait until later. Stick-with-it stillhunting had paid off for us. Seven hundred mile drives can seem like a couple thousand if you never get to fire a shot.

A stillhunting turkey hunter quietly hunts through cover known to be good habitat . . .

What is stillhunting? It is simply what the word means: hunting quietly throughout terrain where the game being sought is known to live. Stillhunting is applied to the hunting of virtually all wild game. A grouse hunter in New York state walks silently toward the abandoned apple orchard, among the hemlocks, and as easily as possible among the thornapples, hoping to jump the feathered rockets at close range. This increases his chances of getting an open shot before the bird can put cover between it and the hunter. The jump-shooting duck hunter paddles his canoe softly around each bend in the stream, intent on bringing his gun to within killing distance of mallards booming upward from the water's edge. Deer, elk, prairie chickens, even cottontail rabbits—all are far easier to approach by the silent hunter than by one making sounds.

Thus, a stillhunting turkey hunter is one who quietly hunts through cover known to be good habitat, trying to place himself in shotgun range through the use of his eyes, his ears, his knowledge of the bird's habits, and his ability to read the woods. To be successful at least some of the time, the hunter must be able to interpret what he sees and hears, and then make a decision on what actions are to be taken. Very often this decision must be made in a split second.

The turkey's eyesight is his number one defense, and a hunter's eyesight is his number one turkey hunting sense. This brings us eye to eye, but as the turkey's eye is more keenly developed, the turkey will eyeball the hunter first. Goodbye, turkey.

There is no substitute for a "game eye." A game eye can only be achieved through countless sightings of the intended quarry, at varying distances, in good light and bad, and throughout the physical makeup of the terrain which it inhabits. As wild turkeys will not let the hunter walk to within several yards before hightailing it, the turkey hunter looks for the whole bird at longer distances. At other times, he hopes to glimpse a slight movement, and then he will focus intently on this area. All such sightings depend greatly on a simple little thing like whether the turkey is facing the hunter, or facing the opposite direction. A bird facing the hunter will appear black at a distance, regardless of sex, and will therefore be readily discernible. But, with the bird facing the hunter, the chance the hunter will be seen increases.

A turkey facing away from the hunter presents its "camouflaged" side, making it difficult to see its turkey form. All of a wild turkey's back, lower rump, and tail feathering is patterned in nature's colors, so that when the bird is hunkered belly-to-the-ground, it becomes all but invisible. The camouflage coloring is present at a very early age in the bird's life, enabling it to hunker frozen, so to speak, and (hopefully) escape, the keen eyes of predators. Coyotes, foxes, bobcats, and man—all will walk within feet,

Stillhunting is simply that: hunting quietly through the woods where the intended quarry is known to be. The technique involves walking slowly, stopping often to listen and look for turkeys and sign. Being able to interpret what you see and hear and the ability to make split-second decisions and actions are keys to being successful.

A sight to make the blood run fast in any winter turkey hunter's veins. These birds have fed onto an open field, so the hunter would need to bide his time until the birds' travels could be studied; then the hunter could make an effort to get in front of them, to intercept them as they fed past. If a kill couldn't be made, there might be a possibility the birds could be flushed and scattered, and one then called to the gun.

and yet not see the hunkered bird.

Amazingly, such hunkered birds have another built-in defense which goes into action. This is eye contact with the predator. Numerous times I have spotted wild turkeys "frozen" on the ground, squatted flat on their bellies, heads usually drawn in on the shoulders at the wing butts, feet tucked underneath where they can catapult the bird skyward. In every instance, the split second that our eyes met the bird has flushed. No waiting, no twisting about to get a good jump, just immediate booming from cover. I've killed a number of turkeys flushed in this manner, one of which was a fine adult gobbler I surprised on bare ground. Obviously the bird saw me just as I popped over the hill, but since I was so near, it apparently thought that in drop-

Purposely posing here just to make the point, Eddie Miller looms white in the sunshine, and would be seen instantly by any approaching turkey. The wise stillhunter, when not moving, should make it a habit to choose a hunting stand in the shadows where his outline will be broken by surrounding cover and where he has good visibility of the surrounding woods.

ping to cover, and remaining motionless it might escape unseen. Sparse cover allowed me to catch a glimpse of a dark hulk on what was otherwise smooth leaf-strewn ground. Unsure of the blob, I turned toward it when my eye recognized that of the bird's. In less than a heartbeat he was up and away. A snap shot somersaulted him back to earth. On another occasion, I rounded a heavy clump of cedars, and noticed a turkey beneath an overhanging bough. The bird was an adult gobbler, and while his body was in the usual hunkered-to-the-earth posture, his head was laid out flat on the ground. Our eyes met and *whoosh*, out he came, all but upending me. An easy kill. I mention these instances to point out that a wild turkey uses its eyesight at all times, near and far.

A turkey's eye seems to detect movement at greater distances than does man's. The bird has a wide field of vision and understands what it sees at a faster rate than do humans. When alert to a danger, it will turn its head so that only one eye is focused upon the subject, at which time it takes a real hard look.

Understanding the turkey's eyesight is a part of stillhunting, as only then can the hunter realize how best to hunt. I've made it a habit to continually scan the woods as far as I can see, intent on dark objects at ground level, along with movement. Cloudy days are preferable, for on bright sunshiny days, there is a vivid contrast between open areas and deep shade. Turkeys have an inclination to remain in the shade, making them less discernible. When walking over hilltops, or from behind any topographical structure, be it rock piles, bulldozed mounds of earth, or solid brush screening thickets, I do so slowly, letting my eyes work back and forth as the terrain before and around me flows into view.

When I pulled the trigger, I was hanging onto a hillside by my fingernails . . .

The stillhunter should make the terrain work for him, which means that he should utilize terrain cover and features to his advantage. It's far wiser to work your way over a hill slightly beneath the highest elevation, as you will be easily seen on the summit. In easing up for a looksee into the next cove, slip up behind a bush, using its screening branches to hide your face as it comes into view of the area. Camouflage is a must for the stillhunting turkey addict, but even then he will need the added concealment found in trees, bushes, rocks, and any other ground cover found within turkey country. I've eyeballed turkeys from behind soap yuccas, dense stands of bluestem grasses, sawgrass, palmetto fronds, blackberry bushes, and a jillion other natural features found throughout this country's turkey habitat. This past spring I heard a turkey gobble, and even though I called, it soon became evident he was not interested. I was interested, so I went looking. He was surrounded by hens. When I pulled the trigger on the old bird, I was hanging onto a hillside by my fingernails, looking down the gun's barrels among a dark scattering of ragweeds, studded with milk thistle.

Long ago I made it a habit to use shadows to my advantage. When I ease over a knoll, drop from the side of a ridge across to the other, or stroll along an abandoned trail,

Lennis Rose walks along an abandoned logging road in a national forest. He will keep constant watch for turkey sign as he travels this road, as the nearby timber and tall grasses make this ideal nesting habitat. If he finds much sign of hens, he knows there will also be gobblers here. Once hatched, young birds will be able to feed along this road for insects and seeds as its surface is open and will not inhibit the small birds' travel. During early fall, Lennis will need be on guard for young birds flushing along this road.

as the country before me comes into view I stick to any available shadows, because these will mask my movements. Additionally, a hunter's camouflage fades into the darkness of shadows.

Many hunters will have an urge to eyeball terrain that is well out of gunshot range, overlooking terrain before it that is within gunshot range. I stillhunt with just the opposite in mind. I make a concentrated effort to only see and study terrain that is within easy killing distance. Once a hunter has done this many times, he will be aware of areas that can be approached in this manner. This is stunningly evident when hunting old logging roads. These will be grown up along the edges with tall weeds, small seedling pines, and myriad quick growth plants. This waist high cover screens a hunter approaching bends in the trail, enabling him to walk around short curves which could place him within gun range of a turkey walking the road. This tactic can be further enhanced by always walking on the inside of these bends, moving to the opposite side of the trail if the bend goes toward that side. Ordinarily, walking on such trails will be very quiet. On this type of stillhunt it pays to walk fast, particularly at the moment when the trail ahead is flowing into view, and it is within gunshot. If the hunt is during the early fall season, when ground and woods cover is still leafy, chances can be quite good for a hunter to walk into killing distance of a drove, whether it is on the trail or off of it in nearby woods. There are hundreds and thousands of acres in Eastern wild turkey range made to order for this technique. I've killed a great many Eastern gobblers while stillhunting in this manner, both on fall and spring hunts. After heavy rains, throughout light rains, during periods of fog, at any and all hours of the day, turkeys walk trails and old abandoned roads.

There is another factor which comes into play during the spring hunt. All human hunters are ground oriented. We seldom look up. If you don't believe me, ask yourself how many times a bowhunter has called out, but you couldn't locate him—*until you looked up*. And, those were the ones who called out. How many others remained silent, while you walked on by?

In never looking up, we're never prepared for the wild turkey which flushes from overhead. Many springtime gobblers roost above old tote roads, logging roads, even little traveled blacktops. Also, spooked gobblers often flop into trees above such trails, standing there on a branch until they're satisfied danger no longer exists. The point is, a stillhunting turkey hunter is very apt to walk smack under one of these birds, which will invariably catch him completely unprepared at its thundering flush. It pays to look up into the trees while stillhunting, more so if it is during the early morning hours, or if it is raining, and if the hunter suspects that other hunters have scattered a drove in the past hour. Stray dogs barking can be an indication of turkeys having been spooked into the trees.

One cold blustery November morning I was stillhunting a creek bottom where a drove of birds had been scattered the day before. I'd come there to call, but as the temperature was dropping, and the wind was building, I'd decided walking would be preferable to freezing to death while sitting backside to a tree trunk, hoping a bird would come to my kee runs. Besides, the way the wind was whistling through the bare limbs, a turkey would never hear a caller. Bare branches and scudding clouds, a dismal morning for turkeying. Dropping down into a dry wash, I had just begun climbing its far side when I glanced up at a slick elm sprawling above me. Hunkered against the wind, not 20 yards distant, sat a big turkey gobbler. I threw the gun to my shoulder and in that instant he half-turned, exposing to my view the bushy beard on his chest. An easy kill, made possible by a chance look-see into the trees, and a wind which killed any sounds I made.

Turkeys have excellent hearing, plus an ability to pinpoint a sound to within feet of its origin. The hunter stillhunting among open forest will be heard well before he walks into sight of the great bulk of turkeys but wild turkeys have favored routes throughout their range and a good percentage of these will be among leaf bearing trees. Invariably the ground beneath these trees will be solidly carpeted with leaves, most often dry and brittle. It's a waste of time and energy to even attempt to stillhunt such terrain. But, if the hunter must cross such areas, he would cause less suspicion among any listening wild creatures if he would walk slowly, stop often, and try to act like another ambling turkey or a deer. A wild turkey hearing the slow steady creeping step made by a sneaking hunter will immediately think the sounds are made by a predator. When I must cross dead leaves, I amble along a ways, perhaps pick up a length of

Larry Marvin, a favorite partner of the author's, is a very successful stillhunter, listening for the sounds of a drove of fall turkeys, and then stalking to where the sounds are coming from. This takes tremendous patience, and the hunter must have plenty of time. Ofttimes fall turkeys are quite vocal and will talk back and forth as they feed and travel over the range. Once the birds are located, then a stalk can be made when the cover allows.

A successful hunter tells his story as a friend listens. The person who hears out each detail can often get an insight into the "how-to's" of the successful hunter, and be more apt to get his share of the game. But as one word can often be the key, it pays to listen closely.

abundance of tracks. Young turkeys will lose scads of small feathers throughout the fall, which can indicate an area being used by a drove almost daily. Many times I have located in an area where I found large quantities of newly dropped feathers, and have invariably bagged turkeys. Such ambushes can take a few hours, or days.

The stillhunter must be quiet for another reason though, and this is so he can hear any sounds nearby turkeys may be making. This could be far off yelping and keeing, made by early morning droves when leaving the roost trees and assembling; or later in the day, he may hear the callings of lost birds, and/or birds that are answering them. It is possible for a springtime stillhunter to hear a gobbler cut loose any time of the day.

There will be times when stillhunting that the hunter will hear the clear unmistakable "putt" or "pertt" of spooked turkeys, birds which have seen the hunter and are alarmed. Young unhunted turkeys may not instantly take flight though they will walk away at a fast pace. Others will invariably run or fly. The hunter should make an effort to identify the birds by sex and age, as these facts could be valuable to him as he continues the hunt, probably by calling.

During fall and winter hunts, I make a run toward spooked birds, going all out in getting them separated from

dead limb, and scratch the leaves with it as I move through the woods. I make every effort to work my way to less noisy ground when at all possible. But, as long as I'm on the leaves, I try to sound like a gobbler feeding. Hunters who have heard solitary gobblers feeding and scratching will agree that these old birds sound identical to a lone human's movements.

A stillhunter working edges will soon know if turkeys have been there . . .

I walk the edges of cultivated fields that border uncultivated areas. Such edges will have weedy cover which, in addition to offering weed seeds as food, will attract insects and bugs. Recently cultivated soils are sometimes used by turkeys in their daily dusting ritual, presumably as a deterrent against mites. The birds will wallow out dish shaped depressions, and lying in these on their sides, will pull the powdery soil up into the feathers with their wings. A stillhunter working edges will soon know if turkeys have been there as he will find feathers, droppings, and perhaps an

Fresh running water is preferred by wild turkeys for drinking purposes over that of ponds, lakes or windmills. This young hunter looks for sign of watering birds along this tiny creek. This rugged cover would be excellent for stillhunting.

each other. In so doing, it's often possible to learn if the birds are a small drove of old gobblers, or if the drove is a hen or two with their young. Too, I'll know how they scattered as all these facts will help to determine what calling methods should be settled upon, and where to call from.

During the spring season when I hear a deep "putt" while stillhunting, I'll usually be able to identify it as a gobbler. If he is alone, and has an inclination to run off through the woods, I'll let him go. Chances are I might be able to cut a ½-mile circle around him and call him to me. But, if he has hens, and I can hear them sounding the alarm, I'll make a run into the birds, spooking them badly which results in a wild flush and hopefully results in the hens being separated from the gobbler. Chances are that if I can get between him and any hens I will hear calling over the next hour, I will be able to call him to me instead. So the stillhunter should train himself to gain all the knowledge he can at every turn which will allow him to use all the wrinkles in the book, so to speak.

Of course, the hunter hopes to spot the birds before they see him, and when this happens, there are a number of alternatives. Number one is to ease to the ground, as this is where a person will be most comfortable, and far less apt to be seen when the turkeys raise their heads. When I see turkeys that appear undisturbed and apparently have not

This hunter has crawled up behind a clump of brush, and brings himself upright on extended arms, but does so with his face screened in the brush. A turkey will have a hard time seeing him so long as he does not move quickly. This works well in all cover, regardless of what turkey is being hunted. Care must be exercised not to get dirt in the gun's action or bore.

detected my presence, I drop to the ground quickly, but do not take my eyes from them in doing this. Thus, as they leave my view I know whether they were pecking at the ground, strutting, or whatever. Or, perhaps one of them spied me just as I sank from sight, and all heads had jerked erect. It makes a considerable amount of difference what is done next if the birds are alerted.

Let's presume the birds had spotted me, but only enough to realize there was a movement they didn't have time to understand. Once I had fallen to cover, I would then want to be extremely cautious in taking a looksee to study the situation. I can't stress how important it is at this time to use terrain to your best advantage while looking over these wary birds. Of course, full camouflage will be of tremendous benefit, but even then the hunter should try to come up behind a screen of brush, grass, a low leafy bush, anything which will break his outline and prevent the birds from noticing his moves. Such moves must be made very, very slowly. Once you can see the birds, stay put. Don't move, because after they decide that there is no apparent danger, they'll go back to whatever they had been doing. Then the hunter can analyze the situation, make a decision on how or what is to be done, then attempt to carry it through.

There are times when slightly spooked turkeys will linger a short time, remain alert and wary, and then decide to leave. They will simply begin walking away, usually at a brisk walk, and strung out in a unit. Such birds won't stop just over the next rise. The hunter must make up his mind as to the next course of action, and quickly, or he can let them walk away. If the birds are within 100 yards or so, and the terrain is fairly level, it's best to run toward them, making a scatter. If the birds are in an area which will cause them to pass from view quickly, there are times when the hunter can wait until they are out of sight, and then run to where he hopes to either intercept them, or to bring himself within gunshot.

If, as I fall to earth, the birds have not seen me, I can then ease behind cover, raise myself behind screening foliage, and study them to decide what action to take. In flat country, a hunter lying on open ground will learn that few turkeys will see him beyond 50 yards.

If the birds are not wary, a hunter can take his time in choosing what to do. Can they be stalked through belly-crawling? Are they coming toward the hunter? Will the turkeys walk behind a solid screen which would allow the hunter to ease within shooting distance? Would it be advisable to call to them? These are but a few of the questions which can and do arise in such circumstances.

I was walking a cowpath late one spring evening, headed for my pickup. Topping a tiny knoll, I eyed a gang of jake gobblers walking at right angles to me, 50 yards away. I sank from view, apparently screened from their sight by my full camouflage, together with a stand of staghorn sumac. All of the facts had gone through my mind by the time I hit the ground. There was one quick chance, which was to call to them. Obviously they were headed for roost branches. The terrain didn't lend itself to my going after them when they walked over the first knoll in their path, nor would the noisy leaves underfoot allow it. Digging a mouthcall from a shirt pocket, I made a series of hen calls which was all that was needed. All six turned and came dead on. I could have killed all of them with one shot, for they came to me like ducks in a row. I began "putting" when they had closed to 20 yards, and they began milling which opened up the formation. Then I made a kill. Had I jumped and run into them when I first spotted the drove, I could have made an excellent scatter for hunting them the following morning. But, I wasn't going to be hunting thereabouts then, so it was a choice of making a kill immediately or not at all.

Big woods with large trees are by far the most difficult for the still-hunter . . .

Osceola habitat is extremely varied, much of it being cypress swamps, strands, heads, and creek swamps. Another part of Osceola habitat is made up of these gnarled live oaks which grow in clumps, or large stands, known as "hummocks." Within these hummocks the ground will be flat, well blanketed with dead leaves and, in many places, studded with palmetto and cabbage palms. Spanish moss will drape from the branches. This is excellent cover for a hunter in ambush.

The old-time method of stillhunting, used in relation to deer hunting, works best in what so many of us know as "big woods." These are heavily wooded areas where the bulk of the trees are mature and where there is a lack of underbrush due to the screening canopy of leaves high overhead throughout the growing season. As soon as fall approaches, with resultant leaf drop, such woods allow visibility. The stillhunter must move very slowly here, taking a few steps, pausing for a few moments either by sitting or leaning against trees. Of course, if the terrain is hilly or has knolls, ridges, gullies, or streams, these features will help the stillhunter to walk within seeing distance of turkeys as compared to tremendous wooded areas where the terrain is flat and open. Nowhere is the advantage greater than if these are a hunter's home woods, where he knows the habits of local droves, or where past experiences can be drawn on for guidance during times when he has not scouted the area recently.

Big woods with large trees, particularly where the terrain

is flat, are by far the most difficult for the stillhunter who is hunting these for the first time, as he has no knowledge of which area the birds are using. And, though it's advantageous for a hunter in strange and new country to move fast to locate birds, in large flat open woodlands he will be seen before he even knows turkeys are there. A hunter on this terrain must have time so that he can ease along like smoke, look for sign, and watch all around him as he listens for turkeys.

The opposite of big, open woods are terrains like those found in Florida, Alabama, Mississippi, Texas, Oklahoma and, in fact, any state that allows turkey hunting, where the roll of the ground, or the denseness of the foliage, allows for a hunter to walk within range unseen. This past fall another hunter and I were stillhunting heavily wooded bottoms in Arkansas. We'd broken out onto a skidding road which hadn't been used in a couple years and had silently glided along it a couple hundred yards when we topped a tiny knoll. The woods exploded in our face. Turkeys thundered up through the mixed pines and hardwoods, and I fell forward, yelling "Shoot! Shoot!" I'd killed my limit 2 days previously. My hunter wasn't ready, but luckily a "late" bird held, and just as it appeared the man wouldn't get a shot, this last turkey boomed skyward, taking not only a course broadside to us, but also one free of even a single intervening branch. This was a wide open dream shot. My friend scored two misses at 20 yards. When last seen, the bird was headed for Missouri at a fast rate of speed. Stillhunting can be this way. Zero one moment, a snap-shooting showdown the next.

Stillhunting has a number of advantages in helping the hunter decide whether he should hunt an area by other means, be it calling or bushwacking. More so if the hunter is working woods he is not familiar with and has no information concerning local turkey populations. Now, I've known endless parties of hunters who, upon driving into

Stillhunting for wild turkeys in sagebrush country involves considerable walking, listening, and maintaining a constant lookout for fresh tracks in the soft sand. Turkeys which have been scared by hunters in this country will thereafter travel from hilltop to hilltop, ever vigilant for signs of man.

such regions, decide that the best method to locate turkeys is to drive backroads until they make visual contact. This is roadhunting, plain and simple, though there are a few hunters who do this only in hope of finding game; then they abandon the vehicle to hunt by ethical means. Fine. But, the main drawback to this technique is that in so many of these areas the droves have been subjected to unrelenting roadhunters and become road shy, thus very few are seen along these paths. A hunter new to the area could drive for mile after mile and never see a bird. This can easily be misinterpreted to mean there are no turkeys or, at best, very few.

Late one fall afternoon I had taken up a calling stand behind an abandoned house, near a small clump of oaks which had been ''plowed'' by feeding turkeys. The leaves had been kicked about so often that it appeared a threshing machine had run amok. I was photographing, so set up a couple cameras with rubber-tube air releases and sat back, making calls quite often. A road ran within 100 yards, but it was out of my view, and I assumed would cause no problems.

Fifteen or 20 minutes later I got an answer which shortly was followed by a hen and her brood walking up to me. They began feeding as I'd cut off the calling. The birds were just getting near the cameras when I could hear a pickup rattling along the road. At first, the turkeys seemed not to hear it, but as it came within 200 yards, they quit feeding, stood alert, then as the truck came nearer, suddenly darted into cover. Aha! Somebody around these parts is roadhunting, I told myself. I gathered up my equipment. Walking back toward the road, I could hear the truck again. Probably the same one, as I was in country where vehicles were not often on the road just before sundown. Quickly I went to where I could watch as the vehicle drove past. It chugged by, two men in the cab, another standing in back, shotgun in hand.

The turkeys knew by the sound of the truck, its speed, and previous encounters what these hunters were up to. Turkeys aren't dumb. A hunter would be hard pressed to get a shot at those birds, particularly from the road. The point I'm getting at is that even though birds are not seen from the roadways that doesn't mean they're not around. If the hunter has reason to believe the area contains wild turkeys, he will need physical proof. Walking will answer the question one way or another.

The most important factor in utilizing sign to determine local drove size is to keep in mind the subspecies . . .

Interpreting sign, then, is the key, and this can open up a whole new can of worms. Finding a lot of droppings, feathers, and tracks, ordinarily indicates a good population of turkeys, but this also can be misleading. The most important factor in utilizing sign to determine local drove size is to always keep in mind the subspecies of bird being dealt with, plus local feeding conditions, and how much acreage may be found in uninterrupted tracts.

For instance, a hunter from West Virginia, spring hunting the Merriam wild turkey for the first time in Arizona, would think he had found a bonanza should he stumble onto a tiny mountain brook where a drove had spent the winter months. Snow on surrounding mountains had perhaps driven them to this area, where the winter afternoon sun melted the snow along the mountain stream, revealing green meadow grasses, and innumerable spring seeps. Nearby Gambel's oak thickets provided scratching for acorns, and a towering ponderosa gave the birds a safe roost branch for the night.

These pile-like droppings are those of fall-hunted young wild turkeys. These are unlike those of the larger adult gobblers which would be elongated and about as large as a pencil. Hens and young turkeys leave an abundance of the droppings shown. The alert stillhunter will notice these things!

A newly found turkey feather can tell a story. This one is obviously a wing feather, and one from a young turkey. Barring and smallness in size reveals this. But we must ask why is it here? A quick search scatters many grasshoppers. Probably the bird was feeding here. We must also not forget to look around the area, because if one or two wild turkeys were here, others much like it could also be around.

The serious turkey hunter never lets up in watching for fresh sign of turkeys. This feather, found near water, indicates the birds were there within the past few hours. Now it's time to find 'em.

(Right) Muzzleloader leaning against a giant oak, the author cuts palm fronds for use in building a hide in Florida's Saint Lucie County. Osceola turkeys travel throughout these stands of oak, searching for foods among the duff on the forest floor, making this an excellent location to lay in ambush.

But, the snows had ceased and gave way before the spring sun's intense rays, and the dry air had preserved the droppings. The birds had drifted to other haunts at higher elevations. Yet a person walking along that trickling water would say to himself, "Hey, man, look at all the sign. Those droppings look like they were made yesterday." Add this to the tracks he had spied in the dust on the logging road, and together it spelled turkeys all around. Of course, as it hadn't rained since the last snow, he couldn't know those tracks were 3 weeks old. A lack of wind and very little traffic can cause few changes. But, the knowing still-hunter, the person who has studied the Merriam before traveling 1,000 miles to hunt it, is aware that these birds migrate up to 40 miles due to weather and feeding conditions. Living in country of varying elevations such as New Mexico, Arizona, and Colorado, where weather varies with altitude, Merriams must travel up and down with the snow line during the winter, as deep snows will prevent them from feeding.

Farther south, the Gould's wild turkey found back in Mexico's Sierra Madre Range, doesn't need to migrate so widely, though it, too, is a high mountain bird. Why? Mainly due to a lack of snow. An abundance of water is the only limiting factor in Gould's range, and this is brought about by lack of rainfall. Nor do Rio Grandes, Osceolas, and the bulk of Eastern wild turkeys wander great distances, in comparison to the Merriam.

On the other hand, a Colorado hunter who has journeyed to West Virginia in November would be hard pressed to find any sign at all. The Eastern wild turkey is not found in large droves, wanders daily across a large portion of its range, and seemingly leaves little to note its having been there. Leaf fall continues to cover droppings as winter progresses. The terrain, with scant patches of bare ground, doesn't make for sighting of tracks. Add to this a greater abundance of annual rainfall, along with tremendous increased hunting pressures, and the Coloradan will come from the woods with the idea that there weren't many turkeys there.

Let's go to Florida, a large cattle ranch in Saint Lucie county, not far northeast of Lake Okeechobee. Or to a spread in west Texas where the ranch buckaroos drive the whitefaces to gathering pens, and chase Rio Grande gobblers from the hurricane deck of the same pony. Turkeys in both localities are apt to be hanging together in large droves, perhaps 30 to 100 to a bunch. The country thereabouts will be solid with tracks, feathers, droppings, and be little different from what one would expect to find at a turkey farm. In fact, the sign can ofttimes be so thick that it becomes confusing, lulling the hunter into thinking he can kill a turkey with his eyes shut. But, fire a shot or two and it's a whole new ball game. Turkeys can see a hunter a mile distant and he'll have to stillhunt with greater respect.

Again, the new hunter to Texas and Oklahoma's Rio Grande is apt to give little consideration to when the last rainfall blanketed out old tracks, for in dry country tracks can appear as though they were made yesterday, when in fact they have been there for weeks. Droppings dry out soon, so there is little to be learned from these unless they're still soft. Feathers which have not been rained upon can stay fresh for weeks. Heavy rains will eradicate tracks, dissolve droppings, and wash feathers into drifted debris. An area abundant with Eastern wild turkeys can appear to be birdless after 2 days of rainfall. The hunter unaccustomed to the region could well think there was no use in remaining there. During an early fall season, when foods are plentiful, and therefore the birds need not scratch for them among the leaves, areas of mixed hardwoods and pine often have scant turkey sign. If the area has no woods roads to walk, very little open ground bare of vegetation, but is made up of creek bottoms, rolling ridges covered with falling leaves, endless roost trees, and only a fair population of wild turkeys, the hunter will again think there are no birds, or so few as to be a waste of his hunting time.

Steven Preston examines a small feather he found where turkeys have been scratching in oak leaves. Finding this feather, and the dished out places among the leaves, will tell him that turkeys are searching here for acorns. This is a clue as to where he should continue looking for them; either by lying in ambush or by stillhunting through the area.

Locals are wont to steer strangers to any place but where the turkeys are . . .

In addition to using sign to determine turkey populations, the hunter can rely on local hunter numbers. The fewer hunters, the fewer birds. Now, I am speaking here of *average* turkey country with its numerous backwoods roads, not of many areas in Rocky Mountain Merriam turkey range, as the human population there is considerably smaller than the great bulk of ranges for the other subspecies of wild birds. Like the turkeys themselves, hunter populations can be related to the number of birds found locally. Merriams are apt to be found scattered greatly across mountain ranges, whereas a mile square area in Virginia may have several native droves.

But, throughout average Eastern wild turkey range, if I notice very few local hunters, though there are small towns scattered about, I realize that I am not within what is considered thereabouts the best place to hunt. Round-about conversation can bring out much information from the locals, though this should be given careful consideration as turkey hunters are wont to steer strangers to any place but where the birds can be found. I know, I've done it.

Game rangers will pass out the whereabouts of droves, particularly in areas where poachers are operating. The last

This old rusted turkey feeder, built from a few poles, some wire, and a 5-gallon paint bucket, is evidence that wild turkeys have been resident in the past. Though feeding the birds in this manner will hold them in an area, a hunter should never shoot over or near the feeder, as doing so will not only drive the birds away, but is also considered by most hunters the same as road hunting, roost shooting, shooting over watering holes, and bunch shooting. In other words, don't do it!

The author finds the water cold and refreshing as it is being pumped up from underground on this windmill location. Very seldom has he known locals to hunt near these watering sites, as this would be considered cheating, taking advantage of the birds' need for water in an area where this may be the only available for miles. *Do not ambush turkeys at watering places.*

(Left) This elaborate wild turkey feeder will attract and hold birds on private property with little attention. The drum section will hold 100 pounds of grain, which is made available to birds through small slits cut into the drum near the bottom. Only turkeys which have flown onto the flat upper section will have access to the grain.

thing a poacher wants is company, especially if it is a stranger. And, while it seems best to hunt in the areas with the greatest number of birds, it should also be remembered that fringe areas, with fewer birds, can produce a better quality hunt. As long as I'm in country with even a fair population of turkeys, I will hunt it rather than go to one with a good deal more birds and an army of hunters.

Large uninterrupted tracts of land, much of which is found today within our national forests, often have small turkey populations, particularly when compared to the amounts of acreage involved. What causes this has been the subject of much speculation among wild turkey biologists. Among the reasons are lack of law enforcement, local attitudes toward poaching, baiting and roost shooting, lack of water the year round, scarcity of preferred foods, and wild turkey lifestyles. I have hunted a region that has huge tracts of national forest which seem to be ideal habitat. Throughout the spring hunt there will be gobblers scattered from end to end, over hundreds of square miles of mixed pine and hardwood terrain. During the fall hunt it is all but impossible to locate a drove in these same woods. Where have all the turkeys gone?

Throughout this area the summers are often hot and dry, causing the bulk of the small streams to dry up. The birds then move to the larger river bottoms. In these areas are found many small farms, which results in cow pastures, cultivated fields, and many woods-lined edges. The birds find this to their liking and can be seen daily by the locals. Local attitudes are "shoot today because you may not see one tomorrow." Baiting is common around the farms bordering the national forests. A game ranger thereabouts is simply butting his head against a stone wall in trying to enforce game laws. Only time, plus an education of young hunters will ever overcome this. Meanwhile, the area is supporting only a portion of what turkeys should be found there.

When the stillhunter is searching for sign, he must keep all these facts in mind. It will help if the fall and winter hunter has hunted the area during the spring, for if birds were gobbling there, it's a good bet they will be nearby at other seasons, except in certain Merriam and Rio Grande areas. But, the hunter must also keep in mind that when finding little sign, this doesn't necessarily mean there are no turkeys; nor does a great amount of sign mean wall-to-wall birds. The hunter should study the birds before beginning the hunt, read all he can about their habits, study game department literature about that area, and then give it his best in the woods. Very often the result of a stillhunter's silent coursing through turkey country will be to see turkeys at a distance, those which have not yet noticed him. Perhaps

Bear tracks surround a water hole laced with tracks of Gould's wild turkeys, far back in Mexico's mountains. Throughout most of the year this high country in Chihuahua, Sonora, and Durango, is extremely dry, with very little rainfall. Such conditions then can concentrate game, though the discriminating hunter will not hunt over nor near the water. This would be cheating, and obviously taking advantage of the birds' and animals' need to go to these locations to drink.

he has eyed them in the shadows of a distant glade while driving a mountain road, or, while trudging back to his vehicle, caught sight of an old gobbler surrounded by hens. As opportunities can be lacking at times, it's best to take advantage of the ones which do arise. So, let's see if we can't sneak into easy gunshot of one of those birds. It's seldom a pushover, but it is far from impossible. I've read a number of times that it took nothing short of a miracle for a hunter to be on the final stalk of a wild turkey, and there are hunters who consider it a feat that cannot be done. Nothing is further from the truth, regardless of subspecie.

Probably the number one quality with which a hunter must be endowed if he is to stalk turkeys is patience . . .

Let's define stalking. To begin with, it's invariably pronounced ''stawk.'' To stalk means to approach behind cover, to hide a person's movements. And that is exactly what it means when hunting wild turkeys. If the hunter doesn't cover himself, he'll never get his gun to within killing range.

Probably the number one quality with which a hunter must be endowed if he is to stalk turkeys is patience. A tremendous amount of time can be required in making a successful sneak. Too often the hunter will try to bring the birds into range too quickly, which results in being seen by them. This happened to me last fall season in the Ozarks. I had spotted a drove of seven birds feeding late one afternoon in a cow pasture which was tucked snug up against a national forest ridge. I had no problem working to a point where I could watch the birds pecking at the ground from about 100 yards. I could tell they were feeding toward a corner near cover so, backing away on my hands and knees, I crawled to where I could walk erect, then slipped through the cedars until I estimated I could sneak to the pasture's edge for another looksee. On hands and knees, then dropping to my belly for the last 30 yards, I wiggled along until I had gained the shaded back of a fallen, dead cedar. The cows hadn't eaten the grass growing up through its stiff colorless boughs, which gave me excellent cover as I raised up to where I could see the turkeys. They were still feeding and the range was now near 70 yards.

But, a light mist had begun falling and evening was coming on fast. Now I noticed that the turkeys were feeding at a faster walk. Because the birds were angling away from me toward the pasture's edge where they would slip into deep woods, I knew I had to move fast if I was going to get in my licks. I would have to take my chance on making for the next cover, which would cause me to pass through small areas which didn't provide sufficient screening. My only hope was that they would continue feeding, and none would raise a head to study the terrain while I made my crawl.

It didn't work. I looked toward them when I reached a screen, but the gang was trotting toward the corner. One of them had eye-balled me. I jumped to my feet. Making for them as fast as I could run, I let out a warwhoop, which made them flush. I watched as they sailed on bowed wings

One of the toughest situations a hunter can face is to have feeding turkeys remain in one spot for a long time. Then it's decision-making time. Scatter the drove? Wait for them to move? Stalk them? It's up to the hunter to assess the problem, then act accordingly. (Photo courtesy of Greg Butts)

into a woods heavy with large pines. Ten minutes later, I stillhunted to where I caught view of one perched on a pine bough, from where I rolled it with a load of No. 6s. I'd won the war, but lost the battle which began it. Had I not run out of time, patience would have won the battle. Good stalking cover surrounded that end of the field, and had the birds been feeding on an average fall evening, minus the rain, I could have eventually stalked to within range.

Seemingly the worst headache for a stalker is that wild turkeys will linger in a place for an hour, then begin walking, perhaps pecking at this and that, but covering a lot of ground. Except for those times when the birds move toward the hunter, which is exceedingly rare, the hunter must initiate another strategy—he must stalk to a point where *he can intercept them*. There he can wait on them. This is ambushing. We'll discuss it later.

I can't overemphasize the importance of remaining behind cover if a stalk is planned . . .

Throughout varying terrains of all five subspecies of bearded and spurred wild turkeys will be areas where the birds can be stalked. The easiest stalking cover is among small rolling hills covered with trees, rocks, and brush. By far the most difficult places are in flat open woods. And, as a turkey has excellent hearing, the hunter must also be quiet, which makes for hard times if the hunter is on dry leaves. Wind is particularly helpful when hunter move-

ments cause too much noise. It also stirs tree branches, brush, grass, and these moving objects minimize moves made by the hunter which could be eyed by turkeys. Rain will obliterate sound as well, though the synthetic materials from which rain gear is made often magnify the sounds of brush and tree limbs brushing against them.

Running streams, tumbling among rocks, hide nearly all sounds. Many times I've worked myself nearer a gobbling spring turkey by walking along a noisy brook. The one setback is that once the hunter begins calling to the bird, it can be difficult to hear its answer, and locate the gobbler.

I can't overemphasize to a new wild turkey hunter the importance of remaining behind cover if a stalk is planned. Though it is possible to stalk a buck deer from out in open terrain, easing along only when the deer is looking another direction or feeding, this can't be done with a wild turkey. Oh, it's possible, but the conditions must be perfect, and then only by a hunter who knows wild turkeys thoroughly. For the average or beginning hunter, a stalk must be made behind cover at all times.

Seldom can a complete stalk be made by a hunter remaining on his feet. Much ground can be covered in a bent-over sneaking position, but when the hunter is covering the last 50 yards, hoping to draw himself to within 30 yards of a turkey or turkeys, the bulk of this distance should be traversed by crawling on hands and knees, or by belly-crawling. Here, it is the hunter's will and desire which will make or break a kill. I can't begin to recall the many physically painful stalks I've made. Anyone familiar with the prairie country's sandburrs, which are a menace to birddog and hunter alike, knows that these pea-sized balls of spikes

(Right) Hunters walk past an old long-abandoned farmstead, with buildings leaning precariously and fences beyond fixing. In parts of the country, these colorful ties to the past are known as "old house-places." Wild turkeys consider them a part of the habitat and do not associate man with them. Hunters can sit out rainy weather within those buildings which could be considered safe. Many wild turkeys have been bagged from such buildings, but it is wise to make sure the end of the gun barrel protrudes beyond the interior. If not, the gun's report will be deafening.

Hunters load up their vehicle as they prepare to leave a parking area on a large ranch near the Cimarron River in western Oklahoma. Turkeys will be difficult to approach on this flat terrain as the mesquite and sagebrush offers little to hide the hunter. The turkey's sharp vision allows it to see well through this vegetation.

Saw palmetto is a nuisance to Florida ranchers, as the vegetation will spread and in time all but take over a grass pasture. Many ranches burn the pastures to rid them of the vegetation. Turkey hunters in Florida will often find themselves hunting among these "burns." Wild turkeys like to feed among these burned-off plants, and old gobblers can strut in the openings. Binoculars are a great help to watch for turkeys in large areas which have been burned.

(Left) The Osceola wild turkey which inhabits Florida is extremely susceptible to the hunter who is expert at stalking. Once the birds have been seen, it is often possible to choose a route which will put the hunter inside of easy shotgun killing distance. This can be done by crawling on hands and knees, or by belly-crawling, often through shallow water. In swamp country, it's not for squeamish folks!

easily puncture the skin and pant legs, and must be removed by hand. A stalker can run amok of cactus, thorns, cow manure, sharp rocks, blackberry bushes, saw creepers, and water. Anyone who's bellied through some of the country's springtime grasses will easily remember the countless tick and chigger bites. Thankfully, I am immune to poison oak and poison ivy, but lots of folks would need to steer clear of these. One morning I bellied 100 yards across a foothigh stand of ragweeds. A hayfever sufferer would have come out of there sneezing for days.

Binoculars are a must for anyone who stalks wild turkeys. Slight elevations that are not easily discernable to the naked eye often become apparent when viewed through field glasses. They also enable the hunter to study the terrain he has decided is a proper course for slipping to within gun range. Further study may reveal a route which, though longer, may present fewer chances of the hunter being seen or heard. There will be times when it's wisest to stay put, and wait to see where the birds go, and then hope to stalk them. This can be a gamble (nothing new to a turkey hunter) as the birds could move into a less advantageous position.

Water in one form or another has cost me shots at a number of turkeys. Invariably this was when belly-crawling. At times the water reached a depth where it was a case

of crawl or swim, and not many turkeys will stand still for a hunter dogpaddling toward them, thrashing about as he tries to hold a shotgun above water. I have bellied through water which was several inches deep, but not so deep that I couldn't keep the gun out of water, or at least the bulk of it. Of course not all hunters want cold water running through their shirt and pants and boots as they wallow from point to point, eyeing a big turkey gobbler as he suns along a rain drenched slew in the deep South. A hunter stalking Osceolas in south Florida could find himself down on hands and knees padding across patches of mud and grass, or slipping into canals where the day before he noted a gator or two, with the ever present cottonmouths, and 3-inch leeches. All these critters and elements come with their respective territories, and to a dyed-in-the-wool turkey addict, are but a part of the hunt. They're to be expected.

Stalking turkeys in snow is as bad or worse, and is best done with white coveralls. Coveralls don't allow the stuff to infiltrate clothing as easily. The greatest hazard of stalking in snow is in getting snow packed up in the gun barrel, though this is a problem faced by any who stalk, and must be guarded against continuously.

Very often, prior to making a sneak, I have had to remove all the items from my pockets and leave them at a designated place, returning for them later. Binoculars can be a nuisance, though I carry them until I'm certain I no longer need their added benefits. My old black powder hunting cronie, Lennis Rose of Missouri, has even been known to leave his possibles bag behind.

Let's pretend you've caught sight of a small band of wild turkeys, either a drove during the fall hunts, or an old gobbler lollygagging with a bunch of hens on an April morning. None of them are aware you are on the premises. It's been a simple matter to get to within about 100 yards by sneaking behind cover and keeping your gun barrel down along your side, so the birds wouldn't spy the the sun's glint from its shiny barrel. Nor would they see it coming toward them like a periscope above the brush.

But, you've come up short. It's hands and knees time. From here on you will need to crawl a few yards at a time, taking extra care to prevent mud or soil from entering the gun barrel, meanwhile being extremely wary of its banging on rocks. You will need to pick a route well ahead of you which is free of noise-making, and hinderances which could prevent your passing. It's often a case of taking the long way around. Throughout this, never for a second forget elevations. Your hat, cap, gun—any part of you—must never be higher than your cover.

Locate a bush, dead limbs, a tiny clump of grass and take a look through these . . .

Stalking takes time. This is what makes it such an exciting hunt. Your heart will pound as you draw nearer. But, what makes stalking so exciting is that all the while you are easing closer, you don't know what the birds may be doing. You could end the stalk looking at a bare woods. So, it's wise to maintain contact with them as you make your sneak. In doing so, you will always run the risk of being seen. This can, however, be minimized and a good

percentage of time virtually eliminated. Choose shadows if at all possible, when you want to elevate yourself to study the birds, but this place *must be* within a part of the terrain above ground features. Crawl right into clumps of grass, weeds, bushes, tiny saplings, vines, until you are so close to it that the stuff brushes your face. You must become a part of it. Don't raise up over a bare log, or peak over a rock; locate a bush, dead limbs, a tiny clump of grass, and take a look through these.

The last bit of raising your head up to where you can see the birds is the delicate part. Do this *slowly*. Then, once you can see them, *freeze*. If the birds seem content, you can study them and plan for your next move. If *they are heads up, one eye toward you, don't move until they relax*. You may need to stay in this position for quite a while, and you may even develop all sorts of cramps and aches. But the slightest stirring could end the hunt with them spooking for the next county.

Once I realize that a bird has zeroed in on where I seem to be hiding, I make like a rock, and remain this way even after the bird has gone back to its activities. Invariably a bird will again look toward any suspicious area, perhaps several times, its head held high. Camouflage is a tremendous asset to a turkey hunter, especially when stalking and stillhunting. Facial camo is especially important. The human face is the part of the body most likely to be seen, this being greatly enhanced by its bright and shiny appearance. It simply shines like a neon sign in turkey woods. Face paint, a camo mask, burnt cork, whatever it takes, the human face requires one of these to make it blend with the surroundings.

Years ago I took up hunting with blackpowder shotguns and put away the camos in favor of clothing which had only dark drab hues to help hide me from the turkey's tremendous eyesight. As stalking is done from behind cover, I had no trouble with it until the time came for a closer look at the birds. I found I was easily detected at distances up to 100 yards, and on countless occasions I was seen at greater distances. The only solution was to use shadows and further burrow into screening cover before rising to

Utility right-of-ways snake all across the United States, like the power lines shown in this photo. Very often these are the only open terrain for miles around, which as such serve a two-way purpose. Turkeys, like all wild things, will gravitate to edges where dense habitat gives way to open treeless areas. Wild turkeys like to feed in these right-of-ways. With them feeding in the open, the birds are easily seen by a hunter, especially if he has binoculars, and can gain a higher elevation where a considerable amount of the right-of-way is visible.

where I could observe the birds. I even fasten tiny oak branches and pine boughs to my hat band and, in general, take all the precautions a soldier would when confronted with an enemy sniper. Nowadays, I smear my face with burnt embers from a dead campfire or let my whiskers grow. What's worse, my whiskers are turning white, so this won't help for long.

All of turkey hunting has endless decisions that must be made, but stalking seems overladen with them. And, once a person has sneaked into easy gunshot, deciding what to do isn't over even then. Can you slip the gun into shooting position without spooking the birds? Are you positive of range? What if you only knock a bird down with the first shot, but it regains its feet or wings, and attempts to escape. Will you be in a position where you can get in a final killing shot? Is the gun barrel free of obstructions?

It is a relatively easy matter to bring a gun into shooting position on stalked turkeys. Before attempting to bring it to bear, make certain of objects nearby which would be brushed in your attempt to aim, and thus which could spook the birds. Positive that you can ease the gun forward, keep your eyes riveted on the birds, and when you are dead sure that none are looking around, slip it into the shooting position. Whatever you do, *don't make any quick jerky moves*. Predators attack like a bolt of lightning, so all birds susceptible to predation take instant action when such moves are detected nearby.

Dick Bland, the author's twin brother, holds aloft a trophy bearded hen. Here it is easy to compare the size and blackness of the large gobbler at his waist with the small lighter colored hen. This hen's beard is as large as this adornment will get on a female wild turkey, exceeding 8 inches in length. He was able to bag these birds by careful stalking and then shooting from the "lay-down" position.

The worst thing a hunter can do is commit himself to the shot, and once having done so, realize the bird is at the fringe of a solid killing pattern . . .

As the average shot at stalked turkeys will be from a crouched position, or perhaps a prone position, a hunter should be familiar with shooting from these positions prior to hunting. I learned long ago that only a handful of people have fired a shotgun while lying on their bellies. The gun will not feel the same, hold the same, or aim as it does when standing. To make matters worse, estimating range is a whole new ball game when the hunter's eyes are but a few inches from ground level. Flat country such as open prairie, palmetto pastures which have recently been burned, large tree-lined meadows, and rolling sage-brush hills, have few reference points to give the hunter something to compare a turkey with. A hunter who has recently put in a spring month chasing adult gobblers can be easily misled by a late-hatched young turkey in October. Chances are he will pass up a shot thinking the bird is well beyond gunshot because at 25 yards it will appear about the same size as did the old gobbler at 40 or more yards. Reverse the situation, and the fall hunter will be blasting at old birds well before they come into range.

On many occasions, I have had to bide my time in estimating range. More than once I have waited until a turkey would be looking away from me, then I'd rise up quickly, standing fully erect on my knees, compare the bird to the surroundings, then duck back behind cover before being seen. Obviously, this is best accomplished with strutting gobblers, facing away from the hunter. The up-raised tails prevent them from seeing the hunter as he takes a look from a raised position to figure the range to the bird. This bobbing up and down is risky but, if the hunter keeps watch on the birds, and does it only when they are feeding or otherwise involved, he shouldn't be seen. I've yet to be "caught," and I've done it a number of times. The worst thing a hunter can do is commit himself to the shot, and once having done so, realize the bird is at the fringe of a solid killing pattern. Or, even beyond it. This is less apt to happen to the hunter who only hunts springtime gobblers of the same subspecies throughout the same type of terrain. Hunters who travel both spring and fall, hunting all ages and sizes of wild turkeys, are the ones who must guard against making bad range judgments. Estimating the distance to a turkey is easy in open hardwoods, more so if these have a slight roll to the topography. The tree trunks can be used as range estimation guides when a bird comes into view. Often this is done without the hunter realizing he is doing so.

Shooting from a prone position automatically eliminates the bulk of out-of-range shots. The reason is that average terrain permits a turkey, including the biggest, long-legged gobbler, to come in rather close to the hunter if there is a reasonable amount of cover. In addition a hunter can very easily raise up and down simply by bending the elbows. This gives him the added advantage of keeping a bird in view as it draws closer, and it can be done so slowly from an extremely low vantage point, that it's rare for a turkey to notice the hunter until the bird is well within easy killing distance. Obviously, when a bird looms up like the proverbial Mack truck, it is where the hunter wants it.

When hunting young turkeys during the fall, it is easy to let them get too near a prone shooter. I prefer never to let a bird walk closer than 15 yards, seldom inside of 20. My black powder shotgun's best killing patterns are at this range, so this is where I make the shots. Today's turkey shotguns are bored Full choke, and any shots at 15 yards are apt to be much like shooting a rifle. True, if the aim is good, and the hunter is holding on the bird's upper neck or head, the bird is dead. But, without a pattern, the bird can be missed.

Why the old bird never heard the *ka-a-a-booming* of my heart is still a mystery . . .

Stalking wild turkeys is a heart pounding experience, not easily accomplished by all, certainly not to a successful end. For the hunter who has never attempted it, I can only say that a person has never hunted wild turkeys until it's been done. Nothing teaches woodsmanship in larger doses. The hunter who studies turkey country and tries to work himself into gunshot of turkeys will begin to understand the what, whys, and wherefores of these birds. The person who has never stalked them will never truly appreciate the turkey's fantastic eyesight, nor will he realize how well these birds hear, and interpret what they hear.

One April morning I was hunting deep in Dixie, near the Louisiana and Mississippi line when I spied a gobbler along a meadow's edge, where some pasture stuck back into the piney woods. From 200 yards away I studied him and determined that he was just loafing. No hens were with him. He would preen his feathers, running his beak through those on his lower back and the wings, all the time stopping from time to time to stick up his head and take a look around. Of course, he could surely be called

Slipping into deeper woods, I cut a course which would bring me to within 100 yards of him. At 80 yards I could catch glimpses of him among the pine trunks, still preening. Settling into cover where I could maintain eye contact, I fetched out a mouth call and clucked two or three times.

The old bird jerked upright and one eyeball zeroed in on me. I sat quietly, knowing he didn't see me. He stood there for 3 or 4 minutes, then walked a step or two, pecking a bit at the meadow. I clucked once again. Then I yelped. None of this had any affect. He walked a few feet this way,

then that, but at last just stood still, puffed up a bit, and then began running his beak through the feathers on his lower back, like the birds do when they seem to be searching out lice.

Thirty minutes later I sneaked in from another quadrant, drawing to a halt at about the same distance, and from there gobbled at the bird. Perhaps if he wasn't up to making love he would like the companionship of those like him. He paid less attention to the gobbles than he had to the hen talk. Worse yet, he walked slowly to the highest hillock in the pasture, and again relaxed. Range now appeared to be some 30 yards beyond any cover at the pasture's edge where it met the woods.

What a fine big Eastern turkey gobbler. The sun sparkled from his plumage, fiery greens dancing among his feathers. What looked to be a fine thick beard in the 10- to 11-inch class jutted from his heavy belly. I drooled all over the pine needles. I hadn't driven 700 miles from western Oklahoma to go home empty handed. What options were left? I could stick around until the old bird left the field. As the morning was getting on toward 10 o'clock, he wouldn't tarry out there too much longer. Of course, there was only 360 degrees in which he could leave the field. Studying it, I could cut that to less than 180 degrees, but that was way too much. Chances of being in the right place were far from ideal. Stalk? Yep. It looked exceedingly risky but, nothing ventured, nothing gained.

Choosing a route which would terminate at the wood's edge nearest the gobbler, I began on hands and knees, though this soon changed to down on my belly. Things went along fine until I had come to within less than 50

The hunter who studies turkey country and tries to work himself into range will be a better hunter for it. It will help him to appreciate the turkey's fantastic eyesight and wariness. This gobbler was taken after a lengthy stalk with a too-long gun, but it worked this time.

yards and crawled into some huckleberry vines. Searching back and forth from left to right, I picked a path and bellied up to where I could see the big gobbler at near 40 yards. He didn't know I was in the county.

Ten yards, if I could gain another 10 yards, he was in trouble. Aside from green pasture grasses and weeds, I'd run out of cover. Where cattle dropped piles of manure, the grasses had grown in slightly taller clumps. Never taking my eyes from the gobbler, I pulled myself along a few inches, but each time he would have one eye in my direction. I'd freeze, head down, hugging the ground, hoping my rear end was not humped up like a sick calf. Why the old bird never heard the terrible *ka-a-a-booming* of my heart is still a mystery. I had long since quit breathing, too. Inch by inch the distance shrank.

That Eastern gobbler never knew when the end came. At about 27 yards I let down the hammer on the priming cap, the blackpowder burned, and the lead hornets killed him in less than a heartbeat. Death had snaked to him in the short grass, then struck with the ferocity of a rattler's blow.

Down through the years I've run, walked, crawled, bellied, elbowed, hunkered and all but dog-paddled my way to where it was a near range shot at all five of the world's bearded and spurred wild turkeys. There've been times when I couldn't pull off a stalk or a sneak, whichever you want to call it. But, there have been lots of days when I could burn powder.

But sudden-like, there he was, all alone, pecking at the ground . . .

From stalking, we can go to ambushing. Have you ever ambushed a turkey? By this, I mean have you ever hidden someplace where you *hoped* a turkey would come, then waited there for the bird? An ambush can be the result of a stalk that has failed, the hunter realizing he can't get within killing distance, so he waits in ambush should the bird come to him. But the average ambush is derived from a hunter's scheming. This is particularly true if the hunter notices a lot of turkey sign at a certain location, causing him to think turkeys come there on a daily basis. This is when it pays to know the habits of wild turkeys, as am-

bushes are best located where the birds travel, feed, and drink. I don't go along with ambushes laid at favored roosting places. Thankfully, only the Rio Grandes and the Osceolas are apt to be limited in terms of numbers of roost sites, but these birds should never be ambushed near these locations.

Laying a proper ambush is not for the average turkey hunting buff. Why? To begin with, today's lifestyle has led mankind into living a fast life! For most of us, it's rush to work, rush at work, rush home, gulp down our food, rush through the evening paper, try to relax for a couple of hours (which are ordinarily spent in rushing around the house doing this and that) jumping in bed, and doing it all again the next day. We live only for the weekends, but these rush by too.

So, we aren't geared to spending several hours idly sitting in the woods, waiting and watching for turkeys we know are there. We'll have the fidgets in an hour. Two hours are an eternity.

I've killed a few turkeys while lying in ambush—less than 10. It is far easier for me to bag one by other methods than to spend hours waiting for a bird to walk past my gun. But, I know men, and I'm sure there are ladies, who enjoy ambushing. It is restful and certainly an excellent way to observe all sorts of wildlife. The few times I've done it, I've been successful. Almost too successful.

One November morning I walked to a huge plum thicket, one I'd seen a large drove of birds pass through 2 days previously. Obviously it lay along the feeding route they were maintaining at the time. I just hoped they would walk through it one more time. Finding a place where I could stretch out on the ground, I made myself comfortable. The birds had been walking through along toward noon, but I was on location nearer 10 o'clock a.m. Just past 1 o'clock

The fall turkey hunter should be always on the alert to foods available which wild turkeys will eat, and watch for fresh sign. Such places are often excellent for lying in ambush. A few of these birds are in a heads-up posture, indicating they are on the alert for possible danger.

I heard a yelp. I'd about give them up, but now they were coming.

I wasn't disappointed. Thirty minutes later I could see the lead hens ambling along as they entered the upper edge of the thicket. Belly down, I had the gun in hand, aimed toward their path as it coursed downhill among the Mexican plum bushes. Thirty or 40 birds were in view, and I'd already noticed a bearded hen when I caught sight of a beard swinging. Aha, an adult gobbler. Things were indeed looking up.

Gently easing the gun higher on drawn elbows, I brought

The hunter who waits in ambush should choose a place which is comfortable, remains shady over a period of hours, and offers enough space so the gun can be swung without hitting any obstructions. Many ambushers carry a camouflaged boat cushion on which to sit, along with lunch and a flask of water. Might as well be comfortable!

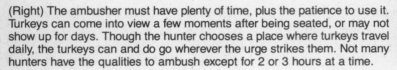

(Right) The ambusher must have plenty of time, plus the patience to use it. Turkeys can come into view a few moments after being seated, or may not show up for days. Though the hunter chooses a place where turkeys travel daily, the turkeys can and do go wherever the urge strikes them. Not many hunters have the qualities to ambush except for 2 or 3 hours at a time.

it to face, looking along the flat between the barrels, past the front bead, to watch turkeys flow past. All were inside of 30 yards. I'll get the old boy when he walks by, I told myself. He came by, sure enough, but hens were all about, plus jakes, young jenny hens, plum bushes, and what-have-you. Suddenly I had the feeling that the whole darned plum thicket, turkeys and all, was bunched up smack dab in front of me. And there wasn't a thing I could do about it. But, suddenlike, there he was, all alone, pecking at the ground. Not a bird on either side for 3 or 4 yards. I triggered a blast. Turkeys went berserk. Scrambling to my feet, I tore through the thicket, right hand and elbow guarding my face against the thorns. I'd got him. If those birds hadn't parted I would never have taken the gobbler. I can easily recall two other instances when an ambush had taken a like turn, but, the birds did not part, and I *didn't* get the bird.

An ambush can be planned for whenever and wherever a hunter wishes, spring or fall. One hot afternoon while hunting springtime gobblers in the Gila National Forest in New Mexico, I decided to sit out the long dusty hot part of the day. I'd noted a place on a little traveled road where it seemed turkeys were walking more often than usual. A small stretch of sandy road tied a ridge to the place where the trail intersected the canyon, and it looked like it could be just the place a Merriam gobbler would pass by should the bird be heading up canyon. I'd not hunted there before and had arrived there too late to hear any dawn gobbling. All I had to go by were an abundance of tracks which angled back and forth across a mountain road. Apparently the area had been subject to numerous hunters during the weekend, as the road dust was well pulverized. But, this was mid-

week, and my "reading" of the road indicated a good number of birds had walked it since then. The size of the tracks revealed that the bulk were gobblers.

I pushed a few logs around at the base of a gnarled juniper, settled back for a long wait, and looked up. A gobbler was tooling down the road. Walked right up to me. Luck can kick a person in the teeth. The person who has any desire to wait in ambush should study wild turkeys intensely. They should study turkey terrain, read all the game department reports which are available, particularly in regard to what wild turkeys feed upon in the area being hunted. There is no finer method to learn turkeys than to spend days in turkey country when the season is closed, especially if this can be done shortly before the season opens. Notice where the birds have been leaving tracks. Can you locate places where the birds have been feeding? Or are they just traveling through? How many foods can you locate? What age of birds made the tracks? Could you be standing in the roost area?

The hunter who thoroughly studies the birds, reads all he can about them from egg to adulthood, and spends what time he can with them in the woods, can set up a successful ambush. He will kill wild turkeys. And besides, a hunter doing this won't come out of the woods so frazzled out as a bunch of us do.

Obviously, the tough birds to sneak, stalk, stillhunt, or ambush, are adult gobblers. All are far more easily hunted by these methods during the spring than in the fall and winter hunts. I attribute this to the bird's intense desire to mate, which causes the adult male to lose a portion of his usual wariness.

(Left) Regardless of what method is being used, hunting wild turkeys on private land is easier than hunting them on land open to the public. This is particularly true for the stillhunter. Birds on private land usually have not been subjected to much hunting pressure, so are less wary.

Once a hunter knows that turkeys are visitng an open field each day, he can wait in ambush for them either hoping the birds will feed within shooting distance, or to plan on stalking the birds.

A person waiting in ambush should carry a camera and keep it handy for such photos as this one. Cattle are curious critters, and if they see a person settle back in cover, they often hang around, continuing to watch the location, often nosing close to the hunter. After a period of time, however, they'll forget his presence. Turkeys pay little heed to cattle, though the animals do chase them at times.

Adult gobblers, whether a single bird, or one in a drove, seem to hone their spooky nature to a razor's edge once the mating season wanes, which together with summer molting, makes backwoods recluses of them by September. Seldom will a person see adult gobblers throughout the summer months—they just disappear. So, when fall rolls around, and the hunting season is on, we have a bird absolutely unmatched for wariness.

These birds can be killed by all of the methods we are discussing, but conditions must be perfect. A bunch of old gobblers that are "nooning," (a turkey hunter term for loafing) may appear to be relaxed, pecking at the mast, or hunkered up asleep, but don't let this fool you. Old gobblers never for a second let down their guard. I swear they sleep with just one eye closed at a time. They do. When I sneak into easy gunshot of a small gang of long-whiskered gobblers, I never raise myself for a looksee from behind cover, I raise up *in cover*. And just as slow as the sun coming up. You can never be any such thing as too careful when stalk-

ing these birds. The hunter who is belly crawling a bunch of them can't get too near the ground. Nor can he be too quiet. Seldom will an entire drove have their heads down, feeding at the same time. And, if one of them gets an inkling a stranger is nearby, you can kiss them all goodbye. Once spooked, you will need all the luck in the stars to get within killing range the next time.

One problem facing a hunter who has sneaked to within shooting range of a drove of adult gobblers is in shooting the best of the bunch. Locating the number one bird is best done at very close range, where beards can be studied and, if possible, the spurs. Quite often the bird with the longest beard will not have the longest, sharpest spurs. Binoculars will be an asset. But, the hunter must do this studying while looking through cover, be it weeds, grasses, bushes, leafy tree branches, or whatever screening cover is available. All movements must be made when the gobblers are looking in other directions or, better yet, when they are heads down, feeding or pecking at the ground.

Chapter 8

Strategems—
Think Like
a Turkey

When available, large boulders make excellent concealment from which a hunter can call to an approaching gobbler. Both Merriam and Gould's turkey ranges have
unlimited terrain with rock-type cover. Here, one hunter
does the calling, and as the gobbling bird comes nearer,
the shooter remains ready.

A PERFECTLY thought out, perfectly executed plan to
bring a wild turkey into easy gunshot is not too often accomplished. Why? Because it is not possible for the hunter
to draw up the perfect strategy prior to the hunt. Only when
he is in the field with the birds at hand can he put together
a hunting stategy. Even then, the plan depends on the time
of year, the number of birds available, and the number of
hunters executing the plan. Other factors affecting a hunting
strategy are time of day and the extent to which the birds
have been hunted. Young unhunted turkeys, for example,
can be a pushover compared to a small gang of old gobblers.

I could say here that whenever so-and-so happens, you
should do such-and-such. This all sounds good when read,
but as we both know, each hunt is just as much an individual event as are all human beings different from each
other. Year after year a hunter might kill an adult gobbler
while sitting against the same tree, but you can bet the
hunter would tell you none of those kills were even close
to being identical. Planning stratagems to bring about a
turkey's demise invariably begins after a turkey is either
heard, or seen. There could be a number of birds involved,
too, and two or more hunters. Let's discuss a number of
these.

Wild turkeys have a habit of seeking high ground once
they have been spooked. Fall or springtime, a single bird
or a drove—turkeys simply hike for "high ground" when
danger is near. The elevation could be nothing more than
a long low hill in prairie country, a short spur ridge in Ozark
mountains, a towering rock strewn crest in Mexico, or a

long rolling summit in Pennsylvania. In low flat river bottom areas the birds often alight in trees. Knowing all these
things, and keeping them in mind, will put birds in
the oven.

One November afternoon, I was hunting on an 800-acre
chunk of ground that was nothing but small up-and-down
hills, cloaked in small scattered oaks, brush, and open
ground dotted with clumps of grass and weeds. About 400
acres appeared to be ideal habitat, the remainder just areas
where birds would flee if hunted hard. I knew the birds had
been hunted, but not to such an extreme. Scouting indicated
a band of perhaps 15 birds to be using the terrain.

Looking for a little bunch of turkeys on 400 acres of
thick cover, in up and down hills, can be time-consuming.
It also takes a dose of luck. What the hunter hopes *does
not* happen is that the birds wander into an area he has
previously searched. The ideal hunt would have the hunter
suddenly coming on the birds in near range, and if not
making a kill on the scatter, then to call one to the gun.

I was hunting the area as fast as conditions would allow,
therefore hoping to make contact before dusk. Trying to
keep the sun somewhere over a shoulder, I began walking
the hills. But I don't just stomp up and down them, busting
over the crest of each like gangbusters. Years ago I made
it a habit to ease over hills in turkey country like the moon
coming up, *very slowly*. I always utilize cover, using trees,
bushes, rocks, weed clumps, cactus, anything which will
break up my outline. When possible, I always use the shadows. I keep my gun barrels down, no use sticking them up
like a periscope for a bird to see. As I gain height on the

The author watches, hand on the wrist of the muzzle-loader's stock, as turkeys feed on a leaf-strewn slope. Extreme care must be taken that the birds do not become spooked. All movements must be made very slowly, and when the time has come to shoot, if these moves are continued, the birds will become alert, and while walking about, will "pert" loudly. Don't make any sudden, jerky movements, as these will cause the drove to instantly flush.

(Below) Binoculars are a must when hunting open plains country such as this land near the Glass Mountains in Oklahoma. The field glasses can detect a wandering drove of turkeys at long range, which will then give the hunter time to study the birds before deciding what action can be taken. Very often a route can be chosen which will take a stealthy stalking hunter to within easy shotgun range of the unsuspecting birds.

their location, and make a killing stalk. But, back to my hunt.

I'd thoroughly covered 100 acres, slipping in and out of coves, basins, over one hill after another when, as I eased up for a look-see on a knifeback ridge, I caught sight of several turkeys trotting up a slope some 200 yards distant. Obviously, I'd been seen. Those birds now knew they had company, and they don't *like* company.

Dropping to my knees instantly, I hunkered behind a clump of waving grass and brought the field glasses to focus. The turkeys stopped only momentarily on the hill's crest and all but one quickly dropped from view down the other side. That one turkey's head remained up and alert for a few minutes, then it also disappeared. Jumping to my feet, I ran as fast as I could to the hill they'd just vacated, slipped up its side, and gently eased to my knees back of a grapevine-draped bush as I reached the top. Studying the terrain across from me, I made out the silhouettes of two turkey heads on the next hillcrest. I froze—both the turkeys and me were seemingly made of stone. Five minutes passed before they made the slightest move. Hardly discernible, I could see one move its head. Let me tell you, those birds were looking things over. I've seen scads of spooked turkeys remain motionless for long periods of time, heads scarcely turning, as they eyeballed the landscape. Such birds are looking for the slightest movement which, if they see any, is all they'll need to tell them to "git." Ten minutes passed before the birds began pecking at the ground, then they ambled from sight, dropping over the other side of the hill.

hill's crest, I scan the opposite hillside as it flows into view, taking great care to study shadowy areas beneath trees for birds feeding on acorns, other mast, berries, and the bugs and insects which are drawn to these foods.

As I rise behind the screening brush, I not only scan the opposite slopes, but also the other side of the one I am on. Turkeys could just as easily be below, perhaps within gunshot. Remember, try to remain in any shadows, make no sudden moves, and make all movements as slow as ice melting. Certainly, this takes time, but if you can't get into easy killing distance, all the turkeys in the county won't do you any good. Among the small hills I was hunting on that day, had I seen a bunch of birds at long distance before they saw me, it would have been easy to fall back, study

Satisfied they were gone, I took off on a dead run. Covering the 70 yards in jig time, I ran up the back side of the hill, thumbing back the hammers on my old blackpowder side-by-side as I reached the top. Busting over the ridge, I ran smack into the little bunch of turkeys just below its crest. They boomed off the hillside, scattering like leaves in the wind. Throwing the gun to face, I sent one sprawling, dead centered in the load. Running to where he'd cartwheeled into a dead snag, I found him flopping in the leaves. A jake. Could have been a hen. Wouldn't have mattered, as both were legal.

None of this came by accident. It was all preplanned. Of course, with this type of hunt, three basic things could occur. I could stalk to within gunshot of a bunch and make the kill then and there. I could scatter a bunch, then call a bird to me. Or, as happened, be seen by the birds, which then required me to get myself into gunshot range by stealth, instant decisions, and quick action.

All of turkey hunting has a tad of luck, risk or the spirit of gambling to it . . .

birds will most often gang up on the sunny side. Ordinarily, such droves of recently spooked turkeys will hole up there for upwards of ½-hour, then they'll go back to wandering and feeding.

The hunter who has the will and the stamina to charge over a hill, knowing birds just walked across it, will very often be rewarded with excellent wing shooting. Of course, I don't recommend this unless you're hunting in an "any turkey" area. Fall turkeys, particularly during an early fall season, are not easily told apart, more so when flying full tilt in the opposite direction. Young gobblers and hens are one and the same under such conditions. Nor do I recommend wing shooting for the hunter who is not a good wing shot. Flushing turkeys are extremely fast to the novice, though, to a veteran hunter who has lived a lifetime of shooting flying targets, they are much akin to shooting at a flying barn. I grew up in a hunting family back in Oklahoma's Dust Bowl, and spent many days trying to outshoot my brother, my dad, and all our cronies. It was a case of becoming a fast-draw shotgunner, or getting no shots at all. Ground sluicing, or shooting at birds on the ground was a no-no, and to this day I like to make turkeys flush, as this is the natural way to kill them. My brother Dick shoots an old "corn sheller" Winchester and has for 50 years. He

This hunter is moving out to where he can see back into a field's recesses, but doing it a step at a time. Camouflaged, he will probably see any birds before they see him. Then, settled back into cover, he can study them, planning further action. This is all part of turkey strategy.

Spooked wild turkeys are not easy to stalk, so it is best to surprise them and do it fast. Catch them in a fast rush, so to speak. I knew that once the birds got over the initial scare, they wouldn't go back to feeding for a while but would simply stand on an elevated area and watch for danger. Past experience told me that one or two might watch from a hilltop, but after remaining there for a while, they would join the main band which would gather on an upper slope. I've come to the conclusion from years of observation that the birds which gather on a high slope are waiting for the birds that are on watch on the hill's summit. Seemingly, the birds who tarry cause the birds in front to do likewise, and in the end, the drove comes together where the main group has assembled. Invariably, this will be just below a hill's topmost elevation. If the day is cold, the

feels the same about it as I do. A hunter should be a good wingshot. If he's not, then he owes it to himself to go to the trap and Skeet range, burn a small mountain of shotshells, and get good at flying targets. True, Skeet and trap are not exactly what the hunter will be up against in the woods, but these sports teach the fundamentals of wing shooting—tracking targets, shouldering the gun, shooting from all sorts of angles and follow-through.

The strategy which I have just described, observing turkeys walking over a hill and then rushing them, is like all turkey hunting strategies— it doesn't always work. I have rushed over hills only to see the birds high-tailing it over a hillcrest 200 yards distant. Numerous times I've busted over a ridge, and the only thing there was me. Zero turkeys. *And*, no way of knowing where they'd gone. So, if you have no gambling spirit, you probably won't try hill busting turkeys. It's risky. But, so what? All of turkey hunting has a tad of luck, risk, or the spirit of gambling to it. Some folks just have a knack for culling out which.

Charging after turkeys can also work on a single bird and can be used in the spring on a group of hens with an adult gobbler. Adult gobblers among a group of hens are easily identifiable, even on the flush. Too, bunches of feeding hens, with the gobbler strutting along with them, move rather slowly, so once they fade from sight, a fast trotting hunter should find them very near where he last saw them. Plus, don't forget that the old bird will usually bring up the rear, being behind the hens a ways. I've popped over hills, rocks, palmetto clumps, you name it, many times, and found myself looking at an old strutter at less than 20 yards, balled out in full blossom. I can recall many times when all the hens would be feeding, the gobbler in full strut, and none of them would even be aware I was on the premises.

All of the methods discussed in this book are far easier brought about by the hunter who carries, *and uses*, binoculars. Nothing in American wildlife has eyesight to match a wild turkey, much less a frail human being. The hunter needs to carry eyes which will be a match for a turkey. A number of times I have watched turkeys fade from view in

Wild turkeys walk old roads, trails, and sometimes even spend a good deal of time on maintained roads which have little vehicular traffic. Such places are ideal for the hunter who prefers to sit near them, hoping turkeys will come along, providing a shot. Turkeys scattered by the hunter along old trails will invariably walk these back toward the scatter point. *Check local game laws before shooting over maintained roadways.*

When the hunter notices open pastures, coves, nooks, and ridges, along his path, he should not blunder out into them, but instead ease forward slowly, studying the area intently as the terrain comes into view. Watch closely in any dark shadows, particularly in the middle of the day, as loafing turkeys often lollygag in shady places. They'll probably be dusting, searching for mites, or pecking at the forest floor.

woodlands, in weedy pastures, on rocky mountain sides, but when I zeroed in on the area with field glasses, a head could be seen here and there. With the naked eye it appeared they had drifted over a hill or into a gulley. Well, their bodies *had* disappeared, but that snakey head on a long neck, had not. Binoculars will reveal all this to the serious hunter.

The hunter who walks, trots, or runs, over a hill in hopes of getting into gunshot of turkeys should make a habit of understanding the path a turkey will most likely follow. For instance, turkeys crossing from one ridge to another, given the choice of dropping down into a deep cut with its rocks, brush, etc., or walking around a long slope connecting the two hills, will always make the walk on the adjoining slope. Pressed hard, they would probably fly across the cut.

Of course, the hunter who year after year stomps old and familiar woods soon learns the travel habits of the turkeys thereabouts and realizes that birds seen traveling in a given direction will, nine times in 10, be making for a certain predictable area. The hunter who hunts strange country won't have this advantage, but if he has been a keen observer, past experiences will help. I killed an old gobbler one October afternoon simply because I knew that all the producing oaks of that late hot summer were very low along the creek bottoms. I'd scattered a gang of four or five old birds when I came around a bend in the trail, and flushed them at 60 yards or so. They flew off on a like course, just up from the bottom 200 or 300 yards. I made a beeline right after them, presumably walking smack through the area where they had flown. Once I was well beyond where

I thought they had gone to ground, or perhaps into a tree, I took up a stand on an abandoned road just alongside the creek. Acorn bearing oaks were scattered along this rocky stream. A couple clucks later I called in two of them, killing the first. Simple. Anyone who watches where turkeys scratch, feed and travel can do it.

So, when you break over a ridge, hot on the trail of a drove of birds that you assume are not within range, let your eyes dart back and forth as the landscape flows into view. You will have to pick your path and watch for the birds at the same time. If they are beyond range, beyond 30 to 35 yards, you will either have to put it in high gear, or shoot into the air, make a scatter, then call one back to you. You may want to do this anyhow if you want to kill only a gobbler.

Kent slammed to a stop and ended the turkey's flight shortly after it had begun . . .

You should be aware that given the proper circumstances, the presence of ample brush, grass, and other low ground cover, the birds might not flush but instead could run from you. And let me tell you, birds on the wing are far easier to hit than birds dodging and ducking around in a bunch of brush. I was guiding Kent Crane one November afternoon, in an area where a drove had been scattered by another hunter. Realizing the birds would gather high, Kent and I were settled in a cedar stand overlooking a long sloping hillcrest. I'd made a few calls, but nobody had answered. Suddenly, Kent whispered that he could see a black-bellied gobbler atop a spur ridge some 50 yards from us. Then, almost as quickly, Kent said the bird had dropped from sight off its far side.

Telling Kent to make tracks, I headed for the turkey's hilltop, running all out. Kent was right with me. He's a savvy hunter, one of those men that guides hope for—an excellent shot and fast gun-handler. Making tracks, I told Kent we'd go over the top and to be ready when we went down the other side. Since the bird had walked off, it meant that it had no intentions of coming to us but had probably heard other birds calling. Kent had said in the earlier exchange that the bird had not appeared spooked, though it had eyeballed our position intently before disappearing. Possibly it had caught a glimpse of movement where we were hidden, too.

Busting over the hill, we both caught sight of the gobbler as he ducked head, and then took off running downhill. Kent couldn't get a shot at him, so he put on a burst of speed which at last made the turkey decide flying would be the best way out of this mess. Kent slammed to a stop and ended the turkey's flight very shortly after it had begun. Had the young gobbler remained afoot, I think it would have made good its escape.

Have you ever shot a turkey out of a tree? *No, no, don't ever shoot one from a roost.* I mean from a tree where it has flown after being scared in escaping danger. Many, many times, when young birds-of-the-year are flushed, they alight on a nearby tree, oftentimes on the topmost part, what is known as the crown. The bird will then sit there, watching and waiting, and once satisfied all danger is gone, will fly back to ground. A rule of thumb is that the older the bird, the longer it will stay there on its high perch. Adult turkeys will stay there until they turn to stone. Leastways, you'll think so. If you like a little spice in your turkeyin', then the next time you flush a drove, keep your eyes peeled for a bird landing atop a tree crown.

Your next move, plus the speed of its execution, will determine whether you carry that bird back to camp. Again,

The author examines strut marks in the dry soil of a Chihuahua mesa. These marks are made by the dragging wingtips of a gobbler in full strut, and are accompanied by an abundance of tracks. The alert hunter will pick up sign such as this with little or no trouble.

you'll need to be a good fast shot, are willing to gamble on a daring chance, are reasonably fast afoot, and regardless of how the episode ends, can go back to camp with a grin on your face, fully aware that you "win some, lose some."

Before that bird gets itself settled on that branch, head for it on a run, marking your course so that when you get inside easy gunshot you will be just off to the side of the tree, where you can angle a shot into its uppermost part. If the leaves are off the tree, you should be able to keep the bird in view until you stop to make the shot. If the leaves are on, the risk is greater that you will lose sight of the bird and may not get off a shot when it flushes. The hunter's running toward the tree seems to freeze the bird, it possibly

There are turkeys sitting in trees and there are turkeys *roosting* in the trees. *Don't ever shoot one from a roost!* Once flushed by the hunter, the birds will often fly to the top of a tree until the danger has passed, then drop back to the ground. Generally, the older the bird, the longer it will stay on its high perch. It pays to look up while turkeyin'. (Photo by Marilyn Maring, Leonard Rue Ent.)

hoping that by remaining motionless it will not be seen. Too, the bird has probably not seen a man running before, and this action is new to the bird's escape senses.

Most of my shots have been at the bird as it still sat quietly atop the tree. I simply run up into easy range, slam to a jolting halt, heave the gun to face lightning fast, get a quick bead, and *bang*, down tumbles the turkey. Easy as shooting fish in a barrel, except you don't get water in your eyes.

When the leaves are still on the trees, the shot will invariably be when the bird flushes, and this high-tree crossing shot is perhaps the hardest to make in all turkey hunting. The bird can present any angle to the hunter as it leaves the tree—going away, to either side, or coming directly across the hunter. A big gobbler can flush fast, gain momentum even faster, and as he booms from a high pine is a veritible hurricane on wings as he heads for the next county.

Hunting in New York state one fall, I noticed a turkey fly up into a tree some 100 yards from me. Gobs of leaves on the trees helped to screen him, so I decided I'd just slowly slip up on the bird. Nobody had shot at it, and since it appeared to be small, was probably very young, therefore not too wary. I hadn't made it halfway to the tree, when the bird decided it wanted to see the other end of the county. After that, I went back to running up on a bird.

The game hog has no place in team killing. His impatience will mess up the plan . . .

Throughout my wanderings across the United States, I've heard of individuals who could sneak a gobbler in a tree, killing it where it stood. I've heard all sorts of tales—boys going barefoot, men in their stocking feet, all of them able to sneak into near shotgun distance of gobbling adults *in full daylight*. Perhaps. I've never seen it done.

Turkeys alighting in trees located on steep hillsides, or inclined mountain slopes, can be hunted by the stealthy stalking hunter, so long as he keeps in mind that such birds, when flushed, will fly either along the side of the mountain or downhill. The exception is the bird that has settled in a tree on the terrain's crest; this bird might choose to fly over the hilltop. Few birds will take this flight pattern though, as the average turkey will perch on a tree on the flank of

(Left) Acorns like these are found throughout Merriam turkey range, often from the Gambel's oak, which is a clump oak. It doesn't grow to a great size, but is a prolific producer of acorns. But the hunter who is new to Merriam's country should keep in mind that this subspecie of wild turkey does not eat acorns as a major part of its diet. A lack of feeding sign in the oak clumps would be nothing to indicate a lack of turkeys, because these birds would probably be feeding on other foods to their liking.

I'd keep the bird gobbling so John could keep track of where the old bird was.

I kept up lots of racket with the calls, yelping loud, and often. This had the double effect of keeping the bird put, and keeping him gobbling. It was simple. John came around behind him, sneaked into easy gunshot, and rolled him from the ponderosa.

Another hunt down in New Mexico's Gila National Forest found us staring up a mountain toward a Merriam gobbler that was whooping it up. The sun was up, but the bird hadn't left his roost tree. John went around behind, came over the mountain, and the bird flew head-on to me. He came down on the second shot.

I would not advise shooting at such birds unless the hunter has made positive identification in terms of sex. Hens are oftentimes perched very near the gobbler, so the hunter must take extreme care in making correct identification. During fall hunts, in "any turkey" legal areas, this would not matter, except to those hunters who prefer not to shoot a hen.

There are a number of strategies two hunters can apply

Retired U.S. Forest Ranger John Waters circled, then stalked this giant Merriam's gobbler, while the author kept the bird's attention with a hen call. Water's shot was a culmination to the teamwork of two hunters, so that one of them could make a killing shot. Many turkeys which cannot be hunted by a single hunter are easy prey for hunters who plan a stratagem as to how the birds might be hunted.

(Right) Lunch time is planning time for the afternoon hunt, especially if someone in the party has made contact with the turkeys earlier that morning. It must be decided beforehand how much calling should be done, by whom, and where from. If the birds were assumed to be an unscattered flock, it may be wise to walk surrounding areas, hoping to scatter them.

a mountain. Mountain gobbler hunters know this and, when a bird refuses to respond to calling, can hope for a shot if they approach the bird's tree from directly downhill. This works extremely well for two hunters working as a team.

John Waters, a long-time hunting buddy of mine, and I have pulled this strategy on numerous gobblers. A turkey is in deep trouble when we decide to hunt him. We heard a gobbler cutting it up just at first break of light. Hearing a response to our calling, we hustled to the area and found an old gobbler high up on a mountainside, gobbling and strutting from a huge ponderosa limb. He wouldn't come to the call but flew a couple hundred yards to another tree where he began his act all over again. We could hear hens yelping too, but none seemed to be near him.

Having two turkeys to kill, and not much time to do it in, we couldn't wait around all day to see what would take place, so we made plans. I told John to sneak around the back side of the mountain, then make his stalk. Meanwhile

to both fall and spring turkeys. Probably the one most used is in pushing, or driving, a bird or birds past another hunter. This tactic works well with all subspecies, at any time of the year. As with all hunting methods employing two or more shooters, teamwork, plus unselfishness, is what hangs birds in camp. The game hog who wants to get in his shot first has no place in team killing of wild turkeys. His impatience will mess up the plan for everyone.

The old-fashioned southern turkey drive is nothing but a group of beaters herding a bunch of birds toward a line of shooters. Very often the birds will be both running and flying. This method should only be utilized in an "any turkey" area, as identification will be impossible when the shooting begins. The size of the drive depends on the turkey population and the number of shooters. The shooters must be excellent and experienced wing shots. I have stood on the "picket line" among retired military men, senators, business magnates, heads of government, cowboys and old long-time duck and goose gunners from Maryland's Eastern shore, watching as a long line of flushed turkeys headed toward the line and, noting the tumbling turkeys as those dead shots swung on them. Cripples? No, but these men were excellent wing shots.

The average drive is done by two buddies who hunt together a lot. It will be an impromptu affair, brought about by the conditions at hand. It seems I've been involved in many of them from New England to Mexico, with any number of friends. All of these hunts have been the result of seeing turkeys positioned so that one hunter could circle behind and push the birds into gunshot range of the other hunter. It must be planned so there is no chance of either hunter being shot, which is unlikely if all parties follow the plan and identify the mark before shooting.

My brother Dick and I were lying on the lee side of a peaked hill one winter afternoon, watching some oak thickets with binoculars. The wind was howling out of the north, but with the sun shining in on our grassy hide, we were comfortable. Long toward sundown, Dick suddenly stiffened, and I swung my glasses to follow his lead. With a

find plenty to eat, and be in that same clump when we got into near range. Much of shinnery country looks alike when a hunter is on foot and on a like elevation. If the birds hotfooted to a neighboring clump, chances were we would spook them while trying to get into shooting position at the original oak clump.

Keeping the topmost branches of the clump marked, I at last came to where I could only continue by belly-crawling through tall grasses. Slowly, ever so slowly, the range to the small oaks diminished. Keeping one eye peeled on my wristwatch, I knew Dick was coming in from opposite the clump, bellying through the grass too.

At 60 yards, I eased up to where I could scan the prairie, my face buried in a tall, thick, waving stand of brown bluestem. Instantly, I caught the sun's glint on a black glistening back. Range—40 yards. The drove had left the oak clump and were headed across my front to another, feeding on weed seeds and dead grasshoppers as they walked. Tall stands of brown bluestem grass dotted the prairie among the oak clumps, and as the birds wandered among these, I began crawling as fast as possible. If the

When two or more hunters are planning to hunt an area, they should discuss the possibilities beforehand that if either should shoot (the signal that turkeys have been located), that will decide what actions will then be taken by the hunter who is not doing the shooting. Turkey hunting can very often be done more successfully by two or more hunters than by the single hunter.

couple of hints from him, I picked up the dark bodies ambling about in a large stand of shinnoaks, what's known in west Oklahoma as a shinnery clump. Blowing sand catches in these oak-leaf strewn clumps, which in time brings the elevation of the clump up a few feet higher than the surrounding prairie. The clumps will average 40 to 80 feet across, and as these are prolific oaks year after year, wild turkeys will feed from one clump to the next, scratching among them for acorns. Visibility for the turkeys is unexcelled. Sneaking coyotes and bobcats would have a hard time catching one of them.

Minutes later a bird walked out to where we could get a decent look. We could see a long beard swinging in the wind. Giving the birds a serious going-over, we then studied the area, planning a pincer movement. Tucking field glasses inside our coats, we separated. I would give Dick 10 minutes to go around the bunch, which we had decided was six adult gobblers. We just had to hope they would

birds got by me, they could make it to a fence beyond which I could not hunt. They were obviously heading for a large roost.

The wind killed any sounds I made as I pushed the gun ahead and pulled myself along. Quickly I covered a good number of yards, at last coming to a large thistle. Hunkered and gathering my knees under me, I eased up for a looksee through it, instantly catching sight of a gobbler walking across a tiny opening not 20 yards ahead. Head down, he hadn't noticed me. Thumbing off the safe, I stood up. Heads shot up. The gun bucked. Down he went. The others flew off. Running to him, I was grabbing for his head when I heard Dick's Winchester thump. Just one shot. Good.

Talking to Dick about it back at the truck, he told me after my shot a bird came flying past him and he downed it. Both birds had 7-inch beards. What a nice afternoon it turned out to be, wind blowing, and all. Teamwork and strategy made it that way.

By positioning him before I left, I then knew where to push the turkeys . . .

Another method which works extremely well with hill country, or mountain turkeys, requires two hunters. The next time you and a buddy encounter a springtime gobbler that keeps gobbling to the call, and yet won't come to it, try this on him. Once you have made voice contact and the bird is answering your calls regularly, you can assume one of two things quickly: either the bird has hens with him, or, he simply wants the hen (you) to come to him. Now, one of you must stay put and call while the other must circle the gobbler, coming in toward him from behind, preferably from higher ground. This can be nothing more than a foot or two in elevation. If the bird is on a hill, make an effort to work yourself into position, *at or above his elevation*. Sneak in as close as possible. Belly-crawl, get down on your hands and knees, whatever it takes to bring yourself to within 60 yards. *Do not call until you are as near him as possible.*

Certain that you are close, you can now make a few hen yelps. This trick has worked each time I've used it, often after one short series of calls. I've called in strutting single gobblers, along with gobblers accompanied by hens. Invariably the birds will come to me a minute or two after the call is made. The ideal situation for this stunt is when you have cranked up a gobbling turkey located above you on a hillside, or along a slope or crest of a mountain. Many of these birds, though located originally on the hill's crest, will work their way slightly off the summit when you call but will refuse to come any lower.

There will be times when the circling hunter can sneak into easy killing distance of the bird, too. A lone hunter can try to work the same trick on the bird, but the one drawback is that nobody is left to call from the original point of contact. Therefore, the bird will often cease gobbling, and perhaps amble off. The lone circling hunter will often spook the turkey then, or lose track of its exact location. When team hunting, we can assume that once the bird was raised, or heard to gobble, both hunters closed the range to within a couple hundred yards. This should place the hunter who remains behind to keep the bird gobbling in an advantageous position to shoot at the bird should the circling hunter spook it. At best, he can watch to see where it goes. Remember, mountain turkeys flush downhill.

Numerous times I have been with another hunter or two, when we saw a drove of wintering birds, or perhaps an old gobbler or two with a passel of hens. Even though there appeared to be nothing we could do about them after watching them for a spell, a plan would slowly evolve. Invariably, this was little more than moving around them and placing ourselves at locations which we hoped would be in their path. By separating, the chances became much greater that one of us would get in a killing shot. There was also

Hunters gather to compare notes after spending the morning tromping a ponderosa forest in New Mexico's Rocky Mountains. The hunting of country which is not familiar to a hunter can be unnerving to many hunters, particularly in "big country," such as areas of the West. An Eastern hunter seeing the Rocky Mountains for the first time will be intimidated by their size. He may feel hopeless in thinking he can find a turkey in such a vast area. Teamwork will put more birds on the table than hunting by yourself, especially in territory such as this.

The observant hunter will notice evidence of wild turkeys in many ways, little things which can reveal the presence of game. Turkey feathers such as these in an abandoned camp fire indicate birds in the area, located along a little used road in Florida. Feathers and bones have told Bland where to expect turkeys to be found in numerous places, including the mountains of New Mexico, Arizona, and old Mexico.

the chance that, if spooked, the fleeing birds would pass the other hunters, or that a bird might fly up into a tree and one of us could make a run for it. At the very least, the birds would probably pass within easy spooking range of someone, and once the birds scattered, the chances for a kill increased. Of course, this applies to spring gobblers, too. As long as the old birds are consorting with hens, the hunter is left out. The bulk of all turkey hunters feel that they must hunt alone, but their chances for success would increase tremendously if they would hunt with a buddy. Having guided for so many years, I have hunted with groups of two to 10 or 20 men, all expecting to get a turkey, and all of them fairly new at turkey hunting. But, by working together, I've been witness to an awful lot of turkeys killed by such groups. And, I have never noted even a near-miss in terms of a shooting accident while engaged in multiple-hunter outings.

David Jackman, an old long-time hunting buddy of mine, and I have a standing joke between us in regard to our

long, but we could take the few minutes required to try a quick ''push.'' Luckily, we were both well acquainted with the area. (So much of the time David and I are hunting woods we've never seen before.) Grabbing a small dead stick, I brushed off a smooth place in the soil, and hurriedly drew a map, pointing out to David what I intended on doing. I'd make a circle and hope to push the birds to my partner. By positioning him before I left, I then knew exactly where the gun was not only for my own safety, but so I knew where to push the turkeys.

Trotting a course which should take me beyond the yelping birds, I soon made the circle, then began walking back toward David. As could be expected, the birds eyeballed me before I saw them because I never did see them. David's gun going off told me the stunt had worked, and when I got back to him, he was standing over a black-bellied young jake turkey. A dozen or so had come past him, fleeing my approach. He picked out a gobbler, and the hunt was a success. Something it hadn't been ½-hour earlier.

By using the "buddy system," these two hunters both scored hits on gobblers. While one kept calling to the birds, the other circled around, flushed them, and both connected with good wing shots.

(Below) A hunter studies turkey tracks at a waterhole. Due to the consistency of the mud, he must be careful in studying such tracks. Quite often a track can be several days old, so it is advisable to make an impression in the mud with a finger, then compare the fresh look of it with that of the turkey track.

many pursuits of prairie chickens. We'll have a bunch of the birds located, and after studying them for a period, one of us is apt to remark, "Let's surround them." Anyone who has put in a lifetime of hunting chickens knows that two men are not going to surround many of these critters. The birds always have a way of sneaking out before either hunter is anywhere near shooting range. But, David and I have surrounded any number of wild turkeys. We've hunted together many, many times, so we each know how the other guy thinks, hunts, and will react. Any number of our teamwork hunts have been so simple and have required but a few minutes to put game on the back porch. I can recall one dreary November morning, along toward noon, when it was drizzling rain, and David and I were walking the mile back to my pickup. It had been a fruitless morning. But, as we skirted thick brush along a draw filled with oaks and other stuff, we heard a couple of turkeys yelp far down the gulley. Time had run out for us to fiddle with them for

Head down, beard swinging the old bird was pickin' 'em up and layin' 'em down . . .

I suppose there are hundreds of turkeys killed each year by hunters who presumed the birds were coming to their calls when in reality, the birds were running from another hunter. A good friend of mine killed his first two birds simply because he was sitting in a line of trees connecting two heavily wooded areas on opening day, 2 years in a row. Too often, the abundance of woods will not allow such situations, but when two good turkey woods are connected by a thin string of trees, or even thick brush, turkeys that are hunted hard will follow this treeline when escaping. At one time I used to hunt a thick woods which was separated from another excellent hunk of habitat by an open stretch of ground, weeds and grass some 60 yards across. I don't know how many turkeys I've seen burst from the woods, one side or the other, and make a hard beeline run for the opposite side. Head down, and feet flying, they would cover that stretch like an overgrown rat. Ken Warner, the same man who is today the editor of *Gun Digest*, gave me a scare one day at this location. I'd been back in the woods calling for a time to a gobbler that was answering me from the other woods. Ken and I couldn't get over there with him because of the open ground. I would call, and the bird would answer. After a long period of this, it became apparent the gobbler was coming near the edge of the far woods.

Suddenly, the bird busted from the woods, running like crazy directly toward us. Head down, beard swinging, the old bird was pickin' 'em up and layin' 'em down. Ken had his gun to shoulder. The bird kept coming, and kept coming. I thought Ken would never shoot. At 10 yards he somersaulted the bird. I swallowed my heart. It had all but jumped out of my mouth. Ken's a good shot, and he had the gun. I didn't, but just wished I could have. I'd have shot a mite sooner.

If you hunt enough, you'll experience what happened to me and Tom Preston one winter morning. We had heard a drove calling to each other in the trees, but by the time we walked to the vicinity, they'd gathered. With field glasses, we could make them out in the deep woods, chasing each other, standing about, preening, and pecking at the river-swamp floor. After so much of this, first a single hen, then another, and another, began wandering off single file which was followed by the complete drove, all headed for whatever it was those first hens had in mind. Droves always begin the day in this manner. One or two hens will set the stage, going toward water or food, and the rest of the drove follows.

We watched them a few minutes, talked it over, then decided we could intercept them. Trotting and running, we soon made a huge arc, at last sneaking in behind a tangle of driftwood among giant, ages-old cottonwoods, part of

Throughout the southern part of the U.S. will be areas where wild turkeys are sometimes hunted from blinds, such as this one located on Brooks Holleman's place south of Montgomery, Alabama. Turkey Hollow, as the ranch is called, has a good number of these timber-tar paper blinds, which are located overlooking feed plots where the birds come to eat. Some Texas hunters also wait for turkeys in blinds, though this type of hunting is too slow for many people. Others consider it unethical. Numerous states do not allow "baiting," though there is some argument as to whether this food-plot hunting could be considered to be in this category.

(Opposite page) Often the best strategy can come from discussing local hunting with folks at hunter check stations. These folks will divulge all the information they have available concerning local turkey concentrations, where most of the birds are being killed, etc. Every little bit of information helps to organize a hunting plan.

the same woods that at one point in time were known as Sheridan's Roost. Shortly we could hear the birds' yelping and located them again with binoculars. Looked as if we'd chosen the right place, as the birds were coming straight toward us. By then, we had eyed a pair of adult gobblers with the bunch of hens and their spring hatched birds-of-the-year. This is not a rarity to find older male turkeys with such a group, but neither can you expect to find them in such a drove every day. Given the opportunity, and the time, it is always wise to look over any fall and wintering drove, just in case there is a long-whiskered bird with them. Certainly all of us would prefer a big gobbler to a lesser one.

Tom and I were hunkered behind brush, looking down gun barrels as the drove flowed past. Sitting side by side, we could whisper back and forth. First, one of us would have an opening at one of the older gobblers, then the other. Both of us couldn't keep one in view as other turkeys would walk between us. It was a case of too many turkeys. Older gobblers always tag along toward the tail end of such droves, so it quickly became apparent the whole shebang was going to be beyond range. I whispered to Tom to take one if he got a chance. Forget me, just shoot when he got the opening. We didn't and wouldn't risk killing additional birds simply so we could both shoot an older gobbler. Seconds later Tom fired. Turkeys scattered toward the river, but we ran out to where a bird was flopping. Just what Tom wanted, a fine adult with an 8-inch beard.

Tom carried the bird back to where we had the pickup, we heated up a cup of coffee, drank it, then decided the drove had probably reassembled. Hiking back to where they had flown across the river, we could hear them calling in heavy brush. They weren't far from an open sandbar jutting into the river from the opposite side. Tom offered to slip around them, thinking that perhaps they would walk onto the sand, where I could get a shot. Sounded okay to me, so he took off.

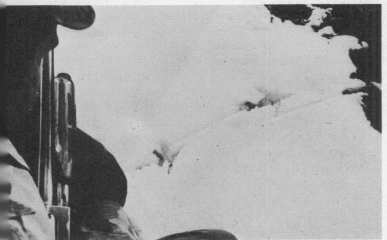

Fresh snow is not uncommon when hunting spring turkeys in Merriam turkey country, and can be a real asset to a hunter who does not know the country. Turkey tracks in a snow only hours old not only tell the hunter the birds are around, but, by studying the sign, the hunter is able to tell the number of birds, which way they were traveling, the size and the sex.

Action soon commenced. First the birds fell silent, telling me they had eyed Tom, or heard him, and then I could hear them flushing. Turkeys came streaming over, high and low, flying all out. Keeping my old muzzleloader at ready, I pulled back the hammers, just in case I needed to shoot. Hens and young gobblers, flying into the morning sun, were easy to identify, many of them passing over me inside of 20 yards. A few of them had run out onto the sandbar, only yards from me and then, on seeing me standing so near, ran to takeoff in flight.

I'd given up on the other big gobbler when a bird ran out onto the sand, and in that instant I noticed the beard swinging on his chest. Up he came, beard streaming back, and headed past me, big black and white primaries cutting huge swaths in the slight wind. I cut down on him, the old bird falling into the cold shallow waters of the North Canadian. Boots and all, I waded out to where he floated down to me. There's nothing so soggy as a wet bird, but the long skinny beard took from some of his wetness.

Teamwork killed both gobblers. Tom's going across the river had brought me mine. My telling him to go ahead, don't wait for me, had brought him his gobbler. Strategy, and helping the other guy, will do it for you.

Digging out a worn call, I stuck it to the roof of my mouth . . .

However, the average turkey hunt is by a single hunter and usually takes place in the spring of the year. The hunter hopes for success through the use of a call to lure the bird to him. The strategy is simple. The hunter hopes to hear a gobbler cut loose from its roost branch, sneak to within a couple hundred yards of it, find a comfortable place to lean back against a tree trunk, make a few calls, then kill the bird when it walks into gunshot. Nothing to it.

We wouldn't have any turkeys left if this technique worked even half of the times it is tried each spring. The birds would all be shot out. But, there are ways to combat the various things which go wrong. Let's say the bird cuts loose like the Bells of St. Mary's just at first day. We get set up 100 yards from him, and he is still in the tree. We haven't called to him. Oh-Oh! A hen sounds off. Her pips and clucks tell us she is in a tree near the old bird. Now we have a problem. What to do? The average hunter will call at this time. The gobbler will gobble back. The hen will continue to cluck and chirp. This goes on and on, the birds fly down, get together, and march off. The hunter gets zip. The hunter would have at least had a fighting chance if he had easily walked in among the roost trees and scattered the birds. It's a dead cinch he wasn't going to bag the turkey if the bunch waltzed off together, so if by flushing them, nothing comes of it later, it's all the same.

But, many times the birds are flushed from the roost area without a shot being fired, chances are good the old bird will soon get over the fright, and commence gobbling again. Having been separated from the hens, he very often is a pushover for a caller. On terrain that lends itself to stalking and sneaking, the hunter could wait for the birds to group on the ground, then attempt to waylay the old adult in this manner. I've done this any number of times.

The one ingredient the average hunter lacks in pulling off such a stalk is patience. The hunter must hold back, studying the group, waiting until they are in a situation advantageous to the hunter. Oftentimes the hunter will not have visual contact, but must rely on keeping track of the birds through their gobbling, the sound of the strut itself, and the talking of the hens. Once the hens begin moving toward their feeding grounds, the groups will move along at a good pace, the old gobbler bringing up the end of the procession. Very often he will be strutting.

During this period when the hens are traveling to wherever it is they have in mind, they will usually be head down, pecking at the ground all along the way. The group is extremely vulnerable *now*. When dealing with droves of birds

up back beneath a huge cedar, hoping to keep a dry thread on me. But, I got soaked. Hotfooted it back to the truck, changed into dry clothes, went back into the area, and after some searching, located the bunch. At last they stopped to sun and preen on the side of a hill, out in the open. I studied the terrain with the field glasses, chose a route with not too much belly-crawling, and went after them.

Moments later I eased up onto my elbows, peeked into the cove, but nothing was there. Then it dawned on me that perhaps I was one cove shy of my goal. Peeking into the next, I stared head on at the backside of a big turkey gobbler. Preening hens stood beyond him.

I couldn't shoot until I had an open shot. Poking the blackpowder burner through the side of dense bush, I waited. And waited. This could have gone on for some time, except that I grew bored, puckered up my lips, and made a whistle much like a very young poult turkey makes. It's a cheeping sound.

The old bird turned, the hens grew to full stature, and when I whistled the second time, the gobbler stepped out

The best strategy when dealing with a drove of wild turkeys far out on open ground is to lay low and wait to see what develops. This can take hours, but in time the hunter may notice that the birds are slowly meandering toward a location which may be conducive to a shot or stalk. Perhaps the hunter can sneak to that location and intercept the birds when they come in range. (Photo courtesy of David Jackman.)

on the move, and the hunter tries to circle them and bring himself into shooting position as they pass him, it is often best to try to waylay the old gobbler who is tagging along behind a passel of hens by coming up on him from the rear. The hens are looking ahead, and the old bird, usually in strut, can't often see behind because of his fanned tail. The hunter who has patience and waits until the group has just passed over a knoll, dropped into a cove, or faded from view behind a rock outcropping can then quickly slip forward, check the birds out, move, check, until the opportunity to kill the gobbler presents itself. Often I have had to whistle to make the old bird stick his head up so I could cut a fine bead on him. Many times all I could see were a few hens pecking at the ground, and the back side of a large fan. All this inside of 20 to 30 yards.

This last spring I located a gobbler at first day, and he was soon joined by four hens. I bade my time. An hour past sunrise, I had closed the distance to less than 50 yards when it began to rain. It poured. I lost the birds while holed

of line with the hens. I thumbed back the right barrel hammer, then burned powder. Charging to my feet, I sensed the hens blowing out fast, and as I ran through the cloud of white smoke, I could see the old bird bounce down the slope in front of me, then tumble from sight as he flopped over a small cliff into a rocky gulley. Side-hopping down into it, I at last laid my hands on him. Field glasses killed that turkey just as much as the gun.

A week earlier, in far west Oklahoma, in Rio Grande turkey country, I had heard a bird gobble long toward middle morning, and soon spied him standing out on a long rolling hill. A few widely scattered junipers were all the company he had. No hens anywhere. Crawling on hands and knees I came to within 100 yards of him, but I was downhill. Obviously, there was no way to get on the bare ridge with him. I called. He gobbled. I called. He gobbled. As this could go on for hours, I quit. Then I laid there watching him. Shortly he began pecking at the pasture, ambling here and there, apparently disinterested in the hen (me) with no place to go. At last he drifted off to the left, bringing an immense juniper between us. Hoping he couldn't see me, I made a beeline for it, crawling with all the grace of a tired crawdad. Bellying into its thick boughs, I edged forward, until I could make out the old gobbler through the lacey foliage. This was looking better. Range was now about 60 yards. All I could hope for was that the turkey would walk behind another juniper.

My problem now was that of being heard as I moved. Small pebbles dotted the gravel-like soil, and I'd noticed a lot of noise in my last moves. Again, it appeared the bird would fade behind an intervening tree which, though to the naked eye seemed to offer a complete screen, might not hold up so well to a turkey's telescopic vision. Could be a chance the bird would pick up a slight movement through the juniper's branches. I'd just have to gamble. The old cuss was drifting toward land where hunting was a no-no, so if I didn't make a play for him, he'd soon be "out-of-bounds." Digging out a worn mouth call just given to me by Buddy Hanks, down near Vicksburg, Mississippi, I stuck it to the roof of my mouth. Buddy had made far the finest turkey talk on it I'd ever had the pleasure of hearing. I prayed some of it was still left in the call. Will Primos, up at Jackson, had made the call.

The second the Rio Grande gobbler stepped from view behind the juniper, I eased to my feet, and keeping the tree lined up with the bird, began walking fast, straight toward it. All the while, I was making that mouth call sing, pouring out a steady conversation of hen talk. The 40 yards to the juniper melted, but when I reached it, I knew the gobbler was still there, as I could hear him clucking to me. Gun up, hammers back, I never slowed, but walked out from back of the big arborvitae to stare the big black turkey right in the face. No gobbler can escape a 12 bore side-by-side scattergun. I rolled the old rascal on about his sixth running step. He hadn't even gotten to wing.

How many times have you read about a hunter who sits still only to have the bird approach from behind? . . .

There are absolutely no end of tricks a hunter can try with turkeys. Some of them are just foolish gambles, coupled with the crazy idea that they might work. Late one April afternoon I was staking out a heavily wooded north slope in some piney woods in Amite County, Mississippi. I had reason to think an old gobbler I'd heard that morning was roosting in those trees, so I would wait to see. Along toward sundown, when the leaves on the hill were washed in a yellowish hue and even the air seemed to be a burnt yellow, I thought I could hear a man coming toward me. I could tell he was coming from darned near right where I thought the bird would walk, so it kinda upset me. What

fool was out in the woods with me? Hadn't known anyone to be hunting thereabouts. Couldn't imagine who it was. About then, I recalled that turkeys oftentimes sound like people when walking on leaves. Perhaps it was *not* a man. I kept my attention riveted to the slope. Waiting patiently there, my memory brought afresh an event that had happened only the winter before, when a small drove of young turkeys had sounded like a bunch of children as they approached my stand, their feet stirring the dead leaves like playing youngsters.

I wasn't surprised when the black old bird drifted into sight, hiking down the slope as sure-footed as a timber cruiser. My, what a fine thick beard I saw swinging back and forth. The slope dropped into a gulley some 40 yards from me, and in seconds the bird had dropped from view into it. I brought the gun to bear on my side. He would pop up on my side in an instant. In the same breath, an inner impulse told me to jump to my feet and charge the gulley. I fought it off, and stayed put, gun up, waiting. I never saw the bird again. Never knew what spooked him, or whether he went down the gulley, or up. Perhaps he wasn't spooked at all. The phrase, "win some, lose some," must have been coined by a turkey hunter. I still kick myself for not following the hunch. I'd have gotten the old rascal. All my hunting life, I have followed hunches—those on-the-spot whims that tell a person to act—and invariably the hunch will prove out.

Insofar as turkey hunting strategy is concerned, I think

A wild turkey's eye can discern color, has extremely fast abilities to make out and decipher objects, and perhaps magnifies movement. Obviously, once a turkey has seen any predator, including a hunter, it will identify that object in a split second and take evasive action. The folks who underestimate the power of a wild turkey's eyes will kill very few turkeys. *If any.*

This young gobbler is safe as it walks between the author and the bunch of whiteface cattle. Notice that one of the calves is walking toward the bird, probably out of curiosity. This bird lived to gobble another day, as the author never could get a clear shot while it walked among the cattle. The best strategy here is just to wait for another chance.

a tremendous number of hunters would make proper decisions, *if they would relax, and allow their minds to think.* A bird gobbling, or a bunch having flushed, then flying to all quadrants, mesmerizes many hunters, causing their thought processes to go blank. From there on, they do the first thing that comes to mind, not turning over all the alternatives prior to acting.

Undoubtedly the one factor which is overlooked is that if the hunter doesn't take a chance, certainly he is not going to be successful. How many times have you read about a hunter who sits still, has called a bird into gunshot only to have the bird approach from behind him? He can hear the turkey gobbling and walking, but can't see it, nor does he attempt to turn toward the turkey. At last, the story ends with the bird walking away, making tracks along with some deep clucks.

Immediately, we can draw some conclusions. First, *why* did the hunter sit there and let the bird walk in on his blind side? Was he so comfortable he just hated to move? Surely not. Could he observe the bird the last 100 yards as it approached? Probably not. Therefore, he could have moved, keeping his gun aimed in the general direction of the turkey. But, if there is no explanation to these, why not make a play for the bird once it has come into easy range? After all, once the bird has walked up too close and spies the waiting gunner, the bird is then spooky, and the chances are heavily against the hunter calling it back into gunshot that day. The fact is, the hunter's chances of dealing with the bird further will be no worse than should the hunter make an effort to bring the gun to bear on the turkey before it is beyond shooting distance.

There is one thing to be learned about dealing with birds near at hand, and this is to make your moves with about the speed you would if you were putting your hand to your face, to brush your hair back. *Do not make quick sudden moves.* All wildlife associates quick moves with predator strikes, and react instantly, hoping to escape. Several times I've fallen asleep, only to awaken with birds inside easy range. On three occasions the birds' cluckings awakened me. I would never have killed any of these birds had I made quick attempts to bring the gun on them. I killed birds in every instance, because I made my moves at a moderate pace, brought the gun to bear, took aim, and fired. Only one of the gobblers was running all out by the time I shot. The others were either walking, or had not taken evasive action.

BOOM! I'd never have killed that big Eastern gobbler if I had not moved . . .

The what-to-do's when turkeys are answering a hunter's calls are probably the trickiest part in all turkey hunting. Fall or spring, it doesn't matter. There have been so many conflicting how-to's on what a hunter should do that all this has just confused a lot of folks. My advice is to read what you can, try to keep it in mind the next time you hear a bird answer, but *think.* Don't try so-and-so just because you read it. Study the situation. Look over the terrain where you are calling from. How would you approach it if you were coming there from where you have heard the turkey? Does it resemble a place you have known turkeys to use? Are you sitting out in a park-like opening against a lone tree with brush scattered about? Could this be a situation where you will be seen first by the turkey? Have you got visibility which would allow you to move if the bird is within what you would estimate as 50 yards? Dense brush does not make a screen for any of the above. You can't see through it, but a turkey can. You can't shoot through it with any degree of confidence. You would not be able to move, as you are not certain the bird wouldn't see you. In such a location, chances are you would never get a shot, as the gobbler would eyeball you before you'd get a shot.

I just mention this in hopes that hunters will loosen up, study the facts at hand, then think themselves into whatever it takes to bag the bird. All of us, given enough time in the woods, will soon weave enough rope to hang ourselves. I'll never forget the first time I suddenly became aware that I was calling a gobbler to me, but the brush was so dense where I was sitting, there wouldn't be the slightest chance I would see him before he would see me. I was holed up in a stand of huckleberries bright with spring's new leaves. If you aren't familiar with them, the bushes are turkey high, perfect to hide a gobbler. The old bird was coming in fast. He'd been hunted earlier that season, in addition to previous years. Leastways, that's what the old gent who owned the spread told me. I'd never set foot on the place before and

This hunter waits for wild turkeys to come to his calling, while making the notes with a mouth call. This leaves the hands free to manipulate the gun. He will need to be aware of the brush when attempting to bring the gun to bear, and to insure that any sharp-eyed turkey does not catch a glint of light reflecting from his wristwatch.

If you don't like a shooting location, find another one you can live with. Bland has often moved to spots *many* times just before the shot. Turkeys move about quite a lot, so it's natural for someone using a call to do likewise. This lucky hunter has just tumbled a nice gobbler. (Photo by Leonard Lee Rue III.)

had started the old gobbler at first day. Knowing the old man's reputation for plain ornery cussedness, I realized that if I didn't prove myself with this old turkey he'd put me on, I might not get invited back.

I'd just called to the bird, his answer seemingly coming from about 60 yards out. Perhaps 70. Glancing around, I spied a small tree some 20 yards from me, with lots of leafy branches down near the ground. It would have to do. I made another call, clucking eight or 10 times, like some noisy hens will do in the springtime. The old boy shot back, gobbling twice. I yelped again, he answered. Crawling fast on my hands and knees, I scooted back under the overhanging boughs, rolled over on my stomach, and aimed the gun back toward the greenery where I'd made the call. His last answer wasn't 50 yards out, and it wouldn't take him a minute or so to cover ground.

The first inkling I had that I had company was in seeing the white flat spot on the upper front of his head. Just a dot of white appeared in the huckleberry bushes. It's gone. There, over there. Looking down the steel track between the gun's barrels, I kept looking, hoping, then I could make out the old turkey's head, eyes, beak, white spot and all. *BOOM!* I'd never have killed that big Eastern gobbler if I had not have moved. There've been others I've taken in the same manner since, but none of them had a 12-inch beard. Yes, I did get asked to come back.

If you have started a bird toward you, "raised a bird," so to speak, but on looking around, don't like anything about your location, get moving. Find a spot you can live with. If the bird is a good distance from you, move toward him a bit if you see a place where you think you can make the kill. I've moved umpteen times in dealing with gobblers. Turkeys move, so it is natural for someone using a turkey call to do likewise. During the spring, hens wander considerably. Calling from one location time after time could make a gobbler suspicious.

Making the actual decision to move is the hardest part of a hunt for many hunters. Possibly there are thoughts dashing madly through their minds as to the bird seeing and/or hearing them. And, while these are distinct possibilities, I learned long ago not to be concerned with them. Few gobblers will see a hunter changing positions at 100 yards, or even at much over 50 yards, due to slight rolls in terrain, brush, trees, and what-have-you. This is evident each time a hunter sits down to call. When he leans back and fetches out "Old Faithful," and before he even makes a note, he realizes he can't see anywhere. Of course, folks who hunt nothing but flat prairie pastures and bald mountain meadows will have excellent visibility, and moving while a gobbler is coming becomes very risky.

The best method for hunting wild turkeys is to get out there in the woods with them and hunt . . .

Ordinarily the hunter hopes to make a few calls, have the bird respond, come to the gun, and the hunt is over. No strategy is required. But, when the bird answers time after time, yet fails to come to the hunter, then it's time to think of what can be done. Chances are fair that the bird is with hens. There is no way of knowing unless they have been heard, or can be seen. I've often noticed that gobblers with hens will be moving, but at a very slow pace. So, if the bird gives you the notion that he is on the move, and doesn't seem to be in a hurry, you should then make an effort to make visual contact. Invariably a gobbler with hens will not answer your calling but a few times, then he is apt to quit. This can mislead the hunter into thinking the bird is coming to him, when it is simply following hens, and no longer gobbles to the hunter's yelps.

The gobbler that answers time after time is often alone. If the bird is moving about considerably, hotfooting from one knob to another, walking back and forth the length of a ridge, it's almost a certainty. The bulk of these turkeys are first year adults, have a beard about 6 to 8 inches in length, with spurs ½-inch long. These gobblers lack but a month or so of being 2 years of age. Who knows why one will act so silly, gobbling at every call, but not coming to the hunter. Numbers of times I have seen these birds walk past hens as if they were invisible. But, the hunter's main clue that he is dealing with such a turkey is that it walks a lot. As mentioned earlier, these kinds of birds are more easily dealt with by two hunters working together, one remaining behind to keep the bird gobbling, the second attempting to waylay it where it stands. Some of these gobblers can be had by intercepting their paths, particularly those which stroll back and forth on a ridge.

Many times these birds have come to where I had

called from, but only after I had left that place and was calling at a new location. In my early turkey hunting years, I presumed I was leaving a calling stand too soon, or perhaps I should shut off all calling, the thought being that the hen had fallen silent and wandered off. So, I tried these tactics on the walking gobblers. But while I might kill one occasionally, very often it's the same old tune, gobble, gobble, gobble, but no turkey came to the call. Walk and gobble.

I have killed them by moving to a new calling location, calling from there several times, making the bird gobble, then running back to my last stand. I never sit down at the exact place where I had made the calls earlier but take a location within 25 yards, and bring the gun to bear on my calling stand. Of course, I can't make a call, as I want the gobbler to think I am still at the place he last heard me. I

Two hunters working together have a greater chance of success than one working turkey woods alone. One hunter keeps the bird gobbling, while the other moves into position and makes the shot. Gloria Merrow of Vermont is all smiles as she admires a young gobbler she bagged.

must point out that the birds I've killed in this manner were standing within feet of my old locations when I pulled the trigger. It's uncanny how a bird can pinpoint sound locations.

I've bushwacked a number of these strolling gobbling turkeys. This required patience above all in waiting until the bird has located on terrain favorable for closing the distance to him. Jake gobblers, those young bucks with beards an inch, perhaps 2 or 3, in length, will also wander about gobbling during the spring hunt. Of course, scads of them are killed by hunters making hen yelps. But, while one may come to calling, the next will seem stone deaf. Springtime jakes are often easily bushwacked, for their gobbling attracts hunters, and sooner or later the bird will find itself in a place where a hunter can sneak into killing distance. They run in bunches, too, so when one answers a call, or comes to it, he could bring lots of company. Only last spring I had a group of six jakes walk up to me. That was followed 2 weeks later by a bunch of four some 700 miles from there. All subspecies of jake turkeys will come to hen calling.

What I've hoped to get across in this chapter is to get the hunter to think. To rationalize, to study what he is planning on doing, *before* he does it. There are times when it's wise not to let the turkey hear your call. There are times when it is best to scratch in the leaves with a stick, imitating a hen feeding, than to make a hen call. Particularly, if the bird you're after has been hunted hard with calls, and you now think he is close on the mountain with you.

But, in thinking, the hunter will also have to realize there will come opportunities which must be taken advantage of with lightning-like quickness, or the chance will be gone. Perhaps it's little else than "skootching" around to bring the gun to bear on another tangent, or to make a run for another tree 30 yards distant. True, with these no-time-to-speculate decisions there is a great amount of risk—the hunter might be seen, and the gobbler may vamoose—but it's far better to try and fail, than not to try at all.

Long, long ago, I learned that so much of this stuff we have heard about waiting in a place for hours, in hopes of a turkey answering our calls, or to not bat an eyelash though the gobbler is not in sight (but could be), is a whole bunch of hogwash. The great percentage of this malarky is put out by folks who have set themselves up on a pedestal as turkey hunters since they have killed a couple or three dozen birds.

By changing calling locations a number of times, Bland has been able to bushwack many strolling gobblers. The birds he's killed in this manner were invariably standing within a few feet of the old locations. It's amazing how a turkey can pinpoint sounds. (Photo by Irene Vandermolen, Leonard Rue Ent.)

Osceola wild turkeys are found on several Florida wildlife management areas which are open to public hunting. The Osceola pays little heed to water, wading in it to a depth of several inches, and often roosts in swamp cypress trees.

The worst way to carry a dead turkey through thick brush is to hold it by the feet, breast forward. With the bird slung over a shoulder, the hunter would find the going much easier.

By far the best method that any of us can develop for hunting wild turkeys is to get out there in the woods with them and hunt. Turkey hunting is a sport of exceptions. Nothing is ironclad, except the coming day, last light, and taxes. Read what you want, but when you get in the woods with a turkey, it all gets back to the old axiom, "Do as I do, not as I say." And, I never know what I'll do, until I do it.

Chapter 9

A Day Here,
and a Day There . . .

The springtime turkey hunter can often expect to wake up to snow, especially when hunting high country in Merriam turkey range. Often these late-season snows are short lived and have no effect on the turkey's mating habits. Though white camouflage might be of use throughout such conditions, there are always shadows, dark tree trunks, and rock piles which will give a hunter places from which to hunt.

FOR MANY years, I had a buddy who was an absolute fanatic about goose hunting. He'd look forward to opening day darned near from the evening it closed in January. By August, he was "bushy-tailed and wild-eyed" to get back in the pit. The big decoy spread had been long since made ready, and all that lay between him and goose hunting were a few days of dove hunting. This was just a prelude to the real shootout. By October, he and I would have the pits cleaned of last season's debris, sprayed for black widow spiders and grass tied to the blind's removable covers. He's dead now, but in his lifetime he killed hundreds of geese. What was so amazing was that he killed each and every one on or over a small tract of 120 acres of land. I never knew him to hunt a goose anywhere else. Seemingly, he never cared to. Being a gypsy at heart, I couldn't understand this.

Throughout all those years, there would be times when the gunning wasn't good over the spread where my buddy hunted, and I'd try my luck in other areas, using other methods. By and large, when compared to hunting from a well-concealed pit, these methods were hard work. Decoys had to be carried long distances, and certainly lying out in a bare wheat field among a stand of decoys was not as comfortable as sitting in a warm pit with a bench seat. During times of below freezing temperatures, such "lying out" was as near to death as a hunter could get, as fences are too far apart to slow a hard prairie wind in the wintertime.

When I wasn't lying out in a field the flocks were using, I'd be looking for bunches that had found feed elsewhere—study them a while, then attempt to belly crawl into gunshot range. Just often enough to keep me doing it, I'd sneak into range and kill a pair. The years went by, and while my hunting partner sat it out on days that were bad at our old stomping grounds, I was killing geese elsewhere. If the birds weren't flying to his decoy spread, he was out of luck.

Late in the season, when the flocks had been hard hunted, skybusted too, if a decoy layout wasn't an exact duplicate of what the geese expected it to be, they'd never toll to the rig. 'Course, my buddy had never lain for hours along fences studying flocks feeding in winter wheat. Nor had he listened to the calls made by a flock as newcomers arrived over the field. January geese he did not kill.

I felt the urge to find the real challenge in "turkeyin'." I found it in new country . . .

Turkey hunting is no different. The hunter who puts in a lifetime killing gobblers in one hunk of woods won't be so good elsewhere. Such hunting tends to close a person's mind, to cause him to quit thinking, to cease asking why. Too, he loses any aggressive qualities, which are perhaps of more importance in turkey hunting than in any other gunning sport. Like the turkeys he has been hunting, the hunter will develop a set of habits, some good, some bad, but all of them geared to fit the area he has become a part

Talking to cowboys Wes McKinney and Ira Davis led the author and another hunter to a sprawling hunk of woods along the Cimarron one morning, where they found Merriam gobblers strutting. Cowhands know the country like few folks know how many moles they have on the back of their hands. Talk to the locals, they'll ofttimes tell you where they've seen wild turkeys.

A great portion of the United States' best turkey ranges are situated where many "edges" are found. As with all wildlife, turkeys love to feed along these edges, where open fields, often in cultivation, lie beside dense wooded areas.

of. Too much of the hunt is taken for granted. Too often, such a hunter will kill a bird year after year, on the same ranch, in the same woods. Though he very often doesn't realize it, the old challenge is gone. He's just going through the motions. Sure, he knows the area by heart, and what the birds that are living there will do. He *should* kill one each time he hunts.

I hadn't hunted turkeys many years before I knew that the sport would lose its flavor for me, providing I just kept drifting along, killing turkeys in the same area year after year. I'd already taken to making birds flush, shooting them on the fly. I'd been raised as a wing shot. Ground sluicing any game bird was strictly for slobs. Wing shooting helped, but I felt the urge to find the real challenge in "turkeyin." I found it when I began hunting turkeys in "new" country—places I'd never been.

One such episode was in my home state of Oklahoma. A young rancher had heard that I was the man who could teach him to call wild turkeys, and he called to invite me to his ranch—hoping I'd hunt with him. Of course, as I was always on the lookout for additional areas to hunt, I accepted. Early the following morning, I pulled into his yard, shook hands, and then we drove down a long lane bordered by big, old cottonwood trees. Daylight was streaking the eastern sky as we walked silently across the sandy sagebrush country, stopping beneath what appeared to be an old apple tree. I noticed my host was carrying an Army surplus .30-caliber rifle. *Humm-mm.*

By now he'd told me the turkeys should be roosting not far from us, in a small grove of soapberry trees. Thinking

it was time we should be hearing from any bird around us, I slipped a call against the roof of my mouth and made a few yelps. Lordy, I wasn't ready for what happened next. So many gobblers cut loose that it was just a big roar. Again and again, the whole hillside in front of us seemed to raise clear off the ground. I thought we were in a turkey farm. It was surely a good thing that broad daylight hadn't yet arrived. I couldn't help but grin so wide that my teeth could have been seen at 100 yards. Whoo-ee-ee! This was gonna be nothing but an old fashioned turkey shoot.

The first day was spent stealing through the woods. Now, I could see that we were crouched behind a tree in what appeared to be an old, long-forgotten orchard with dense brush off to the north, a tiny creek to our east a few yards, open sagebrush country to the south, and scattered brush and trees west. Making several calls, I was up to my neck in good times. Gobblers were shaking the woods to the northwest, seemingly no more than 100 yards from us. The bedlam never ended. Each time one would gobble, they'd all cut loose. There couldn't be less than 15 to 20 of them. From time to time, I could hear a hen, but she'd be drowned out by the gobbler's racket. Then we could hear them flying down, making lots of noise as they left the trees. My thumb kept worrying the safety on my old Fox side-by-side. Whispering to my host, "Don't move even your eyebrows," I made another bunch of yelps. Good gosh, the gobbling all but blew our hats off. Some of them were closer. Hot dogs!

A moment later I called again. Nothing showed, which was kinda surprising. I had presumed we would have to more or less defend ourselves against the onslaught of rushing gobblers. The birds bellered back again. There they were. I could make out several black shapes to the northwest of us, walking back and forth, standing still, and I could see some of them stick out their necks and gobble when I'd call. I whispered to Max Olson, my newfound rancher buddy, "I can't understand what's wrong, they just won't come down here." I'd studied the layout by now, and to me there didn't seem to be a single thing wrong with our location. The grass was pastured off short, and there weren't any vines or high weeds to keep them from coming to us, but all the same, there they were—75 yards away, gobbling and raising hell, but not coming to where we could get a shot. Max whispered, "Yeah, I guess we should've got a little closer to that hog-wire fence. They look like they're walking up and down the other side of it." I all but fainted. *Hog-wire fence!!!**&(???)*

I couldn't believe this was happening to me. It had to be a nightmare. In the growing light I could make out the evenly spaced posts, though I would have presumed the fence was barbed wire.

"Max," I said, "does that fence run all alongside this field?"

"No, it ends right here below us," Max whispered, indicating with a nod of the head the general area where the hog-wire terminated. Maybe, just maybe, those turkeys would come around the end of it. I laid on to the calling, making loud raspy yelps, not even slowing as the birds gobbled. The sagebrush sounded like a turkey convention. While some birds were strutting, others were pacing along the fence, sticking their heads in and out of the wire squares, searching for a way through it.

Suddenly, one of them made a mad dash south, running along the fence. Then others joined the race. I swear those birds threw sand as they rounded the corner where the hog-

wire ended, ducking under the barbed wire, and here they came. Eight or 10 longbeards headed straight for us. Meanwhile, we were squirming around to meet the charge. Max had the rifle stuck up alongside the apple tree, holding it toward the advancing mob. I yelped, hoping it would slow down things which it did. In a second's time, the birds stopped, most of them going into full strut, anywhere from 20 to 30 yards out. Turkeys were still running up and down the fence too.

Hunkered behind my young friend, I watched as he took a long careful aim dead center to the front of us. Gripping my double-barrel, I readied myself 'cause just as soon as he fired, I was going to come out shooting. *WHAM!* Max's gun went off and in that split second his rifle bumped the tree trunk. Missed! Turkeys flew—the whole orchard was a melee of feathers, leaves and flying sand. I swung at an old bird off to the north. *Boo-mmm!* At the shot he went down, thrashing and flopping all over the place. I made a beeline for him, grabbing him by the neck, then the quick flip of the body and I could feel his neck snap. *Wham!* Max's rifle exploded again. Looking around, I couldn't see any turkeys fall. Walking to where I was standing over the dead bird, Max said, "Well, I might have hit one as they ran over the hill. Didn't look like it slowed him down much, though." I agreed that if any bird had been hit, I couldn't see that much damage had been done. "I missed that old bird that was strutting when I first shot at 'em." Max added, "Just as I shot, I didn't realize it but the gun was so near the tree, that I bumped the rifle into it." "I know," I answered, "rifles aren't my idea of anything to hunt a turkey with."

Later than morning Max had a second chance at a strutting gobbler I'd called up to us—again at close range—and missed once more. After that, I had no trouble getting him

(Right) The alligator juniper is a heavy producer of food for wild turkeys in much of Arizona, New Mexico, and old Mexico. Seldom does a year go by when these trees fail to bear juniper berries.

Opening and closing gates are a part of turkey hunting all across the United States. The author has hunted on a ranch which required getting in and out of the pickup 17 times for this chore. Turkey hunting is worth it. *Do not leave the gates open!*

to use my scattergun, and before noon he had killed a gobbler with it. Max and I have been hunting buddies ever since that morning. He's become as good with a mouth caller as anyone I know, and I doubt if he's taken a shot at a gobbler since then with anything but a shotgun. Hogwire fences? Ha-ha! In the years since, I've had all sorts of escapades with fences of all kinds. Hunting in strange country brings them to you.

Turkeys are always doing it to other folks, so I do it to them . . .

Back in my early days when traveling to Dixie, I was hunting in a piney woods one morning in Mississippi. The morning began at first day on a high ridge, but as I heard a gobbler sounding off to the west, I worked my way down into a creek bottom, and eased up onto the gentle slope of the ridge with him. Like so many places, I'd never set foot thereabouts before, but had an idea of what the terrain was like. A person can do this by "reading" the countryside.

A typical far South gumbo road, not easily navigable by vehicles except those with four-wheel drive. But, the worse the road gets, then the chances become greater there will be fewer hunters to reckon with and, perhaps, a greater number of turkeys. Large trees alongside these roads, such as this one on the left, are often used as roost trees, because the open road is an easy place for a turkey to fly up from.

This can be done just as well while traveling in a vehicle as on foot. It's simply studying the terrain as it comes into view. Notice how the land lays. Is it gentle on the whole or is it rough and hilly with lots of water-cut gullies and erosion? Has there been much timbering done recently, or is it from years back and the trees are coming back? What about underbrush? Is there water in all the creeks? What about open fields with those clean grassy edges that strutting gobblers like? Is there any cultivation? There're an endless variety of observations that can be made as a person drives through the countryside which will tell him what to expect if he were on foot hunting turkeys there.

Back to my story. I worked my way to the top of the rise, well studded with mature pines. Obviously the bird had been roosting somewhere thereabouts when I first heard him at daybreak. I called from time to time and he was still answering me off to my southwest, at maybe 200 yards. His muffled gobbles told me he was either behind a knoll, or in a draw. Could be either, as I'd noticed the country had lots of small hills and gullies. Simple. He'd flown down, the hens had come to him, and the whole passel had wandered to where they were now. My first contacts had been from so far distant that I hadn't 'til now been able to tell what the situation was. Calling again, I got another quick answer. Getting a good fix on his position, I sneaked ahead, easing off to the left as I didn't want to risk going straight toward him.

Just in case the bird suddenly decided to come to me, I didn't want to bump into that turkey coming through the woods and spook him off, so I drifted off to one side, more or less a circling move. Turkeys are always doing it to other folks, so I do it to them. If I get to where the bird has been, and he has gone to my calling place, I'll soon know it and can make amends for "standing him up."

Curious hunters stop to look inside an old farm house which has become the home of skunks, 'possums, mice, rats, and rafter-nesting birds such as barn swallows. Cattle will also make themselves at home if the door is left open. These old structures often give hunters shelter during bad weather.

Drawing near to where I thought he was, I called again. His muffled gobble was inside 100 yards. I'd have to be very sneaky from here on in. Didn't want to blow it now. Slipping ahead, a step at a time, I suddenly caught sight of a farm building ahead. That would explain the muffled gobbles. The bird was behind the old barn. A few more steps—what's that? Looks like a car. It hit me in the face like a sack full of mush. I eased forward, taking a look from where the brush ended. Of all the damned fools! There was my gobbler—*my wild gobbler*—in a chicken wire pen. No wonder his gobbles weren't loud and clear. Many domestic turkeys have a gobble which doesn't carry like a wild bird's renditions. Too, he was penned alongside a falling down shed which deadened the sound. I was mad 'cause I'd spent the morning fooling with a tame turkey, but I couldn't help laughing either. I'd been had!

To this day I'm leery of gobblers that won't come to me in areas I've never hunted. I'm always watching for houses and fences if I have to move toward them—and creeks, rivers, streams and beaver ponds, too. It helps to know where these are located, as many turkeys will come to calling, and hang up on reaching water. The larger the body of water, the greater the chance they won't try to cross it. Birds will also react the same to ravines, gullies, draws, cuts and arroyos. Many times I've had turkeys come to me across these obstacles, but it's best to presume the bird won't, if you know the area, and make provisions beforehand. Too often the gypsy turkey hunter finds out such things after the bird has refused to come to him. I called to two gobblers one morning and upon easing toward them came to where I could see a large stream. In short time I could see the two birds pacing the opposite bank, gobbling back at each of my callings. Luckily, they flew across to me after I began a session of non-stop calling. Yet, on a similar occasion, a bird called to an intervening creek wouldn't budge. He could have hopped over if he'd had any gumption. Just stubborn!

I took a compass reading. *Great Balls of Fire*! I was going the wrong direction . . .

The number one rule in hunting Eastern mountain turkeys is to call to them from the same ridge they are on and, if humanly possible, from slightly above them or at least the same level. Of course, if you haven't seen the ridge until you hear a bird whooping and a'hollering from there, you have the odds stacked against you. This is why it's so important to study an area even as you drive through it. Notice how many little side spurs have formed from the main ridge. Are there small coves tucked into mountain sides? Do the main ridges all tend to run in like directions? What about the underbrush—is it open or is it in "new leaf?" Are there lots of dead leaves on the slopes? I lost

Merriam Rocky Mountain turkey habitat is high, rough country, where melting snow causes a babbling brook to turn into a rushing, tumbling stream. If a turkey gobbles across the churning waters, sometimes the only way to cross is by walking on a spanning fallen tree. Don't try it if you are not sure-footed, or if you don't like getting wet.

The hunter must keep in mind the fact that few wild turkeys will cross over water when coming to a hunter's call. The hunter should call from the turkey's side of any water, a fact which the person hunting in unfamiliar country is not always aware of.

A hunter unfamiliar with an area will do well to order topographical maps of the area before the hunt. He should study these intensively to orient and acquaint himself with the area before going into it afoot. This is particularly true in much of the West's Rocky Mountain country, because the hunter who becomes lost here can then be in serious trouble.

(Right) Topographical maps will reveal varied elevations like this ridge to the hunter who is planning a trip to unfamiliar country. By studying such maps thoroughly before making a trip, the hunter will not be a total stranger to the surroundings once he arrives there.

an easy chance at an old Merriam gobbler one morning in the Rockies, simply because the sky was clouded over. I'd been fooling with the bird for ½-hour or so, and it finally became obvious I would have to get above him. I hadn't done so earlier, hoping he'd come down to me. Climbing can be hard work at an elevation of 8,000 feet, but he wouldn't budge, so-oo-oo. . . .

Studying the face of the mountain, I could see that it wouldn't be difficult to back away from where I was calling, make a circle up a dry arroyo to the summit, walk along the backside of the main ridge until I was even with the bird's gobblings, make a call, and shoot him as he came up to me. Any hunter who has done this a great many times is aware that it is easily done. I made it to the arroyo, climbed it until I broke out on the summit ridge, dropped over the backside, and walked the flank around toward where the gobbler had been. He'd stopped gobbling, but with a call I was certain he'd get fired up again. I eased out near where the mountain broke downward and called. No answer. I slipped along 50 yards or so and made another series of calls. I was mystified as to why he wouldn't answer. He had been so cranked up, gobbling time after time, it was unbelievable he had quit. Perhaps the old boy had hotfooted it down to where I'd been earlier. No. If he had, I could easily hear him from where I was. I couldn't understand how, but apparently I'd spooked him. I headed off the mountain.

Moments later I realized that nothing resembled the ter-

rain I'd left. Pulling the compass, I took a reading. *Great Balls of Fire!* I was going the wrong direction. Turning around, I climbed back to the summit. Taking a reading there, I then had the uneasy feeling that somewhere along the way I had taken a wrong turn. Retracting my path, I soon found out what had happened. Not knowing the mountain, I had walked along its backside and had simply walked onto the flank of an adjoining ridge jutting from the mountain's backside. I'd been calling into a canyon that was one ridge removed from the one where the old bird was gobbling. With the course straightened out, I made my way back toward where the bird had been. Never heard him after that. He'd probably gotten disgusted with the hen's ''fiddling around,'' and stalked off looking for another lady friend. Had the sun been shining, I'd have been aware of the change in direction there on the mountain's flank. And, had I been there before, I'd have not made such a goof.

Becoming lost is something a hunter in strange country learns to take in stride. He *will get lost*, if he truly wants to hunt and in so doing, gets back away from it all. I've been hopelessly ''confused'' in Alabama, Mississippi,

Pennsylvania, Arkansas, New Mexico, Oklahoma, Arizona, and in Gould's turkey range in the Sierra Madres in Old Mexico—and I'm not one who easily gets turned around. I go to these places to hunt, so I pull out all the stops once I get into the woods. But, I'm never without a compass, a knife, and my match safe. I've never had to spend the night in turkey woods yet, nor has anyone had to come looking for me. So far, I've been able to find my way out, and hopefully this trend will continue. The fact that I have been able to untangle any mess I've been in is strictly due to earlier observations, together with my knowledge of what I should expect in the terrain where I am at the time. I can't stress one point too often: at the first inkling a hunter feels he is confused about his location, he should immediately stop and make a very serious effort to

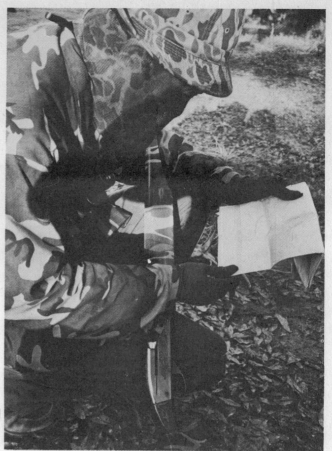

Hunters seeking Merriam wild turkeys in New Mexico can hunt these birds on the Jicarilla Apache Reservation in far northwest New Mexico. First, however, you must obtain a permit from the tribe's hunting department in Dulce, New Mexico.

(Above right) This completely camo'd hunter is wisely carrying a small section of map into an area he has not hunted previously. This will give him instant data on what terrain features surround his location, which will prevent his becoming lost and, at the same time, help him to remain in areas best for wild turkeys. Knowing where he is will allow him to hunt with greater intensity with his mind at ease.

(Below right) Hand-built foot bridges and rhododendron thickets will be unfamiliar to a person from the far West, but these are just a part of turkey hunting throughout the eastern part of the country. Hard pressed and heavily hunted wild turkeys will seek refuge in these "hells," which are all but impenetrable to the average hunter.

reconstruct his actions to the present time. Invariably he will then learn where he went wrong. Together with a fresh compass reading, he should then be able to decipher a *general* direction to civilization. Being accustomed to walking long distances, I'm not concerned about coming out smack dab in the middle of camp. I only want to come out, then I'll find camp. Now, it's silly to get yourself lost, but while you're trying to get out of the woods, you seem to forget about hunting. Could be you're in the best place you'll be for days.

One afternoon I was hunting far back from the road in the Ouachitas, a range in Arkansas. I hadn't been minding my course when it dawned on me that the ridge skylined off to my right didn't look familiar. A little farther along, I noticed again that the mountain didn't look right. It was just after dinner time, and as anyone knows who's spent a lifetime in the woods, a high noon sun can fool you. I could see it as clouds scudded across it from time to time. Digging out the compass, I took a bearing. Oh lands! I'm going

Hunters wait for another member of their party to come out of the woods. Many such waits last until darkness, with the realization then that perhaps the hunter is lost. All members of a party should tell each other approximately where they intend to hunt and give an indication of what time they hope to come out of the woods.

the hill with him. In jig time, I'd walked around the base of the hill, sneaked up the backside, then, trying to pick a route over its rounded top without stepping on too many dry leaves, I chose an old fallen log to call from. The bird gobbled back instantly at my first calling. It sounded like he was just "under" the ridge, maybe 200 yards. I was lying there staring hard when I made out the upper part of the old turkey's fan as he wended his way uphill to me, bloomed out in full display. *Boo-mm-mmm*!

That evening, hunched over the map, I untangled my afternoon's course. It became obvious why that turkey was so heavy. I'd toted him nearly a mile to the road then 3 miles from there back to the truck. Like all fool turkey hunters, I'd be delighted to do it tomorrow, given the chance, and twice the distance.

The real America is found among the little known roads, the back-roads, the small towns and in people's homes . . .

The traveling turkey hunter can do two things that will far exceed all others in preparing to hunt on unfamiliar terrain. Using a map, he can study the region beforehand and then read books on the turkey subspecie that lives there. Both can be done off-season, at home, or riding the commuter train to work. Once a site has been chosen, which needs to be little less than a general area—a national forest, a county or simply one corner of a state—the hunter can then ask for information from that state's game department concerning turkey studies that have been made there, along

back toward Fort Smith, a river town that was in a general northerly direction some 80 miles from where I stood. Correcting my course, I headed southeast, as I knew this would bring me out on a road leading back to the pickup. I had bought a topographical map of the region and had studied it. I highly recommend this practice to anyone intending to hunt in strange woods.

I estimated the distance to where I'd break onto the road at 2 miles, each step through heavy woods, all of it good turkey habitat. No use wasting it. I would ease along for a while, then call. Walk, call, walk, call. Using a wingbone caller, this is easy, as it only takes one hand to work the call while the other handles the gun. A sling on the gun makes this simple, too.

An old bird answered me when I was still well over a mile from the road, but to make things worse, he wouldn't come down. He'd gobble back at me from half-way up a ridge. Knowing that late afternoon gobblers seldom drop lower as the day wears on, I knew I'd have to get up on

Huge ponderosas, along with some scattered conifers, mark this as Merriam turkey country. The Merriam roosts in the big pines, often strutting on large horizontal branches near the tree's crown. Many areas throughout the Rocky Mountains have few roads, so it is wise to obtain maps of the areas before entering. By referring to these quite often, a hunting party can log the route they have followed, also indicating areas where birds have been heard, seen, or which indicate further study.

with annual kill dates, etc. Subscribe to the department's wildlife magazine, many of which are published monthly. Reading these will bring an education in game laws, what to expect in terms of wild animals, trees, flowers and geography, and they'll also give you a general feeling of having been there once you arrive. If a national forest exists, order maps of it. Once the area has been selected, topographical maps can be ordered. These indicate the contours of the area, wooded sections, streams, plus an endless variety of landmarks valuable to an outsider. Many of us want to learn all we can about the flora and fauna thereabouts, so we buy books identifying trees, flowers, grasses and birds. A few years of traveling and hunting for wild turkeys will make a person realize that the real America is found along the little known roads, the backtrails, the small towns and in people's homes.

The five subspecies of bearded and spurred wild turkeys are classified in regions of varying amounts of annual precipitation. Anyone who has studied wild turkeys knows this, which is why anyone who wants to gypsy around over the country hunting these birds should study them intensely. Learn what each one eats at different times of the year. Do they flock together in large droves and, if so, why? Why don't they do it every year? Do they migrate long distances? What about bird saturation per square mile? When are the dry seasons? Would this affect spring hunting?

There is no one book from which a person can learn all there is to know about any one of the subspecies, much less all five. Read all you can, then add to this with your own observations while hunting. For example, though I've never read this in any book, it is a fact that springtime Merriam gobblers are often found scattered far and wide with a mile, or several miles, between gobbling birds. Why? My own deductions are that the range is ideal for turkeys, resulting in what few birds are there using the area to scatter out. Those who have hunted Merriams on such terms consider it just a part of the hunt, but a hunter from

Merriam wild turkey terrain can be intimidating to the "new" hunter. Vast open areas are to the turkey's advantage, allowing the birds full use of their unexcelled vision. Hunting along the Cimarron River, near the juncture of the states of Oklahoma, Colorado and New Mexico, this hunter must use a call to kill turkeys.

Missouri, accustomed to hearing a half-dozen gobblers each morning, would find it unsettling to his nerves.

Consider gobbling, as there is a marked difference among turkeys along this vein, too. Throughout much of the old South, in such states as Mississippi, Alabama, Louisiana, Georgia and Florida, the birds don't gobble as frequently in the late afternoon as do birds in Arkansas and Missouri. However, both are Eastern wild turkeys. Perhaps other hunters have found otherwise, but this has been true in my observations. Nor does the average Merriam gobbler sound off to such a degree during the afternoon and evening hours.

The hunter unfamiliar with Florida wild turkey habitat is often entranced when seeing it for the first time, as it differs remarkably from other turkey terrains. This photo shows the inside of an oak hummock, which is a large clump of live oaks. These oaks have small acorns which are a prime food of the Osceola turkey, the distinct subspecie found in southern Florida. Such live oaks are often huge in size, with sprawling, long branches, usually festooned with Spanish moss and airplants, which have an orchid-like flower.

"Roosting a gobbler" is practiced in many parts of the country, but this sitting quietly in hopes of hearing a bird fly up and gobble would be a waste of time in many areas. Day after day I've hunted Rio Grandes, seldom hearing one gobble at dusk. (They can be located after dark by yodeling like a coyote from time to time. They gobble at coyotes.) Studying and observing will help immensely in hunting and killing wild turkeys on strange terrain. A flat-land turkey's gobble will not carry across the long distances that the gobble of a bird in the mountains will. Very often the gobble will not be heard at 500 yards, less if the bird is behind a slight rise or if a breeze is blowing away from the hunter. An Osceola gobbler, far out among palmettoes, could go easily unheard by a hunter several hundred yards distant. Yet, an Eastern bird on a ridge in Georgia could be heard at four times the distance. Knowing this, a hunter can brace himself to not over-run a gobbler he is going to, spooking it before he can make an attempt to call. In addition, a gobbler can gobble at varying degrees of intensity, which means he can make the sounds so they carry far, or don't carry at all.

My experiences lead me to concur that a wild turkey gobbler gobbles as loud as he thinks he needs to. While on the roost branch during the spring of the year, he gobbles loud in hopes of attracting hens to him. Later in the morning, on hearing a hen nearby, he gobbles only loud enough for her to hear him. Once she has left his presence, he again might gobble loudly, wanting all hens in his area to know his location. Many times I have been slowly walking through heavy woods, calling now and then, hoping to raise a bird and have had answering gobbles from very close, yet the gobble seemed "small," not very loud. There've also been times when I scarcely had time to fall to the ground and get the gun into position when the bird flushed. I can recall other hunts when the gobble would cause me to misjudge the distance, and I would over-run the bird's position, spooking him. Loud, distinct clear gobbling,

This turkey hunter's camp is situated in a National Forest park in New Mexico and is litter-free, with no noisy traffic—obviously a place to enjoy. This is an excellent base camp for a hunt. Individual camping areas are spaced well apart, allowing some degree of privacy. Water can be drawn at a spring, or from a tap. This hunter has the best of everything, including gobbling birds which can be heard from camp.

makes the bird far easier to hunt. Of course, I've been told by ear specialists that I have some degree of hearing loss, so maybe this is all a bunch of malarky.

Reading about the various subspecies, particularly in-depth studies, such as The Wildlife Society's *The Wild Turkey and It's Management,* are of extreme importance to the traveling turkey hunter. Prior to my first hunt for Osceolas in south Florida, I subscribed to that state's game department publication, sent for copies of studies that had been undertaken by the Florida Game Department concerning wild turkeys, and all but memorized what the Society's

Bald cypress are evident at every turn in the turkey trail when hunting Osceola wild turkeys throughout Florida. These trees grow in and around water, which Florida has plenty of. Wild gobblers often roost in the sparse crown of a towering cypress and can be very difficult to see because of the Spanish moss which is invariably draped from these lofty wooded sentinels. Fish hawks (ospreys) and southern bald eagles are prone to building their huge nests in cypress trees.

book had to say about the Osceola and where it lived. During the first 5 days I hunted there, which included my guiding for the hunter with me, I had a total of nine legal birds within 30 yards. Both my hunter and I killed the legal bag of two each. I had never hunted wild turkeys in Florida before that time. All of our success was due to being prepared when it came time to hunt.

One-day hunts are only for the aggressive. And I don't dawdle around . . .

There is a hunt in strange and new country which should be given special consideration, one that I've long referred to as the "one-day stand." Like the old minstrel shows, and circuses of the '20s and '30s, such a hunt lasts but one day, or part of a day. When planned for a bird so wild and wary as a wild turkey, this hunt stands apart when measured alongside its chances of success. This "there is no tomorrow" turkey hunt isn't for anyone who doesn't have tremendous faith in his abilities as a hunter, a woodsman, and his mental and physical skills.

To be successful, most one-day stands require hard hunting, luck, and a knack for always being at the right place at the right time. Many times such hunts will not be of a hunter's own choosing, but the result of visiting newly made acquaintances. Just this past season I was asked to stop by for a visit with another turkey hunter in a state far from my Oklahoma. I could only stay for a day, which didn't hamper his plans in the least. During the course of 3 hours after first daylight, we visited three different woods, heard turkeys gobble at all of them, then went to a fourth and heard one gobble there, and at last sat down to do some calling at number five. I'd scarcely got settled back against a tree when he said, "Let's go." We then high-tailed it to two other areas. Then it was time to go back to camp for a late breakfast. Any turkeys we would have killed that morning would have had to run like hell after us. My host was trying to outdo himself, just wanting me to see the country, and have an enjoyable stay. As my luck would have it, I killed a gobbler after lunch. I shouldn't have, as all the conditions were stacked against it happening. Many, many times I've had a buddy run me from this place to that, but because these men were trying their dead-level best to put me into birds, I have never complained. I've simply learned to swallow hard and say to myself, "Man, what I'd give to hunt that woods all morning by myself."

Being able to only hunt an area for one day, or one morning, will make a finer hunter out of anyone simply because you try harder. As there won't be any "next day," it boils down to making the least chance count. You work your head off for the least little chance. It's no different than the last day of the season, except that if you are hunting new country, you must learn it as you hunt, and you ain't got much time.

Hunters who can't find a place to hunt often must turn to such places as Fisheating Creek Hunting Camp, which offer hunts of short duration, with such options as lodging, butchering of game, fishing, wildlife tours, guides, along with wild turkey hunting. Managed by retired wildlife biologists David Austin (left) and Lovett Williams, the camp offers excellent south Florida hunting for Osceola wild turkeys, plus unexcelled wild hog hunts.

The hunter unfamiliar with Merriam's wild turkeys should remember when traveling to hunt them for the first time, that the gobblers are apt to be much more scattered than the other turkeys he has hunted. Many times a mile, or perhaps a few miles, may lay between gobbling birds. Many hunters carry their camp with them.

I have one tactic which I reserve for such hunts, which is to "cover ground." I put on the best walking shoes I have and when it's streaking first day, I'm going to put some ground back of me by nightfall. This is when the turkeys are not gobbling during the spring season, or when I'm hunting fall and winter turkeys. Long ago I learned that by far the best method for killing fall birds was to find them, scatter them, and make a kill if it hadn't been made on the flush. I'll listen as I hurry along, hoping to hear young birds and hens calling, but otherwise I'll try to walk areas where I think birds might use.

The back-country turkey hunter in Florida will need a four-wheel drive vehicle if he intends to hunt to road's end. Sand holes are very common, and if the weather is dry, these are treacherous. This road is well graded, appearing to be easily traversed by even a passenger car. But, as the author discovered a bit later, with large sandholes scattered along its length, it soon became obvious that none but four-wheelers could drive it safely.

There is no greater thrill to a turkey hunter than to travel several hundred miles, walk into totally new and strange woods, make a few calls, and then see a magnificent gobbler walk into view. Intense study of a game department's past turkey programs can often reveal to the hunter where birds are found, how long turkeys have been hunted there, and what the birds feed upon. Much of the guesswork can be taken out of locating turkeys on unfamiliar ground. Ed LaForce bagged this Merriam within a few hours of setting foot in strange country.

I don't poke along. I walk fast. I've killed a bunch of turkeys doing this, some of them on the scatter and flush, and a good many later, when they'd come to the call. Spring gobblers can be killed in the same manner, particularly later in the morning once they've ceased gobbling. I'll walk the woods at a fast clip, hoping my calling will fire one to gobbling. Too, there is always the chance that my fast walk will bring me within hearing of a gobbling turkey I wouldn't have heard had I been sitting on a calling stand near where the hunt began. Of course, if I'm on a one-day stand, and hear a gobbling turkey at dawn, I hunt him much like I would in any strange country hunt. *But*, I never forget that I won't be back tomorrow. I must plan my hand for each card it holds. Several states don't allow all-day hunting for springtime gobblers, which cuts hunting time to half, or even less. For the one-day hunt this means that any turkey heard gobbling may be the only one you have a chance at. This separates the turkey hunters from the gobble listeners.

One-day hunts are only for the aggressive. As there are but a few hours, I don't have the time to dawdle around,

looking at leaves, flowers, rocks, putting the binoculars on this bird and that, and taking closer looks at lichens. If my hunt is going to end with my getting a shot at an old turkey gobbler at 25 yards, I'll need to hunt first, and if there is time, look at the flora and fauna later. The average hunter may not care for this type of pressure-cooker hunt, which is what it often becomes. A number of times I have been invited to hunt in areas from Arizona to New York, some of them with veteran hunters, some with local hunters. But, my reputation as a turkey hunter usually has preceded me, and when I go into the woods I'm *expected* to come out with a bird. Invariably I've never set foot within miles of the place. The bulk of these hunts begin with a drive to the area before first day, a crude map sketched in the dirt with a stick, and with a few "you can hunt heres," and "don't hunt theres," I'm left standing in the dark.

Twenty years ago I went to Alabama where my first hunt was to be a short half-day affair. It was raining when a friend picked me up, and after a 30-minute drive we pulled into some woods a fair distance north of Tuscaloosa. Hunkered over a bare spot on the woods road, he fetched a stick and drew me a map. "Go around this big dead snag, down through these woods 'til you see a corral. Go through it, and up on this hill you'll come to a gap. Go on through it, and down the long grade from there to the crick. You should hear him up on the ridge to your right." Simple instructions. I asked how far all this was and he told me maybe it was a ½-mile.

Rain gear on, I plodded down the road in the pitch black piney woods, took a wrong fork in the trail which I didn't know was there as it was dark. I never did find the corral, or the gap but did hear a turkey gobble sometime after daylight. The rain was still a steady drizzle, but as the old bird hadn't been but maybe 70 yards from me when he gobbled, I knew to the tree where he was. Slipping forward in the rain soaked woods, I took up a stand behind a big pine. A moment later I clucked the bones caller. No answer. Turkeys seldom talk in a drizzle. I didn't dare make any other calls. I kept silent. Ten minutes later he glided to earth perhaps 50 yards to my left front. Screened by the pine, I clucked again two or three times, quick, as a hen might do on seeing a bird come to ground. He slowly walked off, pecking here and there. His fires had been put out by the cold dreary night. My host picked me up at 11 o'clock, wet, hungry and disgusted with the weather. It's a long way from Oklahoma to Alabama just to stand in the rain. As with so many places I've hunted, I have never seen those woods since, sunshine or not.

Just last spring I made a one-day stand when I was invited to hunt a ranch along the Oklahoma-Kansas line. Larry Marvin, an old buddy from Alva, Oklahoma, had made the arrangements. He and I took off up a creek bottom just after daybreak and as we walked along, I was calling. Four hundred yards from the pickup we got an answering gobble. Two minutes later I shot and that was the end of the hunt. The gobbler was one I'll never forget though as his beard had a beautiful tan band across it about 2 inches up from the bottom.

To me one-day hunts are the supreme turkey hunt. My abilities are tested to the maximum as I don't know the terrain, won't have time to scout it out nor will I be able to study a bird's actions today and use that information against him tomorrow. The hunt is done more or less, on the bird's terms. Such hunts have brought me my finest memories in turkey hunting. There was one in Dixie when my companions were three veteran turkey hunters, one of them the national calling champion at that time. I was in very good company. One of the other hunters killed a nice gobbler at a new location the second morning, but the champion never got a shot. I'd hoped he would kill one. The pressure was on him, hard, but luck wouldn't smile his way.

Lady Luck has been going steady with me for years, and she was tagging along that first morning. Our party was to hunt 'til mid-morning in a vast chunk of lowland piney woods. A gobbler sounded off in my quadrant, so I slipped

The first hunt was Wednesday, the second Thursday, Lady Luck and I were doing fine . . .

Sam Dowery, of Lake Worth, Florida, admires a young gobbler held aloft by David Kelley. The bird was bagged on the Three Lakes Management Area. Camping areas are well marked in Florida and most are confined to small acreages, which results in extremely close contact with neighboring campers.

(Left) Hunting camps or clubs are very popular in parts of the U.S. Members of clubs like this one in Mississippi may belong to three or four different clubs, perhaps two of them being for deer, one for turkey hunting, and one for duck hunting. Most of these hunting camps lease land on a yearly basis from local landowners, while others may arrange to purchase lands.

The hunter from Rio Grande territory will be in an all together different world once he walks into Osceola country. Dark, whiskey-colored water mirrors overhanging bushes, while overhead cypress trees reach far into the warm sky.

(Right) The hunter who has done his homework can expect to bag gobblers like these on back-to-back mornings, even though he has never set foot in that region previously. This can be done by reading and studying the various subspecies, their habitats, foods, and lifestyles.

across the swollen creek on a downed log, hotfooted it quiet like 'til I calculated he was up on a small ridge at maybe 200 yards. I made a call and hoped for the best. Soon he flew down, as the gobbles became flat, but then he quickly walked out onto the ridge facing me, as his gobbling became clear and loud. I made another call on the Turpin yelper. He gobbled. I called again, he gobbled nearer, and I sneaked the gun up on my drawn-up knees. Perhaps 20 minutes after I'd heard him, I pulled the trigger. His head was snow white as I put the front bead on him among the huckleberry bushes. I learned later the old bird had been hunted along that swamp for 3 or 4 years. The man who owned the place said, "I'd know him any place." The gobbler had a small skinny beard about 12¼ inches in length. I'd lucked out.

Two other mornings in Dixie were just like that one. Sometimes I was put out in the dark on turkeys that had been hunted hard, showed how the place lays with sketches drawn on the road in the headlights of pickup trucks, bade goodbye, and left standing there in the dark. The first hunt was on a Wednesday, the second on Thursday, the following morning. Lady Luck and I were doin' fine.

The first bird took until after dinner before I could lay the #6s on him as he came to me in full strut during the heat of the day. The next morning I found the second gobbler exactly where I was told he'd be, but he didn't pull none of the shenanigans on me that I'd been told he was

famous for. I made the yelper sing which, maybe with some Oklahoma sweet talk he hadn't heard before, was too much for him. He was in full strut when I bagged him, too, though the sun hadn't cleared the creek bank. Both gobblers had keen sharp spurs, with beards just under 12 inches. What a fine pair of old birds to take on back-to-back one-day stands. I've never been back to either place.

We sat under the stars and killed a whole bunch of past turkeys all over again . . .

One-day stands during the fall and winter hunts are another story, and for a number of reasons. Number one, there isn't any gobbling to tell a person, "Here I am, come and get me." Number two, all the birds have bunched in small droves and later on in the winter in larger gangs, which makes them harder to find than single birds scattered over the same range. Number three, in many areas the birds will have migrated to another range from where they'd be found during the spring months. Number four, such droves seldom make any calls after the early morning get-together, therefore the hunter is looking for a bunch of birds with umpteen ears with which to hear him, and as many eyes. The better to see him.

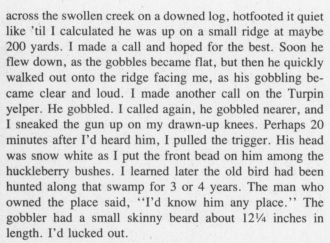

The turkey hunter traveling to unfamiliar country will be more successful if he does lots of homework before making the trip.

(Left) Merriam wild turkey gobblers have a lot of snow-white tips on the tail feathers, along with those on the lower rump. This gobbler, killed by James Frazee (left) from Enid, Oklahoma, also has feet which are white with the fine dust sometimes found when the Merriam's Rocky Mountain range is undergoing a dry spell. These big birds often walk mountain roads, leaving tracks in this powder dust.

One-day stands during the fall in a woods new to the hunter are far more apt to be unsuccessful than a day in the spring. As I mentioned earlier, far the best method for me has been to cover a lot of ground, hoping I'll walk the gun inside of 30 yards, surprise a drove, and make a kill. A lifetime of bird hunting has made me a good snapshot, so if I can get inside of 30 yards on a flushing turkey, he's in trouble. Ed LaForce, a long-time hunting buddy of mine, and I drove to Arkansas one warm October afternoon, getting into the woods long about 2 o'clock. We walked an old woods road to where it forked, him striking out down the right-hand fork, me taking the left. I'd no sooner got into the woods when I noticed fresh droppings, so I knew the birds were around. As I walked along, I found more droppings along with newly dropped small feathers, like a poult would drop as it takes on winter plumage. Fall hunting is ordinarily structured around locating a small drove, scattering them, then calling one back to the gun. Summer was still hanging on in those Arkansas mountains, so the trees had lost none of the leaves. Visibility was poor, which not only would make calling a scattered drove easier, but increased my chances of walking within gunshot of them. I stuck to the old tote road as few leaves were lying on it, and the walking was even and quiet. The sun was high— a beautiful fall afternoon for a stroll in the woods. I rolled up my sleeves. This is the great life.

Ed was somewhere off to the northwest, probably down much lower as I could see that the mountains broke off in that direction where I presumed it ended in a creek. Ed's a good turkey hunter. I knew he'd work that woods while I was working mine. Down through the years we've both heard the other guy shoot lots of times.

Kills can be lightning fast. I had just topped a ridge, dropped down the other side, stepped across a dry creek bed, when there, a flash—a gobbler is running up that hill through the brush. I run hard down the road. Can't get on him. There he is, cutting back to the left. I run hard, the gun up in both hands across the front of me. There he is, still running hard. Hey, he's gonna clear the brush and come out flying. Stop! Up goes the side-by-side, he's running into takeoff, the bead blots him. *Fire! Booo-mm!* Run hard, get to him, grab him by the neck. A flip, I feel the neckbones snap. An old bird. Sharp hooks. What luck. Look at that beard. Twelve inches it looks. Sweat trickles off the end of my nose. A walk in the woods. A turkey runs. A flushing shot, the bird thrashes on the leaves. The ugly stink of burnt blackpowder hangs in a cloud of white smoke.

That night we stuck a measure on the old bird's whiskers, which beat 12 inches, sure enough. We sat under the stars after supper and killed a whole bunch of past turkeys all over again, talked about others which should've met the same fate but didn't, and turned in. Tomorrow we'd try another spot.

To hunt a day here and a day there means that the hunter has all the odds stacked against him. He hasn't the advantage of yesterday, or last fall, or a morning in April when he chased gobbling turkeys over a ridge he knows by heart. The turkey is being hunted on its home grounds, and for only a day.

If you like to know the country you are hunting, then I advise you to stay at home . . .

Don't forget your hunting license, tags, special permits, etc. These are to be on your person and, in several states, must be displayed in a clear plastic case which fastens to the outside of your shirt or jacket. I carry all my licenses and tags in a small leather coin purse, like the one my grandad carried his loose pocket change in, and with them will be my mouth calls, plus a few percussion caps for the muzzleloader.

Study the rules very carefully if you are traveling to a state in which you haven't hunted for a couple of years. Rules can change overnight. It's best to read up on them each time you hunt there. And don't wait until a month before the season to send for non-resident licenses. You

Ranchers like Don Wildman of western Oklahoma are the ones who control wild turkey populations throughout large regions of private land. By keeping tabs of the numbers of hunters allowed on ranches and farm lands, and the birds killed by these hunters, these men can maintain a healthy, sizable turkey flock. Too many hunters with indiscriminate shooting would soon otherwise put an end to thousands of droves on private property.

Many national forests have corrals available for those hunters who use horses. This one, in New Mexico's Gila National Forest, is well maintained and will handle a number of animals. National forests are truly a "land of many uses." Americans should keep constant watch on these public lands, because numerous private interests would like to acquire ownership, or to use them to further financial gain.

This self-explanatory sign will do much toward generating better relations between state-employed wildlife biologists and the hunting public. Hunters who value that sport should do as much as possible to cooperate with game department officials.

unlike those of the remainder of the state. Special permits are often required for hunting these areas. A few states allow turkeys to be killed in roost trees, others allow baiting, and some okay rifles for turkey hunting. Decoys are legal in most, but not all. Study the rules, the latest rules. Could save you some money in fines.

While we are discussing legalities, let's also talk about ethics, as how we act, each and every one of us, has a great bearing on how we appear as a whole to the non-hunting public. There are days on end when a hunter in back country doesn't come in contact with "civilized folks," and the only humans he may see are a bunch of

(Above) Many management areas which don't allow hunting offer excellent opportunities around the outside perimeter to a hunter who is expert with a call. Both gobblers and young fall turkeys can be called from the confines of game preserves and refuges. This one, in far southeast Oklahoma, is a joint venture of the state and federal government.

National forests are truly the answer to many turkey hunter's prayers, because so few private landowners allow hunting today.

may find the state had a permit drawing earlier.

Non-resident license fees have shot up with inflation, which probably has lessened the demand for licenses in the higher priced areas. I've hunted Merriam turkeys in New Mexico and Arizona many times, and hope to continue, but New Mexico's tag costs $75 today, and Arizona's is $109. Both are for *one spring gobbler*. New Mexico has an unusual ruling for their spring hunt. For a gobbler to be legal, the beard must extend 2 inches *beyond* the breast feathers. They've had this rule for years. I recall one jake turkey I called up for a hunter back in 1968. He and I couldn't decide if the bird was legal. The bird was strutting, allowing us to see just the tip end of the beard. I quit calling, and the bird soon began pecking at the ground, giving us enough of a looksee to be reasonably certain of the beard length, so I whispered to him to shoot. Back at the truck, the steel tape said we were legal.

Many states have quitting times that vary, particularly in the spring season, so give these your close attention when traveling to a state you have not hunted. Certain Game Management Areas also may have regulations which are

slobs running up and down the roads, heaving beer cans at pine trees, shooting signs which cost all taxpayers money, and spooking game for miles around. I've never been able to decide who failed, when considering how such people were brought up. When a child enters school, crayons and paper are used to make anti-litter posters. Obviously the message doesn't soak in, for anyone who lives near a grade school has found these hunks of windblown litter tumbling across the lawn. The anti-litter campaign has yet to be stamped into the average American's mind. Look at it this way: you took it in, you carry it out. This world is the only one we got and we must work at keeping it clean.

Recently I hunted a number of public hunting areas in a southern state. Management areas are what some folks call these. Roads were marked which could be traveled. Rules were even posted on the front of the check stations. Nowhere have I seen less regard for what a state has attempted to provide in hunting acreage than there in Florida. Four-wheelers and three-wheelers charged in and out over every trail on that area. Fire breaks, disked feed strips, walking trails, you name it. By the end of the first day's hunt, there wasn't a path that hadn't been raped a hundred times. To boot, there were grumbles all about the camping areas that evening about the scarcity of game! The spring season there will last only 5 weeks, and obviously such extremely visual and noisy disturbances will drive all the turkeys from there onto private lands.

On that opening day, in an area considered to be good turkey habitat, 105 hunters bagged one gobbler. The flagrant disregard for other hunter's rights didn't end at dusk because then it was time to turn the radios up, or jump on the three-wheelers to tear through camp. Before I left the area, I learned that the state was on the verge of losing all that acreage to private interests, which seemed to me to be a blessing in disguise.

The next time you get to feeling sorry for yourself about local conditions, that there are too many hunters and not enough turkeys, gas up the old pickup and take a trip to a neighboring state. Buy a turkey tag and see what they have to offer.

If you have been noticing that the sport doesn't thrill you as it did when you first began, chances are that such a trip will put back all the zest into it that you care for. But, take it from someone who's been there—if you like to know the country you are hunting, what the birds thereabouts are apt to do, and you don't like surprises, then I would advise you to stay at home. You will just be one less hunter for me to have to put up with *when I get there*.

Locked gates are becoming common barriers to today's turkey hunter, which forces him to look elsewhere for hunting. This, and the want of a greater challenge are what caused the author to begin making trips to new or strange country, as hunting turkeys on unfamiliar grounds put all the challenge anyone could want back into the sport. In doing this, he found that there are many areas open to hunters, without locked gates.

(Left) A hunter breaks camp at a management area in Florida. Florida has several areas which would support good populations of wild turkeys, though the hunting is not what many hunters would consider of good quality. This is because there is too much abuse of the areas by off-road vehicles, mainly three-wheelers. Littering is widespread, as is the loud use of radios throughout the camp areas. These actions are just putting ammunition in the propaganda guns of the anti-hunting community.

Chapter 10

Gould's Turkey— King of the Mountain

DEATH ANGELS on the merry-go-round. Circling, wheeling, always circling. But, these birds were low. So close I could make out their eyes on the naked heads. I'd spooked the black vultures off a kill. Then I got a whiff of it. *Whooo-oo-eeee!* There sure enough was something dead, and it had to be nearby.

Studying the drag trail I'd been following, I already had a sneaking hunch what I'd find at its end. I'd come upon the trail while easing across a manzanita studded flat, atop a mesa, far back in the Sierra Madres of Chihuahua, Mexico, one hot May afternoon. I was searching for an old turkey gobbler that had been giving me the raspberry. The ground was heavily marked with turkey tracks, droppings as big as your little finger, and the parallel lines we turkey hunters know as strut marks. Smack in the middle of all this I came upon what appeared to be an area where something heavy had been dragged along the ground. Noting which way the grass was bent, I decided to see where the trail went, hoping to learn what had happened. Seventy-five yards further I spooked the buzzards.

Hearing a swarm of blowflies as I forced my way through thick tangles of manzanita and madrone brush, I suddenly saw a black object on the ground in front of me. Yep, a dead heifer. A black angus. She was covered with brush and leaves, but I could see the ear tag which I knew the rancher would want. I cut it free, and at the same time, twisted the animal's head. Broken neck. Old *el leon* had cut the young cow down in a whirlwind charge, eaten his fill of one flank, and was probably lying up right now in the immense rocky needles that were towering toward the

cloudless sky off to the southeast.

Mountain lions that kill cows aren't popular anywhere, and deep in Mexico's mountains even less so. Cattle aren't easy to come by back in the high Sierras. My guess was that within a few days a bunch of cowboys, and a pack of dogs, would come calling on old Mr. Mountain Lion.

A sudden sound made me whirl. Running to a slab-sided gray rock, I scrambled up on it. Standing still, I looked off toward the west, ears cocked. Aha-ha. There that turkey goes again. That cottonpicker has switched mountains. ''Muchos Gobbles'' was at it again. I'd nicknamed the old bird for his relentless gobblings. He'd found a mesa to his liking with roost trees studding its north face. There wasn't time to go after him so late in the afternoon, but I knew he'd be there come first day on the morrow.

''Muchos Gobbles'' would be known among learned turkey people as *Meleagris gallopavo* Mexicana Gould, the fifth member of *Meleagrinae* family, not so well known among turkey hunters as the other four, *silvestris* (Eastern), *Osceola* (Florida), *Merriami*, and *intermedia* (Rio Grande). *Meleagris* differs from all other birdlife in that the males have both spurs on the legs and a growth of rudimentary hair on the chest—a beard. The Gould's wild turkey truly is the King of the Mountain, as he is the giant among wild turkeys, both in stature, and in his reign of towering rock strewn mesas, which make him a worthy adversary. I'd arrived in camp on a Friday morning in May, first heard the old bird at daybreak the next morning, again that evening, the following morning, and at sunup on the day I found the dead cow.

The Mexican Gould's wild turkey grows to a size in total length and wingspan unmatched by any of the other four subspecies of bearded and spurred wild turkeys. This gobbler's wings spanned 73 inches.

The author demonstrates the use of a wingbone call to Antonio Corrales while in camp in Chihuahua, Mexico. Bland has never seen any indication that natives have any knowledge of calling wild turkeys in the Sierra Madre mountains.

I'll fool that old gobbler this time. Fools are made, not born and I was being made . . .

That first morning found me climbing the mountain to where he was cutting loose, hoping to call him to me. It quickly became apparent I could forget such foolishness, for several hens joined him. Not giving up without a fight, I then tried bushwacking, but after making my sneak to within easy gunshot of the birds, I was spied while trying to bring the gun to bear on the gobbler.

Late that afternoon he took to gobbling like crazy again, but I didn't try to call him. Instead, I hung back, planning to wait for him and his ladies at the creek the following morning. They'd all sashayed down there once they'd given me the slip the first day, so perhaps they'd do it again. Next morning at first day I went back to the creek. "Muchos Gobbles" was on top of the mountain, called the hens to him, and faded from hearing. Noon found me still waiting at the creek. Phooey. You guessed it. That evening he fired up, gobbling all over the place. Wouldn't pay any attention to my calling, so I "listened" him to bed. I'll get him tomorrow.

Monday morning finds me above him at first hint of coming day. Nope, he ain't coming up. He heads for the creek the second his feet touch down. I scramble around the side of the mountain. I'll fool that old gobbler this time. I'll be waiting for him at the creek. Fools are made, not

born, and I was being made. I never heard him until near noon. He was going back uphill. He'd gotten a drink, but not from any of my hospitality.

Monday evening, "Muchos" gobbles from another nearby peak. And, again, and again, and again. I could hear laughter, too. Not many hunters can hear a turkey laugh when he cuts loose, but I could that evening. Tuesday morning. Like an overgrown alarm clock, the crazy turkey goes off just at first day showing. Smack on top of a ridge at near 9,000 feet. I seldom use a horseshoe mouth caller, but fished one from my shirt pocket, stuck it in my mouth, and clucked back at him. Here we go again. The mountains rang with gobbling, first above me, and off to the left, then he'd pause straight above my hide, then go off to the right a little, and holler like heck from there. I slapped my hands on my pants, which makes a sound somewhat like a hen turkey flapping her wings. Darned if the gobbler didn't cut back at that, too.

Having studied the situation good by now, I could tell that he was perhaps ¼-mile up a very steep grade of loose shale, oak leaves, rocks, cactus, and brush. Where the tenacious things had taken root were scattered pines, oaks, mountain mahogany, and whatever else dared hang onto life in the arid surroundings. Off to the west I could hear the cooing of a band-tailed pigeon.

I could forget making an attempt to get up on the high ground with him, which probably wasn't a ridge but was the beginning of a small mesa that flowed off gently toward the south. Oh, I could get there, but I'd have to make a circle comparable to the travels of Cortez.

Though seldom seen by the average hunter, there are times when hen turkeys will seemingly strut, much like a gobbler. The author interprets this as an aggressive behavior and has seen three hens in a group in this display, pirouetting around each other, purring while doing so. These were Mexican turkeys. The bird pictured is a Rio Grande. (Photo courtesy of David Jackman.)

(Right) Horses and mules are often used for getting back into turkey country in the far Southwest and Mexico. These local animals are accustomed to walking in this rough country, so they're extremely sure-footed. This picking their way among rocks takes time, so the hunter must leave camp with this in mind. When returning to camp, particularly at high mountainous elevations, it is much easier to tote back a big gobbler tied to the saddlehorn, than it would be to carry it by hand while on foot.

Noticing a huge rock butted in near the base of the mountain, I made a yelp or two, then ambled toward it. "Muchos Gobbles" shot back his answer, several times in fact. Again at the rock I called. *Gob-obb-ooble*. Two times, three times. Each time I thought he'd quit, he'd rack the mountains again with his yodeling. I kept my mouth shut. Then, slowly, like snow beginning to fall, a feeling ran hot through my veins. The old bird wasn't calling. You could cut the mountain air with a knife. What's that? A leaf crunched far up the slope. Again, a tiny sound. A rock moving. Another. Gently, oh, so very gently, I snaked the 12-bore forward, cradling it in my hands where they rested atop the rock. A thumb smothered the safety, and I could feel it slip to the fire position. I shot him as he tried to strut on that steep mountainside.

Throughout the areas where I have hunted this turkey, the terrain is volcanic in origin with some steep faulting on north, northeast, and northwest slopes due to uplift when the earth was cooling. South slopes are gradual, with mesas predominating at the peak, gradually giving way to southern quadrants at a lesser degree of grade. Invariably these northern slopes contain predominant roost sites, which are chihuahua pines and, if left undisturbed, will be used year after year by these birds. Too often the local hunters roost-

shoot the birds, causing them to move. This roose-site information seems to be passed down from one generation of hunters to another, and if it wasn't for a lack of guns and shells, there wouldn't be any turkeys. From my contacts with Tarahumara Indians in Mexico, they obviously never forget where the birds roost, and can go there on the darkest of nights, without artificial light to show the way. Once at the roost site, they have no qualms about building a fire to keep themselves warm while awaiting better light to shoot. Roost trees are invariably just below the summit and are not as large a tree as many we would find in areas in the United States. Like all of the civilized world, Mexico's virgin forests were timbered off way back when, and due to scant precipitation, large trees are few and far between.

North slopes are often extremely rugged in character with rock outcroppings and rock walls heavily cloaked in un-

Two gates side-by-side, one a cattle guard made of pipe laid over a trench, the other a wire gate closing a gap in the fence. This ranch is in Chihuahua, Mexico. The sign *El Coconito* translates into "Little Turkey." The bottom line also tells any passersby that hunting is strictly prohibited. The native Mexicans and Indians who inhabit the rough mountain country hunt wild turkeys when the chance presents itself, and when they happen to have a gun and shells. All three, guns, shells, and turkeys are scarce in Mexico.

(Left) Manzanita berries are a favored food of the Gould's wild turkey, the bird found in the mountains of Chihuahua, Sonora, and Durango. Manzanitas are clump-like bushes which grow in extensive thickets on the flat top of mountains in Mexico's Sierra Madres Occidental Range. This flat area is often known as a "mesa," which is Spanish for table.

gerfield's famous remark, "Don't get no respect."

The gradual slopes of the southern quadrants from the roost sites have reddish to brown soils, strewn with rock which appears volcanic. These mesas are dotted with various junipers, scrub oaks much like the shinnery oaks found in the ranges of the Rio Grande turkey, or Gambel's oak which grows in Merriam habitat. Manzanita and madrone are found in abundance, both excellent turkey foods. Manzanita grows into a large shrub or bush, has a smooth red bark, and a small berry. The madrone grows into a small crooked tree which has scaly red bark and a reddish-orange berry. Both are prolific, bear fruit most years, and are a favorite of all wildlife in the high Sierras. Among the junipers, the alligator juniper is far the most productive, having a large brown fruit with the consistency of a nut when ripe. These brown fruits will often carpet the ground beneath a mature juniper. The tree gets its name from its bark configuration, which looks like the armor plating on an alligator. This tree is found in much of New Mexico's and Arizona's Merriam turkey range, but in all my wanderings there, I've never seen them in the abundance of those found in the Sierra Madres. Each time I see one I can't help but recall those I've seen in Arizona's Sitgreaves National Forest. These have a small brown sign posted on them, designated them as "Wildlife Trees," and protecting them because of the shelter and food value that they provide for nature.

derbrush. Much of the slopes are covered with loose shale rock, which makes walking difficult. During the spring hunt, gobblers will often be heard sounding off along these high rims.

In many instances a stream will be trickling down the canyon along the base of the north slope. It's hoped by the hunter that the bird will come down once he has called together his entourage of hens, saving the hunter the horrendous climb. What usually happens is that the birds are heard assembling, then march off out of hearing range, traveling out on the gradual inclines to the south of the roost areas. If the hunter decides to fool 'em and makes the climb in the dark before sunrise, then very often the birds gather below the roost sites, on the steep brush-cloaked slopes just below the summits, and drop to the valley floor for an early morning drink. Reminds me of Rodney Dan-

Gould's turkeys will travel long distances each day to seek out a cultivated field . . .

Throughout Gould's range, ground cover is lacking in vines, creepers, and grass carpet. I've seen Apache Rose on rocky slopes along with a small thorny bush known as Johnny-Jump-Up, derived from the way its thorns grab at you when you brush against it. Much of Mexico is deemed open range, though the term in Mexico has a different meaning than the term used to describe the cattle country of the United States. "Open range" in America means that it isn't cross-fenced, therefore a traveler touring by vehicle should be alert to cattle on the road. "Open range" in Mexico allows local inhabitants to pasture cattle on such lands. Should you notice 100 head of cattle on a mountainside and inquire as to ownership, you could be told they belong to any number of individuals in a nearby village.

in the crops of Gould's turkeys, so obviously the bird finds them to its liking.

Gould's turkeys are no different from other turkeys. They seek out cultivated foods, particularly corn and maize. Up among the rugged mountain chains, very few cultivated fields are found and when they are, they are often small. Even in this age of modern machinery, these fields are still farmed with horse-drawn tools. For example, the planting of corn is a two-man operation. As one farmer cuts the furrow with the single-share plow, the other walks alongside him dropping corn into the trench from a bucket he carries. Before you belittle this method, you must remember that transporting heavy machinery back into Mexico's mountains is an arduous job, and once the machinery is there, repairs and fuel will be costly. Crop productivity will not support such expenses.

Gould's wild turkeys will travel long distances each day to seek out a cultivated field and will make daily excursions to a field long after its crop has been harvested. On a winter hunt several years ago I observed a large drove which hiked

A turkey hunter who travels far and wide in quest of the five gobblers which make up the Grand Slam of bearded and spurred wild turkeys will come in contact with customs which may seem outdated. These Mexicans are planting corn, one driving the team of horses, while the other drops beans, one at a time, into the funnel which allows the bean to fall into the furrow immediately behind the plow. It's an out-moded method, but it works.

This often results in severe over-grazing, which together with a low rate of annual rainfall, allows no time for grasses to regenerate. Such over-grazing, could, to a degree, be a limiting factor for Gould's turkeys at lower elevations. Throughout the higher elevations, where cattle are less likely to graze, grass growth can be found in poor to excellent degrees.

On ridges where there is excellent grass growth, chances are much greater that you will find turkeys. Invariably, the choice pastures, insofar as productive cattle range is concerned, are those in private ownership. It's not unusual to drive through a gate back in the mountains, and find one side of the fence bare of grasses, while on the other side grass clumps protrude everywhere from among the volcanic rock. Predominant grasses are of bunch-grass formation, what I would classify as muhly grass. Another grass is what would be termed a short white grass, much like our buffalo grass here in western Oklahoma, and still another is similar to our tickle grasses. I've found large balls of these grasses

each day to a field some distance from its roost site, beelining for it each morning. Once there, they seemingly spent no end of time scratching and wandering about, and as the corn crop had been taken some weeks earlier, it would appear the birds were having little success. On my treks through the field, I would scan the ground, but to me there wasn't enough food there to feed a bunch of mice. I killed two hens there one morning, the first a young jennie, a bird-of-the-year, and the other was an older adult. Though neither had been in the field long, both had surprising amounts of grain in their crops. I couldn't help but think and compare how sorry my vision was in comparison to those feeding turkeys.

Gould's wild turkeys have been raiding man's fields for centuries. In recent times, between 700 AD and 1300 AD, when these regions were inhabited by peoples known today as the Paquime Indians, it's certain the birds stole from their tiny crops. I've noticed in many arroyos stones piled across a gulley which in due time caused a soil buildup on

Antonio Corrales points to a "parrot rock" lying on the ground amid pottery shards where Mexican natives have been searching for ancient Indian pottery. The parrot rock, which has a hole in it, was built into the side of an adobe enclosure which, with its reed roof, was a cage for the birds which were traded northward by natives in Southern Mexico. The birds were fed and watered through the hole, which was kept plugged with a short section of log the remainder of the time. The large dished out rock is a *metate*, in which maize was ground, as this was the Indians' principal crop and means of food.

(Left) When hunting up among the peaks of Mexico's Sierra Madre mountains, a person is going to come upon areas where others have searched for the graves of ancient Indians. The pottery found in these graves is highly sought, so it brings a good price in border towns. This Indian skull was unearthed by these pot-hunters. The dig area is known as a "montezuma." The gobbler was killed near the montezuma, and is a Gould's wild turkey.

the upstream side of these dikes. Apparently each of these small areas was then prepared and planted with maize though back in those times this crop did not resemble the one we know today as corn, nor was it as prolific. The Paquime Indians were farming peoples, and even today it is very rare when a pointed implement such as an arrowhead is found among ancient ruins of that tribe. "Montezumas," as such ruins are referred to today, are invariably found along streams, and it is thought that there must have been greater rainfall in that region during those times. Many of these streams nowadays have very little water in them, and then only after moderate rainfalls. These people lived by agriculture, which means the wildlife benefited from their efforts, regardless of how small the scale. So it makes sense why the Gould's turkey travels to a corn field, even those back in the far reaches of the Sierra Madres, for the bird's ancestors were doing this perhaps thousands of years ago. On numerous occasions while hunting among the ruins of past civilizations, I have noticed the tracks of wild turkeys.

What irony lies in the cold hard fact that whereas the Pacquime Indians have long since vanished from the earth, innumerable generations of wild turkeys have trod those mountain halls in the time spanning the centuries.

A hunter intent on hunting the Gould's should give his health a good second look . . .

The Gould's habitat encompasses areas within the Upper Sonoran zone, with elevations from 4,500 to 7,500 feet and extends into the lower reaches of the Transition zone, closely resembling the habitat of the Merriam subspecie. The Merriam's habitat, often referred to as the Ponderosa zone, is subject to great temperature change and, further north, to extreme snow fall, heavy summer showers, and

Allen Hawkins, of Mexico, totes a big Gould's gobbler into camp, tied to the saddlehorn. Horses are used daily in work and in hunting turkeys back in the Sierra Madres. Ancient Indians thought the Spanish horses were meateaters and brought the Spanish conquorers turkeys to feed to the horses. Horses were unknown on the American continent until the arrival of the early Spaniards.

Sections of one of Mexico's maguey plants can be cooked and eaten, much the same as cabbage palms are eaten in Florida. Allen Hawkins totes this one toward the road. These giant spears are dead ringers for giant asparagus.

bitter cold during winter months. The arid peaks of the Sierra Madres are not subject to these heavy amounts of moisture, so the turkeys need not migrate to lower elevations during times of deep snow. Anyone who has spent much time studying or hunting the Merriam wild turkey has gained a deep respect for this bird's ability to travel long distances to stay alive. This is particularly true along the Mogollon plateau's south rim, which wends its way across Arizona and southeastern New Mexico. An extreme geophysical landmark, the long slope leading down from this uplift is breath-taking the first time it is viewed. Merriams caught on top of this plateau by a sudden heavy winter snowstorm will migrate under the rim, dropping to the lower elevations where food and higher temperatures can be found. Such migrations have been known to exceed 40 miles. The Gould's turkey does not make these migrations.

Gould's turkeys feed on the tiny green grasses at spring seeps and along streams, exactly as does the Merriam. Wintering droves of both subspecies apparently do much loafing at these locations as the earlier droppings of younger birds, plus more recent signs, are liberally scattered where there has been water during winter months. This small green meadow grass is taken as a variation in diet and for roughage.

Among the oaks found within the Gould's range are both white and red, which are known locally as "sweet acorns" (red oaks) and "hog acorns" (white oaks). Among these are the Mexican blue oak, Arizona white oak, grey oak,

silverleaf oak, and the Fremont oak, which has bark much like the Alligator juniper. The Sonoran fantailed deer utilizes these acorns, as do the many squirrels found in the Sierra Madres.

Meleagris gallopavo Mexicana Gould, like all turkeys found in Mexico, goes by many names. I've heard them called *pavo*; as well as *guaya*, and *guajolote*, which is pronounced "wah-ya-loh-ti." Further south in Mexico the birds are known by the names of *totoe* and *pipilo*. Back in the high Sierras I've never heard them by any name other then *cocono*. The hen is *cocona*, and the young bird is *coconito*. Along this same vein, water holes are *lagunas*, and roosts are *dormitorio*.

A hunter intent on pursuing a Gould's turkey should give his health a good second look. Far back in the high Sierras is not the place to decide it's time to go to the hospital, as there aren't any. First aid is just as far unless you or someone in your party is equipped with a first aid kit. When you pack it, remember that it could be subject to scrutiny at the border when you enter Mexico, and unmarked drugs could mean a delay. If you wear eyeglasses, carry an extra pair in your coat pocket. The same goes for hearing aids.

The Gould's wild turkey lives in extremely rough, rugged mountain country. Elevations vary but can reach 9,000 feet. You must remember this if you have any type of heart trouble. Breathing can be difficult on a long, hard climb before daybreak, when the early morning air, always cold, seemingly burns holes in your lungs as you gasp for breath.

Many times I've stood there in the dark asking myself, "Just what the hell turkey is worth all this?" The answer is always the same, but the following morning I'll probably ask again. A cold dark mountain isn't the place for a heart attack. Don't run the risk if you have a history.

Folks with back or leg trouble would be wise to stay out of the high Sierras. These old mountain gobblers have a liking for hiking up and down the steep slopes, and though I've never understood how they've come by steel legs, I keep looking at the dead ones to see if that is what they are outfitted with. The chill air encourages leg cramps, which are also brought about by sitting too long before continuing the climb. Take it easy when you first begin your hunt, and after a few days time you'll get both your legs and your lungs accustomed to the thinner mountain air. This is even more important if you are wearing a back pack or fanny pack. I can recall early predawn climbs that required being ready to assault the slope an hour prior to first day, and on which has been carried the following: gun, shells, flashlight, canteen of water, box call, two oranges, small box of raisins, two cans of Vienna sausage, a can of spam, several slices of bread (or tortillas), two small cans of fruit juice and a couple of candy bars. This is for each hunter and it'll be gone well before it's time to come off the high mesa at dark later that day. It's enough to make a grown man cry to ask him to drop off the mountain for lunch, then go back after noon. The not very smart hunters have been known to chase the birds up and down the mountains from dawn 'til dusk, but I would not endorse this foolishness. (Do what I say, not what I do). Thankfully, any bird killed on the mountain will be carried *downhill*.

Anyone interested in hunting in Mexico will need to contact a Mexican embassy . . .

I never leave camp without a belt knife, a small belt bag which contains a compass, and a small match safe, plus an extra mouth "horseshoe" call. The bag also contains a small pocketknife, and one of the new breed of very compact full-frame 35mm cameras. I never leave camp without a sling on whatever gun I'm toting. I've taken simple leather strips with me, and on more than one occasion, custom tied a sling then and there. This leaves both hands free, particularly for the predawn climb, when one hand will be needed to aim the flashlight, and very often the other is needed full-time in fighting brush, grasping limbs to haul yourself up-mountain, etc. Should you decide to make any hunts from horseback, the sling comes in very

(Above) "Gringos" (North American hunters) should take water with them into the backwoods mountain country of Mexico. Here, Dwain Bland draws water from a portable plastic water bag. By bringing water with him on his forays into Mexico, he has never suffered any health problems.

Water is a priceless comodity in much of the great Southwest, extending into Mexico. Every effort must be made in this age to keep this water pure and uncontaminated. Experts predict that the day will come when water will be far more widely sought than can be imagined at this time.

It is unusual to find a place to take a hot bath back in Mexico's high Sierras, especially when the water comes from a spring already heated by nature. This small bathhouse encloses such a spring at Ramon Garcia's hacienda, where the author and Allen Hawkins had a refreshing dip. Turkey hunters seldom have it so good.

handy then. Too, if hunting from a horse, you could make an overnight hunt in some remote region, requiring a sleeping bag. Small, extremely compact bags are best, along with an outside tarp wrapping which can be used as both a ground cloth and in case of rain, provide some protection. Rain isn't a great concern in the arid mountains of Mexico, though.

Additional items to pack are extra boots, long-handled underwear, gloves, soap and towel, and a collapsible water container. I have one that holds 5 gallons of water, which I have found fits perfectly in a amall Army surplus shoulder bag. This gives it added protection for hauling in the back of a pickup, and with the carrying strap a way to hang it up. These water bags have a spigot and are excellent for camp use.

Undoubtedly, you have heard many tales about the water in Mexico. Though I'm certain many are true, if proper precautions are taken, little different than those taken anywhere, I don't think many of these unfortunate occurrences would happen. I always fill water jugs prior to leaving the United States or, if in Mexico, at deep wells. High in the mountains, water is taken from the streams which are also supplying the local cattle and horse populations. This water *must* be boiled to be made safe. As such, it has never done me any harm.

But, for the average North American hunter, the "gringo," I would very highly recommend his lugging along what water he requires. Sharing can be done, but, invariably one party will think the other is cheating. You'd be surprised at how much water you use in a week's time. Of course, this is strictly for consumption. Washing your face requires more. A bath? Ha-ha!

Clothing required for a mountain hunt for wild turkeys is much like what you'd take along on a deer hunt, insofar as warmth. I don't mean a deer hunt in old Mississippi but one to the Pennsylvania hardwoods. Early morning and late afternoon hunts can be cold and will be on a winter hunt from November through February. Afternoon can be pleasant, but as in all mountain hunting, at dusk the temperatures plunge.

A hunter is wise to carry along his own mess kit, including a spoon, knife and fork set. You'll appreciate having your own drinking cup. Don't forget your camera and extra film. Special foods, paper plates, throw-a-way cups, these items are all up to the individual. Some folks carry water purification tablets. A new item on the camping market is a small tube which can be stuck in a shirt pocket, through which water can be drunk from a stream. It has its own built-in purifying system. You don't want to be in a hurry when drinking with one of these, though.

Gun and shells? Take my advice, locate a guide who already supplies these things. It's not worth the hassle to lug them through customs. If you do want to use your own gun then I would suggest you get in touch with the nearest Mexican embassy well in advance of when you plan on entering Mexico. They will supply you with the information to begin the procedures for obtaining a firearms permit. Anyone interested in hunting in Mexico will need to contact a Mexican embassy for the requirements needed to buy hunting permits, also. I want to stress that these things must be done well in advance of the planned dates afield. Six months, at least.

Once you are at the border crossing, you will need to obtain a visa, and you will be shown into a building where a Mexican border authority will ask for your proof of citizenship. The average tourist will provide a simple voter's registration card. This will suffice. After leaving the border crossing, you will soon come to additional check-points, where you will be asked for the visa. *Keep it with you until leaving Mexico, and don't give it to anyone.*

Do not attempt to sneak any guns or shells across the border in your luggage, or even on your person. A friend of mine tried this on one hunt, and we spent a couple extra hours at the border, until he decided it best to pay a heavy fine so we could be on our way. The little box of .22 shells cost him an extra $113 right there. Sneak in a gun? Ha! Be sure you leave your will where someone will find it back home.

Hunting the Gould's often leads to the true meaning of the word hunting . . .

The Gould's turkey is a large black and white turkey, truly a regal "King of the Hill." It is the fifth member of the world's huntable populations of *Meleagris*, the other four being the Eastern, Rio Grande, Merriam, and Osceola wild turkeys. All of these subspecies within *Meleagris* are distinct from all other birdlife in that the males have spurs on the legs, and a rudimentary hair growth protruding through the feathers of the upper breast. This adornment is known among turkey hunting addicts as a beard. It is considered the ultimate trophy by the average turkey hunter. Its trophy value increases with its length. Beards in the 11- to 12-inch range, thick and bushy, are what all turkey hunters dream of.

In truth, the spur should be considered the ultimate trophy, but as spur growth varies among the subspecies, more so than beard development, the beard has never relinquished its hold in the average turkey hunter's heart as the trophy of killing a fine old gobbler.

Spur growth of the Gould's turkey is on par with that of the Merriam Rocky Mountain turkey, which is far short of the spur length found on comparably aged birds of the Eastern and Osceola races. Merriam gobblers seldom have spurs exceeding 1-inch in length, and this holds true for Gould's Mexicana, *if* the bird has spurs. Many adult gobblers I have examined in the mountains of Mexico had no spurs, while others had slight bumps, or knobs, indicating the location

The author with an adult hen bagged back in Mexico's high Sierras. Notice the pure white tips of the tail feathers and those on the lower rump. The shuffling box call in the authors' pocket is a very old Lynch box.

The outspread feet of a Gould's turkey gobbler are huge, as are all measurements of this turkey found in Mexico. Spur growth, however, is on a par with that of the Merriam Rocky Mountain turkey.

(Left) Mexican cowboys are a part of camp life while hunting turkeys in the mountains of Mexico. This *caballero*, Ramone Garcia, has ridden for a ranch continuously over a period of 50 years, his principal tasks being to check wild cow traps for newly caught animals, and to see that the cattle do not stray. He also keeps a sharp eye for brush fires in the dry country.

of spurs which had not developed. The Gould's wild turkey has feet which easily exceed in size any of the other subspecies. I've seen tracks in mountain soils which I could hardly believe were made by a wild turkey, particulary after arriving there from a recent hunt for Eastern birds in the old South. A Gould's hen will leave a footprint as large as that of the average southern gobbler from Mississippi, Louisiana or Alabama. Bigness carries over into other measurements when comparing the Gould's to the other birds of *Meleagris*. For example, an average primary wing feather from a Gould's gobbler will measure 20 inches, while that of any other subspecie will be in the 17–18 inch classification.

Hunting the Gould's wild turkey often leads the hunter to the true meaning of the word, "hunting," for it's just that. And, it can be as hard as any he'll do in his lifetime. Many of the birds are exceedingly wild. In areas where they are exposed to local hunters, they are shot at whatever chance presents itself. I've yet to know inhabitants of the small Mexican mountain villages who had a permit to kill wild turkeys, or deer, or who had considered when the season allowed hunting. Government pressures on firearms and ammunition has a tendency to keep guns out of the hands of many of the people, but the men who do have them will "take a cut" at a game animal or turkey when they get the chance. Though this has the effect of making

the birds as wild as a billygoat, I want to emphasize that the meat is shot for the table, and won't be wasted. It's expected to find feathers where a bird has been picked near a cowboy's line shack, as the *vaqueros* life is nothing but day after day of riding fence, checking wild cow traps to see if one of the wary critters has been caught, or looking over the herd. Day after day the Mexican cowhand eats tortillas and beans, and refried beans, so a change of menu shouldn't be criticized by outsiders. Many times I've examined the coals of campfires along the edges of meadows where a summer herder had lingered, finding evidence of turkeys having been consumed.

Sitting up, we looked at each other, grinned and made ready to go get the bird . . .

One April morning several years back, David Jackman and I before daybreak had made the hard struggle to the crest of a mountain in Chihuahua, breaking out on the mesa in time to recover our wind before a bird cut loose. Taking up a calling stand inside 100 yards of where the bird was treed, we hoped to call it to us. April is too early to hope

Though you may not know the language, any hunter will recognize a "No Hunting" sign. This one was posted along a small ranch in western Chihuahua. The Mexican word for hunt is *casar*. It helps to know a few words, though, to stay out of trouble.

Wild cow traps are built back in Mexico's mountains to try to catch half-wild cows and bulls which are not accustomed to man, and evade the cowboy *vaqueros* at gathering time. The animals are enticed into the trap with granular salt placed in the center of the enclosure. These traps are built with logs cut on-the-spot, hand cut with an axe, and tied throughout with baling wire. The gate is balanced so the animal can walk through the narrow opening, but, like a fish trap, once inside, the animal can't escape because the sharp points face inward on the gate poles.

for such success in Gould's range in Chihuahua, as flock breakup is just beginning. Prime gobbling season for the Gould is throughout May, as compared to April which is peak gobbling time throughout the range of Merriam turkey in Arizona and New Mexico. What causes this? Mother nature looks after her offspring. In this case, summer rains in the arid mountains take place during the months of July and August, so the poults must not pip the shell until this time. The young birds thus come into the dry mountain world when conditions are at the very best, with water trickling among the rocks and new green grass bringing life to small mountain meadows. Starker Leopold, the great naturalist, advanced the theory many, many years ago that deer births and egg laying of the mountian's Harlequin quail was retarded to correlate with summer rains. Obviously, his studies were dead center.

David and I were aware of Leopold's theories at the time, but season dates that year meant that we hunt in April or not at all. The old bird began gobbling like crazy, which fired up another bird or two, and it soon was obvious that just under the rim, all along our northern flank, the mountain was infested with turkeys. Hens were yelping too, which we didn't want to hear, as the gobblers would group with them, dashing our hopes of calling one to us. But, once in a while a gobbler will leave such groups, so this kept us calling. The sun was peeking over the mountainous

horizon when the birds began flying down. We laid on heavy with the calling, but in no time, we could tell the birds had assembled and were ambling down-mountain, as the sounds suddenly took on a muffled note. Nothing to do but follow them, 'cause if you don't, and lose contact, it can easily be the last you'll see or hear of them. Mexico's mountains are big, and there are endless chains of them. We sneaked in and out of the manzanita and madrone brush, passing through some big pines, and beyond them onto the mountain's brushy north face. A bird saw us and flushed 100 yards lower. That blew the whole thing as birds flushed all across the steep slope.

Sitting down, we watched through field glasses as the birds spanned a huge valley, hitting the far slope on a dead run, uphill. A huge gobbler caught my attention. What a sight. He wound his way up the mountain among rocks, brush, trees, and on coming to a short rock wall, never slowed, but with two or three flaps of those tremendous wings, he simply boomed upward, and, feet touching atop the wall, scrambled ever upward. Again, a rock outcropping, and as though he had springs in his feet and pinions, he jumped and flew above it, resuming his journey to the summit. My respect for Mexican mountain turkeys had grown a thousand fold by the time he crested out, trotting from view. Those were the wildest bunch of turkeys I'd seen anywhere. Surveying the situation, I had two choices:

Food in a turkey hunting camp can come in endless varieties. The flour tortillas here are being cooked on top of an oil drum wood stove. These were made in camp by a Tarahumara Indian boy and are fine eating when covered with homemade apple sauce or peach preserves. This is but one unusual (to Americans) custom back in Mexico's mountains.

This small Mexican boy has killed and skinned a squirrel for the family table, knocking the animal from a pine tree with his slingshot. Food is not plentiful in Mexico's high mountain villages, so this morsel will be highly valued, if the lad can get it home before his two dogs take possession.

go look for others, or go after these. I asked David if he wanted to go after 'em. His answer was no, but, thank you. Hell no!

What had taken the turkey perhaps 3 minutes to cover, I scrambled up in a little under an hour. More dead than alive when I gained the mountain's top, I then slowly worked my way among the oaks, junipers, and manzanita on its mesa, finally choosing a place to sit where I could make a call. Could be that since the birds were well split apart a gobbler would come to me. Fishing the bones caller from my shirt front, I licked the tip a moment, then made a couple or three yelps. The bird fired straight back, telling me he was off to my left front at some 300 to 400 yards.

I never heard nor saw him after that. Probably a hen went to him once he gobbled at me, causing him to forget me. My calls went in vain. Two hours later I began the long, often hazardous climb back down, then back up, to where David was still waiting. He'd heard the gobble and then hoped to hear the lonesome *dooo-mmm-mm* of a shotgun blast. Soaked with sweat, my sole consolation was that I'd given it a hard try. Sadly, spring dates in Mexico are too early, resulting in conditions exactly as mentioned. Flock breakup is not complete. The hens are not laying, much less sitting the clutch of eggs. Gobblers are not easily swayed into leaving them.

Far the wisest thing to do is to scatter the birds, *then* attempt to call one to the gun. If, at the time of the scatter, the hunter can identify the course of a gobbler as he flies

away, this will help no end, as then an attempt can be made to go after him quickly, hoping he has been cut off from the others and will respond to early calling. The size of the mountains and the time and effort involved in pursuing such birds works against the hunter, but this is part of the hunt. These same circumstances surface all too often when the hunter finds ideal gobbling conditions. Gould's turkeys seemingly are prone to roost in close proximity, and at the break of day, the hens are invariably in voice contact with the gobblers. Assembly takes place on flydown, scuttling any quick plans of calling a bird. Bushwacking the bunch seldom has any chance, due to the deathly silent mountain air at dawn, plus the ever-present noisy gravel, loose rock, and dry leaves underfoot.

Later in the morning the hunter's chances for calling will be better. Two years ago, David and I were lying alongside a long-since harvested cornfield, having for 2 hours watched a pair of hens as they pecked around the field. Visible to surrounding mountain slopes, we had hoped a gobbler would see, and join, them. Nothing showed up. They finally drifted into the brush. David hadn't killed a bird. I'd shot one at the dawn flydown earlier that morning, which had come to a hen I'd called to me. She was clucking back and forth to me from about 20 yards when here comes the old boy, and though he'd never gobbled, I'd heard his drumming with the strut. I readied myself to give him a greeting blast with the 12 bore, and bowled him over.

The sun was getting higher, and we were stretched out

in the shade. It was short of noon a bit when far, far to the east, a gobble rolled across the mesa to us. Sitting up, we looked at each other, grinned, began stuffing hunting paraphernalia into pockets, and made ready to go get the bird. David buckled on the fanny pack he wears, grabbed his gun and we took off. Gobbling a couple times, the bird made it easy for us to maintain a course to him. Satisfied with a small ridge just above an arroyo, I located a hide for David, then settled down a few feet behind him.

The old bird hooted right back to my first rendition on the bones call. He also answered the second call a moment later, this time nearer. I could see him shortly after the third calling, as he strutted toward us through the mountain cover. I could see a hen and a jake were coming along too. An easy, classic, kill.

Last spring David and Antonio, a Mexican friend of ours, heard one of these late day gobblers cut loose while sitting on a mountain-side taking a breather. David made a series of yelps with his old Latham shufflin' box, and though the birds didn't walk up to them, David and Antonio could see the two gobblers and two hens ambling along the mountain's face. The bunch would pass by inside 40 yards. David "knows" the gun, so he bided his time, allowing the best gobbler to walk into an opening, made the shot, and a kill.

Many times we have heard gobblers sounding off throughout the spring season, and sometimes we attempt to get closer in order to try a calling kill. But, ordinarily the birds will be on another mountain, or will have dropped down to a stream. Going down is a toss-up decision, due to the time that is often consumed in getting to where the bird is calling. On the hunter's arrival 20, 30, maybe 40 minutes later, the bird could have wandered away, shut up, or both. I heard a bird sounding off time after time from a small basin and realized I would have to make a large circle in order to drop down to his level in a side canyon where my descent wouldn't be heard, and then come into the basin from a draw that fed a creek. I never heard the bird once I'd worked my way to the area. My two hunting partners were on an opposite mesa, and afterward they told me he never shut up. He did wander away, but not far, and had been gobbling all the while in a saddle around the mountain. The intervening slope was nothing but a soundproof barricade insofar as I was concerned.

Whenever you think you're up to it, hike yourself off to lands south of the border . . .

Hunting the Gould's turkey during the fall and winter months is a far different ball game. There isn't any gobbling to tell you where to find the birds. So, you begin looking. If you are in strange country you haven't hunted, you have your work cut out for you. It becomes a matter of finding sign—tracks, droppings, feathers and what-have-you—and following these to where they become thick. Then, you'll know you are in the area of the roost site. You will be on a mesa, and somewhere along its northern face where the mountain drops off steeply, you'll find scattered pines, perhaps both Apache and Chihuahua pines. If the stand of pines is small, dotted here and there over only several acres, and you feel up to clambering around over the steep mountainside where these trees are located, you can drop off the rim and search beneath them for droppings. These young mountain turkeys leave very small droppings which, together with being a dull green color making them blend with the pine needles, look somewhat like an alfalfa pellet used for cattle feed in the United States. If you locate sev-

Due to the nature of the terrain, binoculars are a must when hunting the mountains of Mexico. The slopes of opposing mountains can be studied, particularly when a gobble has been heard.

The ancient Spaniards taught the primitive Indians the art of silversmithing, which is carried on widely in these modern times. Bowguards, worn on the arm to protect it from the recoil of the bowstring, were and are made, these being fashioned from silver, often embellished with turquoise. Because of its beautiful blue color, turquoise was known by the Indians as "turkey stone" because the color is like that found on the wild turkey's head.

eral trees with these near the base, your chances are improving. You haven't won the game, but, you haven't struck out. You can then take up hiding on the mesa nearest where you've seen the greatest amount of sign, and hope that a turkey will walk by on its way to roost. *If* any turkeys roost there.

Once you've hunted an area for several days, you will have located several of these roost rims, with adjoining mesas, and you can rotate among them until you make contact with a drove. This can be done at first day, providing you can find your way in the dark, and again late in the afternoon. You won't know all the locations where a traveling drove spends the nights, but if you can alternately stake out several *dormitorios* you'll get a shot. I certainly don't advise anyone sitting under the roost trees and banging away at one after it has flown up. You may wish to hunt the area again, or perhaps your partner hasn't been lucky, so don't ruin the roost.

David Jackman and Antonio had walked both legs off one winter afternoon, so they decided to take a stand on the mesa near a roost, and trust to luck. Just at sundown David heard a yelp nearby, and glimpsed a black shape wending among the manzanita. The young gobbler passed him by at a range many lesser experienced hunters would have considered inside gunshot range. Darkness then began

to close in. Obviously the one chance for a kill had gone a'kiting. Suddenly, a second jake gobbler showed, hurrying along, directly at my two buddies.

I was standing by the old woodstove, warming a tortilla on its redhot lid, when they came into camp shouldering the big young black and white turkey. We built a bonfire near the log cabin, and I watched Dave field-dress the bird.

If you want to keep busy during the midday hours when the birds are not near the roost areas, you can look for dust sites along old cultivated fields, or along dry washes. Once you've located a dust area, you can check it from time to time for birds. You can search for where the drove is feeding, though with such an abundance of foods, this can be all but hopeless. Again, concentrate on areas where you find the greatest amount of fresh signs. Mountain air will dry the droppings very quickly, so don't be deceived. Tracks remain for long periods too, as there is little wind to disturb them. Tracks 2 to 3 weeks old can appear to be made yesterday, or a couple days ago. Once you've found lots of sign, search around among it and look for other indications of age. Have any leaves fallen on the tracks where they pass under overhanging bushes? A tiny grass blade is growing from the bottom of a track. Look, and closer examination reveals that the soil at its base is undisturbed. It's popped up since the track was made. That dropping, it looks very fresh. If you don't want to pinch it with your fingers, as us old turkey hunters are prone to do, then use a stick. It's soft. Heh, that bird has been by here today.

Should the winter hunter after Gould's turkeys locate, and scatter a drove, and take up a calling stand at the scatter location, he'll find the birds are not difficult to call. Few wintering droves in Old Mexico have been subjected to calling, so the experienced fall and winter turkey caller will find the setup to his liking.

So, whenever you think you're up to it, and you've got a hankering to hunt the King of the Mountain, hike yourself off to the lands south of the border, to Mexico. Go west to the mountains that straddle the states of Sonora, Chihuahua, and Durango. Hunt with somebody who knows the country.

I had to give up a trip down there last year, as the soldiers had found "marrywanna" in that old cornfield where I'd killed a couple birds several years ago. Those Federales then went on a search for more of the pot, and raised a ruckus all over those mountains. Just wasn't the time or place for a gringo turkey hunter to be caught lollygagging along the backroads.

They say there's gold in the Sierra Madres. As vast as the range of mountains is, I don't doubt that. These days the cash crop is marijuana. The only gold I want to see back in those hills is the yellow glint of sunlight bouncing off the feathers of a big old Mexico gobbler. I prefer my smoke in smoked turkey.

Chapter 1

The Hazards of Hunting Wild Turkeys

Turkey hunters should develop aggressive attitudes because this will not only give them the will "to hang tough" when things are not going well, but will also give them the physical strength to hunt when conditions are far from ideal. Wild turkeys are tough and wary, and conditioned to living a raw, hard life in the outdoors. The hunter who can understand this and can challenge the birds on their own ground will have the best chance to close to within easy shooting distance.

TO ME, the greatest danger facing a turkey hunter are fences. These man-made demons can do more to mess up a day's good times than any other thing on dry land. One spring morning I'd called in an old bird, but at the blast of the old muzzle-loading 11 bore, he flopped over, rolled around once or twice, and headed across the woods with me in hot pursuit. I had the other hammer cocked on the gun, and if the percussion cap would just stay in place through the footrace, I intended on giving him that barrel's contents. I hadn't known about the race until the bird had a head start, so I had some catching up to do. The turkey and I had just taken one obstacle in stride. Well, he took it in stride, I took it in the face, as we went in and out of a thorny plum thicket. What came up next was there all the time, but as I'd never set foot there before, only the turkey knew about it—a three strand "bob-wire" fence.

I learned the fence was there when I hit it going full speed ahead. The fence stopped my legs, but from there on up, I kept going. I did a perfect full twisting half-gainer—an Olympic diving event only mastered by champions. Here I did it without even trying. Dazed, I looked at the gun in my hands. The hammer was still cocked. Then I remembered, I was in a footrace.

Jumping up, I looked around. There the old bird goes, down through the woods. Away I went. Very soon I noticed the wet grass seemed to be wetter'n it had been. This was because most of my pants were no longer with me, but were back at the three-strand. By now I was making a vengeful pursuit. This thing had taken on a personal grudge, like a duel.

Barbed wire fences are a very real hazard to a hunter trotting toward a gobbling turkey, particularly if "first day" is yet a faint glow on the eastern horizon. The hunter who is in unfamiliar country should be alert to this menace. A deep scratch or cut by a dirty, rusty barb has been known to cause the dreaded Lock Jaw. Westerners know the wire strands as "bob-wahr."

I began gaining ground. The race had been taking some time as we'd covered some country new to both of us. Forty yards, 35 yards, hey-hey, I'm closing the gap. Any marathoner would have been envious. I was really picking 'em up and laying 'em down. When I was within 20 yards of the gobbler, I decided it was time for what is known in elephant hunting circles as "The Moment of Truth." Now or never, and all that rot.

I'd heard of one-shot antelope hunts, and one-shot whiskey glasses, but this was going to be one shot 'cause that's all there was. I slammed to a stop, heaved the old stump blower to face, and "hauled steel." The gobbler disappeared in a cloud of smoke. If you've ever shot a muzzle-loading shotgun, your first reaction to its going off is, "it went off." Only after you've patted yourself on the back for being such an expert among black powder buffs does it strike you that it must have been going off at something. Running under the smoke cloud, I could see the old bird flopping.

Not all fences have been hazardous for me, as two I can remember were bad for turkeys. In both instances the birds were trying to find a way through them, walking the fence until they bumped into my brother, Dick, and me. We were sitting maybe ½-mile apart, and we'd scattered a bunch of birds. Being wise to what would probably happen, we'd both taken up stands inside gunshot of the hogwire fence and sure enough, both of us killed adult gobblers who were searching for a hole.

Tom Preston, another sidekick of mine, who is married to my daughter, Sherry, was with Max Olson one April morning, and they made the mistake of calling an old turkey up to a hogwire fence, just out of shooting distance. They fooled with this turkey for some time before the gobbler found a way to them, where he was shot for his trouble.

appeared to be solid timber and underbrush. Turning to Randy, I said, "Let's get out of this open field, and go up to this small bunch of trees with that brush in them, then I think we'll see what we can do about that turkey." Randy was all for it. He's hunted turkeys a few years, but wants to learn all he can about the sport. I wasn't packing a gun. Randy would do the honors.

The clump was good hiding for the two of us, so I then hauled out my old Latham shufflin' box, the one made of poplar, sold by the Penn's Woods turkey call people, and chalked the paddle good with blue carpenter's chalk. Rounding the box's calling edges with sandpaper, I then chalked them. Having used the box for nigh on to 20 years, I can rely on it to make exactly the sound I want, and these notes can be extremely loud if I desire. Stroking the box hard, I made a long series of 12 to 15 notes. Far to the east I could hear the turkey gobble. I didn't wait, but made another series, then another and another. I'd hear the bird gobbling from time to time, but I didn't pay much attention. I just kept the box going. Moments later I could already tell a difference in the gobbler's gobbling, he was obviously coming our way. I lit into the calling again, calling over and over. Many mornings I've called hens to me that would stand nearby and yelp time after time, loud raspy yelps, notes that could be heard for a good distance. Other times I've heard hens at a distance calling in this same manner, yelping incessantly, making lots of noise.

Though this appears to be a two-headed gobbler, it is two birds walking side-by-side along a woven wire fence. Wild turkeys will wander along a fence for some time, poking their heads in and out of the hog-wire trying to get through. A hunter who is calling near such obstacles should be certain to locate within easy gunshot, because the bird may not overcome the barrier.

Here he came, dead center down the road. Beard swinging, he was in a hurry . . .

Fences can be bad news in many ways, particularly if there are turkeys beyond one, and it's heavily posted. Of course, this is where a turkey call can come in handy. Randy Willems and I were hunting spring gobblers one morning, but didn't hear any in the woods we'd laid our hopes on, so we began looking and listening elsewhere. The sun was on the eastern horizon when we finally got an answer to my callings. The direction sounded bad, but we hurried anyhow, hoping the wind was fooling us. It wasn't. The bird was far inside a hunk of posted land, well fenced, and from the signs nailed to the posts, it was one of those places where they don't just say, No, but "HELL NO." Leaning on a post, I made another call. The bird gobbled back. As best as I could tell, he was back near the center of a mile square section of land. From where we stood it

watched a party of hunters scatter a drove on neighboring lands, which had ''No Hunting'' signs tacked darned near on each post. It was obvious I wasn't welcome there. From time to time I would hear a shot or catch a glimpse of a hunter. It was cold that day but I stuck it out, hoping they'd leave and, after what seemed an eternity, I heard a pickup start, then another, and listened to the trucks fade in the distance. Telling the two hunters with me where to sit, I began calling, making the lost kee runs of very scared

More and more of these kinds of signs are popping up on fences all across America. This one needs no explanation.

(Right) This hunter's bulletin board is well plastered with signs alerting the hunters to local rules and regulations. It also shows maps of the area and landmarks which will tell a wandering hunter approximately where he is. Sadly, too many slobs among us are not paying any attention to any of this, which brings the country nearer to the end of public hunting with each passing year.

It seemed like we'd not gotten settled good when I realized we'd best get ready for company, as the gobbler was bee-lining for us. Posted signs be hanged, we'd get that bird anyhow. The gobbler came into view about 100 yards from us, stepping out onto the little used county road which lay between us and the other farm. He stood still, eyeballing the surroundings. I stroked the box. Straight back, he fired a gobble, and here he came, walking dead center down the road. Beard swinging, he was in a hurry. Out of the corner of my eye, I could sense Randy's tensing, gun still low, but ready to be brought to bear.

I whispered, ''Wait 'til he comes through the fence, then take him.'' Soon the bird broke over to our side of the road, dropped from sight a moment as he dropped into a ditch, then he came back into view, ducking under the barbwire. Scattered tall weeds and old sunflowers dotted the flat, but he was easily discernible from where we were hunkered. Range? Less than 30 yards, and closing fast. ''Take him when you're ready,'' I whispered to my partner. Randy stood up, freezing the gobbler for an instant, which was too long, for the shot bowled the turkey over backwards. Somebody else's turkey was now trespassing on us, and had paid the price.

Down through the years I've called a lot of turkeys from within ''signed'' property, both private and government. One afternoon I tolled four gobblers from the confines of a National Wildlife Refuge. Another morning an old longbeard brought two hens with him. One fall afternoon, I

Have you ever tried to call a turkey to you which was located beyond a hog-wire fence? A fence you did not know was there? Never locate with one of these fences between you and the turkey. The bird will walk along it, and unless it finds a hole large enough to walk through, the bird most often will not cross through the woven wire.

young turkeys. In jig time I got an answer, then I could see the bird running toward us, weaving in and out of the trees and the brush. I didn't need to tell one of my hunters to shoot. He did. Bird number one. They thought we should then move, but after telling them the shot wouldn't upset my plans, they sat down and I went back to calling.

A bird called back a while later and wouldn't walk toward us but several yards at a time, then it would stand there and call. The bird wanted us to come to it. We just couldn't do that, so I leaned on the kee runs, which would get the bird coming our way a little farther. Sounded like a young gobbler, and when he walked into sight, we could tell that it was. We had quite a show as the bird eased to us, yelping and keeing. Ten minutes later my second hunter stretched out bird number two on the leaves—the two young gobblers identical in size and plumage.

Things seemed to be going my way, so I once again tuned up the kee runs, putting all I had into them, trying to make them keen and clear, like the beautiful, plaintive whistling kees of a young wild turkey. I was using a mouth horseshoe call. Shortly a bird whistled back, the sounds coming from perhaps 300 yards inside the posted land. I called again. Then, suddenly I could see a bird flying straight at me. The turkey landed not 10 yards from me. But, as I jumped to my feet it flushed, probably a very surprised bird. I killed it on the wing at 20 yards. Bird number three. All were taken with the knowledge of what scattered wild turkeys will do when exposed to calling. Had we not been able to do this, the bunch would have gotten together behind the no-no signs, and we'd truly have been left out in the cold.

Prickly pear cactus is common throughout the ranges of the Rio Grande, Gould, and Merriam turkeys. Hunters must be careful when walking across land dotted with this plant, particularly during darkness, as a fall into it could result in a trip to a hospital emergency room.

Turkey terrain everywhere is well laced with thorny trees, bushes, and vines. It's very important that the hunter protect his eyes when going through these thorns as it doesn't take much to ruin your eyesight.

A turkey hunter hunts turkeys where turkeys are, often the best place for insects, too . . .

Another problem area the average turkey hunter must contend with is insects. Many insects could be avoided, but a turkey hunter hunts turkeys where turkeys are, and all too often this is the best place for insects, too. Swamps, along meandering creeks, all sorts of areas that hold water, is where a hunter expects to find turkeys, and these are ideal breeding grounds for mosquitoes. Today's hunter can spray himself with aerosol repellent or apply the kind that can be rubbed on the skin. Recently, camouflage creams with bug repellent added to the ingredients have become available. In addition to these, the hunter can also choose from a variety of headnets. Take your choice, mosquitoes can be dealt with effectively.

The buffalo gnat is another all but invisible insect which is nothing but one big biting mouth. I've known a great many people who were allergic to the bite of these gnats and when bitten suffer from large raised red bumps on the skin. The best repellent is vanilla extract.

Ticks are one insect which defy all repellents to a degree. I've never found a spray or lotion which could be relied on to keep them off. What is worse, tick bites can be fatal as ticks carry Rocky Mountain tick fever. Nowhere will a hunter find ticks in such numbers as in parts of southeastern Oklahoma and southwestern Arkansas. Sitting on a calling stand, I've found them crawling up my pant legs in waves, ignoring the spray and sulphur powder on my boots. Far the best defense against them is simply to be on the lookout for them where you must hunt. Ordinarily you won't find them in short grass nor on open soil. But, you will find them in deep woods, in leaf mast, in high weeds and particularly around areas where there have been animals, especially if manure is scattered among the leaves. Ticks, like mosquitoes, are most often reckoned with during the spring season, but not if the spring has been cold. Anyone hunting in tick country should always inspect his body each night. Ticks found can then usually be easily removed with alcohol. Ticks dig in, burying their heads under the skin after many hours on the body, but if found soon enough, will have not managed to do this. Very often, if the head is left imbedded under the skin, the area will become red, swollen, and will itch, sometimes becoming an infected sore.

Parts of the country have chiggers, a tiny insect that can cause much torment, as the bites become red, and itch unmercifully. Chiggers are invariably found in dense weeds and grass. Stay out of these, and you probably won't be bothered by them. I hate chiggers worse than all the other pests put together. Fingernail polish will kill them.

Bumblebees, hornets, fire-ants—the list of creepy crawlers is endless, but most won't bother a hunter unless he bothers them. Simply being careful where you sit or lean will eliminate most dangers.

Spiders are not much danger to the average hunter, but, there is one which causes trouble for a great number of people each year, the brown recluse or fiddleback spider. This spider likes darkness and therefore will take up residence in sleeping bags, boots, coats, bedclothes, and camping equipment. So, it is wise to shake these out when camping, and be careful when reaching into dark places where a spider may lurk. The bite will have only one puncture hole, as opposed to two with snake bites. Ordinarily, the area around the bite will soon become inflamed and swollen, and can turn from red to purple, then to black in a few days time. Once the bite progresses to this stage, the victim can expect sloughing off of flesh. Like snake bites, spider bites should be considered dangerous, and medical treatment should be sought quickly. Both my grandson and my brother have been bitten by fiddlebacks. They both agree, "Don't fiddle around with a spider bite—go to the doctor."

Another critter that many find repulsive are leeches. These are blood-sucking worms which will attach themselves to a person, ordinarily while in water. The hunter who wades swamps, ponds, and any slow moving rivers or creeks where there are lots of waterlogged trees with leaves coating the bottom, can expect leeches to attach to his legs. Florida swamps rate at the top of the list if you're looking for leeches. A hunter seeking out Osceola turkeys in the cypress heads and strands can count on having these "riders" after a hunt. Just pull them off. I've never known the bite to cause any problems.

A large hornet's nest hangs above an alligator hole in south Florida. This nest has been torn open, exposing the egg-holding cells. A large nest such as this one, bumped accidentally by a hunter, would bring forth a raging swarm of hornets—a real hazard if they should sting.

At that instant the stick broke, and in less than a heartbeat I felt the rattler's fangs go deep into my hand . . .

Snakes are what a good many hunters fear, though the chances of tangling with one are very poor. And, while the average hunter expects to find them in the spring, the chances of being bitten are higher during an early fall hunt. During April, the month spanning the greatest number of turkey seasons, snakes are still sluggish from hibernation. Of course, many areas in the country don't have the snake problem the southern hunter faces.

In less than an hour's time, David Kelley and I while in Osceola country stepped over, or around five nasty looking cottonmouths in the watery confines of a grassy marsh. All of them threw up their heads and opened wide the white-

Copperhead snakes are perfectly cam-ouflaged for lying motionless on leaves or rocks. This poisonous reptile is not an aggressive snake, though it will bite if provoked. It's best just to give them a wide berth.

Rattlesnakes are present throughout the bulk of the country's wild turkey ranges. Often these poisonous snakes hunt during the morning hours, but are always present throughout the day, except during extreme heat or cold. Rattlers do not always rattle a warning before striking. A hunter who is bitten should seek help and get quick medical attention.

as-cotton mouth which looks like it's on hinges. None of them tried to strike. The morning was cool, and a light mist was falling. I suppose one would have struck at a person's leg, if his heavy boot had come down across its body.

Anyone who keeps his eyes open when hunting near water in the southern states will notice cottonmouths, as there are lots of them. They have one habit which is very unsettling to some folks. Artificial light attracts them. If you are using a flashlight with a strong beam to find your way through a swamp, chances are you could look back and a snake will be trailing along after you. They'll do the same thing if you're running banklines from a johnboat on a hot summer night. It's nothing to get excited about. They'll only come so close, then stop.

Copperheads are also a very common poisonous snake throughout the South. Like the others, they only bite when threatened. Copperheads are splendidly camouflaged to match dead leaves, so a hunter does need to look before he sits. I suppose the chance of sitting down on one would be one in 10 million.

Rattlesnakes are found throughout a great deal of all turkey range in the United States, and also in the Sierra Madre range of the Gould's turkey. But, not a handful pose a threat to any turkey hunter. Probably the greatest danger with rattlers comes when hunting Osceolas in Florida's palmetto flatlands. The huge Florida diamondback calls this country home, and his bite is very lethal. Florida would be over-run with this chimera if it wasn't for the palmetto pasture burnings to keep this shrub-palm from taking over a ranch's cattle pasture.

There's one unwritten rule about snakebite: if you are not certain what kind of snake has bitten you, at least get yourself out of the woods, tell your hunting buddies, or summon help. Nine times in ten you won't get sick, but don't take chances with snakebite. Late one fall afternoon I had a small rattler nail its fangs into my hand, and later that night kinda wished I'd gone to the doctor. I was hunting in Arkansas, the fall weather was hot, and while leaning against a tree on the side of a ridge, noticed a little timber rattler crawling past. Rick Greene, a turkey-hunting buddy from New York State, was not far away, so I thought I'd just catch the little critter, and carry it over toward Rick. It was a beautifully marked rattler. The snake was very active, so I knew if I didn't catch him quick, he'd escape on the leaf strewn slope. Glancing around for a forked stick, I grabbed the first one I saw, and that was my mistake. It was a small dead pine branch. Breaking away the surplus, I slipped the fork down on the snake's neck, then grabbed the reptile behind the head with my free hand. At that instant the stick broke, and in less than a heartbeat, I felt the rattler's fangs go deep into my hand as the snake pulled free before I'd gotten a solid hold on his head. Instinctively I looked at my hand, then quickly sucked on the bites, spitting out what venom I could draw from the punctures. I thought, it couldn't be too bad as the snake wasn't that big. Having caught snakes all my life, and with no bad results, I'd gotten careless.

Showing the snake to Rick, I then told him I was heading back for the pickup for some ice in the ice chest, and I would make an ice pack; perhaps that would help. The bite was burning, but not yet uncomfortable. The walk was perhaps a ½-mile, but when I got to the vehicle, the bite was becoming painful and swollen. I applied the ice, then waited for Rick and the other boys who were hunting in our party.

At dusk they gathered and, since due back home, bid me farewell. I assured them I was not in much pain and would be okay. I ate a bite, rolled out the sleeping bag, but couldn't go to sleep. Tossing and turning, I at last decided I'd feel better sitting up. By midnight the pain was excruciating, and then I noticed a large red area on my upper arm, along with another on my chest. Considerable swelling had enlarged my hand. At 9 o'clock the next morning I was in a doctor's office in a nearby town. He was as friendly as anyone could be with someone whom he'd never seen, and who should have been there hours earlier. He remarked that I should have come to town just after the incident, whereon he would have put me in the hospital. I answered, "Yeah, and I probably saved myself several hundred dollars just by gritting my teeth all night." This made him mad, and we never did hit it off from that moment on.

He told me that the worst was over since I'd made it that far. He looked me over, gave me a couple of shots, along with prescriptions to pick up at the local drugstore and sent me on my way. Swollen hand and all, I killed a fine old adult gobbler that same afternoon. But, I would advise anyone who is bitten by a poisonous snake to go to a doctor right away. I was very lucky. I got nailed by a little rattler, and probably also was able to suck some of the venom from the bite. Even so, the pain I sat up with all that night was what some would best describe as "hurt like Hell." No dawn looked so glorious, no rising sun so gorgeously red. These days I cut live branches for my snake catching sticks.

One damp morning in Mississippi, I turned and scared the heck out of a bobcat . . .

Wild animals are not of much concern in turkey hunting country. I watch for bear, mountain lions, bobcats, coyotes and what-have-you, but with the exception of the coyotes, seldom see any of the others. I did sneak up to within a few feet of a monstrous 'gator a few years back while hunting Osceolas one morning. He (or perhaps it was a she) was sunning alongside a deep hole back in a swamp. Lots of small black-and-yellow 'gators were snaking around in the shallow end of the pond. Coyotes are a common sight while hunting turkeys, and any number of times I have had them come within several yards to my calling. One damp morning in Mississippi, I turned and scared the heck out of a bobcat that had sneaked to within 10 feet of me. I suppose the greatest hazard from animals would be in getting bitten by a rabid skunk, as there has been an upturn in this disease among wild animals. Skunks are the common carriers, though raccoons are also a serious threat.

Packs of wild dogs have been known to attack hunters, particularly in the South. Georgia had a serious problem

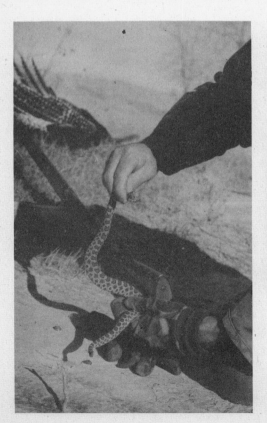

Accidents are bound to happen regardless of how careful a hunter may be. Hunting rough terrain can lead to all sorts of injuries, such as sprained ankles. This hunter is having an ankle taped and, though it will slow him down, he will be able to continue to hunt.

(Left) The author's heavy bullhide boots deflected the strike of this small but deadly prairie rattler. There are snake leggings made expressly for hunting in country which has numerous poison snakes, along with a number of heavy-weight leather boots that will resist their fangs.

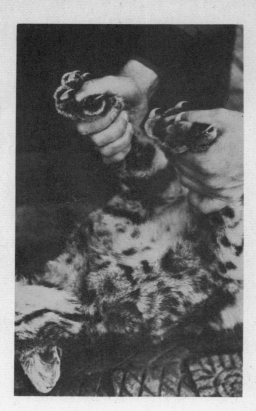

Earl Woodbury, a veteran Oklahoma turkey hunter, holds a large bobcat killed with a load intended for a turkey gobbler. Bobcats are considered a serious predator of wild turkeys.

The bobcat is perhaps the number one wild turkey predator, aside from man. Few turkeys will escape, once claws like these are sunk into the bird's sides. Bobcats often live near established wild turkey roosts, rearing their young within the bird's territory. The cats normally own't bother hunters, except maybe to scare them a bit.

with free-running packs of dogs several years ago. These are house pets gone wild, and strays dumped along country roads. These dogs gather in bunches, take to running deer, and have been known to seriously injure people.

Another domestic animal to keep an eye on are cattle. This may sound ridiculous, as those among us who are regularly exposed to cattle consider them harmless. True, the cowlot is full of docile white-faced bulls, and black angus will often not even look up as you wander by them as they graze. But a friend of mine who would agree with this assessment and who has been a dairyman all his life, spent months in the intensive care unit of our local hospital, hanging between life and death after a Holstein bull got him down one morning. Only his wife's heroics saved his life. Another man of my acquaintance has a zipper-like scar running across his face, the aftermath of a fracas with a bull "that wouldn't hurt a fly." Brahmas? All of them demand respect.

I'll freely admit I've been lost, and I probably will be again . . .

Getting lost is the number one turkey hunting hazard. According to most hunters this is the worst thing that could happen to them, and the one with the best chance of happening. The fear is so great for some that they will not hunt in areas where getting lost is a possibility. For those of us who like to hunt the backcountry areas, other's fears work to our benefit. The fewer the hunters the better the hunting.

A person can also become thoroughly lost in country he's hunted for years. Several years ago a man and wife from my hometown went quail hunting on the same ranch they have hunted birds on for many, many years. During the course of the afternoon they became separated, which is easily done in the type of country where they were—small rolling sandhills covered with sagebrush, a few chittumberry trees, and little else. It all looks alike. A late afternoon fog settled in and she soon knew she was lost. She couldn't walk a straight line far enough to bump into the fence which surrounded the place, so at dark, she sat down beneath a tree, and was still there the next morning when the search party found her. She wasn't hurt, probably not too frightened, but just tired of sitting all night in quail country.

Such incidents happen year after year. She was aware of this, and took it in stride. There are fools who think they have a sense of direction, and are often heard to say, "I'm one of those people who doesn't get lost." To which the only answer is, *Hogwash*. I'll freely admit I've been lost, and if I live as long as another season or two, I probably will be again. I hunt hard, like to walk, and if my feet can take me farther from the road where the turkeys are, and where I know there are fewer hunters, that's where I go. I don't worry about getting lost, but the reason I don't worry is because I have already begun taking precautions against that possibility long before I climb from the pickup.

During the planning stages, when I know I'll be hunting in strange country, I order maps of the areas and study them. I don't just glance at them and stick them in the desk. I study them many times, trying to pinpoint areas where I think turkeys might be, locating landmarks, timbered areas, creeks, backroads, pipeline right-of-ways, fire towers, predominant elevations, anything which will make me feel more at home when I get there. I'll make notations on the maps if need be, or draw circles around an area that needs a closer look.

I don't leave the maps at home in the desk. Anyone who hunts with me will vouch for this. The maps are on a clipboard, lying on the front seat of the truck. On leaving the pickup, I'll fold the map and stick it in my pocket if I feel the need. Ordinarily, I'll take a good hard look at it, imprint some outstanding features of the area I plan to hunt in the following hours, and plunge in, looking for turkeys.

I'm also one of those people who has a sense of direction, a way of knowing which direction to take to get to camp. But, I'm aware that no one is born with this aptitude. Such a knack is no more than always observing what lies around a person as he makes his way through the country. The woodsman is always conscious of the sun, stars, the wind, watersheds, the contour of a distant ridge, which sides of a mountain various tree species can be found on. He notices things as he travels, always alert, forever looking. In many parts of the West, the trees will have a slight bend toward the north, due to the strong south winds blowing across the prairie during the summer growing seasons when the tree

that's tucked in the matchsafe. It is one made by an old Arkansas buddy, Bill Kimes, of Mountainburg. Bill is a tough, bearded, ridge-running Arkansan, just like the turkeys he "train wrecks" on those Ozark hills.

These few items will see me through, as I can build a fire, and then after a night of keeping the fire company, use the compass to "strike a line," and walk out. You've noticed I said, strike a line. The person who is lost, whether he's studied the area on a map beforehand or not, could not care less about where he comes out into civilization, just so long as he comes out. Much of the United States, darned near all of it east of the Mississippi River, will take little more than a 10-mile walk to break onto a road. Simply by taking a reading on a compass from time to time, a person can walk a fairly straight course to safety.

If you had studied the map intensely, perhaps you noticed a road that was to the south of where you intended hunting, so it would be much quicker to walk a southerly direction. Too, you would then have an idea of where you were in relation to your vehicle, once you broke out of the woods. So, strike a line due south. Perhaps a river caught your attention on the map, as it wound through the country east of where you expected to hear a gobbler. Once you have found it, you can follow it downstream to civilization.

There are many areas across the United States where a turkey hunter can easily become lost. Chasing after a gobbling turkey can cause a hunter to soon become disoriented, especially if the day is hazy or cloudy, as in this picture. Any hunter who is hunting unfamiliar country should carry a compass, and familiarize himself with his location with a map of the area before entering.

Turkey hunting is like most hunting—get up early and go to bed late. After a few days of this, everyone is bone tired. Probably the best solution to this is to lie down after lunch and take a long nap. Wild turkeys often loaf during the midday hours too, holed up in the shade, dusting, or just lollygagging beneath trees on a high ridge. (Photo courtesy of Greg Butts.)

is soft. Not all trees will do this, but the woodsman knows this too. By fall, the blowsand will be piled up along the north side of trees, rocks, etc. After a hard winter wind, it'll be on the south side.

As I walk into the woods, I will be carrying three very small items which could see me through, should I have to spend the night there. A compass, a pocketknife and a matchsafe. Oh, one other item. I carry an extra mouth call

Never go upstream, if you are truly lost, as the stream will only grow smaller, and branching tributaries could only confuse and worsen your predicament. I've made this mistake many times after chasing a gobbler into unknown woods. Some have taken me into further unknown woods where I didn't now north from sic'em. It's so easy to think, "I'll just follow the crick back up to where I was this morning, when I heard him gobble," but after taking a

Hunters trudge along a recently used logging road which carried the timber from this clearcut area. Clearcuts are simply that, all timber has been taken from a tract varying from 40 to perhaps 200 acres in size, leaving little or nothing but wildlife. This practice is becoming widespread, along with the reforestation of these areas with nothing but pine trees. When mature, these so-called "pine orchards" will be very nearly void of all wildlife.

(Right) The author with a Gould's turkey gobbler bagged high in Mexico's Sierra Madre mountains. Hunting these birds can become hazardous due to mountain people raising marijuana in small cultivated fields. When the Mexican soldiers (*Federales*) search for these fields, any white North American (*gringo*) will be looked upon with suspicion. Especially if he should be carrying a gun.

couple wrong forks in the creek, you realize the surroundings are not the ones you'd expected. It's all part of the hunt. I've hitchhiked rides all over the United States trying to find my way back to where it had all begun. I'll undoubtedly have my thumb up again, and someone will take pity on this turkey-chasin' Okie, and give me a lift.

If you have been hunting, and suddenly it smacks you in the face that you're lost, don't go any farther. Sit down on a log and take a break to gather your thoughts. Carefully study the country in every direction and you may unravel your location. If you are carrying a compass, lay it flat where the metal of your gun won't affect its reading, and see what direction it says is north. Now, if you are lost, you won't in any way agree with what the compass has just told you. You'll instantly disagree, as you are positive north is over in so-and-so direction. Of course, you are wrong.

This is the worst part of being lost, as you will have a difficult time adjusting your mind to the directions on the compass. I've read any number of articles written by people who have never been lost, about what to do when lost, but

These spurs on a Merriam gobbler, bagged by David Jackman, are sharp enough to inflict serious injury to an unsuspecting hunter. Never grab a downed gobbler unless precautions are taken to prevent the bird from flopping. The sharp ends of the large primary feathers on the wings and the spurs can cause serious injury.

they have no idea how difficult it is to reorient your mind to a compass reading when your mind has another quadrant deeply embedded as the right one and points you in that direction.

If you are hunting in a large area that lacks criss-crossing roads, and you have no compass, your only hope is to try to strike a straight line and walk it, hoping it won't take you too many miles to break free. This is done by lining up geographic reference points well ahead of you and keeping them lined up as you walk forward. You will need to keep these features in line as you come to them (and pass them), and in so doing, you can walk a fairly straight line. Nobody can walk a straight line without help, and if you don't think I'm right, have one of your friends drop you off some pitch-black night in strange country. Oh yeah, be sure you take a flare gun, so he can come get you after a while. Better yet, tell him to stay at the road and honk, or you'll both be out there walking in circles.

If you're lost and it is near dark, stay put. Build a fire. You surely didn't leave the car without matches, *did you?*

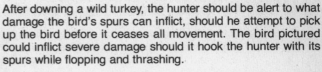

After downing a wild turkey, the hunter should be alert to what damage the bird's spurs can inflict, should he attempt to pick up the bird before it ceases all movement. The bird pictured could inflict severe damage should it hook the hunter with its spurs while flopping and thrashing.

(Left) Hunters examine a campfire to ensure that those who recently camped there have extinguished all embers. Many areas in the eastern part of the country are dry during the fall months, which presents a forest fire hazard. All campfires should be either fully covered with dirt or doused with water, or both.

Don't shoot up all your shells the minute you think you are lost. Nobody will pay any attention to your shooting until you don't arrive back at camp, or your vehicle. If you've wandered into an area without anyone's knowledge, it could be that no one will be looking for you at all. Nobody knows you are there. Then it becomes a matter of, you got yourself in this mess, now it's up to you to get out of it. You won't get out if you panic.

If you are certain you would panic in such a situation, then my advice is to hunt within sight of the road. *Don't hunt in strange country.* Of course, you could get lost while driving some backroad, as all of us have done. Miss the turn, or take the wrong fork, or else we didn't interpret the directions correctly. People who live in an area take it for granted. Everybody just naturally knows that, "You should turn at the mailbox by that big white oak, and once past it, you cross that little spring branch, the one that's just got a trickle in it now. Then after you go past old man Downey's place, you take that road that turns to the right. You'll find where I'm talking about, a mile, no, maybe it's a little

further'n that, right down that road. *You can't miss it!*" All the while, they're drawing you a map of this in a smoothed out place in the road. Good luck!

The truth is the average hunter gets too much to eat and too little exercise . . .

One hazard which is overlooked is ourselves—our health. Just ask of your buddies, "Are you in good shape physically?" Darned few will admit they aren't. A recent national survey revealed that 88 percent of the American public felt like they were in good health. The truth is a great percentage of all Americans haven't been to a doctor in heck knows how long for a complete physical checkup. The average hunter gets too much to eat and too little exercise. He's fat and flabby. Worse yet, he drinks too much.

The Sierra Madre mountains of Mexico are massive, imposing ranges, intimidating to a hunter not accustomed to such terrain. This kind of country, found throughout the length of the Continental Divide, the home of both the Merriam and Gould's wild turkeys, is for the hunter who does not mind strenuous walking and climbing while in the pursuit of turkeys. Hunters with heart trouble or breathing difficulties should not tackle this type of terrain.

The first thing many of us think of when health is mentioned is the heart. Fine, but have you done anything about it? Have you had a cholesterol test made recently? When was the last time you had your blood pressure checked? As you grow older these things should be done more often. I have three good friends who have had heart disease in one way or another, have had by-pass operations, yet today all

three are very active turkey hunters. True, it has changed the way they hunt, but they are aware of their limitations. These men learned about their problem before it felled them in the woods, maybe for good. They've killed lots of turkeys in the years since. Good turkey hunters? You'd recognize them in an instant if I spelled out their names.

Heat stroke is another high risk potential during spring turkey season in many areas, or even during an early fall hunt. I've walked many Arkansas trails on early October afternoons when the sweat trickled from under my hat. High humidity makes it worse. And, though we all know that light colored clothing, particularly white, is the coolest to wear when it's hot outdoors, we turkey hunters are doing just the opposite. We dress in dark clothing head to foot.

The simplest way to prevent heat stroke is to slow down, and during the afternoon's hottest time, lie down and take an afternoon snooze. Not being a hunter who wants to miss any chances, I never take a nap at camp or at the pickup parked alongside the road. I catch my catnaps in small doses, scattered throughout the woods. During a day's time, I might sleep five or six times, according to how many days I've been hunting.

My method for sleeping and hunting while I'm doing it, is very simple. Finding a good location, one where I can stretch out in front of a large tree in the shade of its trunk, I first study the surroundings. Sitting against the tree, gun at my side, I'll make a call. If I haven't heard anything, I'll call again a few moments later. If, after a few minutes, I still have had no answer, I'll stretch out on my back in the shade, pull my hat over my eyes, and relax. Along my left side, (I'm a southpaw shooter) with my fingers around the pistol grip, will lay my shotgun, barrels pointed away from my toes. Having trained myself to sleep in the open woods, I'll drop off in a minute or two. I don't have any idea what or who has walked up to me while "dead-to-the-world," so to speak. I snore badly, which could attract passersby. I don't know how many turkeys have eyeballed my slumbering figure and slipped away. I can recall five

Fall turkey hunting can be a strenuous sport, requiring a great deal of walking over rugged terrain. Coffee and lunch breaks are important, as the hunter will need considerable food and fluids in hot weather to maintain strength.

which didn't walk away, as these clucked when very near, and all were shot by me as I came up shooting. It is easy to come up to a sitting position from lying on one's back, with the gun already in hand, and heave it to face, and fire. In one instance, I had to jump to my feet to be able to bring the gun on the bird, but as the gobbler was within 6 feet of me when his clucking woke me, this was easily done. Fortunately, or maybe it is unconsciously, I don't awaken with a start from these naps. My eyes simply come open, and I instantly assess the situation. The hat goes flying, as I'm never aware of it until gathering my gear for the walk back to the truck. No, I don't mind taking a nap in the woods. Maybe I'll get a shot.

Nasty falls would never have entered my mind as being a hazard, until I'd had surgery, leaving me with no feeling in parts of my right foot and leg. I'd lost much of my balance on that side of my body. Making a hunt to Pennsylvania the following fall, I'm certain I either fell over, or on, a great many of the rocks in that state. Much of this was due to the rocks being covered with leaves.

The wind had freed a "widow maker," and it had given me Hail Columbia . . .

Rain and snow can make hazardous conditions worse when hunting on steep slopes, especially if these slopes are part clay, which becomes slick as greased glass when wet. One cold winter day, many years ago, Maurice "Monty" Montgomery, then the outdoor editor for *The Boston Globe*, and I were hunting some steep mountains near Pawlett, Vermont. It was snowing, and never before or since have I encountered such treacherous conditions underfoot. Monty and I got off those mountains only through the use of walking sticks, long straight poles we picked up in the woods. The conditions came near to being a complete whiteout, and though we lucked out in not getting lost, everyone else in our party did. We soon forgot the turkeys. Our main concern soon became one of getting off the snow-covered mountain without a broken leg. Or worse.

Though the average turkey hunter has little difficulty in gettng around, there are many places where a serious fall could result in injuries to careless hunters. Steep banks resulting from land erosion can give way when the hunter walks too near the edges, and, in some cases, can be undermined by swift waters. The hunter who goes into these areas during dark hours should carry a flashlight.

Poison ivy can cause profound misery to anyone susceptible to the vine's pollen. The stuff grows in clusters, often in dark woods, with "runners" extending up into the trees. If you're affected by it or poison oak, be sure to pack along the proper topical ointments to alleviate any problems.

Hunters in many areas of the country have often found themselves in the clutches of a greenbriar tangle or in wild blackberry vines. Anyone who thinks he'll just bust on through has got another thing coming. Far the best thing to do is to make a slow retreat, then look for a path around. The same goes for laurel and rhododendron thickets, "hells," as some folks who know them will often refer to them. Poison ivy, sumac, and poison oak also cause a good deal of grief to people allergic to them. I'm thankful none of these bother me, otherwise I would have to sidestep an awful lot of turkey woods.

Warm clothing is a must if hunters are to enjoy the sport and stay healthy while doing it. Sudden storms are always a hazard when hunting wild turkeys, and these storms bring wind, lightning, rain, snow, hail, the works. If a person takes shelter near trees, make certain these are not the largest ones in the immediate area. Such trees will attract lightning and support huge branches which can be loosened by wind gusts.

The hunter hurrying toward a gobbling turkey will slow down real quick when running afoul of any of the wicked, thorned vines which lace the country's turkey woods. Eastern wild turkey country is where most are found, and they can be a real menace.

Sudden storms are another danger. I was hunting in Arkansas one afternoon and had noticed a darkening of the sky, but having a rain slicker tucked in my possibles bag, I didn't pay it much mind. When the drops began to patter, I slipped on the raincoat, and backed against a big pine, still intent on watching an area where I'd found lots of fresh sign. The wind began coming up, blowing harder all the time, but as there wasn't any lightning, I wasn't worried about leaning back against the pine tree.

I never heard it break. All I can recall is that suddenly I was on my knees, badly staggered. Rubbing my neck, I felt something wet. No, it wasn't rain, it was blood. Getting to my feet, I looked around to see what had happened. A big dead limb was lying where none had been earlier. The wind had freed a "widowmaker," and it had given me Hail Columbia when it came sailing down out of the treetop.

Dust storms, tornadoes, downpouring rains, all are a part of turkey hunting. George Pullen and I spent a good part of one morning driving backroads in Mississippi, looking for fallen limbs across powerlines. An April tornado had skipped around those parts during the night, and George's job as a Mississippi lineman was to keep folks in electric service. A torrential downpour kept me, Ted Trueblood, Johnny Nance, Ed Norwood, Vernon Cade, Tom Preston and Bruce Brady, holed up for the better part of 2 days one April up near Union Church, again in ole Miss. When we did get to the woods, we needed Noah's ark as the whole country was underwater. That was the year that the freshets kept me and an old turkey gobbler from getting together. I bellied out into a pasture 'til I got to the floodwaters and called him as far as he would come, but the swollen creek between us was about 60 yards wide. I couldn't shoot him that far away, and it ended that way. I couldn't swim over, and he wouldn't fly over.

I've sat out many rainstorms in old barns, in fallen-down sheds, and one in a leaning outhouse. Ed Merrow, an old Vermont turkey hunting buddy, and I were backed into a long hay shed one cold drizzling April morning, when suddenly here comes a gang of jake turkeys. Ed jerked the welcome mat back when he rolled one of them in the cowlot. I've huddled beneath rock overhangs along the Buffalo River in Arkansas, the rock walls blackened from Indian fires of long ago, and got my face blackened over a pinewood fire while waiting a bitter cold dawn along a road back in Mexico's high Sierras. Last spring, Ed Merrow, Ed LaForce, and I got run out of New Mexico's Gila National Forest by a raging snowstorm. But, that wasn't the first time I've had to drop to lower elevations when hunting Merriam turkeys during the springtime.

Bad weather brings on bad roads which can slow down a hunt. Sudden cloudbursts can flood them, too, though in much of the country this won't last long, as runoff will soon allow you to continue. One fall afternoon I was caught far from the pickup by a real gully-washer, so I waited it out in a cowshed. Once the rain quit, I took out for the truck, but when I got to the main creek, what had been a stream I could step across hours earlier, was now a raging torrent. I found a sturdy 6-foot pole and waded across. The pole probed the deep places, which I would then skirt around. The remainder of the time I used it for balance, and to prevent my being swept away. Had the creek been to the dangerous stage, I wouldn't have attempted the crossing. Having grown up as a farm boy near a creek that flooded quite often, I'd learned to read such streams to a degree. Floodwaters are like quicksand—they look very innocent.

Turkey hunting is a sport which has all the ingredients for danger . . .

Far the most deadly hazard awaiting the turkey hunter is *another turkey hunter*. Those of us who have only been sprayed with shot are the lucky ones. Situation: It is a beautiful spring morning, and just as day is breaking a turkey gobbles. A hunter heard the bird and slips his call from his pocket. Hopefully he can call the bird to him. He is on private land. Farther down the creek, another hunter has heard the bird. He realizes he must get nearer. He, too, begins sneaking through the dense stand of cedars bordering the stream. He is on private land, though the rancher told him there could be another hunter or two hunting that day.

The hunter strikes the box, making several yelps. The old bird gobbles. The second hunter hears the yelping. Silently, he slips nearer, the dew-drenched grass silent under foot. Suddenly, there in the cedars, a movement. That's where he heard the turkey. Slowly, surely, he brings the 12 gauge to bear. There, the turkey moved again. *Boomммmm.* The rolling boom of a single shotgun blast echoes among an omniously silent forest. A man rolls over, swallowed in the deadly swarm of No. 4 chilled shot. He was dead when his hat hit the ground. The box call clatters

Hunters take a rest next to a dairy farmer's barn. Hunters must strive constantly toward making better relationships between themselves and the landowners. Too often a hunter has left a gate open, scattered litter, or caused other havoc on such lands, turning many landowners against the hunting public.

These hunters are together planning the next segment of the hunt to insure safety, while allowing each to enjoy the hunt without interfering with others in the party. Small Nos. 4, 5, or 6 shot can travel a considerable distance, so each hunter should know where others are located at all times.

against a tree trunk. A tiny rivulet of blood wends among the leaves. Running steps fade into the distant woods. On a faroff ridge, still another hunter mutters to himself, ''Well, somebody got himself a gobbler.'' There has become too much turkey hunter killing in the United States. Too many people are shooting first and looking second.

Turkey hunting, in its very manner of execution, is a hunting sport which has all the ingredients for danger if the participants don't take precautions to make it safe. And, though these precautions are so simple that any small child would have no trouble in abiding by them, each year we have hundreds of grown adult American hunters who don't. At times I think nobody has had the number of guns aimed at them that I have in the past. Being the first hunter to push the use of turkey calls in Oklahoma, I could almost count on somebody trying to do me in each and every day I hunted. Oklahoma hunters that heard a turkey went after it. The thought never crossed their minds that the sounds might be made by another hunter. I can recall one winter day when I had five hunters in sight, closing on me from three directions, because they knew turkeys used the area, and heard me calling from a large stand of shinnoak. Back then I hunted quite often from a shallow pit, much like a layout blind used for killing honkers over a decoy spread. I'd also become aware of camouflage, and with face blackened, have had hunters all but step across me, never realizing my presence, then walk on past me, still searching for the turkey they'd heard. All five hunters worked past me, crossed a nearby fence, disregarding its No Hunting signs, and the last I saw of them, they were fanned out in the brush, looking for turkeys.

The best defense against other hunters would be to stay home. Being extremely alert will prevent you from being shot a great deal of the time. Being alert also includes taking precautions about where you call from. Do you move slightly while calling? Do you try to locate with a large area of dry leaves or loose gravel behind you? Are you always scanning the far woods for movements?

There are several things you can do to prevent being shot, once you are aware another hunter is within shooting distance of you, and is looking for that turkey he heard. Freeze, and by this, I mean *don't move*. He won't shoot until he sees a movement.

Don't open your mouth, instead begin humming a tune. Hum the ''Star Spangled Banner.'' Hum it loud. Make yourself known in this manner. *Don't make a sudden move*. It could be your last. If you are hunting private lands, try to learn who else is there. *But*, private lands attract hunters, so you can expect trespassers. Many of them will be staying in thick cover, so they won't be found. Make sure of your turkey before you shoot. Poachers should be shot, but leave that to the law.

Education is the number one defense. Try to make your hunting buddies understand that if they will shoot at all game at close range, identity is certain. And, with game that is close, small shot can be used. Small shot won't kill a man at 40 yards. The hunter who kills his turkeys inside

Father and son, Tom and Steve Preston, hold adult gobblers bagged by each on a spring morning hunt. Fathers all across the United States have begun taking their children turkey hunting, as this gunning sport is an excellent one for teaching them about hunting and the outdoors. Boys and girls are learning that if it had not been for sportsmen's dollars the past 100 years, there would be very little wildlife of any kind in this country today. However, today's hunter must make these young people aware of the continuing loss of wildlife habitat.

that distance won't either. If you'll always shoot small shot at turkeys inside of 30 yards, the only thing you'll kill are turkeys. *Think about it*.

What this whole chapter boils down to is the cold hard fact that far the worst hazard in the woods to you, the hunter, is you. You'll have to watch for the snakes, and not stumble into hornet's nests. Study the maps before making a hunt to save yourself from getting lost. Stay alert. This could save your life. Get plenty of rest, take a nap when you want. A hunter who is bone tired is apt to make mistakes.

Anyone, who hides near a place where grain has been scattered for bait is cheating . . .

Probably the toughest thing any turkey hunter will face is cheating. There will be times when the opportunity is there, wide open for him to enhance his chances of bagging a wild turkey, and all he need do is bend the rules a tiny bit. I doubt if there are many hunters who have not done this on occasion. After all, what is playing by the rules, insofar as turkey hunting is concerned? Baiting? Legal or illegal? Good or bad? Right or wrong?

Baiting is probably practiced to a far greater degree than most of us realize. I have found bait (scattered grain, feed containers, cultivated food plots, etc.) virtually everywhere I have hunted, except in the Rocky Mountain areas. Much baiting was being done openly, though local and state laws forbade such practices. Along with this, I also know of many highly respected hunters who were shooting regularly over baited areas. To me, anyone who hides near a place where grain has been scattered, or a food plot has been planted for the purpose of enticing birds on a regular basis, is cheating by all of the ethics of wild turkey hunting. You be the judge. Do you ever shoot over bait?

What about riding down a backwoods road on a quiet April morning. You have a buddy driving, and you're rid-

Many hunters will disregard this sign and leave the gate down. After enough of this irresponsible action, the Forest Service may then fence the gate closed and allow no entry. Obey the signs!

(Left) Several states do not allow all-day hunting for wild turkeys, which gives hunters time to compare notes after each morning's hunt. The afternoon hours can also be used to great advantage in studying the hunting areas nearby, looking for sign, readying equipment for the following day, and in practicing with the turkey calls.

ing in the passenger side, gun stuck out the open window. It's loaded. Suddenly you round a bend in the road, and there trotting through the woods is a granddaddy red-headed gobbler within easy gunshot. Quick as a cat you throw down on him as he begins scooting for cover. You take a shot, then another. Missed him this time. But maybe the next time . . . !! Cheating? Illegal?

Read the rules as they apply in your state, and read them word for word. I've hunted areas where road-hunting was against the law, yet every hunter thereabouts seemed to indulge in the practice. Why? Mainly because it was easier

to get a shot in this manner than to go into the woods, and work for a shot. The unspoken local code was why walk when you can ride.

What about roost shooting? And, while you're at it, tell me, exactly what is roost shooting? Is it shooting a wild turkey on the exact branch it spent the night time hours? Is it shooting a wild turkey in any tree? Could shooting a turkey in a tree be considered roost shooting if done within legal shooting hours, though it was a known fact that the bird had roosted the previous night among the branches of said tree?

Many wild gobblers sound off well into the morning during the spring hunts, remaining in the tree where they spent the night hours. These old birds gobble time after time, telling all hunters in hearing distance where they are. Many of these birds can be stalked to within easy shotgun killing range. And, though legal shooting hours may begin ½-hour before sunrise, very often the woods thereabouts will be sufficiently dark to allow such a stalk. So, the hunter begins his stalk within legal shooting time, and rolls the old bird from the tree, the same tree where it spent the night. Legal, or illegal?

Rules governing late evening or early morning shooting are ordinarily spelled out when defining legal shooting hours. Various states spell out rules which outlaw roost shooting, though the term ''roost shooting' is not actually defined. My home state of Oklahoma, for example, does not allow roost shooting, though on opening day during the fall hunt, it is a common practice for gangs of hunters to surround a known roost and begin blasting away as soon as the birds can be made out against the morning sky. Shooting hours? Ha! I have yet to hear of one of these episodes ending in anyone's arrest, though these ''turkey shoots'' take place well before legal shooting time. This isn't turkey hunting; this is a slaughter.

If a hunter doesn't study the game laws governing the hunting of wild turkeys, in whatever state he is hunting, he or she will be running the risk of breaking a law. Shooting hours vary, and, in particular, quitting times during the spring seasons. Legal weapons and ammunition vary as well. Oklahoma allows rifles for turkey hunting during the fall season, but rifles are a no-no in the spring. Shotgunners are limited to No. 2 shot or smaller.

But, regardless of what your state laws spell out regarding the hunting of wild turkeys, you could be a cheater if you violate a few of the old timeless ethics which are heritage to the sport. Perhaps these are not known to many of today's new turkey hunters. Certainly, as turkey hunting has become the popular gunning pastime we know today, such ethics are sometimes exceedingly difficult to maintain. For instance, it's been an unwritten rule to back off if you realize you are infringing upon the calling efforts of another hunter who is trying to call a turkey to himself or his party. This rule is often ignored, especially on public lands, where the birds are considered public property and the turkey is considered there for the hunter who can bag it. Perhaps four hunters hear the bird make its first gobble at daybreak. Who is to say which of the four should be allowed to make a concentrated effort to call it into gunshot.

Hunters on private land, and known to each other, often recognize another's calling efforts and will give way to the hunter who is hunting a given territory, or who has made the initial contact. The older hunting clubs have strict rules which, if disregarded, can lead to a member being ousted from the club simply because he can't (or won't) hunt within reasonable bylaws.

Sneaking in between a hunter and the bird which is responding to his calling is another ethic being violated today.

From what I've been told, this has become a headache to a great many who hunt public lands. Again, it boils down to a bird on public land not wearing anyone's tag on it until placed there. Like it or not, the hunter who is not aggressive in today's woods can either take his lumps or pass them out. Possibly, you won't like me for stating this so bluntly. I am simply telling the hard truth.

In the end, man presents the greatest hazard to the future of the wild turkey . . .

A wild turkey hen with two small poults. The average nest will contain 10 to 12 eggs, but some of what are laid may not hatch. Of those which do hatch, the young birds are susceptible to death from cold rains, hail, cold temperatures, snakes, dogs, cats, raccoons, skunks, and an endless list of other predators, along with diseases and other dangers. This hen has two birds which have survived to this age. All ground nesting birds face such predation. (Photo courtesy of Greg Butts.)

Scattered throughout the country are hunters who will not shoot hen turkeys, and who argue that to do so is ethically wrong. To men who have studied wildlife extensively, such arguments fall in the same category as those which oppose the hunting of doe deer. The wildlife biologists who have brought about the return of the wild turkey all across the face of America are the same people who recommend season bag limits. If there is a hen surplus, then taking hens is allowable. Unlike does, hen turkeys will be skimmed off by Mother Nature if there is a surplus. A given range will only carry so many wild turkeys.

Oklahoma is an excellent example of this. For years we

have had an "any turkey" fall season throughout the bulk of western Oklahoma. Both rifles and shotguns are allowed. A hunter can shoot any bird which pops in front of his sights. Fall turkey hunting is exceedingly popular, so when opening day rolls around, an army of hunters takes to the outdoors. Only a small percentage will make a stringent effort to take only gobblers. Yet, few states have the excellent wild turkey populations that we boast of, and this is because the bulk of these hens taken during the fall season would have died of natural predation during the ensuing winter months. Like all states, Oklahoma does not allow the killing of hens during the spring hunt, nor would any hunter want to shoot a hen at this time. Ethically speaking,

Vehicles should remain on Forest Service roads which are signed for this purpose. This creates a greater degree of quality hunting for those who are willing to walk back a distance from the trails. Too often today's hunter is not willing to walk even a short distance, and drives these roads despite the law. This is all part of hunting ethics.

(Right) This old campfire location was within a few feet of a well traveled national forest road. It presents a disgusting and disturbing sight to many who pass this area. Not only have those who camped here left litter, but they also tore down a sign, therefore leaving a closed road open to any and all who desire to travel it. These are the things which give hunters a bad reputation.

if your state allows hen turkeys to be taken during a fall hunt, and you won't shoot hens then you are as guilty as the hunter who will not shoot a doe and, then bemoans the fact that the state is overrun with deer. Leave it up to the men who know, the wildlife professionals.

I was brought up back in the days of Oklahoma's infamous Dust Bowl, when it was a no-no to shoot winged game on foot. "Ground sluicing" it was called, or "pot shooting." By my way of thinking, turkeys should be shot on the wing. Obviously, it would be far more ethical, and certainly very sporting, if all hunters were to shoot turkeys on the wing. Why don't we?

Ethics. It's okay to shoot a turkey while it's on foot. This is a holdover from "the good old days" probably because few hunters had the courage to flush a bird which had been so difficult to draw to within easy killing distance. This is a fact today. Very few hunters, regardless of how good they maintain they are at hunting wild turkeys, will stand and flush these game birds.

Wild turkeys face many predators besides man. Bobcats kill turkeys, both big and small. Watch for cat tracks where you see lots of turkeys—they'll be there. Fox and coyotes hunt them. Raccoons bust up nests, eating the eggs, as do crows, skunks, opossums, and other predators. Forest fires take a toll, as does drought, and yet, on the other hand, too much rain can kill young turkeys, as do severe hail storms. And from the skies comes another danger, the great horned owl, who can kill both young or old birds. But, in the end, it's man who presents the greatest hazard to the future of the wild turkey, along with the rest of today's wildlife across these United States.

It can be summed up in one word—*greed*. The greed for money is gulping down chunks of America at a rate which will doom sport hunting along with many outdoor related pleasures in another two or three decades. Shopping centers, leap-frog developing (by-passing large acreage within urban areas), oil well sites, strip mining, clear cutting large areas by timber companies, and large block leasing to cattle conglomerates are but a few of the dangers that may wipe out America's wildlife. I know—I was here to see and hunt

50 years ago. In that short time, at least three-fourths of the ground hunted on then *is gone today. Gone forever.*

But hunters are part of a worsening problem. They disregard regulations, litter, and are in effect, driving the nails in their own coffins. I know, you say it won't happen here. Turkey hunting will last forever. They said that about the buffalo, too. Have you hunted buffalo lately?

These are but a handful of the problems and hazards facing both the turkey and the turkey hunter today. Perhaps some of them would best be described as "pains-in-the-neck." Of course, for many hunters, the turkey is the worst pain-in-the-neck of all.

The author dry-picks an Osceola jake turkey near water. When the feathers have been removed, he will field dress the bird, which means to remove the entrails, but a thorough cleaning will not take place until the bird is in camp.

Chapter 12

After the Hunt— Pluckin' and Eatin'

EATING a wild turkey is, to me, one of the fine rewards of hunting this game bird. If the bird has been properly taken care of from the time it was shot, through the dressing and cleaning stages, and in cooking, a wild bird has a wholesome flavor harkening back to its wild life in the backwoods of this country.

The first thing to do after shooting the bird, and perhaps taking pictures, is to remove the entrails. This is known as field dressing. Lay the bird on its back and with a sharp knife cut a circle around the vent, or anal area, about 3 inches in circumference; the entrails can then be drawn out through this opening. Like Charlie Elliott says, ''They'll come out kinda like a rope.'' You can then take both hands, and by doing a little stretching, widen the opening you've cut, reach up deeper inside the bird, and pull out the gizzard, heart, and liver. Many folks save these, and you may have stuck a small plastic sandwich bag in your billfold just for this purpose. The gizzard, about the size of a slightly flattened lemon, is cleaned by cutting all the way around the outside, through the meat. It can then be opened like you would open an oyster. There is a whitish skin lining which can then be peeled from the gizzard, which is the inner wall or lining of the organ. You may ask, ''What is a gizzard, anyhow?'' If you'll notice on cutting open this organ, it is full of coarse sand, gravel and tiny pebbles, which together with the organ's powerful muscular walls, can exert tremendous pressures. This grinding is what helps the bird digest such things as acorns, pecans, and even hickory nuts. Anyone who has hit a hickory nut with a hammer will understand the forces a gizzard can exert.

Place the heart in the bag along with the gizzard and liver. Do be careful in cutting away the small dark green gall which will be attached to the side of the liver. If it's punctured, you'd just as well throw away these pieces. The gall juices will give them a bitter taste. These parts can be washed thoroughly when you get back to such facilities.

Some folks cut through the bird's neck area when field dressing to bleed the bird, also removing what they can of the windpipe. Others will remove the crop. I've field dressed hundreds of wild turkeys and have never done this to one yet. Of course, such actions will ruin the bird for any further photo sessions. I was with a retired Army general one morning, and he had killed a fine old long-bearded turkey. Obviously, he was pretty proud of the gobbler, as probably he hadn't killed many such trophies in his wanderings. A young fella was with us who knew nothing about turkey hunting, but had killed lots of deer. The general and I walked over to the pickup to get a cup of coffee from my thermos bottle and to get my camera for some pics. We left the gobbler lying on the ground beside the young man's vehicle. We walked back around the truck to take the pics just in time to see our friend tying the old bird to a low-hanging branch of a hackberry tree.

Presuming it needed the same treatment he had apparently been giving to the deer carcasses he'd come by, he had cut its throat, split the bird part way down the front, removed the windpipe remaining from my field dressing, then hung the bird in the tree, so it could bleed out. Very little blood remains in any bird after field dressing, but what was in the gobbler was trickling down soaking the beard.

Hunting wild turkeys is but one part of the enjoyment for hunters. After the hunt, the cooking and eating of the game is probably the final reward of all the effort and time spent while trying to bring the bird to bag. This young hunter can look forward to enjoying a great turkey dinner.

A guide field dresses a wild gobbler while the hunter watches. Quickly removing the entrails from a downed gobbler will ensure the bird's not spoiling, particularly in warm weather. This is easily done by cutting around the anal opening and then pulling the intestines from the body cavity through this opening. Care must be used in searching with the fingers in the body cavity, to ensure removing the lungs and other meaty organs found there. Though water is within inches in this picture, it is for washing the hands and knife afterward. The author never washes the body cavity until the bird is completely cleaned.

I'd been the beneficiary of some very well presented "chewing outs," while in the Army, but the one the general gave that guy made mine seem almost complimentary. The boy had it all coming, and then some. Nobody should mess with another hunter's game unless given permission.

You should keep the bird as cool as possible after field dressing, hanging it in the shade where air can circulate around it. Of course, most winter kills won't require this concern, but spring killed gobblers in many areas will spoil due to heat. Blowflys will be attracted to the bird and, unless black pepper or other preventatives are placed in the body cavity, will lay eggs there. I place loose green grass, pine needles, a wad of long brown bluestem grass, or something of this nature in the body cavity. Cheesecloth works as well. I never wash out the body cavity until I have the bird where, once it is completely picked and washed, can be placed in the refrigerator or freezer.

There is only one easy method for picking a wild turkey after its feathers have "set" . . .

There are two excellent methods for picking a wild turkey. The first is field picking, as it can be picked clean as a whistle, just after it's killed. No, I don't mean 3 hours later, though there will be times on warm spring days when a turkey can be picked easily several hours after being shot. If I intend to pick the bird in the field, what many of us

Dr. Dennis McIntyre, a hunting buddy of the author's, dry picks a young fall-killed gobbler. Dry picking is easily done within an hour of when the bird was bagged. Once the bird has been dead for a few hours, the feathers will "set," and then dry picking will cause the skin to tear.

older turkey hunters refer to as "picking it dry," I'll pick the bird within ½-hour of its being killed. I'll simply hang the bird in a tree at eye level, often tied there by one leg with my bandana, and by getting after it, will have it picked in a short time. Even the big wing pinions will come free. I want to stress one thing: *Do not remove the head, beard, or one leg, as these are identifying characteristics to game law enforcement agencies.* Any hunter should know local laws, and dress any turkey with these kept in mind. What one state will allow, the one next to it might class as a no-no.

There is only one easy method for picking a wild turkey after it's been dead long enough for its feathers to have "set." A person can quickly learn if the feathers have set by taking hold of a few on the breast, and trying to pull them out. If the skin begins to tear, you may as well begin heating some water. Some of today's hunters will skin the bird, but, being from the old school, I still want to pluck my turkeys.

(Above left) These hunters examine a gobbler while waiting for water to heat on the propane-fired outdoor heater. The water must be near 160 degrees to make picking easiest. Cooler water will not allow the feathers to come free easily, while water too hot will scald the meat.

This turkey is being completely immersed in hot water and allowed to remain there for a few minutes, ensuring the hot water has penetrated all of the feathers. This will allow all of the feathers to be pulled free without much effort. The water must be heated to about 160 degrees.

After the turkey has been sloshed around in the hot water, even the large black-and-white barred wing feathers pull free easily. These large flight feathers are also known as primaries, or primary feathers.

I have an old copper wash boiler which I place on the kitchen stove, half-filled with water, and then heat it to 155 to 160 degrees. Carrying this outside, I slosh the bird around in this for several minutes, hang the bird in a tree by one leg, and it can then be picked clean with little effort. If the wings have been well soaked, the wing feathers will come free easily. Only then do I cut off the head, remove the crop from the front of the bird, and cut off the legs. After a good thorough washing, the turkey is ready for cooking, or to be placed in the freezer. Invariably I'll cut open the crop to study what the bird has been eating, and this will be filed in my memory against the day I hunt such terrain again.

I should point out that if a hunter is in an area where he is allowed two turkeys, perhaps three, it is good thinking to open up the crop on the first bird killed, providing the bird has been killed after it has had time to feed. Any bird taken near noon will have fed, though perhaps not on its primary source. I've known many turkeys that were killed

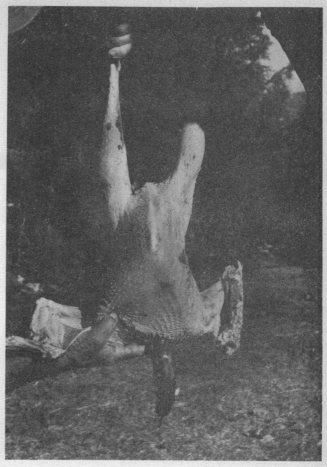

A dry-picked young gobbler shows but a single pellet mark, indication that the bird was shot at reasonably close range. All that remains to be done before washing is to cut off the feet and remove the craw.

(Left) A sharp knife severs the last joint on the turkey's wing with its group of primary flight feathers. This portion of the wing has virtually no meat that is edible so it is just as well discarded.

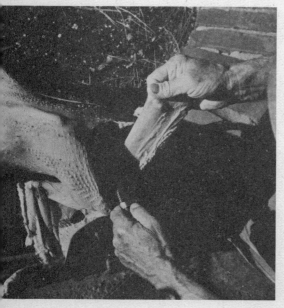

To remove the craw, simply pull on its loose skin, beginning the separation with a sharp knife.

By pulling, and with a slight cut from time to time, the craw will come free. Leaving it on the bird would allow the craw's juices to permeate the meat, causing it to sour.

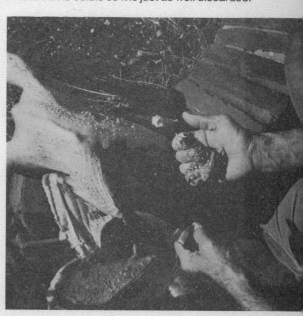

(Left) The best place to hang a downed gobbler, if it is not to be cleaned soon, is in the shade, and where a breeze can keep air circulating around the body. The bird should always be hung head down, and the wings pulled forward toward the head, allowing air to get behind them. Pine needles or long loose grasses can be stuffed loosely into the body cavity if flies are a problem. Never leave the bird under plastic, or directly on the floor of a vehicle where transmission, exhaust pipe or differential heat are present.

(Right) Once the feathers have "set" on a wild turkey's carcass, the bird can then be scalded and picked, or it can be skinned. Skinning is simple. The bird is hung securely, the skin is cut between the wing and thigh, and then removed by pulling it free.

(Below right) Wingtips are cut off, the craw removed with the skin, and then the head is severed at the neck.

(Below) Having removed the entrails in the hunting field, all that remains is to give the bird a thorough washing in cold water. The feet are cut off last.

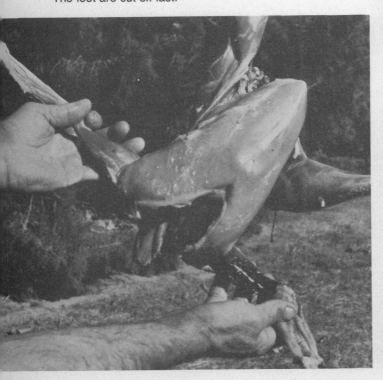

It seems most hunters prefer to dry pick their birds in the field shortly after shooting them. Doing so eliminates a lot of mess around camp or home and it doesn't require heating cans of water for the other method. Buddy Lawrence prefers to cook and eat birds with the skin still on them.

David Jackman and I were hunting Gould's turkeys back in the high Sierras of Chihuahua, Mexico, one spring, and we had thought the birds were feeding on grass pannicles, acorns, and such stuff. David killed a gobbler late one afternoon, so we cut open the crop. A whole cupful of alligator juniper berries was in the bird, each about the size of a very large pea. We didn't hunt low afterwards, at least not later than noon. The alligator junipers are found in great abundance on the high mesa, so we hunted afternoon gobblers on the high flats.

Back in the good old days, before any fowl was cooked, it had to age . . .

If you mention the eating of a turkey to anybody in this country, you can bet big money he'll invariably think of roast turkey, because that's the way it's fixed for Thanksgiving, or Christmas, which is when the bulk of all domestic turkeys are eaten. We raised turkeys on the farm with the idea that one of them would end up on the Thanksgiving table. Roasted, just like I said.

There are a great many ways that turkey meat can be prepared, some of them far tastier than roast turkey, but such cooking also takes more time. I've eaten wild turkey which was slow cooked in a hole in the ground, as the Indians and Mexicans do it in old Mexico. This is back up in the mountains, where there is no modern cookstove, nor a roaster-broiler. The bird was fine eating, though once a hunter has been back in the mountains living on tortillas, fried beans, and scrambled eggs and potatoes for a week, he just may not be the one to judge what's good or bad to eat. Strips of *venada* (venison), are added if a carcass is in camp.

Back in the good old days before any fowl was cooked it had to age. This invariably brought about arguments about which tasted best, a bird that had been hung by the neck, or by the feet. Birds were often hung under an eave, in the shade, for several days. Too, there were people who thought the meat had a finer flavor if the entrails were left in the bird while aging. Others felt "the innards ought'r come out soon as poss'ble." Among those who hung birds by the neck, there were some who left the birds hanging 'til it fell to the ground, the body weight and the bird's "condition" bringing this about. Today's modern American citizen has not got such an ironclad stomach, so we couldn't endure meat so well aged.

I often let fall and winter killed turkeys hang for 5 to 6 days in full feather, but with the innards taken out. I hang the bird in a small shed so it is never exposed to any light or heat source. I have hung them for this long during the spring, but only when the weather is cool in the daytime, and drops down into the 40s at night. I've never had ptomaine poisoning yet.

near lunch time that were very near to the feeding objective when shot, having hunted them previously. But, whatever food is in the crop (or craw, as it's always been known to me) will give the hunter a clue as to where to find birds during the feeding hours.

One fall I killed a bird which had been feeding on hackberries, nothing else. Two days later I was guiding a hunter, and he killed a young gobbler as it teetered in a low hackberry tree. For the remainder of the season I looked nowhere but out in the sandhills, where the hackberry trees were scattered, for the droves of feeding birds.

On another fall hunt, I scattered a small drove of young turkeys, just before noon. I examined the craw of the young hen and found she had been eating crabgrass and grasshoppers. I killed her along an old abandoned road. It was easy to put two and two together. Along the roads was far the best place to find crabgrass in that heavily wooded country. Nor would you expect to find many grasshoppers back in deep woods where there isn't any crabgrass. Killing the other two birds was as simple as falling off a log; hunt the old roads. Both of them fell to my gun in the afternoon, and I counted nearly 200 small grasshoppers in the craw of each.

The carcasses of wild turkeys hanging in a hunting camp are an indication that somebody is doing things right. But, how long can the birds be left this way? So long as the birds are hung in the shade and the entrails have been removed, they can be hung this way without damaging the meat for 24 hours, even in warm weather. The author has hung birds in a shady place, where a slight breeze could be felt, for up to 48 hours, and this when the temperatures were in the 60- to 70-degree range.

If I'm off 1,000 miles from home and am traveling by commercial airlines, I will take an extra Army-surplus duffel bag along, then any birds I bag can be packed in it with newspapers for the flight home. I will make arrangements to freeze the birds before flying, and then they can be well wrapped, then packed, with old newspapers, which will keep the birds frozen stiff. I seldom pick birds which I intend to bring home in this manner, as the feathers are the best insulation known. I never travel without a number of large plastic bags equal to what will be my allowable limit of birds.

When I'm traveling by pickup or car, I lug along a big 48-quart ice chest, which serves as a clothes chest until the return home, and then I pack the birds in it with packed ice. Or, as I did just recently on heading home from an Arizona-New Mexico hunt, I packed the birds in snow from the huge snowbanks along the roads in Arizona. I have brought home birds in full feather packed in the ice chest, but, I try to make it a point to dry pick turkeys immediately after killing. Again, I do not remove the head, feet, or beard. Several years ago, Stella and I were driving home from a trip to Show Low, Arizona, and were stopped at a roadblock near Magdalena, New Mexico. The highway officers were checking for driver's licenses, and the game department was looking in ice chests for trout. They admired the old gobbler in the chest, okayed the Arizona tag, then told me where I could find birds in New Mexico without needing to drive so far. Haven't tried the place yet, but....

Here're a couple or three other recipes that are favorites of ours . . .

Many of the ways my wife prepares turkey dishes is to simply substitute cooked and deboned turkey in recipes calling for chicken. Chicken tetrazzini is turkey tetrazzini at our house. Chicken salad sandwiches are something we haven't had in heck knows when, but I eat turkey salad sandwiches very often. Chances are nine in 10 that if you have a sandwich with me during turkey season, spring, fall, or winter, it will be either roast sliced turkey, or turkey salad.

Here are a couple or three other recipes that are favorites of ours:

Wild Turkey and Wild Rice

3 cups of cooked and diced deboned turkey
1 cup Uncle Ben's mixed long grain with wild rice
1 lb. sliced fresh mushrooms
1 chopped onion
2 tablespoons butter
2 teaspoons salt
¼-tsp. pepper
3 cups turkey broth
½-cup sliced blanched almonds
1½ cups of heavy cream

Wash rice thoroughly. Pour into pan, cover with boiling water, let stand for 1 hour. Drain well. Sauté mushrooms and chopped onion in butter for 10 minutes. Mix rice, onions, and mushrooms, salt, pepper, turkey and almonds in a greased casserole. Add broth and cream. Cover and bake at 350 degrees for 1½ hours.

Turkey Buffet Casserole

3 cups cooked and diced deboned turkey
1 cup cubed American cheese
1 cup chopped celery
½-cup chopped onion
1 can mushroom soup
2 eggs beaten
¼-tsp. salt
½-tsp. pepper
1 tsp. sage
4 cups turkey or chicken broth or bouillon
4 cups round butter cracker crumbs

Mix turkey, cheese, onion, mushroom soup, eggs, salt, pepper and sage. Mix in bouillon (mixture will be very thin). Place half the cracker crumbs in a 3 qt. casserole. Spoon in turkey mixture—top with remaining crumbs. Bake in 350-degree oven for 1 hour.

Old-Fashioned Turkey Pie

3 cups of large chunks of cooked turkey (these can be just as taken from turkey after roasting)

¼-cup flour
¼-tsp. paprika
¼-cup water
2 cups turkey stock
¼-cup light cream
Salt
Pepper
Baking powder biscuit dough

Start heating oven to 450 degrees, blend flour, paprika and water in saucepan. Add stock gradually, cook—stirring—until thickened. Stir in cream. Season to taste with salt and pepper.

Arrange turkey chunks in 1½-qt. casserole. Pour hot sauce over turkey. Prepare baking powder biscuit dough, using enough milk or light cream to make it easily handled. Roll, or pat out ⅛-inch thick, to fit top of casserole, then arrange over casserole, sealing edge. Make slits in top. Bake at 450 for 15 to 20 minutes, or until done.

For variation—¼-cup of chopped onions can be added to the top biscuit dough.

Scratch biscuits can be laid on top of the turkey mixture, in place of the dough topping.

Wild Turkey with Broccoli and Rice

3 cups chopped, cooked turkey
chicken broth
½-cup uncooked rice
½-cup chopped onion
½-cup chopped celery
2 Tbs. cooking oil
½-cup fine dry bread crumbs
Two 10 oz. pkg. frozen broccoli, cooked
¼-tsp. pepper
1 pound American cheese cubed
One 10 oz. can cream of mushroom soup

Cook rice according to package directions, using chicken broth in place of water. (Broth from roasting the turkey would be preferable, but if frozen turkey is used, this may not be available.) Sauté onions and celery in oil. Mix cooked rice, broccoli, turkey and pepper. Pour into greased 4-qt. casserole. Combine cheese and soup in small saucepan and heat over low flame until cheese melts. Pour over turkey mixture. Top with crumbs. Bake uncovered at 325 for approx. 50 min. Serves six to eight.

Wild Turkey Casserole

Begin with 4 cups of boned cooked turkey. Place a layer of turkey in a large Pyrex pan. Add one can cream of mushroom soup and 2 cups precooked egg noodles, one can English peas, or corn. Add another layer of turkey and a can of cream of chicken soup. Top with grated cheddar cheese. Salt and pepper to taste. Bake in 350-degree oven for 35 to 45 minutes. Serves eight to 10.

There are times when we will "rob" the breast meat from a big gobbler, but in not wanting to lose any of the meat for other recipes, Stella will take the remaining parts of the bird, (wings, thighs, legs, etc.) and cook them in the pressure cooker. Stella makes absolutely delicious homemade noodles, and the boned meat from these parts often is cooked with the noodles. What do we do with the meat we've robbed from the turkey's breast?

Fried Turkey Breast

Take slices of raw turkey breast (½- to ¾-in. thick) and roll in flour. Dip in beaten egg. Roll in crushed corn flakes, and fry in skillet with hot oil. Let cook on low flame until turkey is tender and brown on both sides. Whoo-EE-ee! Makes me hungry just thinking about it.

Turkey Salad for Sandwiches

2 cups boned chopped turkey
2 hard boiled eggs, chopped
Chopped sweet pickles to taste
Chopped onion to taste (some folks like lots of both, some don't). Mix ingredients in large bowl, then add Kraft Miracle Whip until of good spreading consistency.

Chapter 13

Fond Memories—Trophies and Mementos

Homemade powder horns are a part of black powder scattergunning. This one was a gift to the author, made by longtime friend and black powder shooter John Glass of Sand Springs, Oklahoma. A nice memento, indeed.

A WILD TURKEY doesn't have to weigh 35 pounds, and sport a 15-inch beard to be a trophy. Nor does it need 2-inch spurs which are shaped like fish hooks to qualify. Too much emphasis has been placed on these things. A few feathers from a small hen can be a trophy to the hunter who has put in 3 or 4 hard days in getting the bird into gunshot.

Each time a hunter looks at the trophy from a hunt it should bring back all the memories of a grand time in the woods. Recently I was reading the accounts of a young man who obviously was born into a very wealthy family, and of his hopes to kill a member of each game animal found on the North American continent. Money was no object. The article related to his prowess as a hunter, and yet, it was apparent he was running from this place to that, hiring guides and outfitters, mowing down animals left and right.

The article stated, "He had gotten the easier animals out of the way soon after realizing his ambitions." I would hate to think any hunter is shooting animals simply "to get them out of the way," and thereafter be able to say, "I've killed every kind of game animal in the Americas, what do you think of that?" How very sad. Nowhere, never, should an animal—fish or bird—be a number. Yet, I've never been to a hunter's convention where numbers were not mentioned.

I've been asked many times, "How many turkeys have you killed?" Why? You won't find a scoreboard in my den. You fill find a room full of trophies, mementos, pictures, all memories of good times and the friends who made them so.

A full-mount bearded hen overlooks my desk. When I look at her I think about Tom Preston and I hunting on Ivan Jellison's place, and the two times we hunted that drove before I got her on a flushing shot one cold, winter day. I'd lain in wait as the drove walked across in front of me, but as I tried to get the bead on the hen I was eyeballed by one of the birds, and in the blink of an eye, they boomed off the ground. I didn't dare take my eyes from the bird as she took flight, catching her in full flight about 30 yards out.

Her beard has the usual kink found so often in the beards of wild turkey hens. It's small, as are most such beards, about 7 inches long. She's a beautifully plumaged adult Rio Grande hen turkey. Ivan's gone now, but each time I look at her, I think of him and what a grand old boy he was, and the fine times I had on his ranch.

A big Osceola gobbler stands behind her, a simulated tree mount with a wisp of Spanish moss dangling from the limb on which he is perched. I'll never kill another gobbler in south Florida to match him, either in size or in the hunt which brought him to me. Hens, an alligator, a small creek, and high noon, all these things come to mind as I gaze at his gorgeous plumage and the dark barring of his primaries. It was a classic hunt with all the ingredients—hens leaving him, his strut, my slipping into the creek where I'd just scared the 'gator, bellying into the sawgrass, thumbing back the hammers on the old muzzleloader, and the last thought as I squeezed the trigger, "Boy, I hope Old C&G didn't get wet in that creek." C&G stands for Cough and Groan, a nickname I tagged on that old gun. Full-sized flying or standing mounts of wild turkeys are to me an outstanding tribute to the memory of a bird high in the hunter's memories of past hunts. Certainly it is not cheap to have such taxidermy performed.

Wild turkeys which a hunter considers of trophy status can be taken to a taxidermist and positioned favorably for display on the den wall, or perhaps in the hunter's office. These are perhaps the best, most vivid reminders of a great hunt.

Taxidermists tell me they would prefer all birds brought to them to be whole and frozen . . .

Field care of a bird intended for taxidermy is extremely important. Blood should be wiped away with a warm wet rag or paper towels, being careful to remove all blood stains before they mat and dry. And, in this day and age of home freezers, it is best to freeze the bird whole rather than risk damage in field dressing. Taxidermists tell me they would prefer all birds brought to them to be whole and frozen. They invariably have a backlog of work, and will need to freeze the bird for a time before working it into the schedule. Comb the plumage down with the contour of the feathering. This can be done with a knife blade, a small wire, or even a small tree branch. Lay the bird flat on its back, gently tuck the head down over a wing butt, and then slip the bird into a large plastic bag, making certain the tail is straight. Place the bird in the freezer in this manner and until you can get it to the taxidermist, don't lay other frozen food packages on it. If one should puncture the bag, leakage

A wild turkey wing is easily dried for display by spreading it to the shape desired, and then tacking it with small nails in that position. Powdered Borax is then spread on any meaty areas, and then it should be hung to dry in a shed or other like area until there is no odor.

(Left) Having been powdered with Borax and then left to dry, these trophies of the hunt are now completely odorless. They are the next best thing to having the whole bird mounted.

(Left) The tail of this adult hen will make a beautiful fan once it has been dried with Borax. Notice the comparison of the breast feathers of these two birds. The one on the left is a gobbler, with nearly solid black breast feathers. The hen on the right, with the spread tail, has light-tipped breast feathers.

To remove the tail from the bird, simply grasp the tail as a complete unit, and sever it from the body. This will result in a small amount of meat being visible, most of which can be cut away with a sharp knife.

(Above) The tail is then fanned out on a board with the rear of the feathers facing up, then tacked to the surface with small nails. Powdered Borax can then be sprinkled on any meaty areas, and the board can be tacked up out of harms way. Any of these displays which require Borax should be checked from time to time, and additional Borax added when needed.

The tail feathers of this adult gobbler make a perfect half-circle when spread, tacked, and dried. The author has simply rough-sewn a hunk of soft leather over the base of the tail, and then inked a few facts about the bird and the kill on this surface.

could damage the plumage. The taxidermist can only do his best with what you bring him.

Many of today's taxidermists don't use the skin of the turkey's head, but will substitute a plastic head. I prefer the old method, but this is because I don't want to degrade a memorable hunt with space-age plastics.

You may want a specific wood for the base, or want the bird to be mounted with it facing a certain direction, perhaps due to damage to the plumage or of a wing. Go over these points with the taxidermist. Too many hunters simply drop off game at a shop, but when they come back for it, they are unhappy about posture, etc. Nine times in 10, the taxidermist has had to use his own judgment, as he had no instructions otherwise. You can expect to pay a stiff down payment toward having taxidermy work performed, brought about by too many hunters leaving game to be mounted, and then never going back after it. Many states will not allow game to be sold, so the taxidermist is stuck with a trophy which means nothing to him except lost money.

Once you get a life-size mount at home, you can best care for it by never touching it, nor allowing people to pull on its feathers, or pat its plumage. Dust it lightly from time to time, but otherwise just admire it. An old Eastern gobbler glares down at me from on the corner of my desk, a reminder of good times 15 years ago with my old turkey hunting buddies, Charlie Elliott and Dempsey Cape, both from Georgia. After all those years, the bird is still in good condition.

Wings and tails alone can be spread or fanned out and left to dry in that position, which are easily looked after, and will take considerable abuse hanging on a den wall. I always nail these to the wall of a shed and leave them there for several months. During this time I apply powdered Borax to areas where meat has been exposed. Once dried, a piece of leather folded over any objectionable area can be hand sewn in place. Dates, where the bird was killed and any other information can be inked on the leather.

Feet can be cut off at the first joint up from the foot, and then after driving a 16-penny nail into a post, the foot can be pushed down alongside the post, spreading the toes exactly as if the bird was walking. Then it is tied there, with the leg bone alongside the nail, and left to dry for a few weeks, it will hold this position. Numerous hunters dry the feet or legs of those turkeys with the best spurs.

Turkey beards are often displayed by gluing them into empty shotshell hulls. I'll take a nail punch and knock the old primer free, then glue a small brass cup hook in that hole. I'll hang the shell by this. Anyone wanting to use shells should go to a gunshop which has a variety, and gather a few 20 gauge hulls, along with some .410s. The average turkey beard will fit into one of these. Once in a while you may need a larger hull, particularly if you hunt in Missouri or northern Arkansas, as these areas are where the largest beards can be found. For small jake beards a hunter can use .44 caliber rifle brass, or even .38s. I identify each beard so I will be able to tell what bird it came from.

A stone grinding bowl I found while hunting Gould's turkeys in Mexico holds a handful of alligator juniper berries from an old gobbler I bagged there. A plastic license

The feet of wild turkeys can be kept as trophies simply by shaping them to suit, and letting them dry for several weeks. Here, the author has driven 16-penny nails into a board, pressed the feet down against the board with toes outspread, and then wired them securely to the nail.

(Right) Various types of shell casings and cup hooks can be glued together for making a device in which wild turkey beards can be displayed. The cup hooks are glued into the hole once the primer has been removed.

back-tag from West Virginia holds an old license from there, along with a handful of beechnuts I took from the crop of a hen I killed there one winter afternoon. Wayne Bailey was sitting down the gully from me a ways when I shot the bird. It rained on us walking out that evening.

Feathers from another Osceola gobbler are tied Indian fashion to the handmade shotgun carrying case that holds my old muzzleloader. Spurs are fastened to it for adornment, too. A bunch of the huge black and white primary feathers from the wings of Gould's gobblers hang on a wall hook, for when I want to send a friend one, hoping he'll take the time to compare it to one from a bird he's killed.

An old hornet's nest hanging from a ceiling beam brings back crazy memories . . .

Mementos of a hunt can be whatever a person desires. There are old plantation bricks in my sidewalks, and water oaks I've dug up in the old South. A climbing wisteria came from an old house place on a hill overlooking the Homochito River in Copiah County, Mississippi. Grinding stones from the long extinct Paquime Indian tribe take me deep into the mountains of Chihuahua, Mexico, where the ancestors of turkeys those Indians hunted are now hunted by me. Stone axes remind me of afternoons David Jackman and I sat on stone metates, waiting for wild gobblers to come into a clearing alongside a fallen down log house. Probably that's the only time in the history of man that a metate, used by ancient Indians for grinding corn, has ever been used for a seat by turkey hunters. Two of the metates came home with me.

An old hornet's nest hanging from a ceiling beam brings back crazy memories of an afternoon with a great Missouri turkey hunter, Lennis Rose, of Washburn. Lennis and I had been hunting turkeys down below the Pea Ridge National Park, which commemorates a battle during the Civil War. Lennis' brother, Harley, had driven down with Lennis, while Tom Preston had come along with me. We had a tent camp set up and though it had been a cold fall night prior to Arkansas' opening day, the day dawned clear bright. We split up, going in all directions, meeting back at camp for lunch. Nobody had seen anything. After lunch, Tom and Harley headed off down a ridge to the west, Lennis and I dropping off toward a bottom to the south.

Near a stone outcropping, we spied a big hornet's nest not far off the ground in a small tree. It was a dandy, big around as a basketball, and in perfect condition. I told Lennis it would look good hanging in my den. We carried a fair-sized log down the slope, and bending the sapling over, eased it onto the trunk with a "thud." Boy, oh boy, we did stir up a hornet's nest. We both made a fast retreat to a safe distance, where we watched the humming swarm that was searching for whoever was creating all the ruckus. We sat still, and after a while, the hornets settled down.

Obviously, we weren't going to get that hornet's nest until a later date. We were still hanging around there studying on how we'd separate the critters from their home when we heard a shotgun blast, then another, and another. Had to be one of our bunch, so we forgot the hornets to go see about turkeys.

Harley had scattered a small drove, making a kill while he was at it. The next morning we all made kills, after which we broke camp and went our separate ways. I soon forgot the hornets nest. The next spring, Lennis pulled in my yard one afternoon as he and I had a date to hunt gobblers in far west Oklahoma. What a surprise! He was

If this old plantation house could talk what turkey stories it could tell because there have probably been hundreds of them told, over and over, on the long porch. Now a hunting camp, it smells of hunting gear, boots, and the smoke from wood fires. Though the old oak provides shade, the long forgotten horse-drawn buggies no longer discharge visitors from under the porch's overhang.

Good times, such as this lunch break, are forgotten soon if not caught on film. After all, whoever heard of a "mountain man" sipping Dr. Pepper, or worst yet, eating a *sandwich*. What happened to all the grizzly "bars?"

Turkey hunting is spending the night at Tom Pierotti's camp up in Pennsylvania, and wondering who's the best snorer in the loft. 'Course, you can't hear yourself. Better yet, it's bacon and eggs before first day, stuffing your pockets with roasted peanuts, and heading into turkey woods. Having a camera along helps to preserve all these fine memories. To hunt wild turkeys is to meet all the fine people of America.

carrying the one memory of that hunt which I had hoped to get. He'd waited until winter set in, gathered up a large plastic bag, and after picking up Harley, they'd driven back to the area. It was no trouble to slip the bag up around the nest and cut the limb. With the bag safe in the Bronco, they headed back home. By the time they got there, the bag was humming with mad hornets. They'd really got warmed up. Lennis killed them with a bug killer.

Lennis and I have had many good times. Speaking of trophies and beards makes me think of Lennis when he hadn't been hunting turkeys but a few years. My wife Stella and I on our way back from a drive over to Roaring River State Park where we'd had a fried trout dinner stopped at Lennis' place. Corliss, Lennis' wife, rounded out the foursome, and, she insisted Stella and I come in for a while to visit. We'd been talking about this and that, when Corliss called my attention to a long cedar board which had small cup hooks its entire length. The cedar board was long and narrow, had been sanded and varnished, and obviously was for hanging a bunch of something on.

"Good times" is what turkey hunting is all about. Vernon Cade, the hunter on the far right, keeps these hunters laughing with his squalling renditions of a raccoon fight.

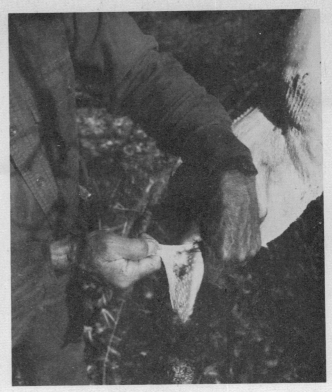

Removing a beard from the carcass of a wild turkey is easy. (Top left) Grasp the beard firmly with the thumb and forefingers of one hand, while the other hand holds the bird's neck. (Bottom left) While gripping the whole beard as a unit, pull it directly away from the bird's neck. (Above) The beard will come free as a unit. (Below) This beard has pulled free, complete as a self-contained unit, which can now be placed into the open end of a fired shotshell, and glued there for displaying. This short beard is from a young gobbler, or "jake" turkey.

Western Oklahoma rancher Max Olson works long days while feeding and caring for cattle, which together with planting a considerable acreage to wheat harvest, leaves him little time to hunt. He gives ultimate protection to wild turkeys on his "spread," which were started there with a small release of birds many, many years ago. Many of his close friends have bagged great numbers of birds from his flocks.

Corliss was laughing by now, and chiding Lennis about his turkey beards. I couldn't help but laugh too, as Lennis had made this thing for hanging turkey beards. Lordy, the board was 6 to 7 feet long, and it would hold a batch of turkey beards. We all got to gigging Lennis about filling that board, razzing him about how old he'd be by the time he had killed all those turkeys. If he lived that long.

Lennis has already got the board full. You never saw a finer, bigger bunch of wild turkey tassels in your life. Lennis Rose is a pretty mean turkey hunter. I envy him living in the area of the country where the largest, thick, whisk-

broom-like bearded turkeys are found. If you don't think I know what I'm talking about, you need to go see that board in Lennis' den.

Good times and meeting new people will soon fade from memory if the facts aren't written down . . .

Memories won't be complete if a person forgets the little things. Few people can recall what happened the past spring. Dates are definitely forgotten, along with all the details. About all that is remembered are the kills and a few incidents when a bird gives the hunter the run-around. Many years ago I began carrying a small notebook and a pencil tied to it with a short string. I'll jot down happenings from time to time, and it's amazing when I read these years later, as all sorts of things happen which a person forgets. I would never have remembered that Louis Maus was shooting a double-barreled L.C. Smith when he killed a gobbler with me one April morning nearly a decade ago. Louis is one of those good Alabama turkey hunters, and he'd come west to hunt Rio Grandes. Nor would I have remembered the exact day I toppled an adult hen out of a big sugar maple, during a fall hunt to Vermont, if I didn't have it in my notes. I'd already killed a jake that October 21, 1978, and the reason the hen was in the tree was because Ed Merrow had scared her there. He'd called in a small drove with the barrel of a fountain pen, after he realized he'd left his Turpin yelper at home. Nor would I have recalled that the next morning, October 22, there was a light skiff of snow in Vermont's Green Mountains, and that I killed two "pats" that day. "Pats" are partridge to New Englanders, ruffed grouse to us outsiders. Both were

Story telling time is as much a part of turkey hunting as the hunt itself. Tom Preston, left, enjoys the story being related by Buddy Hanks, right, as Ed Norwood listens with a scowl on his face. Perhaps the joke is on him! This is *good times*.

Late night action around many turkey camps is a few hands of poker, or several games of dominoes. The later these hunters play the games, the greater are the chances that no turkeys will be shot the next day. Get your rest—you'll need it for turkeyin'!

(Right) Ben Horst, a turkey hunting guide from Garland, Texas, wears a necklace of old trade beads, wild turkey spurs, and a shotshell with a wild gobbler's beard glued inside. Spur necklaces are extremely popular among turkey hunters because the spur is the ultimate trophy of the wild turkey. The spurs shown here, the long ones nearest the shotshell, are long and sharp, and indicate that the gobbler from which these came was perhaps 4 to 6 years of age. Ben is a good hunter, because these old gobblers are seldom taken by anyone who is not.

of the gray phase. October 23, I shot a woodcock with my old muzzleloading 11 gauge.

Good times, meeting new people, all these things will soon fade from memory if the facts aren't written down. I wish I'd done what my old lifelong partner John Waters has made a practice of doing. He has kept hunting notes ever since he got out of college. As an example, he's run 477 boxes of shells through his shotgun, and has a 53 percent kill ratio at doves, quail, and ducks. If you aren't aware, that is excellent shooting. I realize there will be many hunters who will read this statistic and mutter to themselves, "That ain't so good, I've been out several times and got 10 for 10," or some such score. Yep, and those are the ones we all remember because we want to. We soon forget the times we got five for 20, or six for 30. We don't talk and brag about those hunts, so we erase them from our mind. Keep notes, you'll be surprised in your old age what took place years ago.

Undoubtedly the finest rewards I have had down through the years in wandering around the United States and Old Mexico, are the friends I've made. The backwoods turkey hunter sees little of what an average tourist sees, but at the same time meets the heart-and-soul of this great country of ours. You learn how these folks make a living, what are

accepted practices, and a jillion other things. Now, I don't mean that all the people are country folks, not by a long-shot. This country wouldn't exist if it wasn't for the guy in the steel mill and the janitors sweeping our school rooms. It takes all of us, and so goes turkey hunters, people from all ways of life. Rich men, poor men, game wardens, turkey biologists, girls with camo paint smeared faces instead of lipstick, and kids, too. Boys who have watched dad go hunting, so they want to go, too.

Not many hunters will take the time to learn how maple syrup is made, from the time it is tapped from a tree until it is poured on pancakes. But let me tell you, once you know, it's far easier to understand why it brings the price stamped on it in the grocery store. Did you know Florida has some of the finest cattle ranches in this country? And some fine cowboys too? Have you ever watched folks spend a Sunday afternoon catching crawfish for Monday dinner? Or, that it takes about 15 pounds of live crawfish for a good meal for three grown people?

I'll bet you haven't eaten squirrel pie. I'll bet you didn't know that some folks are proud to be "coonasses?" Just ask a Cajun native. Until I'd been making some plantation tours in the deep South, I never knew that food was prepared in a building behind the owner's home, and then carried along ''the whistle walk'' by servants bringing it to the master's table. The slave carrying it to the ''big house'' was supposed to whistle while carrying the food to let his master know that he was not sampling the meal enroute. I've stood in the ruins that were once Mark Twain's home. It overlooked a bend in the Mississippi River. Burned to the ground one night after a guest apparently threw a cigarette in a waste basket. Some thanks for being invited to the party being held that evening.

I'd been taking these lousy smile-at-the-birdie pictures for several years when it dawned on me . . .

Of course, photography rates at the very top for recording events whether it's high school graduation day, or a snapshot of a big old turkey gobbler being held by a very happy hunter. Photos, slides, transparencies, snapshots—all are a material image which can be kept throughout a hunter's lifetime, left to the generation to come. I suppose some-where in time that a distant relative of mine, who perhaps I'll never know, will have an occasion to study an old photo of me, and though he may know very little else about me, he will get the idea I was a turkey hunter. The fact is, anyone who walks into my den would probably think I do nothing else in life. (How I wish that were true).

There are undoubtedly thousands of folks who don't take photos simply because they have the idea that this would require a great outlay of money, but more importantly, that today's camera is too sophisticated for the average person to operate. Nothing could be further from the truth. In fact it's just the opposite. Today's camera shops have tremendous selections of fully automatic cameras, and Polaroid cameras which do everything but push the button, and say ''cheese'' for you. Some of them can be purchased for $20 to $30 and with the film available today, will take amazingly detailed snapshots, indeed so, when you consider how little money is involved.

I first began taking snapshots with one of the small Kodak Brownies. I knew so little about cameras that it was imperative I use one which could be loaded much like a shotgun. Simply push a button, open it up, roll in some film, close, and it was ready for picture taking. You guessed it—all of my pictures were of various buddies

Outdoor shows made for television have become exceedingly popular all across the United States. Here, Don Wallace of the *Wallace Wildlife Show*, from a TV station in Oklahoma City, hoists a wild gobbler taken on a televised hunt.

Many films have been made about the comeback of the wild turkey, which has spread even into places where it had not lived earlier, and on present day hunting of the bird. Such films do much to educate the non-hunting public about the American hunter and his responsible awareness in bringing conservation to all of nature.

holding up dead game or fish, and staring at the camera. If their heads happened to be in the developed print that was great, but sometimes they weren't, and I would have a group of bodies, some belonging to a bunch of dead ducks, the other bodies being nameless as they had no heads. Sometimes I'd get most of the boys in the picture, but maybe cut off an arm or so. But, today when I look at those old photos, it's easy to recall how the birds flew that day, or how we laughed as we hauled in the channel cats. My dad, Orin Bland, Whitey Killam, Dick Lyons, Chuck Athey, all of them are gone now—but not from my memories.

I'd been taking these lousy smile-at-the-birdie pictures for several years when it dawned on me that maybe I could take pictures like I was always seeing in *Sports Afield*, or *Outdoor Life*, and *Fur, Fish, and Game*. So I began experimenting. Let me tell you, I was *not* an overnight success. Photo composition was a foreign critter to me. My early attempts at getting things "arranged" were often terrible in the finished product, with telephone wires crisscrossing a clear blue sky, and hunters so far away that nobody could recognize them. My attempts at taking still photos of a wild turkey, with gun and call, looked more like a pile of coal on a sandbar. What I didn't realize was that to become even a fair photographer, a person must take lots of pictures. Or, take courses in photography. Heck knows when I would have learned this, maybe never, if it had not been for Charlie Elliott.

One spring I was sitting at the supper table, having just come in from turkey hunting, and was telling my wife about the day's happenings. She got up to go see who knocked at the door, then came back to tell me two men wanted to see me. I didn't know Cliff King, who then was a photographer for the Oklahoma Game & Fish department, but I had read articles written by the man with him, whom he introduced as Charlie Elliott. Somehow they had gotten

hold of my name in their search for a hunter who could put them into wild turkeys. Telling me this, Charlie said he was doing a story for *Outdoor Life*, about hunting the Rio Grande. Cliff was wanting photo material for the department and for his personal files. I told them I couldn't promise them anything, but if they were willing to risk it, I'd be more'n happy to give it a try.

Lady Luck was kissing me on the back of the neck in those days, and she outdone herself in the 2 or 3 days that followed. Charlie laid out a grand old gobbler, and both of them took so many pictures, I presumed they had half interest in Kodak.

Right off I'd learned any number of things. One being that outdoor writers are very capable hunters. Charlie Elliott proved to me he was as good a turkey hunter as there was going (still is). He was also a first class gentleman, a woodsman of the first ranking, and obviously knew a few things about photography. Both he and Cliff King were carrying what I presumed to be very expensive cameras, enclosed in leather cases, plus bags full of gadgets I'd never laid eyes on, and roll after roll of film. My ears hurt from listening to those guys talk about settings, f-stops, and numbers. Now and then I'd catch the phrase, "film speed," which was baffling to me.

For the first time in my life, I was told to do all sorts of crazy things while one or both would take pictures. "Walk toward us, but don't look at the camera, look back over yonder." "Stand over there by the fence, and study that No Hunting sign." "Hold your binoculars up to your eyes

(Right) Though these two turkey hunters have gone on to "The Turkey Woods In The Sky," their memory lives on in pictures such as this one. Orin Bland, the author's late father, and his longtime hunting cronie, Henry J. "Hank" Lyons, admire a pair of jake turkeys which fell to their guns. The author was fortunate to have captured them on film.

Photographs are lifelong keepsakes, recording good times and fond memories. The time to take hunting photos is when afield, as these hunters are doing in Florida's saw palmetto country.

Picture taking sessions sometimes include a nosy bird-dog, and the photographer must be careful of what is included in a camera's viewfinder. But, photos are a record of an event, so it could be an interesting photo if this photographer included the dog.

(Left) Photographs such as this one can never be replaced, particularly for hunters like Tom Preston, on the left. With him here is the late Ted Trueblood, the veteran outdoorsman who was long associated with *Field And Stream* magazine. Trueblood's memory will live on with the many men who had the privilege to share hunting trips with him.

and look over this way, toward that clump of shinnery.'' And, they wouldn't be happy with taking just one or two photos of each pose, they'd do it over and over. Seemed like an awful waste of film, but in the years to come, I could understand why they had gone to all this trouble.

It all added together when Charlie's story came out in *Outdoor Life*. I could so quickly relate to how each photograph had been made, all the pains that Charlie and Cliff had gone to, for what amounted to just four pictures that were printed with the article. What pictures though! They helped tell the hunt. Not just a bunch of mugs staring at a camera, with a dead turkey held up in the middle. The binoculars, the sign on the fence, these made the story take on the atmosphere of having been there to anyone reading it. After the two of them went back to Oklahoma City, from where Charlie would fly back to his beloved Georgia, I made up my mind I needed to make some changes. I began asking all my buddies to ''walk toward me with that turkey slung over your shoulder,'' and that kind of stuff. Immediately, I could see a change in my photos. They got worse!

The camera had to be the culprit. It didn't have all the numbers on it that Charlie and Cliff talked about, so I got one that did. I bought a small used job for $15, and though it wasn't automatic, it was a start. I began experimenting with various settings, read a book on outdoor photography by Erwin Bauer, and tried numerous films. Where in the beginning I'd been strictly a black-and-white picture taker,

Like so many of today's Americans, the author's wife does not hunt but she loves the outdoors. Stella has tromped many miles with him and driven a thousand country roads, but she could not care less about shooting a gun. She doesn't move an eyelash, though when Bland whispers, "Sit still," she knows who "The Boss" is in the family.

I soon could see why Charlie liked films known as Ekta-color and Ektachrome. Foliage color was magnificient, hunting pictures began to look like what I would see while hunting. Composition fell into place as the numbers of photos grew. From my mistakes I soon learned about balancing, distances from the camera, blur, plus a jillion tiny things a photographer must always be alert to.

A long time ago I learned that the hunter never has his camera with him when he wants it most . . .

I took many, many pictures, taking a hint from what Charlie told me on another hunt. Once a person finds the setting he thinks is the best for the intended photo, make that one, then take two others, one at the f-stop below that setting, and one above. Everything taken into consideration, shadows, light and dark areas in the background and on the subject, movements which could blur, and overall composition, should balance out on one of those three pictures. Invariably one, or more, will be what you were wanting. True, this can be expensive, but too often a person will never again have the opportunity to make that individual photo again. So many photos are a once-in-a-lifetime situation, therefore it's get it now or not at all.

Astronaut Wally Schirra with a bearded hen taken by him in far west Oklahoma. Schirra is an avid backer of The National Wild Turkey Federation. Bland's having his camera along on the hunt preserved the memory.

A long time ago I learned that the hunter who wants to take pictures of the hunt never has his camera with him when he wants it most. It is back at camp, or in the pickup. Invariably, this is the case when he has hunted out onto a rocky point with a fantastic view of the country, is kneeling beside a blooming wild flower in the spring, or wants to photograph a bunch of old rusting syrup buckets in a maple woods. All of us can recall those hunts on which not a single photo was made, and how we now wish for those photos.

There certainly isn't any reason for today's hunter to be anywhere without a camera. Why? Because of the wide selection of very small compact cameras. I carry an Olympus, which is about the size of a package of cigarettes, won't weigh much more, and slips easily into a shirt pocket. I sewed together a rectangular belt bag in which to carry mine, and in this little bag is also a pocketknife, a compass, and a match safe. Anytime I see something which I want a photo of, I dig out the little camera and take a shot or two. This particular camera is a full-frame 35mm. I load it with a 36 exposure roll of Ektachrome, for slides, and Ektacolor for color prints. An extra roll of film also fits into the belt bag. Whereas most of these tiny compacts

Chantell Preston watches, as grandad autographs copies of his last book, *Turkey Scratchings*.

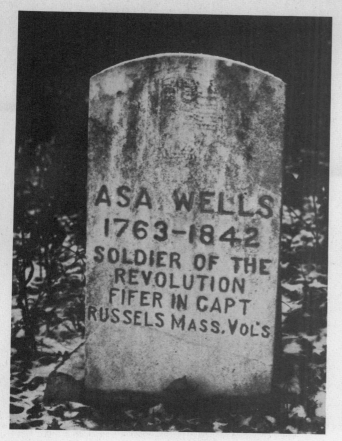

Having a compact camera tucked away in a hunting coat pocket allowed the author to photograph this old tombstone during a fall hunt. Such markers denoting the burial place of people from long ago dot the width and breadth of this land. Don't leave home without a camera. Carry it with you. You won't be sorry.

clampods and tripods which will do this admirably, but these are just other items to carry.

Another problem when using a self-timer is that the hunter can't see how he'll look in the photo. He simply has to hope it will come out okay. Too, he will need an object at an equal distance from the lens to focus on, so that when he takes his place before the camera he will be in focus.

The last time I was hunting gobblers in Arizona I made several pics of myself crossing a stream on a log spanning the creek. None of them are what an editor would buy for use in a hunting magazine, though I will keep them for home viewing. I took several hoping one would be excellent. None were, for any number of reasons—couldn't see the gun, too much glare off the water, too far across in two pics (which unbalanced the picture too far toward the direction I was walking), and one was no good because I was nowhere in sight. I hadn't thought the release had been properly pressed, and ran back to check, then it took the shot before I could get on the log. A self-timer may have its problems, but these are the greatest things since zippers on pants. I waste film fooling with them, but I've taken a batch of pics I would never have gotten if it hadn't been for the timer *and, having the camera with me*.

Now, if you are going to run out and buy a camera because you want to take pictures of turkeys, wait just a minute. You are opening up a whole can of worms if you do that. Turkeys don't like to have their picture taken. Take

utilize rolled film cartridges, Kodak has recently brought on the market a small compact which uses a disc. Again, like so many of Kodak's products, the camera is a good buy for anyone who is not schooled in photography. This little job is extremely simple to operate, enabling the average person to enjoy past happenings through photography.

My Olympus also has a self-timer, which can be of great importance to a hunter who wants to be a part of his own photos. A self-timer will allow you to press the shutter release and give you about 10 seconds to position yourself within the camera's field of view. There are two problems which crop up when taking these pictures. The first concerns keeping the camera aimed at the subject matter while the release is depressed. I have learned that the finest base for the camera is a handful of soil placed on a log or a rock, and then if your handkerchief or bandana is laid on this, the camera can be pressed lightly into this base, and it will remain there while you make the focus and the photos. Of course, the camera must be placed in an elevated position so that you can see through it for focusing and composition, and to bring the lens up to a height that will eliminate ground clutter. There are small devices known as

The safest method for crossing fences while carrying guns is to let another member of the party hold the gun, as each hunter in turn gets across the wire strands. *Whoops!*, you tore your britches!

my word for it. But if you must do this, tell the person selling you the merchandise what you want to do so he can show you his line of telephoto lenses. These are like a binocular or rifle scope, magnifying the turkey, while taking its picture. You won't need to be so close.

To take photos of wild turkeys with the average camera lens would mean that the lens will have to be within 15 yards for the turkey to be seen on the print. Don't be surprised if you can't see the bird well, even at that distance. Seven or 8 yards or closer would be best. In taking these pictures, focusing is extremely important, for if the bird is not clear and sharply defined, you might as well have stayed home. The slight movements in focusing are easily seen by a turkey, so unless you do your photography from a blind, you will need to be very careful in making any adjustment while the bird is close. You'll also need lots of luck.

Turkey hunting is everything that is the good life . . .

Anyone who spends his life in turkey country is going to get chummy with a snake sooner or later. The bulk of them will be harmless, but the remainder are the ones we all will remember. Snakes are one part of turkey hunting which I like to recall, so these critters are part of my trophies. Visitors to my den quickly become aware of this, as there are always two or three dried snake skins hanging someplace. Let me tell you how it's done. Once you've found the snake you want, search about for a small pencil-sized switch, 2 or 3 feet in length, one that has lots of "whip." If you strike the snake with this directly behind the head, it will kill it quickly and mercilessly. Just two or three quick strikes.

Roll the reptile over on its back, and then by inserting the thin blade of your pocketknife under the skin just below the mouth, an incision can be made the length of the snake. Or, this can be done in reverse, running the knife forward as you hold the snake in place by standing on the tip of the tail. It is then easy to work the skin from the body. Soak the skin for 3 days in a strong saltwater solution. Then remove, wash thoroughly in fresh water, and tack to shape on a wooden board, the side of a shed, or the garage. The skin will dry in a few days and can then be glued or sewn to a piece of canvas, and the edge of the canvas cut to shape with pinking sheers. Or, the skin can be displayed on a weathered board, or simply left loose, and draped over furniture. (This can cause close encounters, screams, near heart failures, etc.)

Glancing around, I can see the hides of three copperheads hanging in my den, along with the skin of a nigh 6-foot canebrake rattler, but no cottonmouths. Lots of them in the South, but I have just never gotten around to doing one in and skinning it out. Probably the prettiest snake I have seen was a giant Mexican corral snake which I came on one hot afternoon in the high Sierras. Sadly, I was so intent on looking at the creature that it began crawling into a rocky retreat before I realized it was escaping. I grabbed it by the tail, but couldn't pull it free without perhaps separating the tail, so I let it go.

Indian relics—arrowheads, axeheads, smoothing stones, mixing bowls—all of these ancient artifacts are often found by observant turkey hunters. Many such relics grace my home and bring back memories of great hunts. Each time I gaze at a cream colored flint arrowhead, I recall bellying along a sandy wash in far western Oklahoma. An old gobbler was grazing in an open meadow not far from the wash, and I had high hopes of easing into killing position. Suddenly my hand came down on a sharp object in the soft dry sand, which I discovered was this arrowhead. Generals Custer and Sheridan chased the Cheyennes and Comanches all across those Antelope Hills, and it just could have been from an arrow fired in anger.

Turkey hunting is everything that is the good life. It's moonshine whiskey from an iced-tea glass, and a guzzle of clear cold water from a tiny brook high on a New York ridge. It's wishing for one less shirt on a scorching, windless Arizona afternoon, and wishing for two more the next morning at first daylight, when the temperature has fallen below freezing. And, have you ever been to Brooks Holleman's stomping grounds down south of Montgomery, Alabama? Brooks makes a ceremony of getting everyone out of bed each morning. I think he works at it. Nowhere are the nights so short as at Brook's "Turkey Hollow." God should've made more like him.

Turkey hunting is holding a guy's gun while he tears his pants on a fence. Or, perhaps unloading it while he ain't looking. Turkey hunting is changing a tire on Ed LaForce's Wagoneer while a couple of local pulpwood cutters offer advice and a drink from their bottle.

APPENDIX—A
Wild Turkey Seasons and State Game Commissions

State	Seasons	Subspecies

The following states offer hunting for wild turkeys during the spring season, and some of them offer fall and winter seasons, as well as spring. License fees are not listed due to the constantly changing prices. A hunter interested in hunting wild turkeys in any state should send for the rules and regulations governing that season, and study them very carefully. Maps can be purchased from the state game departments.

Several of the states have additional subspecies to those listed, and a number of states have hybrids. But, because they are found primarily on private property, many of these subspecies are small in numbers. The birds are not easily accessible to the hunting public.

State	Seasons	Subspecies
ALABAMA Department of Conservation and Natural Resources 64 Union St. Montgomery, AL 36130	Spring/Fall	Eastern
ARIZONA Game And Fish Department 2222 West Greenway Rd. Phoenix, AZ 85023	Spring/Fall	Merriam
ARKANSAS Arkansas Game and Fish Comm. 2 Natural Resources Drive Little Rock, AR 72205	Spring/Fall	Eastern
CALIFORNIA California Department of Fish and Game 1416 Ninth St. Sacramento, CA 95814	Spring/Fall	Rio Grande Merriam
COLORADO Colorado Division of Wildlife 6060 Broadway Denver, CO 80216	Spring/Fall	Merriam
CONNECTICUT Connecticut Department of Environmental Protection State Office Building Hartford, CT 06115	Spring	Eastern
FLORIDA Florida Game and Fresh Water Fish Commission 620 South Meridian St. Tallahassee, FL 32301	Spring/Fall	Osceola Eastern
GEORGIA Georgia Game and Fish Comm. 270 Washington St., S.W. Atlanta, GA 30334	Spring/Fall	Eastern
HAWAII Hawaii Game and Fish Division 1151 Punchbowl St. Honolulu, HI 96813	Spring	Rio Grande
IDAHO Idaho Dept. of Fish and Game Box 25 Boise, ID 83707	Spring/Fall	Merriam
ILLINOIS Division of Wildlife Resources 605 State Office Building Springfield, IL 62706	Spring	Eastern
INDIANA Division of Fish and Wildlife 615 State Office Building Indianapolis, IN 46204	Spring	Eastern

State	Seasons	Subspecies	State	Seasons	Subspecies

IOWA
Iowa Conservation
  Commission
Wallace State Office
  Building
Des Moines, IA 50319 — Spring/Fall — Eastern

KANSAS
Kansas Fish and Game
  Comm.
Route 2, Box 54A — — Rio Grande
Pratt, KS 67124 — Spring/Fall — Eastern

KENTUCKY
Department of Fish and
  Wildlife Resources
Capitol Plaza Tower
Frankfort, KY 40601 — Spring/Fall — Eastern

LOUISIANA
Department of Wildlife and
  Fisheries
Wildlife and Fisheries
  Building
New Orleans, LA 70130 — Spring — Eastern

MAINE
Inland Fisheries and
  Wildlife Licensing
284 State St.
State House Station 41
Augusta, ME 04333 — Spring — Eastern

MARYLAND
Maryland Wildlife
  Administration
Tawes State Office Building
Annapolis, MD 21401 — Spring/Fall — Eastern

MASSACHUSETTS
Massachusetts Division of
  Fisheries and Wildlife
100 Cambridge St.
Boston, MA 02202 — Spring — Eastern

MICHIGAN
Michigan Wildlife Division
Dept. of Natural Resources
Box 30028
Lansing, MI 48909 — Spring — Eastern

MINNESOTA
Division of Game and Fish
Box 7, Centennial Off.
  Building
St. Paul, MN 55155 — Spring — Eastern

MISSISSIPPI
Mississippi Game and Fish
  Comm.
P.O. Box 451
Jackson, MS 39205 — Spring/Fall — Eastern

MISSOURI
Missouri Dept. of
  Conservation
2901 North Ten Mile Drive
Jefferson City, MO 65101 — Spring/Fall — Eastern

MONTANA
Montana Dept. of Fish and
  Game
120 East 6th St.
Helena, MT 59601 — Spring/Fall — Merriam

NEBRASKA
Nebraska Game and Parks
  Commission
P.O. Box 30370 — — Rio Grande
Lincoln, NE 68503 — Spring/Fall — Merriam

NEW HAMPSHIRE
New Hampshire Game
  Department
34 Bridge St.
Concord, NH 03301 — Spring — Eastern

NEW JERSEY
Division of Fish, Game,
  and Wildlife
CN-400
Trenton, NJ 08625 — Spring — Eastern

NEW MEXICO
New Mexico Dept. Game
  and Fish
State Capitol
Santa Fe, NM 87503 — Spring/Fall — Merriam

NEW YORK
New York Fish and Wildlife
  Div.
50 Wolf Rd.
Albany, NY 12233 — Spring/Fall — Eastern

NORTH CAROLINA
Wildlife Resources
  Commission
325 North Salisbury St.
Raleigh, NC 27611 — Spring — Eastern

State	Seasons	Subspecies	State	Seasons	Subspecies
NORTH DAKOTA North Dakota Game and Fish Dept. 2121 Lovett Ave. Bismarck, ND 58505	Spring/Fall	Merriam	**TENNESSEE** Tennessee Wildlife Resources Agency P.O. Box 40747 Nashville, TN 37204	Spring/Fall	Eastern
OHIO Ohio Division of Wildlife Fountain Square Columbus, OH 43224	Spring	Eastern	**TEXAS** Texas Parks and Wildlife Dept. 4200 Smith School Rd. Austin, TX 78744	Spring/Fall	Eastern Rio Grande
OKLAHOMA Oklahoma Dept. of Wildlife Con. P.O. Box 53465 Oklahoma City, OK 73105	Spring/Fall	Merriam Rio Grande Eastern	**UTAH** Utah Division of Wildlife Resources 1596 West Temple Salt Lake City, UT 84116	Spring/Fall	Merriam
OREGON Oregon Dept. of Wildlife P.O. Box 3503 Portland, OR 97208	Spring	Rio Grande Merriam	**VERMONT** Vermont Fish and Game Dept. Montpelier, VT 05602	Spring/Fall	Eastern
PENNSYLVANIA Pennsylvania Game Commission P.O. Box 1567 Harrisburg, PA 17120	Spring/Fall	Eastern	**VIRGINIA** Virginia Commission of Game Box 11104 Richmond, VA 23230	Spring/Fall	Eastern
RHODE ISLAND Rhode Island Division of Fish and Wildlife Group Center Wakefield, RI 02879	Spring	Eastern	**WASHINGTON** Washington Department of Game 600 Capitol Way Olympia, WA 98504	Spring/Fall	Merriam
SOUTH CAROLINA South Carolina Wildlife Resources Department P.O. Box 167 Columbia, SC 29202	Spring/Fall	Eastern	**WEST VIRGINIA** West Virginia Department of Natural Resources 1800 Washington St., East Charleston, WV 25305	Spring/Fall	Eastern
SOUTH DAKOTA South Dakota Department of Game, Fish and Parks Anderson Building Pierre, SD 57501	Spring/Fall	Merriam	**WYOMING** Wyoming Game and Fish Dept. Box 1589 Cheyenne, WY 82202	Spring/Fall	Merriam

Topographical Map Directory

Topography map index, and maps, may be ordered from:

For map areas east of the Mississippi River:
U.S. Geological Survey
Map Distribution Section
Washington, DC 20242

For map areas west of the Mississippi River:
U.S. Geological Survey
Map Distribution Section
Federal Center
Denver, CO 80225

United States Forest Service Maps can be ordered from:
United States Forest Service
Washington, DC 20250

And/or from Field Offices of The Forest Service:
Eastern Region, National Forest Service
633 West Wisconsin Ave.
Milwaukee, WI 53203
(National forests in Illinois, Indiana, Ohio, Michigan, Minnesota, Missouri, New Hampshire, Maine, Pennsylvania, Vermont, West Virginia, Wisconsin.)

Southern Region, National Forest Service
1720 Peachtree Rd., N.W.
Atlanta, GA 30309

(National forests in Alabama, Arkansas, Florida, Georgia, Kentucky, Louisiana, Mississippi, North Carolina, South Carolina, Tennessee, Texas, Virginia.)

Northern Region, National Forest Service
Federal Building
Missoula, MT 59807
(National forests in Idaho, Montana.)

Rocky Mountain Region, National Forest Service
11177 West 8th Ave.
Box 25127
Lakewood, CO 80225
(National forests in Colorado, Nebraska, South Dakota, Wyoming.)

California Region, National Forest Service
630 Sansome St.
San Francisco, CA 94111
(National forests in California.)

Pacific Northwest Region, National Forest Service
319 S.W. Pine St.
P.O. Box 3623
Portland, OR 97208
(National forests in Oregon, Washington.)

Turkey Call Manufacturers

Key: **B** — Box type calls (also shuffling box, gunstock, push-pin, small striker)
C — Can type calls (snuff cans, tubes)
M — Mouth type calls (diaphragms)
S — Slate type calls
Y — Yelper type calls (trumpet yelpers, wingbones, suction types)

Delta Calls—(B)
1221 McLean St.
Greenwood, MS 38930

Companion Outdoor Products—(Y)
Box 156A
Rohwer, AR 71666

K-Hill—(Y)
P.O. Box 24
Addison, IL 60101

Tom Gaskins—(B)
Box TC
Palmdale, FL 33944

Scotch Game Call Company—(B, M)
6619 Oak Orchard Rd.
Elba, NY 14058

Evans And Sons—(M)
4048 Summerhill Square
Texarkana, TX 75503

Rod Benson Turkey Calls—(C)
3137 Putnam Rd.
Muskegon, MI 49445

Borderline Bosses—(M)
Bruce Rigard
347 Walnut St.
St. Mary's, PA 15857

Borderline Bosses—(M)
East Eschbach Road
St. Mary's, PA 15857

Al Willis Turkey Calls—(B, M)
Route # 1
Travelers Rest, SC 29690

Stowe Away Turkey Calls—(S)
Lewis Stowe
10 Barnes Drive
Belmont, NC 28012

M.S. Turkey Caller—(B, M, Y)
Route # 1
Box 146A
Weiner, AR 72479

Big Turk Turkey Calls—(B, S)
J. S. Shaw
Route 1
Box 220
Sturgis, MS 39769

Knight And Hale Game Calls—(C)
Box 468
Cadiz, KY 42211

P.S. Olt Co.—(B, M, S)
P.O. Box 550
Pekin, IL 61554

Johnson Game Calls—(Y)
V. O. Johnson, Jr.
Route 2
Gould, AR 71643

Old Jake Products—(C, M)
Box 97
Pawlett, VT 05761

Bill Tannehill Turkey Callers—(S)
P.O. Box 1234
Staunton, VA 24401

Ben Horst—(M)
P.O. Box 462411
Garland, TX 75046

Li'l Jake Turkey Call
Polecate Manufacturing Company
P.O. Box 327
Jenks, OK 74037

Lloyd Greer—(B)
Walker Valley, NY 12588

Frank Hanenkrat—(B)
Route 2
Box 136
Appomattox, VA 24522

Kelly Kallers—(B, M)
P.O. Box 49-T
Picture Rocks, PA 17762

Mountain Hollow Turkey Calls—(M, S)
Box 121
Cascade, MD 21719

Super Yelper Turkey Calls—(B, S)
Richard M. Shively
Box 236, Route 2
Stephens City, VA 22655

Primos Yelpers—(M)
260 Highland Place Drive
Jackson, MS 39211

Turkey Systems, Inc.—(B, C, M, S)
4055 Bohannon Drive
Menlo Park, CA 94025

Cedar Hills Game Calls—(B, M)
Route 1
Box 463
Farmerville, LA 71241

Penn's Woods Products, Inc.—(B, C, M, S, Y)
19 West Pittsburgh Street
Delmont, PA 15626

Lost John Turkey Calls—(B)
John T. Grayson
103 Mount Vernon Road
Bristol, VA 24201

Quaker Boy, Inc.—(B, M, S)
6426 West Quaker Street
Orchard Park, NY 14127

The Forney Brothers—(S)
P.O. Box 6396
Akron, OH 44312

Moss's Double Tone—(B)
P.O. Box 1112
Sedalia, MO 65301

Perfection Diaphragm Turkey Calls, Inc.—(M)
P.O. Box 164
Stephenson, VA 22656

Ben Lee Calls—(B, M, S)
P.O. Box 27
Coffeeville, AL 36524

M. L. Lynch Co.—(B, M, S)
Liberty, MS 39645

Neil Cost, The Gobbler Shop—(B)
P.O. Box 1444
Greenwood, SC 29646

Larry Hearn—(B, Y)
Box 217
Medon, TN 38356

APPENDIX—D
Hunting Equipment Directory

AMMUNITION (Commercial)
Activ Industries Inc., P.O. Box 238, Kearneysville, WV 25430
Cascade Cartridge, Inc. (See Omark)
Dynamit Nobel of America, Inc., 105 Stonehurst Court, Northvale, NJ 07647
Estate Cartridge Inc., P.O. Box 3702, Conroe, TX 77305
Federal Cartridge Corporation, 2700 Foshay Tower, Minneapolis, MN 55402
Frontier Cartridge Division-Hornady Mfg. Co., Box 1848, Grand Island, NE 68801/308-382-1390
Remington Arms Co., Inc., 939 Barnum Ave., P.O. Box #1939, Bridge-port, CT 06601
RWS, (See Dynamit Nobel of America)
Service Armament Co., 689 Bergen Blvd., Ridgefield, NJ 07657
Weatherby's, 2781 Firestone Blvd., South Gate, CA 90280
Winchester/Olin, Shamrock St., East Alton, IL 62024

AMMUNITION (Foreign)
Dan/Arms, 275 Commerce Dr., Suite 300, Port Washington, PA 19034
Dynamit Nobel of America, Inc., 105 Stonehurst Court, Northvale, NJ 07647
FFV Norma, Inc., 300 S. Jefferson, Suite 301, Springfield, MO 65806
Hirtenberger Patronen, Zuend-huetchen- & Metallwarenfabrik Leo-bersdorfer Str. 33, A-2552 Hirtenberg, Austria
Paul Jaeger, Inc., P.O. Box 449, 1 Madison Ave., Grand Junction, TN 38039
Kendall International Inc., 501 East North, Carlisle, KY 40311
Laupa (See Kendall International, Inc.)
Norma (See FFV Norma, Inc.)
PMC (See Patton and Morgan Corp.)
Patton and Morgan Corp., 5900 Wilshire Blvd., #1400, Los Angeles, CA 90036
RWS (Rheinische-Westfalische Sprengstoff) [See Dynamit Nobel of America; Paul Jaeger, Inc.]
Sports Emporium, 1414 Willow Ave., Philadelphia, PA 19126

BOWHUNTING EQUIPMENT
American Archery, P.O. Box 200, Florence, WI 54121
Barnett International, Inc., P.O. Box 934, Odessa, FL 33556 (also crossbows)
Bear Archery, RR 4, 4600 S.W. 41st Blvd., Gainesville, FL 32601
Black Widow Bow Co., Box 357-1, Highlandville, MO 65669
Bohning Co., Ltd., 7361 N. Seven Mile Rd., Lake City, MI 49651
Browning, Rt. 1, Morgan, UT 84050
Cabela's, 812 13th Ave., Sidney, NE 69160 (also crossbows)
Cobra Mfg. Co., P.O. Box 667, Bixby, OK 74008
Easton, 7800 Haskell Ave., Van Nuys, CA 91406
Gander Mountain, P.O. Box 248, Wilmot, WI 53192 (also crossbows)
Golden Eagle Archery, 104 Mill St., Creswell, OR 97426
Muzzy Products, Inc., 501 107th St., Gulf Marathon, FL 97426 (Turkey Thumper Broadheads)
Saunders Archery Co., Box 476, Columbus, NE 68601

Stuart Archery Products, Inc., P.O. Box 1587, Easley, SC 29641
Tru-Fire Corp., 732 State St., N. Fond Du Lac, WI 54935
Wasp Archery Products, 9 W. Main St., Plymouth, CT 49651
York Archery, P.O. Box 110, Independence, MO 64051
Zwickey Archery, Inc., 2571 E. 12th Ave., N. St. Paul, MN 55109 (Zwickey Scorpio Turkey Grappler)

CLOTHING AND ACCOUTREMENTS (Old Timey)
Buffalo Hoof Trading Co., Box 103, Gowrie, IA 52302
The Buffalo Bull, P.O. Box 8, Marion, IA 52302
Connie La Lena's Sunflower Studio, 2851 Road 51B½, Grand Junction, CO 81501 (custom makes frontier clothing from homespun materials of the era)
Mountain Man, 1001 Manitou Ave., Manitou Springs, CO 80829
Mountain Man's Trading Post, 3713 Waterway Drive, Hudson, FL 33568
River Junction Trade Co., 312 Main St., McGregor, IA 52157
Salish House, P.O. Box 27, Rollins, MT 59931
Tecumseh's Frontier Trading Post, Box 369, Shartlesville, PA 19554

EQUIPMENT FOR THE TURKEY HUNTER
B&K Outdoor Supply, Tr.1, Box 220, Vandalia, MO 63382
Cabela's, 812 13th Ave., Sidney, NE 69160
Gander Mountain, Inc., P.O. Box 248, Hwy.W, Wilmot, WI 53192
Wing Supply, P.O. Box 367, Greenville, KY 42345

GUNS (Foreign)
Aimpoint U.S.A., 201 Elden St., Suite 302, Herndon, VA 22070
Allen Firearms Co., 2879 All Trades Rd., Santa Fe, NM 87501
Anschutz (See PSI)
AYA (Aguirre y Aranzabal) [See Wm. L Moore] (Spanish Shotguns)
The Armoury Inc., Route 202, Scottsdale Airpark, New Preston, CT 06777
Armes de Chasse, 3000 Valley Forge Circle, #1051, King of Prussia, PA 19406
Armsource, Inc., 6 Donald Drive, Orinda, CA 94563
Armsport, Inc., 3590 N.W. 49th St., Miami, FL 33142
Beeman Precision Arms, Inc., 47-GDD Paul Dr., San Rafael, CA 94903
Benelli Armi, S.p.A., via della Stazione, 50, 61029 Urbino, Italy
Beretta U.S.A., 17601 Indian Head Highway, Accokeek, MD 20607
British Guns, P.O. Box 1924, Corvallis, OR 97339
Browning (General Offices), Route 1, Morgan, UT 84050
Browning (Parts & Service), Rt.4, Box 624-B, Arnold, MO 63010
Caprinus U.S.A., Inc., 100 Prospect St., Stamford, CT 06901
Conco Arms, P.O. Box 159, Emmaus, PA 18049
Connecticut Valley Arms Co., 5988 Peachtree Corners, East, Nor-cross, GA 30071
Davidson Supply, 2703 High Point, Greensboro, NC 27403
Des Moines Imports, 21 Glenview Dr., Des Moines, IA 50312
Dixie Gun Works, Hwy. 51, South, Union City, TN 38261

Dynamit Nobel of America, Inc., 105 Stonehurst Court, Northvale, NJ 07647

EMF Co. Inc., 1900 East Warner Ave., 1-D, Santa Ana, CA 92705

Euroarms of America, Inc., 1501 Lenoir Dr., P.O. Box 3277 Winchester, VA 22601

Excel Arms of America, 14 Main St., Gardner, MA 01440

Firearms Import & Export (FIE), P.O. Box 4866, Hialeah, FL 33014

Flaig's Inc., 2200 Evergreen Rd., Millvale, PA 15209

Frigon Guns, 627 W. Crawford, Clay Center, KS 67432

Armas Garbi, Urki No. 12, Eibar (Guipuzcoa), Spain

Gun South -Dept. Steyr, 7605 Eastwood Mall, Box 6607, Birmingham, AL 35210

Heym, Friedr. Wilh. (See Paul Jaeger, Inc.)

Incor, Inc., P.O. Box 132, Addison, TX 75001

Interarmco (See Interarms)

Interarms Ltd., 10 Prince St., Alexandria, VA 22313

Paul Jaeger, Inc., P.O. Box 449, 1 Madison Ave., Grand Junction, TN 38039

Jenkins Imports Corp., 462 Standford Place, Santa Barbara, CA 93111

Kassnar Imports, 5480 Linglestown Rd., Harrisburg, PA 17110

Kawaguchiya Firearms, c/o La Paloma Marketing, 4500 E. Speedway Blvd., Suite 93, Tucson, AZ 85712

Kimel Industries, Box 335, Matthews, NC 28105

Kleinguenther's Distinctive, Firearms, Inc., 2485 Highway 46 No., Seguin, TX 78155

Lanber Arms of America, Inc., 377 Logan St., Adrian, MI 49221

Lanchester U.S.A., Inc., P.O. Box 47332, Dallas, TX 75247

La Paloma Marketing, 1735 E. Ft. Lowell, Suite 7, Tucson, AZ 85719

Morris Lawing, 150 Garland Court, Charlotte, NC 28202

Leland Firearms Co., 13 Mountain Ave., Llewellyn Park, West Orange, NJ 07052

Mandall Shooting Supplies, 3616 N. Scottsdale Rd., Scottsdale, AZ 85252

Mannlicher (See Steyr Daimler Puch of Amer.)

Manufrance (See Armsource, Inc.)

Marathon Products Inc., 1331 Silas Deane Highway, Wethersfield, CT 06109

Wm. Larkin Moore & Co., 31360 Via Coinas, Suite 109, Westlake Village, CA 91360

Navy Arms Co., 689 Bergen Blvd., Ridgefield, NJ 07657

Outdoor Sports Headquarters, 967 Watertown Lane, Dayton, OH 45449

The Parker Gun, Div. of Reagent Chem. & Res., 1201 N. Watson Rd., #224, Arlington, TX 76011

Parker-Hale, Bisley Works, Golden Hillock Rd., Sparbrook, Birmingham B11 2PZ, England

Precision Sales Intl. Inc., P.O. Box 1776, Westfield, MA 01086

Precision Sports, P.O. Box 708, Kellogg Rd., Cortland, NY 13045

Quality Arms, Inc., Box 1947, Houston, TX 77224

Richland Arms Co., 321 W. Adrian St., Blissfield, MI 49228

Rottweil (See Dynamit Nobel of America)

Savage Industries, Inc., Springdale Rd., Westfield, MA 01085

Steyr-Daimler-Puch/Gun South, Inc., Box 6607, Birmingham, AL 35210

Stoeger Industries, 55 Ruta Court, S. Hackensack, NJ 07606

Valmet Sporting Arms, Div., 7 Westchester Plaza, Elmsford, NY 10523

Ventura Imports, P.O. Box 2782, Seal Beach, CA 90740

Weatherby's, 2781 Firestone Blvd., South Gate CA 90280

Winchester, Olin Corp., 120 Long Ridge Rd., Stamford, CT 06904

GUNS, U.S.-made

Bighorn Rifle Co., P.O. Box 215, American Fork, UT 84003

Browning (General Offices), Route 1, Morgan, UT 84050

Browning (Parts & Service), Rt. 4, Box 624-B, Arnold, MO 63010

Leonard Day & Co., P.O. Box 723, East Hampton, MA 01027

Du Biel Arms Company, 1724 Baker Rd., Sherman, TX 75090

Firearms Import & Export (FIE), P.O. Box 4866, Hialeah, FL

Hatfield Rifle Works, 2028 Frederick Ave., St. Joseph, MO

Hopkins & Allen Arms, 3 Ethel Ave., P.O. Box 217, Hawthorne, NJ 07507

Ithaca Gun Co., Ithaca, NY 14850

Jennings-Hawken, 326½-4th St. N.W., Winter Haven, FL 33880

Kimber of Oregon, Inc., 9039 S.E. Jannsen Rd., Clackamas, OR 97015

Marlin Firearms Co., 100 Kenna Dr., North Haven, CT 06473

O.F. Mossberg & Sons, Inc., 7 Grasso Ave., P.O. Box 497, North Haven, CT 06473

Mowrey Gun Works, 800 Blue Mound Rd., Saginaw, TX 76131

Navy Arms Co., 689 Bergen Blvd., Ridgefield, NJ 07657

Oregon Trail Riflesmiths, P.O. Box 45212, Boise, ID 83711

Ozark Mountain Arms, Inc., P.O. Box 397, 141 Byrne St., Ashdown, AR 71822

Pecos Valley Armory, 1022 So. Canyon, Carlsbad, NM 88220

Pennsylvania Arms Co., Box 128, Duryea, PA 18642

Remington Arms Co., Inc., 939 Barnum Ave., P.O. Box #1939, Bridgeport, CT 06601

Ruger (See Sturm, Ruger & Co.)

Savage Industries, Inc., Springdale Rd., Westfield, MA 01085

Sturm, Ruger & Co., #1 Lacey Place, Southport, CT 06490

Tennessee Valley Arms, Inc., P.O. Box 2022, Union City, TN 38261

Thompson-Center Arms, P.O. Box 2426, Rochester, NH 03867

Trail Guns Armory, 1634 E. Main St., League City, TX

Ultra Light Arms Co., P.O. Box 1270, Granville, WV 26534

U.S. Repeating Arms Co., P.O. Box 30-300, New Haven, CT 06511

Weatherby's, 2781 Firestone Blvd., South Gate, CA 90280

Winchester (See U.S. Repeating Arms Co.)

HUNTING AND CAMP GEAR, CLOTHING, ETC.

Bob Allen Sportswear, P.O. Box 477, Des Moines, IA 50302

Eddie Bauer, 15010 N.E. 36th St., Redmond, WA 98052

L. L. Bean, 386 Main St., Freeport, ME 04032

Big Beam / Teledyne Co., 290 E. Prairie St., Crystal Lake, IL 60014

Browning, Route 1, Morgan, UT 84050

Brush Hunter Sportswear, Inc., NASCO Industries, 3 N.E. 21st St., Washington, IN 47501

Camp-Ways, 1140 E. Sandhill Ave., Carson, CA 90746

Chippewa Shoe Co., P.O. Box 2521, Ft. Worth, TX 76113

Coleman Co., Inc., 250 N. St. Francis St., Wichita, KS 67201

Converse Rubber Co., 55 Fordham Rd., Wilmington, MA 01887

Danner Shoe Mfg. Co., P.O. Box 22204, Portland, OR 97222

Dunham Co., P.O. Box 813 / RFD 3, Brattleboro, VT 05301

Durango Boot (See Georgia/Northlake)

French Dressing Inc., 15 Palmer Heights, Burlington, VT 05401

Game-Winner, Inc., 2625 Cumberland Pkwy., Suite 205, Atlanta, GA 30339

Gander Mountain, Inc., Hwy. "W", P.O. Box 248, Wilmot, WI 53192

Georgia Boot Div., U.S. Industry, 1810 Columbia Ave., Franklin, TN 37064

Georgia/Northlake Boot Co., (Durango), P.O. Box 10, Franklin, TN 37064

Gokeys, 84 So. Wabasha, St. Paul, MN 55107

Gun Club Sportswear, Box 477, Des Moines, IA 50302

Gun-Ho Case Manufg. Co., 110 East 10th St., St. Paul, MN 55101

Kap Outdoors, 1704 Locust St., Philadelphia, PA 19103

Kenko International Inc., 8141 West I-70, Frontage Rd. No., Arvada, CO 80002

La Crosse Rubber Mills Co., P.O. Box 1328, La Crosse, WI 54601

Langenberg Hat Co., P.O. Box 1860, Washington, MO 63090

Peter Limmer & Sons, Box 66, Intervale, NH 03845

Marathon Rubber Prods. Co., Inc., 510 Sherman St., Wausau, WI 54401

Marble Arms Corp., 420 Industrial Park, Gladstone, MI 49837

The Orvis Co., Rt. 7A, Manchester, VT 05254

Quabaug Rubber Co., Vibram U.S.A., 17 School St., N. Brookfield, MA 01535

Quoddy Moccasins, Div. R.G. Barry Corp., 67 Minot Ave., Auburn, ME 04210

Ranger Rubber Co., 1100 E. Main St., Endicott, NY 13760

Red Ball, P.O. Box 3200, Manchester, NH 03105

Red Head Brand Corp., 4949 Joseph Hardin Dr., Dallas, TX 75236

Refrigiwear, Inc., 71 Inip Dr., Inwood, L.I., NY 11696

W. R. Russell Moccasin Co., 285 S.W. Franklin, Berlin, WI 54923

Safariland Hunting Corp., P.O. Box NN, McLean, VA 22101

Servus Rubber Co., 1136 Second St., Rock Island, IL 61201

Stearns Mfg. Co., P.O. Box 1498, St. Cloud, MN 56301

Teledyne / Big Beam Co., 290 E. Prairie St., Crystal Lake, IL 60014

Ten-X Mfg., 2410 East Foxfarm Rd., Cheyenne, WY 82001

Thermos Division/KST, Thermos Dr., Norwich, CT 06360

Norm Thompson, 1805 N.W. Thurman St., Portland, OR 97209

Utica Duxbak Corp., 815 Noyes St., Utica, NY 13502

Walker Shoe Co., P.O. Box 1167, Asheboro, NC 27203
Weinbrenner Shoe Corp., 108 Polk St., Merrill, WI 54452
Wenzel Co., 1280 Research Blvd., St. Louis, MO 63132
Wolverine Boots & Shoes, Div. Wolverine World Wide, 9341 Courtland Dr., Rockford, MI 49351
Woods Inc., 90 River St., P.O. Box 407, Ogdensburg, NY 13669
Woodstream Corp., P.O. Box 327, Lititz, PA 17543
Woolrich Woolen Mills, Mill St., Woolrich, PA 17779

KNIVES AND KNIFEMAKER'S SUPPLIES—FACTORY and MAIL ORDER

AC Enterprises, 507 N. Broad St., Edenton, NC 27932
Alcas Cutlery Corp., 116 E. State St., Olean, NY 14760
Atlanta Cutlery, Box 839, Conyers, GA 30207
Bali-Song (See Pacific Cutlery Corp.)
L. L. Bean, 386 Main St., Freeport, ME 04032
Benchmark Knives (See Gerber)
Boker, The Cooper Group, P.O. Box 30100, Raleigh, NC 27622
Bowen Knife Co. (Div. of Adventure Products Inc.), P.O. Box 1929, Waycross, GA 31501
Browning, Route 1, Morgan, UT 84050
Buck Knives, Inc., P.O. Box 1267, 1900 Weld Blvd., El Cajon, CA 92022
Camillus Cutlery Co., 52–54 W. Genesee St., Camillus, NY 13031
W. R. Case & Sons Cutlery, 20 Russell Blvd., Bradford, PA 16701
Charlton Ltd., P.O. Box 448, Edenton, NC 27932
Charter Arms Corp., 430 Sniffens Lane, Stratford, CT 06497
Chicago Cutlery Co., 5420 N. County Rd. 18, Minneapolis, MN 55440
Collins Brothers Div. (See Bowen Knife Co.)
Colonial Knife Co., P.O. Box 3327, Providence, RI 02909
Crossman Blades, The Coleman Co., 250 N. St. Francis, Wichita, KS 67201
Custom Knifemaker's Supplies, P.O. Box 308, Emory, TX 75440
Custom Purveyors, M. Devlet, P.O. Box 886, Fort Lee, NJ 07024
Dixie Gun Works, Hwy. 51, South, Union City, TN 38261
Eze-Lap Diamond Prods., Box 2229, 15164 Weststate St., Westminster, CA 92583
Gerber Legendary Blades, 14200 S.W. 72nd St., Portland, OR 97223
Golden Age Arms Co., 14 W. Winter St., Delaware, OH 43015
Gutmann Cutlery Co., Inc., 900 S. Columbus Ave., Mt. Vernon, NY 10550
H&B Forge Co., Rt. 2, Geisinger Rd., Shiloh, OH 44878
Russell Harrington Cutlery, Subs. of Hyde Mfg. Co., 44 River St., Southbridge, MA 01550
J. A. Henckels Zwillingsworks, 9 Skyline Dr., Hawthorne, NY 10532
Imperial Knife Associated Cos., 1776 Broadway, New York, NY 10019
Indian Ridge Traders, Box 869, Royal Oak, MI 48068
J. A. Blades Inc., an affiliate of E. Christopher Firearms, State 128 & Ferry, Miamitown, OH 45041
Ken Jantz Supply / Ken Jantz, Rt. 1, Sulphur, OK 73086
Jet-Aer Corp., 100 Sixth Ave., Paterson, NJ 07524
Ka-Bar Cutlery Inc., 5777 Grant Ave., Cleveland, OH 44105
Ka-Bar Knives, Collectors Div., 434 No. 9th St., Olean, NY 14760
Keene Corp., Cutting Serv. Div., 1569 Tower Grove Ave., St. Louis, MO 63110
Kershaw Knives/Kai Cutlery, Stafford Business Park, 25300 SW Parkway, Wilsonville, OR 97070
Knifeco, P.O. Box 5271, Hialeah Lakes, FL 33014
Knife and Gun Finishing Supplies, P.O. Box 13522, Arlington, TX 76013
Koval Knives, 822 Busch Ct., GD, Columbus, OH 43229
Lamson & Goodnow Mfg. Co., 45 Conway St., Shelburne Falls, MA 03170
Lansky Sharpeners, P.O. Box 800, Buffalo, NY 14221
Al Mar Knives, Inc., P.O. Box 1626, 5755 SW Jean Rd., #101, Lake Oswego, OR 97034
Matthews Cutlery, P.O. Box 33095, Decatur, GA 30033
R. Murphy Co., Inc., 13 Groton-Harvard Rd., Ayer, MA 01432
Nordic Knives, 1634-C Copenhagen Dr., Solvang, CA 93463
Normark Corp., 1717 E. 78th St., Minneapolis, MN 55423
Ontario Knife, Queen Cutlery Co., P.O. Box 500, Franklinville, NY 14737
Pacific Cutlery Corp., 3039 Roswell St., Los Angeles, CA 90085
Parker Cutlery, 6928 Lee Highway, Chattanooga, TN 37415
Plaza Cutlery Inc., 3333 Bristol, #161, South Coast Plaza, Costa Mesa, CA 92626
Queen Cutlery Co., 507 Chestnut St., Titusville, PA 16354
R&C Knives and Such, P.O. Box 32631, San Jose, CA 95152
Randall Made Knives, Box 1988, Orlando, FL 32802
Rigid Knives, Highway 290E, P.O. Box 816, Lake Hamilton, AR 71951
A. G. Russell Co., 1705 Hiway 71 North, Springdale, AR 72764
Bob Sanders, 2358 Tyler Lane, Louisville, KY 40205
San Diego Knives, P.O. Box 326, Lakeside, CA 92040
Schrade Cutlery Corp., 1776 Broadway, New York, NY 10019
Sheffield Knifemakers Supply, P.O. Box 141, Deland, FL 32720
Smith & Wesson, 2100 Roosevelt Ave., Springfield, MA 01104
Jesse W. Smith Saddlery, N 307 Haven St., Spokane, WA 99202
Swiss Army Knives, Inc., P.O. Box 846, Shelton, CT 06484
Tekna, 1075 Old Country Rd., Belmont, CA 94002
Thompson-Center Arms, P.O. Box 2426, Rochester, NH 03867
Tommer-Bordein Corp., 220 N. River St., Delano, MN 55328
Tru-Balance Knife Co., 2155 Tremont Blvd. NW, Grand Rapids, MI 49504
Utica Cutlery Co., 820 Noyes St., Utica, NY 13503
Valor Corp. of Fla., P.O. Box 10116, Hialeah, FL 33010
Washington Forge, Inc., Englishtown, NJ 07727
Wenoka Cutlery, P.O. Box 8238, West Palm Beach, FL 33407
Western Cutlery Co., 1800 Pike Rd., Longmont, CO 80501
Walt Whinnery, Walt's Custom Leather, 1947 Meadow Creek Dr., Louisville, KY 40218
J. Wolfe's Knife Works, Box 1056, Larkspur, CA 94939
Wyoming Knife Co, 101 Commerce Dr. #2, Ft. Collins, CO 80524

MUZZLE-LOADING GUNS, BARRELS or EQUIPMENT

Luther Adkins, P.O. Box 281, Shelbyville, IN 46176
Allen Firearms Co., 2879 All Trades Rd., Santa Fe, NM 87501
Anderson Mfg. Co., Union Gap Sta./ P.O. Box 3120, Yakima, WA 98902
Antique Arms Co., 1110 Cleveland Ave., Monett, MO 65708
Antique Gun Parts, Inc., 1118 So. Braddock Ave., Pittsburgh, PA 15218
The Armoury Inc., Route 202, Scottsdale Airpark, New Preston, CT 06777
Armsport, Inc., 3590 N.W. 49th St., Miami, FL 33142
Bauska Rifle Barrels, Inc., Box 511, 105–9th West, Kalispell, MT 59901
Beaver Lodge, 9245–16th Ave. SW, Seattle, WA 98106
Blackhawk East, #C2274 POB, Loves Park, IL 61131
Blackhawk West, Box 285, Hiawatha, KS 66434
Blue and Gray Products, Inc., RD #6, Box 362, Wellsboro, PA 16901
Jim Brobst, 299 Poplar St., Hamburg, PA 19526
Ted Buckland, 361 Flagler Rd., Nordland, WA 98358
Butler Creek Corp., Box GG, Jackson, WY 83001
C.N.S. Co., P.O. Box 238, Mohegan Lake, NY 10547
Cache La Poudre Rifleworks, 168 N. College Ave., Ft. Collins, CO 80524
Challanger Mfg. Corp., 118 Pearl St., Mt. Vernon, NY 10550
R. MacDonald Champlin, P.O. Box 693, Manchester, NH 03105
Chopie Mfg. Inc., 700 Copeland Ave., La Crosse, WI 54601
Connecticut Valley Arms Co., 5988 Peachtree Corners, East, Norcross, GA 30071
Earl T. Cureton, Rt. 2, Box 388, Willoughby Rd., Bulls Gap, TN 37711
Homer L. Dangler, Box 254, Addison, MI 49220
Leonard Day & Co., Box 723, East Hampton, MA 01027
Dixie Gun Works, Hwy. 51, South, Union City, TN 38261
Dixon Muzzleloading Shop, RD #1, Box 175, Kempton, PA 19529
Peter Dyson Limited, 29–31 Church St., Honley, Huddersfield, West Yorks. HD7 2AH, England
EMF Co. Inc., 1900 East Warner Ave., 1-D, Santa Ana, CA 92705
Euroarms of America, Inc., 1501 Lenoir Dr., P.O. Box 3277, Winchester, VA 22601
Excam Inc., 4480 East 11th Ave., P.O. Box 3483, Hialeah, FL 33013
Andy Fautheree, P.O. Box 863, Pagosa Springs, CO 81147
Ted Fellowes Beaver Lodge, 9245—16th Ave. S.W., Seattle, WA 98106
Firearms Import & Export (FIE), P.O. Box 4866, Hialeah, FL 33014
Marshall F. Fish, Rt. 22 North, Westport, NY 12993
The Flintlock Muzzleloading Gun Shop, 1238 "G" So. Beach Blvd., Anaheim, CA 92804
Forster Products, 82 E. Lanark Ave., Lanark, IL 61046

Frontier, 2910 San Bernardo, Laredo, TX 78040

C.R. & D.E. Getz, Box 88, Beavertown, PA 17813

Goex, Inc., Belin Plant, Moosic, PA 18507

Golden Age Arms Co., 14 W. Winter St., Delaware, OH 43015

A. R. Goode, 4125 N.E. 28th Terr., Ocala, FL 32670

Green Mountain Rifle Bbl. Co. Inc., RFD 1, Box 184, Center Ossipee, NH 03814

Guncraft, Inc., 117 W. Pipeline, Hurst, TX 76053

The Gun Works, 236 Main St., Springfield, OR 97477

Hatfield Rifle Works, 2028 Frederick Ave., St. Joseph, MO 64501

Hopkins & Allen Arms, 3 Ethel Ave., P.O. Box 217, Hawthorne, NJ 07507

The House of Muskets, Inc., 120 N. Pagosa Blvd., Pagosa Springs, CO 81147

Steven Dodd Hughes, P.O. Box 11455, Eugene, OR 97440

JJJJ Ranch, Gun & Machine Shop, Route 1, Star Route 243, Ironton, OH 45638

Jennings-Hawken, 326½ 4th St. N.W., Winter Haven, FL 33880

Jerry's Gun Shop, 9220 Ogden Ave., Brookfield, IL 60513

La Chute Ltd., Box 48B, Masury, OH 44438

Morris Lawing, 150 Garland Court, Charlotte, NC 28202

Leding Loader, R.R. #1, Box 645, Ozark, AR 72949

Les' Gun Shop, 105–9th West, Box 511, Kalispell, MT 59901

Lever Arms Service Ltd., 572 Howe St., Vancouver, BC V6C 2E3, Canada

Log Cabin Sport Shop, 8010 Lafayette Rd., Lodi, OH 44254

Lyman Products Corp., Route 47, Middlefield, CT 06455

McCann's Muzzle-Gun Works, 200 Federal City Rd., Pennington, NJ 08534

McKeown's Sporting Arms, R.R. #4, Pekin, IL 61554

Mike Marsh, 6 Stanford Rd., Dronfield Woodhouse, Nr. Sheffield S18 SQJ, England

Maurer Arms, 2154–16th St., Akron, OH 44314

Michigan Arms Corp., 363 Elmwood, Troy, MI 48083

Mountain State Muzzle-Loading, Supplies, Inc., Box 151-1, State Rt. 14 at Boaz, Williamstown, WV 26187

Mowrey Gun Works, 800 Blue Mound Rd., Saginaw, TX 76131

Muzzleloaders Etc., Inc., 9907 Lyndale Ave. So., Bloomington, MN 55420

Numrich Arms Corp., 203 Broadway, West Hurley, NY 12491

Kirk Olson, Ft. Woolsey Guns, P.O. Box 2122, Prescott, AZ 86302

Olde Pennsylvania, P.O. Box 17419, Penn Hills, PA 15235

Oregon Trail Riflesmiths, P.O. Box 45212, Boise, ID 83711

Ox-Yoke Originals, Inc., 130 Griffin Rd., West Suffield, CT 06093

Ozark Mountain Arms, Inc., P.O. Box 397, 141 Byrne St., Ashdown, AR 71822

Pecos Valley Armory, 1022 So. Canyon, Carlsbad, NM 88220

A. W. Peterson Gun Shop, 1693 Old Highway 441, Mt. Dora, FL 32757

Phyl-Mac, 609 N.E. 104th Ave., Vancouver, WA 98664

Provider Arms, Inc., 261 Haglund Rd., Chesterton, IN 46304

R.V.I., P.O. Box 1429 Sta. A, Vancouver, BC V6C 1AO, Canada

Richland Arms Co., 321 W. Adrian St., Blissfield, MI 49228

Salish House, Inc., P.O. Box 383, Lakeside, MT 55922

Shiloh Products, 181 Plauderville Ave., Garfield, NJ 07026

Sile Distributors Inc., 7 Centre Market Place, New York, NY 10013

C. E. Siler Locks, 7 Action Woods Rd., Candler, NC 28715

C. Sharps Arms Co., Inc., P.O. Box 885, Big Timber, MT 59011

Ken Steggles (See Mike Marsh)

The Swampfire Shop, 1693 Old Highway 441 N., Mt. Dora, FL 32757

Tennessee Valley Arms, Inc., P.O. Box 2022, Union City, TN 38261

Tennessee Valley Mfg., P.O. Box 1125, Corinth, MS 38834

Ten-Ring Precision Inc., 1449 Blue Crest Lane, San Antonio, TX 78232

Traditions Inc., Saybrook Rd., Haddam, CT 06438

Treso Inc., P.O. Box 4640, Pagosa Springs, CO 81157

Upper Missouri Trading Co., Box 191, Crofton, NE 68730

J. S. Weeks & Son, 4748 Bailey Rd., Dimondale, MI 48821

Fred Wells, Wells Sport Store, 110 N. Summit St., Prescott, AZ 86301

W. H. Wescombe, P.O. Box 488, Glencoe, CA 95232

Thomas F. White, 5801 Westchester Ct., Worthington, OH 43085

Williamson-Pate Gunsmith Serv., 117 W. Pipeline, Hurst, TX 76053

Winchester Sutler, Siler Route, Box 393-E, Winchester, VA 22601

York Cnty. Gun Works, R.R. 4, Tottenham, Ont. LOG 1WO, Canada

SCOPES, MOUNTS, ACCESSORIES, OPTICAL EQUIPMENT

Action Arms Ltd., P.O. Box 9573, Philadelphia, PA 19124

Aimpoint U.S.A., 201 Elden St., Suite 302, Herndon, VA 22070

Alley Supply Co., Carson Valley Industrial Park, P.O. Box 848, Gardnerville, NV 89410

The American Import Co., 1453 Mission St., San Francisco, CA 94103

Anderson Mfg. Co., R. R. 1, Royal, IA 51357

Apollo Optics (See Seno Corp.)

Armsport, Inc., 3950 N.W. 49th St., Miami, FL 33122

Armson Inc., P.O. Box 2130, Farmington Hills, MI 48018

B-Square Co., Box 11281, Ft. Worth, TX 76109

Bausch & Lomb, Inc., P.O. Box 478, 1400 N. Goodman St., Rochester, NY 14602

Beeman Precision Arms, Inc., 47-GDD Paul Dr., San Rafael, CA 94903

Bennett Gun Works, 561 Delaware Ave., Delmar, NY 12054

Buehler Scope Mounts, 17 Orinda Highway, Orinda, CA 94563

Burris Company, Inc., 331 E. 8th St., Box 1747, Greeley, CO 80631

Bushnell Optical Corp., 2828 E. Foothill Blvd., Pasadena, CA 91107

Butler Creek Corp., Box GG, Jackson, WY 83001

Kenneth E. CLark, 18738 Highway 99, Madera, CA 93637

Clearview Mfg. Co., Inc., 20821 Grand River Ave., Detroit, MI 48219

Compass Industries, Inc., 104 E. 25th St., New York, NY 10010

Conetrol Scope Mounts, Hwy. 123 South, Seguin, TX 78155

Cougar Optics, P.O. Box 115, Groton, NY 13073

D&H Products Co., Inc., P.O. Box 22, Glenshaw, PA 15116

Davis Optical Co., P.O. Box 6, Winchester, IN 47394

Del-Sports Inc., Main St., Margaretville, NY 12455

Dickson (See American Import)

Fontaine Industries, Inc., 11552 Knott St., Suite 1, Garden Grove, CA 92641

Griffin & Howe Inc., 589 Broadway, 4th Fl., New York, NY 10012

H. J. Hermann Leather Co., Rt. 1, Skiatook, OK 74070

J. B. Holden Co., 295 W. Pearl, Plymouth, MI 48170

The Hutson Corp., Optics Division, 104 Century Drive No.,

Import Scope Repair Co., P.O. Box 2633, Durango, CO 81301

Interarms, Ltd., 10 Prince St., Alexandria, VA 22313

Paul Jaeger, Inc., P.O. Box 449, 1 Madison Ave., Grand Junction, TN 38039

Jason Empire, Inc., 9200 Cody, P.O. Box 14930, Overland Park, KS 66214

Jennison TCS (See Fontaine Ind., Inc.)

Kahles of America, Div. of Del-Sports, Inc., Main St., Margaretville, NY 12455

Kenko International Inc., 8141 West I-70, Frontage Rd., No., Arvada, CO 80002

Kowa Optimed, Inc., 20001 So. Vermont Ave., Torrance, CA 90502

Kris Mounts, 108 Lehigh St., Johnstown, PA 15905

Kwik-Site, 5555 Treadwell, Wayne, IN 48185

T. K. Lee Co., 2830 So. 19th St., Off. #4, Birmingham, AL 35209

E. Leitz, Inc., Rockleigh, NJ 07647

Leupold & Stevens, Inc., 600 N. Meadow Dr., P.O. box 688, Beaverton, OR 97075

Jake Levin and Son, Inc., 9200 Cody, Overland Park, KS 66214

Walter H. Lodewick, 2816 N.E. Halsey, Portland, OR 97232

Lyman Products Corp., Route 47, Middlefield, CT 06455

Marble Arms Corp., 420 Industrial Park, Gladstone, MI 49837

Millett Industries, 16131 Gothard St., Huntington Beach, CA 92647

Nikon Inc., 633 Stewart Ave., Suite 1006, New York, NY 10022

Nite-Site Inc., P.O. Box 0, Rosemount, MN 55068

Orchard Park Enterprise, P.O. Box 563, Orchard Park, NY 14127

Oriental Optical Co., 605 E. Walnut St., Pasadena, CA 91101

Pachmayr Gun Works, 1220 So. Grand Ave., Los Angeles, CA 90015

Ken Patable Enterprises, P.O. Box 19422, Louisville, KY 40219

Pilkington Gun Co., P.O. Box 1296, Muskogee, OK 74401

Pioneer & Co., Marine & Optical, Div., Marketing & Research, 216 Haddon Ave., #522, Westmont, NJ 08108

Ranging Inc., 90 N. Lincoln Rd., East Rochester, NY 14445

Ray-O-Vac, Willson Prod. Div., P.O. Box 622, Reading, PA 19603

Redfield, 5800 East Jewell Ave., Denver, CO 80222

S&K Mfg. Co., Box 247, Pittsfield, PA 16340

Schmidt & Bender (See Paul Jaeger)

Seattle Binocular & Scope Repair, P.O. Box 46094, Seattle, WA 98146

Senno Corp., 505 E. 3rd, P.O. Box 3506, Spokane, WA 99220

Sherwood Intl. Export Corp., 18714 Parthenia St., Northridge, CA 91324

W. H. Siebert, 22720 S.E. 56th Place, Issaquah, WA 98027

Simmons Outdoor Corp., 14205 SW 119th Ave., Miami, FL 33186

Southern Precision Instrument Co., 3419 E. Commerce St., San Antonio, TX 78220

Stoeger Industries, 55 Ruta Court, S. Hackensack, NJ 07606

Supreme Lens Covers, Box GG, Jackson, WY 83001

Swarovski Optik, Div. of Swarovski America Ltd., One Kenney Dr., Cranston, RI 02920

Swift Instruments, Inc., 952 Dorchester Ave., Boston, MA 02125

Tasco, Inc., 7600 N.W. 26th St., Miami, FL 33122

Tele Optics, 5514 W. Lawrence Ave., Chicago, IL 60630

Thompson-Center Arms, P.O. Box 2426, Rochester, NH 03867

John Unertl Optical Co., 3551 East St., Pittsburgh, PA 15214

United Binocular Co., 9043 S. Western Ave., Chicago, IL 60620

Vissing (See Supreme Lens Covers)

Weatherby's, 2781 Firestone Blvd., South Gate, CA 90280

Weaver/Omark Industries, Box 856, Lewiston, ID 823501

Weaver Scope Repair Serv., P.O. Box 20010, El Paso, TX 79998

Wide View Scope Mount Corp., 26110 Michigan Ave., Inkster, MI 48141

Williams Gun Sight Co., 7389 Lapeer Rd., Davison, MI 48423

Boyd Williams Inc., 8701-14 Mile Rd. (M-57), Cedar Springs, MI 49319

Carl Zeiss, Inc., Consumer Products Division, Box 2010, 1015 Commerce St., Petersburg, VA 23803

TAXIDERMY

Jack Atcheson & Sons, Inc., 3210 Ottawa St., Butte, MT 59701

Doug's Taxidermy Studio, 2027 Lockport-Olcott Rd., Burt, NY 14028

Jonas Brothers, Inc., 1037 Broadway, Denver, CO 80203

Kulis Freeze-Dry Taxidermy, 725 Broadway Ave., Bedford, OH 44146

Mark D. Parker, 1233 Sherman Dr., Longmont, CO 80501

APPENDIX—E
Books About Turkeys and Turkey Hunting

Some of these books I have read, some I haven't. When I first began hunting wild turkeys, there was not a single book on the market which had been done in recent times. The first book I found was in a store which sold old books, and I paid $6 for a copy of McIlhenny's *The Wild Turkey And Its Hunting.* Not long afterward I found a copy of Davis' book for a ridiculously low price. Today, both are high dollar collector's items. *Dwain Bland*

The World of The Wild Turkey, by James C. Lewis, J. B. Lippincott Co., Philadelphia and New York City.

The Wild Turkey, Its History And Domestication, Publishing Division, University of Oklahoma, Norman, OK.

The Education Of A Turkey Hunter, by Frank Hanenkrat, Winchester Press, Piscataway, NJ.

This Love Of Hunting, by Frank A. Jeffett, Tejas Press, Dallas, TX. Some chapters on turkey hunting, good reading.

Tenth Legion, by Tom Kelly, Spur Enterprises, Monroe, LA.

Spring Gobblers, by John Lowther, McClain Printing Co, Parsons, WV.

The Grand Spring Hunt For America's Wild Turkey Gobbler, by Bart Jacob and Ben Conger, Winchester Press, Piscataway, NJ.

The Voice and Vocabulary Of The Wild Turkey, by Lovett E. Williams, 2201 S.E. 41st Ave., Gainesville, FL 32601.

Advanced Wild Turkey Hunting And World Records, by Dave Harbour, Winchester Press, Piscataway, NJ.

The Book Of The Wild Turkey, by Lovett Williams, Winchester Press, Piscataway, NJ.

The Complete Book Of The Wild Turkey, by Roger Latham, Stackpole Books, Harrisburg, PA.

The Complete Turkey Hunt, by William Daskal, El-Bar Enterprises Publishers, New York, NY.

Hunting Wild Turkeys In The Everglades, by Frank Harben, Harben Publishing Co, Safety Harbor, FL.

Bowhunting For Turkeys, by Jack Brobst, available from Jack Brobst, R.D. 2, Box 2172, Bangor, PA 18013.

Modern Turkey Hunting, by James F. Brady, Crown Publishing Co., New York, NY.

On Target For Successful Turkey Hunting, by Wayne Fears, Target Communications, Mequon, WI.

The Wild Turkey Book, by Wayne Fears, Amwell Press, Clinton, NJ.

The Old Pro Turkey Hunter, by Gene Nunnery, available from Gene Nunnery, Meridian, MS 39301.

Turkey Hunting With Charlie Elliott, by Charlie Elliott, David McKay Co., New York, NY.

Turkey Hunting, Spring and Fall, by Doug Camp, Outdoor Skills Bookshelf, Nashville, TN.

Turkey Hunter's Guide, by Byron Dalrymple, The National Rifle Association, Washington DC.

The American Wild Turkey, by Henry E. Davis, available from Old Masters Publishers, Route 2, Box 217, Medon, TN 38356.

The Wild Turkey And Its Hunting, by Edward A. McIlhenny, available from Old Masters Publishers, Route 2, Box 217, Medon, TN 38356.

Tales Of Wild Turkey Hunting, by Simon Everitt, available from Old Masters Publishers, Route 2, Box 217, Medon, TN 38356.

The Turkey Hunting World of Ben Lee, by Ben Lee, available from Gander Mountain, Inc., Box 248, Wilmot, WI 53192.

50 Years, Hunting Wild Turkeys, by Wayne Bailey, available from Wing Supply, P.O. Box 367, Greenville, KY 42345, or Penn's Woods Products, 19 W. Pittsburgh St., Delmont, PA 15626.

Some Turkey Scratchings, by Dwain Bland, available from Wing Supply, P.O. Box 367, Greenville, KY 42345, or Penn's Woods Products, 19 West Pittsburgh St., Delmont, PA 15626.

Tall Timber Gabriels, by Charles S. Whittington, Spur Enterprises, Monroe, LA.

Tom Tells Tall Turkey Tales, by Tom Gaskins, available from Tom Gaskins, Box 7, Palmdale, FL 33944.

We Talk Turkey, by Tom Gaskins, available form Tom Gaskins, Box 7, Palmdale, FL 33944.

The Complete Turkey Hunter, by W.N. Bledsoe, available from The Long Hunters, 11334 Crest Brook, Dallas, TX 75230.

In Search Of The Wild Turkey, by Bob Gooch, Great Lakes Living Press, Waukegan, IL.

Happy Times Hunting In The Beautiful Woods Of Alabama, by Gesna Griffith, available from Gesna Griffith, Route 1, Box 229, Camden, Al 36726.

Talking Tomfoolery, by Earl Groves, available from The National Wild Turkey Federation, P.O. Box 530, Edgefield, SC 29824.

Long Beards, Long Spurs, And Fanned Tails, by Bob Clark, Northwoods Publications Inc., Boiling Springs, PA.

High Ridge Gobbler, by David Stemple, William Collins Publishers, New York, NY, and Cleveland, OH.

Dealer's Choice, by Tom Kelly, available from Wingfeather Press, P.O. Box 50, Spanish Fort, AL 36527.

Bearded Bird, by Larry Hudson, available from L. F. Hudson, 2013 Lansdowne Way, Silver Springs, MD 20910.

The Turkey Hunter's Guide, by Leon Johenning, The Humphries Press, Inc., Waynesboro, VA.

The Turkey Hunter's Book, by John M. McDaniel, available from The National Wild Turkey Federation, P.O. Box 530, Edgefield, SC 29824.

Hunting The Wild Turkey, by Tom Turpin, available from Penn's Woods Products, #19 West Pittsburgh St., Delmont, PA 15626.

The Ted Trueblood Hunting Treasury, by Ted Trueblood, David McKay Co., Inc., New York, NY.

Mr. Anonymous, by Charlie Elliott, Cherokee Publishing Co., Atlanta, GA.

Brogans, Clothespins, And A Twist Of Tobacco, by K. Maynard Head, Pine Mountain Press, West Allis, WI.

In Search of L.L. Bean, by M.M. Montgomery, Little, Brown and Co., Boston, MA.

The Complete Black Powder Handbook, by Sam Fadala, DBI Books, Inc., Northbrook, IL.

The Muzzleloading Hunter, by Rick Hacker, Winchester Press, Piscataway, NJ.

Black Powder Gun Digest, by Jack Lewis, DBI Books, Inc., Northbrook, IL.

Advanced Muzzleloader's Guide, by Toby Bridges, Stoeger Publishing Co., S. Hackensack, NJ.